Cover:

Diagram of the mummy of Tutankhamun. At his death, the king (who was never a pharaoh, let alone an Egyptian) became an Osiris bearing the title of SA-RÂ, son of Ra, which is also read IS-RÂ-GOD in the hieroglyphs, origin of Israel. The mummy was removed after its discovery in 1923 by Howard Carter (research financed by Lord Carnavon).

I have voluntarily compared the royal mummy with the diagram of a Jew wearing the prayer shawl and tefilin or phylactery, because the Jewish secret tradition assimilates them to the sacred ornaments of the kings of Israel. One of the great secrets of Kabbalah reveals that all the kings of Israel were crowned with the crown of the serpent of Amun. This crown constitutes the **"perpetual testimony to recognize the kings of Israel"**[1]. Only the kings we use to call «Pharaohs» fit this explanation.

---

1   Le Zohar, tome II, collection 'les dix paroles ». Traduit par Charles Mopsik. Vayera, Hayé Sarah, Toldot, Vayetsé, Vayichlah. Verdier, 1984, p. 116.

Around 280 BC, the Greek pharaoh Ptolemaos Philadelphos outlawed the cult of Osiris throughout the Middle East. Osiris, the gods, hieroglyphs and the square Hebrew were forbidden to the Jews. They were forced to encrypt their knowledge, hiding the Mystery of Osiris in the Septuagint and the Torah. The religion of the Nile Valley sank into demonization and magical and occult practices. The Egyptologist Jan Assmann attests that in the Ptolemaic period, the Law and the cult of Osiris were kept secret:

"For the Egyptians, the paradigm of secrecy is the corpse of Osiris, which must be protected by all means from the attacks of Set. The role of Set as discoverer and potential destroyer of Osiris' corpse became in the late period the emblem of a general threat to all gods and their cultic secrets. In the late period, as we have said, there is an EXPLOSION OF SECRET IN THE EGYPTIAN CULTES." [2]

The Septuagint, the Torah, the Bible, the Gospels and the Koran are the legacy of the death of Osiris, the ancient Israel.

---

2   Jan Assmann. *Moïse l'Égyptien*. Éditions Aubier. 2001, p. 193.

Roger Sabbah

OSIRIS

IS

ISRAEL

The incredible discovery

FROM THE SAME AUTHOR

Secrets of the Exodus

Secrets of the Jews

Secrets of the Bible

The Jewish Pharaoh

The Secret of the 3rd Millennium

Ancient Egyptians were the Jews

Series director : Daniel Guersan, professor of political science from the University of Montreal.

Self-published in July 2022, Bourg-la-Reine, France.
ISBN: 978-2-9584227-1-4

For more than a century, millions of visitors to the Cairo Museum have been victims of the greatest historical and scientific deception in the world: the name Israel is, according to Egyptologist Sir Flinders Petrie, engraved on the stele of Pharaoh Merenptah (also known as Mineptah), grandson of Ramses II. The alleged reading of the name "Israel" on the stele of King Merenptah does not read Israel. The phonetic reading, letter by letter, does not read Israel, but ASSYRIARY. According to the Bible, in the Book of Genesis, Israel means "the one who fights with God" and in the Book of Exodus, the "Son of God". Nothing in common with the stele falsely qualified as a stele of Israel.

But for the Jewish esoteric tradition and for the ancient Greeks, the Bible is an oracle of God. Several texts state that the first Torah of the Jews was modified by Pharaoh Ptolemy Philadelphus. The Torah is the coded text of a lost first Torah, concealing another truth. For Kabbalah, Israel means God, the light, the River, the Father, the divine Shekhina, the sun and the moon, the cosmos. The Children of Israel form the Body of Israel. Israel is confused with Osiris, at all levels of reading and interpretation. The name of Osiris is broken down into SA RÂ the sacred goose, the Son of RÂ, or IS' RÂ the solar cosmic egg[3] ◯. RÂ is the vision, the light and the symbol of God, EL.

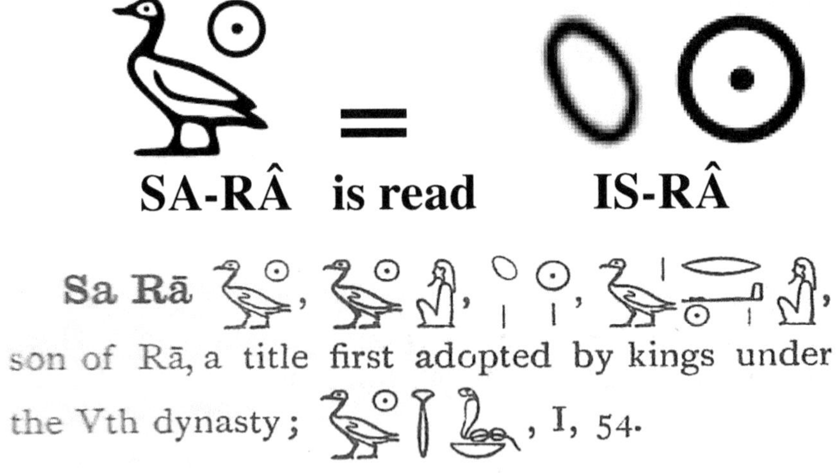

---

3 Egyptian hieroglyphic dictionary. Wallis Budge, Dover Publications, inc, , 1978, 583a, M 217; N 589.

Roger Sabbah

OSIRIS

IS

ISRAEL

How the ancient Greeks made Osiris-Israel disappear from the collective memory of humanity by modifying the Septuagint and the Torah, by inventing the "Egyptians", by fixing them in the Septuagint making Osiris the eternal enemy of Israel.

CONTENTS

PREAMBLE

Egyptology has dragged all humanity into an unprecedented lie. The ancient Nile Valley constituted the true, the verus Israel in its universal dimension where humanity lived in harmony with God and his representatives, the gods. The ancient Greeks caused the collapse of the Nile Valley civilization by inventing the Pharaohs, Egypt and the ancient Egyptians. They fixed these names for eternity in the Septuagint and in all the books of the world, in order to monopolize the land of the Nile Valley for good. For these names refer to Greek gods. If I were to tell you that the inhabitants of the Nile Valley were the "ancient Jupiterians", you would jump up and reply: "No! The ancient Jupiterians never existed! Yet Egyptologists recognize that the words Egypt, Egyptians and Pharaoh are Greek deities that were deliberately introduced into the Septuagint, the Greek Bible. To say that the ancient Egyptians and Pharaohs existed means that they are the symbolic children of the Greek god Ægyptos, which is historically impossible. And yet, we naturally accept this assumption. How did mankind come to this point, frozen in the ignorance of hieroglyphics?

From the Assyrian, Babylonian and Persian invasions to the Macedonians, researchers have concluded that several million Jews inhabited the Nile Valley. A study of the Egyptian origins of Roman civil law in relation to the Hebrews points to a historical fact of the first order:

"But in the interval between the time of the Assyrians, whose invasion drove so many Jews back into Egypt, according to the prophets, and the time of Ptolemy, when they were numbered by millions in the Nile valley, and precisely at the time of Apries and Amasis... ...What is quite certain is that then the Hebrews [Jews] were as numerous in Egypt as in the famous Babylonian captivity..."[4]

---

4   Les origines égyptiennes du droit civil romain. Eugène Revillout. Forgotten Books publishers, page 21.

In the first century, the historian Flavius Josephus already raised the greatest mystification in human history. Addressing the Greek and Roman historians, he said, **"Why, if these people are Egyptians, do you call them Jews?"**[5] There is no doubt that Flavius Josephus had books, now lost, which testify that the Egyptians were called "Jews" by the Greek historians. Many testimonies attest that the books of the ancient Greeks were used to deceive humanity by inventing Egypt and the Egyptians. The *Letter of Aristaeus* confirms that the Jews (YAHOUDS) were called "Men of God" by the Egyptian priests. Only the "Men of Osiris" correspond to this honorific title. This expression is translated by IS-RÂ, said Osiris, designating the true "Egyptians". The Hermetic texts and Diodorus of Sicily denounce the incredible mystification of the ancient Greeks, a schism, a holy imposture known as Septuagint, or Hellenization. A real brainwashing initiated by the Lagid kings, in the third century BC. The Greek king Ptolemy Soter, father of Ptolemy II Philadelphus, ordered the scribe Manetho to write an Egyptiaka: a falsification of the History of the Nile Valley, where Egypt and the Egyptians replace the real builders of the Nile Valley civilization.

An imposture where Jews and Egyptians become age-old enemies. The Letter of Aristaeus denounces the schism that arose during the Hellenistic period when Ptolemy Philadelphus enslaved the Jews and stripped them of their possessions before imposing on them the Septuagint, the revealed Oracle that would become the Torah[6], the Bible. But the seventy-two scribes of the Septuagint managed to encrypt the myth of Osiris, both in the Septuagint and in the Hebrew Torah. Thus, the fight of Jacob against the angel conceals the myth of Osiris, the fight of the sun against the serpent of darkness. The patriarchs Abraham, Isaac and Jacob form an immense cosmogony. An allegory of the Light that settles in Egypt, while the Children of Israel symbolize the gods, the stars of the sky, the souls of humanity. This index is important to decode the message of the scribes.

---

5   Flavius Josèphe. Contre Apion. Éditions Les Belles Lettres, 2003. Première édition 1930. Chapitre XXXV § 314, p. 57.

6 Les cinq premiers livres de l'Ancien Testament écrits en lettres hébraïques.

INDEX

EGYPTIAN: This word is formidable because it misleads us. Since the third century B.C., by the criminal will of Ptolemy II Philadelphus, we have been conditioned by thousands of books to apply it only to the inhabitants of the ancient Nile Valley, as if they were distinct from the whole population of the Kingdom of the Two Lands which extended into Canaan, later renamed Palestine by the Romans. The words "Egypt", "Egyptian" and "Pharaoh" never existed in hieroglyphics. The inhabitants of this kingdom called themselves "Sons of Osiris". We are obliged to use the word "Egypt" because we have no other, while scientifically demonstrating to the reader that its use is wrong. However, thousands of books written by Egyptologists do not question this fundamental error, which leads to a false vision of the whole of history and Egyptology.

JEWISH: In the same way, this word misleads us. Its meaning has been largely falsified, and when it is used, it only applies to the Jews of the Bible, 99% of whom are called Children of Israel and very rarely Hebrews. This last word also absent from history before the Septuagint, dating from the third century B.C. On the contrary, we will discover in this investigation that the word "Jew" came from the hieroglyph of the reed, the Yod ▌, which represented, according to Maspero and Enel, the identity and individuality of each inhabitant of the kingdom of the Two Lands, in a universal vision where each individual is a **"Reed"**. **This idea was shared by Pascal who declared: "Man is only a reed, the weakest of nature; but he is a thinking reed"**.

In other words, for the ancient Egyptians, all men are Jews, since they are all Yods, Reeds, born in water, drawing their roots from the ground and rising towards heaven. When Ptolemy Soter and his son Ptolemy II Philadelphus, in order to achieve the syncretism to which they aspired between Greek and "Egyptian" society, enslaved in the third century B.C. the Jewish notables who were the guardians of tradition (clergy, officials, scribes, administrators), the word "Jew" changed its meaning by the power of the Septuagint. From then on, "the Jews", which previously referred to all the inhabitants of the land of the Two Lands, renamed Egypt, was only applied to this caste, which became distinct from its people. This caste became a population socially excluded from the rest of humanity because the Law of Moses was imposed on it, in a double separation both in terms of identity and geography. In this work, care must be taken to understand that the word "Jew" takes on different meanings depending on whether one is before Ptolemy Philadelphus, where it means "inhabitant" of ancient Egypt, or during and after Ptolemy, where it takes on a much more restrictive meaning, sometimes even torn from its hieroglyphic origin, from its semantic root under the name of "Hebrew". It is astonishing that the majority of Egyptologists have ignored the very essence of the basis of their discipline: the Yod ◢, the image of God and Mankind.

YAHOUD : This name designates in the Hebrew Bible the Jewish sons of the tribe of Judah, Yahouda יהודה. But the corresponding hieroglyph Yahoud or Yahout designates among the ancient Egyptians, before the Ptolemies, the dignitaries (or officials) of the Nile Valley. "Yahouda", "Yahoudaé" in Aramaic, 'Youdaïos" in Greek, mean "dignitary", "notable", which considerably changes the meaning of the verse.

HEBREW: This name, whose root EVER' עבר means "to pass" from one country to another, does not exist in ancient pre-Ptolemaic Egypt. It only appears in the Septuagint in the third century B.C. It then designates the Children of Israel, the Sons of Jacob, as "passers-by", strangers in Egypt. But the Targum often translates "Hebrew" as "Yahudae (dignitary) instead of using the true Aramaic translation "Ibrae", as if the scribes were pointing out that the Hebrews are dignitaries, sedentary people, the real inhabitants of the Nile Valley.

ISRAEL ישראל : When we talk about Israel today, we are referring to a *geographical territory*, and possibly to the population of this territory. It will be difficult for the reader to abstain from such a representation, as it is so much imprinted in our collective unconscious. However, its original meaning is quite different. In the Bible, *Israel* is the name of Jacob, who received this name after defeating the angel of darkness. Jacob/Israel was buried in a royal sarcophagus and mourned by the Egyptians. But for the secret tradition, the Zohar or the Kabbalah, Israel *is the god of the Nile valley*, under the term "divine Shekhina" (the divine light, the winged sun), who came down to Egypt with forty-two angels (his court), which makes Israel a memory of Osiris/Prince/Son of Râ, SAR 𓊹𓅮𓏤𓀭 in hieroglyphics, and of his forty-two judges. We will see that the myth of Jacob/Israel agrees with that of Osiris on many points, and that the name of Osiris is read IS-RÂ-GOD (EL) in hieroglyphics, especially the name SAR of Osiris is the root SAR שׁר of Israel ישׂראל , meaning "Prince" or "Son of King".

MITSRAIM מצרים : This Hebrew word reads in Greek MISRAIM Μεσραιμ **and cannot be translated as Egypt** whose root Ægyptos is the name of the Greek god Αἴγυπτον. To come out of Egypt is to come out of a geographical territory, GREEK, while to come out of MISRAIM is to come out of the "Pyramid" the celestial, uterine Matrix MESS, where the sun RA is born as well as all kings and men, the Maternal Womb of the celestial mother Isis/Nout, the celestial ocean (YAM). In this work, we will mention the explanation of the Kabbalah/Zohar according to which the people of Israel, when they came out of Egypt, came out of the Tree of Life located in the middle of the Garden of Eden, symbolizing the other History, the other family tree: Egypt. Indeed, the pronunciation MITSRAIM מצרים is the same as the Hebrew MÉ-ÈTS-AHAÏM מעץ החיים (Gen. 3, 22-24) when Yahweh expels Adam and Eve from the Garden of Eden and forbids access to it "for fear of consuming the Tree of Life" which conceals the prohibition for the Children of Israel/Jews to return to the Nile Valley.

TRIBE: Here is another word that lends itself to interpretation. In the collective representation, and thanks to big show movies, tribes appear as numerous groups of nomads, living under the tent of the breeding of their herds or hunting, under the guidance of their venerated clan chiefs, and actually quite primary. It should then be remembered that in Athens as in Rome, the tribes constituted a political, military and social framework. In Athens, the tribes corresponded to well-defined geographical territories and the men of the same tribe fought together, for example. Nothing to do with backward people living in the desert under tents. In the pre-Ptolemaic era, this was also the case. According to Jewish tradition, certain Jewish tribes were entrusted with particular functions, for example the priestly caste, such as the Levites who formed the clergy (of Osiris).

HELLENIZATION : After the conquest of the Middle East by Alexander the Great, the first Pharaohs Ptolemy programmed the "conquest of knowledge", an appropriation associated with the deculturation of the Jews, namely the Egyptian officials of the ancient Nile civilization. Thus when we speak of the ancient Greeks, we are talking about the Hellenes.

ÆGYPTIACA: Around 320 BC, the pharaoh Ptolemy Soter' asks his historian Manetho to reconstitute a "pseudo-hellenized history" of the ancient Nile Valley in order to create, to invente Egypt and the ancient Egyptians, and especially to legitimize his taking of power over the Nile Valley. The objective being double. On the one hand to make the Greeks look like the legitimate inhabitants of the region, the Egyptians (Ægypton' Αἰγυπτίων) becoming the ancestors of the Greeks. Thus the ancient names of the kings were hellenized, SA-RÂ into Pharaoh, Amenhotep into Amenophis, Tutmes into Thutmosis, Senusert into Sesostris, Sethy into Sethos, etc., in order to appear as those of whom the Ptomemies could be the legitimate heirs. On the other hand, to make the Jews a "race" of foreigners in the country renamed Ægyptos.

SEPTUAGINT (LXX): It includes the first five books of the Old Testament written around 270 B.C. by the seventy-two Jewish scholars in the tower of Pharos in Alexandria, on the orders of Pharaoh Ptolemy Philadelphus. It is a second Ægyptiaca which makes the Jews - in the new meaning of this word - the heirs of the Hebrew slaves of Pharaoh, a myth invented for the occasion.

KYRIOS: κύριος: This is the name of God in the Septuagint. It is usually translated Lord, but several verses attest that it is the only divine name allowed to the Jews Yudaios by the ancient Greeks. In ancient Athens, κύριος Kyrios is the legal guardian of women, dividing the family estate.

RACHI: Famous French Talmudist, exegete and commentator of the Torah, the Aramaic Targum and the Babylonian Talmud, born in Troyes in the 10th century (1040-1105). The commentary of Rachi is a reference for its contribution to the ancient vocabulary of the French language.

MIDRASH : Considered as a higher level than the literal reading of the Bible, the Midrash forms a literary corpus which gathers the commentaries of the Torah and the Targum accumulated over the centuries since the Greek Septuagint.

RABBI SIMEON BAR YOHAI : Living in first century Safed, Rabbi Simeon is considered by rabbinic tradition to be the most prominent author of the Zohar, or rather of an important part of it, since some of his work has been lost. Rabbi Simeon places the secret tradition of the Torah - the Zohar - at the highest level of all forms of interpretation. The Zohar or "Oral Law" embodies the "royal crown" of understanding of the sacred hebrew text, but also the very symbol of the Tree of Life, whereas any literal reading of the Torah refers to an imprisonment of the mind in the Tree of Knowledge of Good and Evil.

THE OSTRACA OF ELEPHANTINE: Following the French excavations at Elephantine in Upper Egypt, conducted from 1906 to 1911 by Charles Clermont-Ganneau, assisted by Jean Clédat and, more episodically, by Jules Couyat and Joseph-Etienne Gautier, scholars discovered papyri and pottery shards or ostraca on which were written in ancient Aramaic the letters forming a correspondence between the Jews of Jerusalem and the Jews of Elephantine where the temple of Yhaou (Yahweh), the god symbolizing Osiris, the light of the world, stood. From the data of this correspondence, the scholars of the CNRS have established that the Jews of the time practiced the cult of Osiris.

THE LETTER OF ARISTAEUS TO PHILOCRATES :

This historical document tells, in Greek, how Ptolemy II Philadelphus summoned seventy-two Jewish sages versed in Hellenistic culture in order - allegedly - to translate the Torah of Moses into Greek. Aristaeus is said to be a Hellenized Jew - which is why he is called the "pseudo Aristaeus" - who had recounted on a hundred pages the details of the birth of the Septuagint preceded by a great banquet of seven days where seventy-two questions were put by Ptolemy to the 72 sages. Even if the Letter of Aristaeus was written - either rewritten or reworked - late (around -160 according to the low hypothesis), it gives us vital information on the historical religion, "Osirian" of the Jews developed in the Middle East, as well as the perverse motivations of king Ptolemy to settle the "question of the Jewish books".

MASSORA or TORAH: This is the text of the first five books of the Old Testament, written in Hebrew square letters, known as the Masoretic text. The Torah was canonized in the first century of our era. In its secret reading, it is a cryptic language of the Septuagint, known only to the initiated rabbis. But in its literal reading, it is in total ignorance of the true past of the Jews as the Egyptian ruling caste before the Ptolemies.

ARAMAIC TARGUM: This is the translation of the Bible by Onklelos at the beginning of the second century, into Aramaic (a Semitic language close to Hebrew). The Targum is written with square Hebrew letters. It is considered to be an interpretation of the Torah, since it provides additional information. The name of God is not Yahweh or Elohim as in the Hebrew Torah, but is written with two ׳׳ or three Yods ׳׳׳ and thus refers to the multiplication of the primordial reed from which the universe was created, which corresponds to the Principle of the great Ennead of Heliopolis.

KABBALAH: This is the secret tradition of the Torah dating back to the time of the Septuagint (around 270 AD). The word Kabbalah means "that which is received". The Kabbalah, also called the "oral tradition", is a body of esoteric knowledge, is a corpus of esoteric knowledge, reporting the great secrets that the initiated Jews, resisting and rebelling against the Assyrian, Babylonian, Greek and Roman dominations, transmitted to each other either orally or in writing. Thus, the Kabbalah is considered as a forbidden reading before forty years, even "idolatrous reading" by the rabbinic authorities, because it often deconstructs the text of the Torah, going so far as to designate the god of the Jews as the god of the ancient Egyptians. The Kabbalah is the hieroglyphic reading grid that has remained unexploited by modern Egyptology.

ZOHAR and TIKOUN AZOHAR: It is the set of works gathering the fundamental texts of the KABBALAH in Aramaic at different times. When I use the word "Kabbalah" in my works, I always quote the Zohar text as a reference. Jean de Pauly and Charles Mopsik translated the Zohar into French. The TIKUN AZOHAR is the most secret part of the Zohar, and therefore of the Kabbalah, which questions the characters of the Torah. The latter are - as in ancient Egypt - solar characters, the Children of Israel are the twelve constellations that came to settle in Egypt. Joseph is the nourishing River of Egypt, Abraham was born in Egypt, in the house of his father - Terah, the famous merchant of idols - who is none other than Yahweh, the god of Egypt. Jacob is renamed Israel, because he is the sun illuminating Egypt, etc. These few pieces of information make the Zohar the «Secret Code» of an « Egyptian » or even hieroglyphic reading of the Torah, and therefore of our Bibles. The Zohar constitutes a fundamental basis for the study of the ancient Nile Valley, a basis that modern Egyptology has never deigned to exploit.

ADONAI אדני: It is in the liturgy and the reading of the Torah the pronunciation of the sacred name YHVH יהוה. ADONAI means at the same time "My Lord" and "My Lords" and for the Cabala, the root Adone refers to the worship of the sunlight (Aton' or Adon' in hieroglyphs). The Jewish tradition gives the hieroglyphic name of Abraham Etan' Ezrahit' meaning the Sun ⊙ at the Eastern Horizon ⌒, corresponding to the hieroglyph of Aton.

ANOKHI אנכי: First word of the ten commandments, it means I when God speaks. This sacred name is considered the «I of God» according to the Midrash Rabbah, or the «word of the Egyptian words» according to the Rebbe of Lubavitch. ANOKHI is broken down into AKNH ☥ the LIFE and YOD ▐ , God. It is found in all Egyptian liturgy in the form but it also exists in the form ANKHI meaning the Spirit of Ra. We find in this hieroglyph the two Yods ⎍⎍ of the god of the Aramaic Bible יי (Targum of Onkelos).

Ānkhi ☥ ～～～ ⎍⎍, Ṭuat X, the god of time and of the life of Rā.

Anokhy, the God of the eternity of Ra's life[7].

ELOHIM אלהים :

First name of God in the Hebrew Torah. It is read "the gods" because it is the plural of EL. אלהים is broken down into EL אל "HE" ה and YAM ים, the HE ה is the breath of God EL, coming from the celestial waters YAM, like Atum, the Egyptian demiurge Yod ▐, coming out of the waters of the primordial ocean, the Noun ～～～. In the hieroglyphs, ELOHIM corresponds to the Neteru 𓊹𓊹𓊹, the three gods meaning God and the gods.

NETER' 𓊹 (God) or NETEROU 𓊹𓊹𓊹 (the gods):

These words are generalized by modern Egyptology to mislead mankind about the true meaning of the word GOD in the hieroglyphs. We will demonstrate, with several examples, that the ideogram 𓊹 "GOD" and its plural, the gods 𓊹𓊹𓊹 refer above all - and this is perfectly obvious - to Atum. Atum or TAM is the creator god, the Demiurge who generated the gods

---

7   Egyptian hieroglyphic dictionary. Wallis Budge, Dover Publications, inc, New York. Published by General publishing Company, 1978, p. 125b.

- the priests, the builders - as well as the whole creation, and whose hieroglyph of the First Principle is the YOD ▟. . Atum - the One who became three - claims to be the origin of the creation of the gods, either by childbirth or by the begetting or tripling of the YOD. I will come back to this enormous error of Egyptology which has blinded humanity because of false postulates, prisoners of conventions.

For example, Thoth, the god symbolizing writing, Knowledge, is written either with the sacred ibis, or with the sacred Yod ▟. followed by the figurative ר

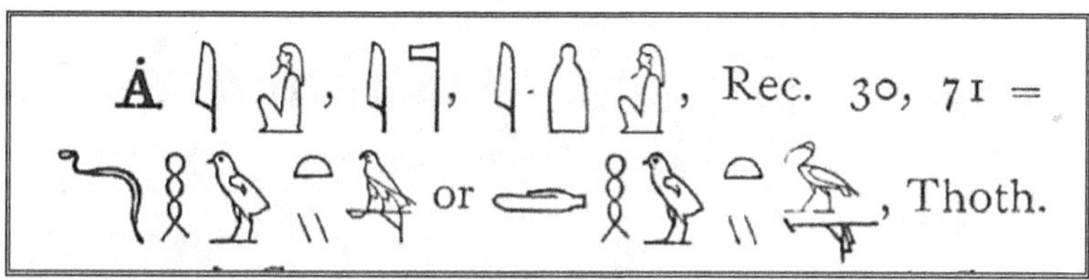

YAHVE יהוה :

Also written YHVH, Yahweh, it is the second name of God in the Hebrew Torah. According to Jewish tradition, YHVH is unpronounceable, although it is pronounced Adonai, Jehovah, and Yahu or Yaho in ancient Jewish texts. We recognize the semantic roots Yod, Yah, Yahou used in hieroglyphs to designate the divine light or the flood of the Nile.

The Kabbalah compares YAHOU/YHVH יהוה to the primordial light and the course of the sun ☉ across the two horizons ◠. The hieroglyph of יהוה is inscribed in the most sacred writings as well as in the name of Aten. The symbol of YAHOU is found in the royal seal of king Hezekiah, in the form of the winged sun with three rays (the winged sun is engraved on most of the temples of the Nile valley, as we shall see in the second part of this trilogy).

Hieroglyphics of Yahu, origin of Yahweh (YHVH) the light of Ra-Osiris with the figurative of the sun with three rays[8].

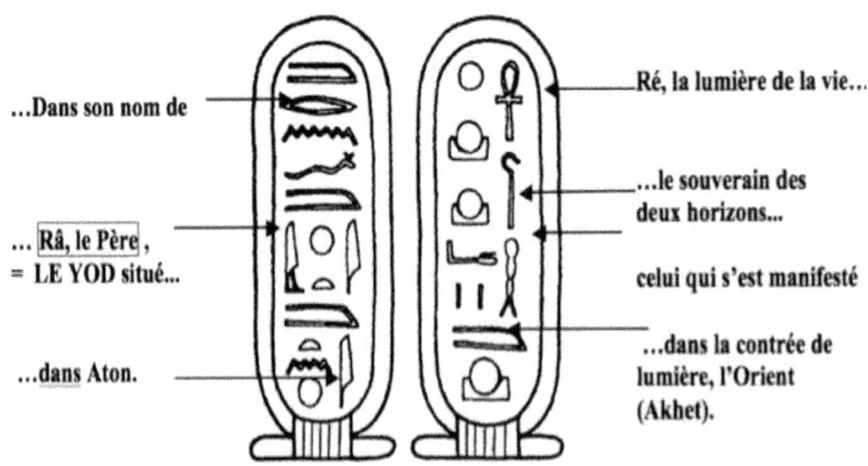

Second didactic form of the name Aten. God is symbolized by the Light of Ra ☉ running through the two horizons .

---

8   Egyptian hieroglyphic dictionary. Wallis Budge, Dover Publications, inc, New York. Published by General publishing Company, 1978, 23 a.

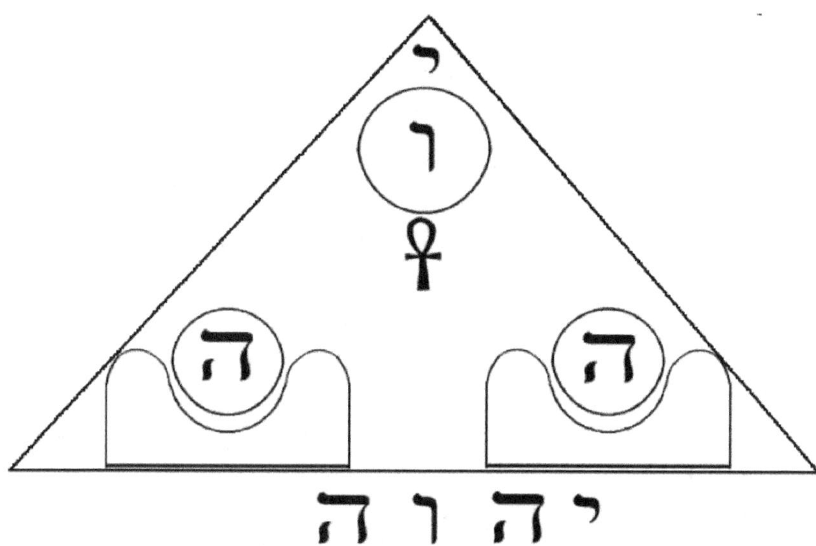

Pyramid of the Tetragrammaton at the origin of the universe from the hieroglyphs of the name Aton according to the Kabbalah.

Royal seals of Hezekiah (Hazak-YAHOU power of YAHOU in Hebrew and hieroglyphs) king of the Nile Valley engraved by the hieroglyph of the winged sun or of the winged scarab meaning Yahu, the Light (RÂ, Aton, Amon) origin of Yahu.

TREE OF LIFE עץ החיים :

This is the supreme tree, allowed to Adam and Eve in the Garden of Eden, the image of happiness for humanity. Even if this story is very short, the Tree of Life עץ החיים contains the essence of God, the word Life being written with two Yods יי. like the two Yods of the God of Egypt. It symbolizes in the Kabbalah the first lost Torah, symbolically broken by Moses, the wisdom of Egypt, and finally the land of Egypt from where the Children of Israel were expelled to Canaan to receive the other Torah, the other "Tree", the one of the Knowledge of Good and Evil, which is why it is said in Psalms (80,9-12): "The Torah is a Tree of Life for him who grassps it" for him who grasps its hidden meaning, the SOD in Hebrew. This means that the two trees in the Garden of Eden symbolize two family trees, the passage from the ancient Jewish civilization, the so-called 'Egyptian' of the Tree of Life, to the new Jewish civilization linked to the Septuagint and later to the Torah/Massora.

THE TREE OF THE KNOWLEDGE OF GOOD AND EVIL עץ הדעת טוב ורע:

Regarded as the tree forbidden by God to Adam and Eve in the Garden of Eden, this tree symbolizes the root cause of the expulsion from paradise, the original sin of Adam ; but also of all Israel and by extension of all humanity symbolically expelled from Egypt equated to the Garden of Eden. For the Kabbalah, this tree represents darkness, the "death of the world", the disappearance of the light of the ancient wisdom of Egypt called "Supreme Wisdom", identified with the Tree of Life. However, a part of this light remained coded, encrypted in the second Torah of Moses, when the latter is read from the data of the Kabbalah and we will see it from Egyptology.

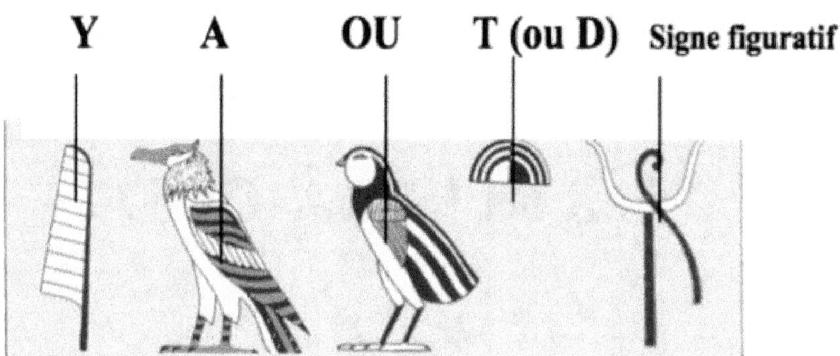

Symbol YAHOUD consecrating the dignitaries - the substitutes of the serpent uræus - and the kings of the Nile Valley.

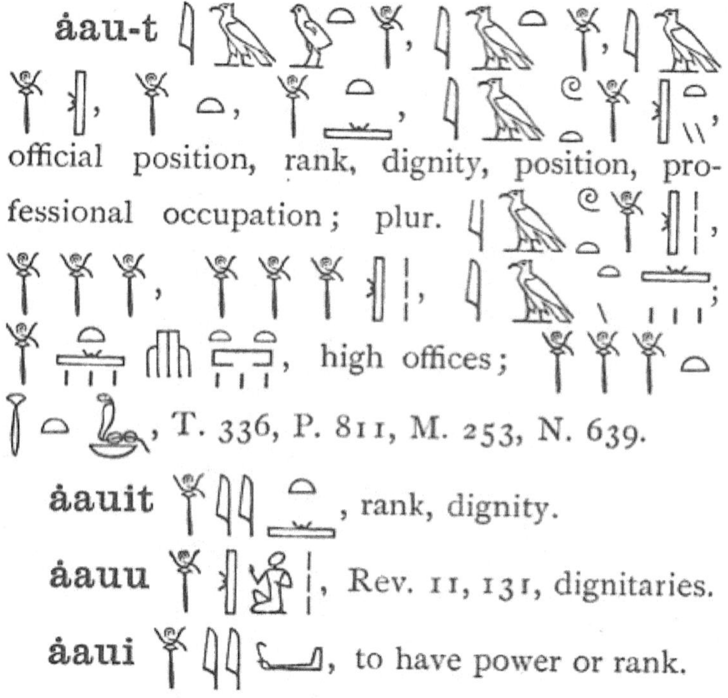

åau-t official position, rank, dignity, position, professional occupation; plur. high offices; T. 336, P. 811, M. 253, N. 639.

åauit rank, dignity.

åauu Rev. 11, 131, dignitaries.

åaui to have power or rank.

Hieroglyph Yahoud, Yahoudi or Yahout, Yahou, origin of the word "Jew" meaning the function, the initiation, the priestly office, the dignity, the worship of the god of light, etc.[9]

---

9 Egyptian hieroglyphic dictionary. Wallis Budge, Dover Publications, inc, New York. Published by General publishing Company, 1978, pp. 18-23-24.

Analogies of Osiris with Israel

The name of Osiris

is read IS-RÂ-GOD[1]

The name of Osiris SA-RÂ is read IS-RÂ-GOD origin of Israel[2]

Solar Egg = IS

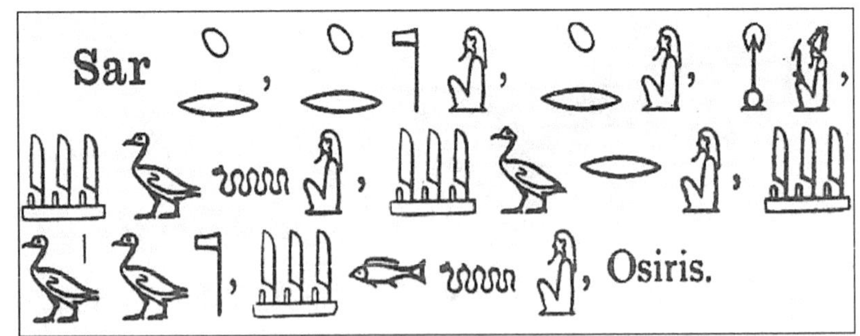

---

1   Egyptian hieroglyphic dictionary. Wallis Budge, op. cit, p. 583a, M 217; N 589

2   Dover Publications, inc, New York. Op. cit., Wallis Budge, 1978, tome 1, p 83 a.

OSIRIS	KABBALAH ISRAËL
IS-RÂ-GOD : SON OF GOD.	ISRAEL/JACOB: SON OF GOD.
EARTH = SA-RÂ = IS-RÂ (EGYPT)	LAND OF ISRAEL
MAKES THE WATERS OF THE NILE RISE	MAKES THE WATERS OF THE NILE RISE
THE JUST 42 JUDGES	THE JUST 42 ANGELS
SUN ATON	SUN OF THE YEAR
FAUCON	FAUCON RAÂ or EAGLE
FIRST MAN DEAD AND RESURRECTED	FIRST MAN DEAD AND RESURRECTED
SON OF TOUM=ATOUM, PERFECT MAN	SON OF ADAM, TAM PERFECT MAN
42, 26, 14, OR 12 PARTS OF GOD INCLUDING THE PHALLUS	42, 12 SONS = 12 PARTS OF GOD JOSEPH = PHALLUS
Rivalry with his brother Set.	Rivalry with his brother Esau.
Osiris fights at night against the serpent Apophys.	Jacob/Israel fights against the serpent Esau at night.
Osiris is the light which drives out Apophys the darkness	Israel is the light that chases Esau, the darkness.
TREE OF LIFE DJED PILLAR	TREE OF LIFE PILLAR OF THE WORLD
At night, Osiris confuses two sisters and marries them	At night, Jacob confuses two sisters and marries them
ISIS AND NEPHTYS: Sirius Sothis Venus.	RACHEL (day) and LEA (night).
Annual flood of the Nile.	Raises the Nile's waters
Happiness, prosperity, abundance and fertility in Egypt.	Happiness, prosperity, abundance and fertility in Egypt.
Father of the twelve regions of the cosmos.	Father of the twelve tribes = 12 constellations of the cosmos.
Embalmed in a sarcophagus in Egypt.	Embalmed in a sarcophagus in Egypt.

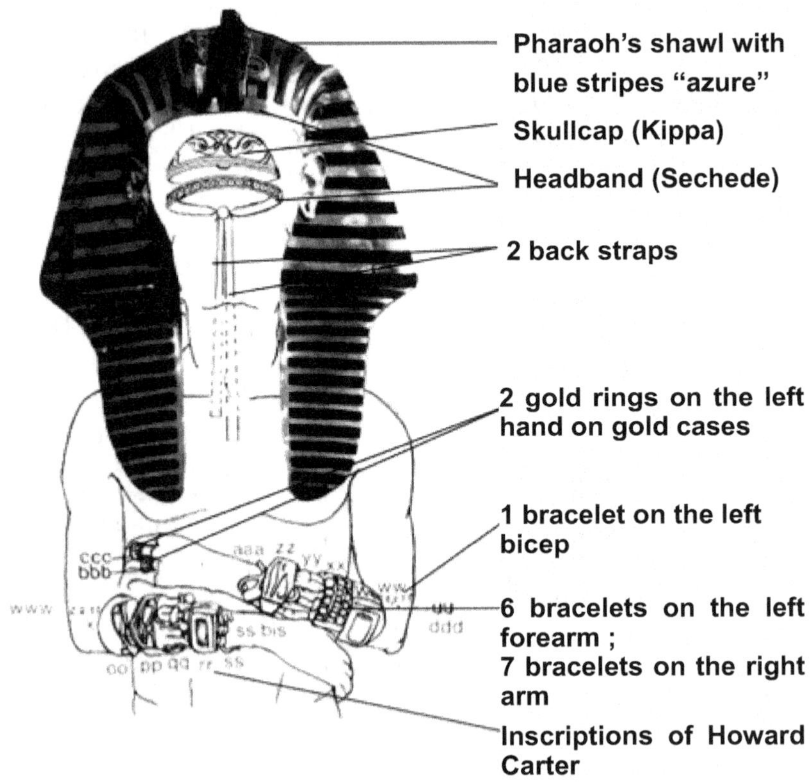

Mummy of Tutankhamun IS-RÂ-EL with the Jewish divine symbols.

Osiris/Israel/Yahoud

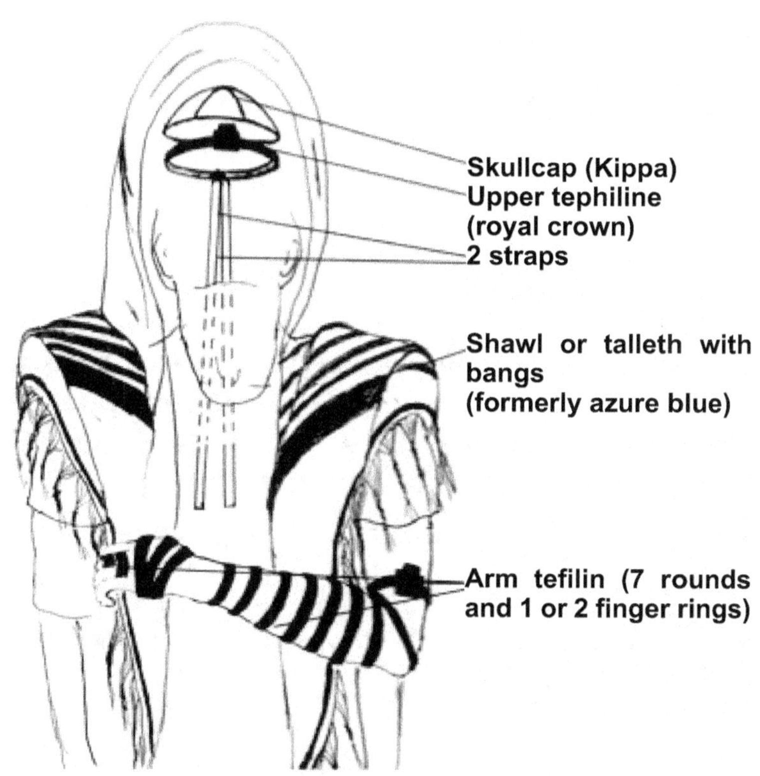

Jew wearing the prayer shawl (tallith) and Tefilins, considered the royal and divine adornment and crown of the kings of Israel, wearing the crown of Amun.

Israel/Osiris/Yahoud

It is essential to remember that Jacob, renamed Israel after his symbolic fight against the angel of darkness (named Elohim), and his son Joseph, were embalmed and placed in an "Egyptian" sarcophagus, by Pharaoh's doctors. The sarcophagi of Joseph and Israel are therefore designed in the image of Osiris. Israel and Joseph are buried under the image of Osiris by means of the sarcophagus. In the Torah and in Jewish tradition, the sarcophagus, far from being considered as an idol, as it should be (we saw it in the first part of this trilogy), is looked upon by the Kabbalah (the Zohar) as the universal sarcophagus of the Righteous, the sarcophagus of the Fathers, the sarcophagus of the kings of Israel, the other Ark of the Covenant of Israel is the sarcophagus of Osiris...

"Notice that the holy side is called «Ark of the Covenant», and it is appropriate to enclose the body of Man in it. That is why the great zealots [the wise men, the kings of Israel] had been enclosed in a sarcophagus after death."[1]

"The Jews do not practice embalming today [...] In truth, it is customary concerning the kings [of Israel] so that their bodies may endure, to embalm them in the anointing oil superior to all oils...[...] So it was with Jacob/Israel, for he is the Body of the Fathers [...] It is written, «He was put in a sarcophagus, for he was a Righteous One"[2]

The Zohar confirms that the kings of Israel wore the crown to the serpent of Amon, they were embalmed, placed in a sarcophagus, and this was for the purpose of bringing the soul of the dead to the heavenly court of Israel in order to be "justified". This is the memory of the Book of the Dead, in its foundation, the very essence of the so-called Egyptian civilization. Ancient Judaism and Egyptology form only one civilization, that of the celestial journey of the sarcophagus into the afterlife. A revelation that calls into question archaeology, Egyptology, but also any literal reading of the Torah. A challenge to our three monotheistic religions based on the Revelation of Yahweh at Mount Sinai, and on the demonization - without any foundation - of the Nile Valley civilization.

---

1 Zohar, tome IV, Le livre de la splendeur, op. cit., p. 225.
2 Le Zohar, tome I, collection « les dix paroles ». Traduit par Charles Mopsik. Verdier, 1981, 250, b.

Old Kingdom -2600 BC.
First kings SA-RÂ, son of SA-RÂ Osiris.
The names Egypt and Egyptian do not exist.
First pyramids built by the priests of On'.
Middle Kingdom -2033
Kings SA-RÂ/Osiris, never «Egyptians».
Book of commandments of SA-RA (Osiris).
New Kingdom -1600
Kings SA-RÂ, sons of SA-RÂ, no Egyptians.
Late Period -1000

Greek period -300: After the conquests of Alexander the Great, Pharaoh Ptolemy II Philadelphus enslaves the Jews and falsifies their history. The king invents the history of the pharaohs and the ancient Egyptians.

The Nile Valley is named ÆGYPTOS, the name of the son of Zeus. Ptolemy forbids the Jews to worship Osiris. He falsifies the history of the kings Sons of RÂ. The Jews are demonized. On' becomes the Greek Heliopolis.

The Jewish priests of On'/Heliopolis and Amun are chased out of Egypt in the Septuagint.

Ptolemy orchestrates the great miracle of the Septuagint, the Greek Bible with 72 wise men, Jews from the great ancestral priesthood of Heliopolis.

Commandments of Kyrios
given by Moses.
History of the Hebrews and the kings of Israel.
Disappearance of the history of the SA-RÂkings.
Disappearance of the priests of Heliopolis.
Disappearance of the sons of SA-RÂ/Osiris.
Disappearance of the Book and the Laws of Osiris.
Osiris/SA-RÂ is put in secret.
The secrets of ancient Israel and the SA-RÂ are preserved in the Kabbalah.

Creation of synagogues.
The Jews study, read, pray and sing
sing the Bible in Greek.
Ptolemy worships in the Septuagint
through the Holy Double Drachma.
The universal god of the Jews, priests of On',
becomes the political god of the exit from Egypt.

Adam, Noah, Abraham, Isaac, Jacob, Joseph,
Moses, become the founders of Israel.
1st century AD
Massacre of the Jews of Alexandria.
Separation between Jews and future Christians.
Jews abandon the Greek Septuagint.
THE HEBREW TORAH IS CANONIZED
(the first five books of the Old Testament)
Abandonment of the name Kyrios.
Reappearance of the name Yahweh in the Torah.
Birth of the Babylonian Talmud.
6th Byzantine century
The emperor Justinian definitively forbids
hieroglyphs and the cult of Isis/Osiris.
BIRTH OF THE KORAN
Appearance of the Koran between the 6th and 9th centuries.
Allah returns the land of Misra to the Sons of Israel.
19th century
Champollion: birth of Egyptology.

THE ANCIENT EGYPTIANS HAVE DISAPPEARED

Jean-François Champollion is not followed in his request to study the Sacred Criticism of the Bible. Ancient Egypt is studied as a dead civilization, without any filiation with the religions.

Chapter I

DECIPHERING THE HIDDEN MEANING

IN THE PERSIAN ERA AND BEFORE, JEWS PRACTICED THE CULT OF OSIRIS

The ostraca found at Elephantine in Middle Egypt included part of the correspondence between the Jews of Jerusalem and the Jews of Egypt. CNRS scholars are certain that in the 6th and 5th centuries BC, the Jews practiced the cult of Osiris. In the letters discovered, the Jews bless themselves in the names of the gods of Egypt and do not make the slightest allusion to the Law of Moses... which they did not know.

The scholars of the CNRS in their conclusions on the Elephantine correspondence (dating from the 7th to the 4th century B.C.) had the honesty to recognize that the Jews of that time practiced the cult of Osiris. Therefore, they followed the forty-two commandments of Osiris, the syncretic, single and multiple god of the Nile Valley, following the trail of their ancestors.

"The gods of Egypt were worshipped by the Orientals who resided in the country, AND EVEN BY THE JEWS before the reform introduced around 520 B.C. However, THE THING IS ATTESTED BY TEXTS ONLY FOR THE CULT OF OSIRIS"[10]

---

10 Some letters attest that the most important Jewish priests swore by Yahô, Ptah, Knoum, Osiris. Aramaic documents from Egypt. Littératures Anciennes du Proche-Orient. Éditions du Cerf, 1972, p. 345.

In the said correspondence, the Jews swore and blessed each other in the names of Yahô, Ptah, Khnoum, Isis, Osiris, the latter worshipped under the name of Yahô or Khnoum, Amon, because of the importance of the syncretism of Osiris:

"I bless you to Ptah, that he may make me see your face again in good health. Hail Bet'El-Natan»!" [11]

"Blessed be 'Abâ son of Hûr and Ahatabû daughter of Adiyâ, both of whom (are) blessed and honored. May they have access before Osiris the god! Absallî son of Abâ, whose mother is Ahatabû spoke thus in the year 4 of the month of Mehîr, of Xerses king of kings; (Executed) by the hand of Pamin."[12]

The Jewish and Egyptian names are mixed in a symptomatic way, affirm the scholars of the CNRS. It is important to note that the religion of Osiris was widespread throughout the Middle East in Persian times. Because of its universal character for all men and especially because of its syncretism, any god could naturally be identified with Ptah, Amun or Osiris (like Baal). The Torah of the Jews was none other than the Book of the Exit to the Light, falsely named *Book of the Dead*:

"This devotion to Osiris was widespread in all the Middle East: it aimed at obtaining for the pilgrims immortality in the afterlife, as it appears from the Book of the Dead... ...One notes that the devotion to Osiris is alive, in this Egypt where men of all races were mixed"[13]

---

11   Documents Araméens d'Égypte. P. 160, inscription n°28.

12   Ibidem, p. 341, inscription n°85, épitaphe courante sur vases à libation.

13   Documents Araméens d'Égypte. Littératures Anciennes du Proche-Orient. Éditions du Cerf, 1972, p. 340 ;343.

It is clear that the scholars of the CNRS denounce a «pagan» Judaism, generalized, Osirian, inherited by the ancestors of the Jews... who were the real Egyptians.

"The Jews of Egypt therefore did not have to innovate to become pagan; all they had to do was to continue in the footsteps of their immediate ancestors and to perpetuate the forms of worship that had become generalized under the reign of Manasseh"[14]

Scholars have noted that in the 5th century BCE, the Jews who were subject to the Persian invaders were ready to execute and impose the Law of the King, according to the Talmudic principle «The Law of the Kingdom is the Law» (Aramaic Dina di-malkhouta Dina). The new Law of the King/God Darius II served as a royal decree to subdue the small population:

"But when one remembers the bastardized character of the [Jewish] cult of Elephantine, strongly marked by syncretism (cf. no. 89), one has the impression that the high authorities of Judaism took advantage of the circumstances to introduce a cultic reform with the support of the power"[15]

More than a century before the Ptolemies, Darius imposed a new law. To the Jews and not to the Egyptians. This Law is not yet the Torah of Moses! Even less so with the support of the so-called prophets, whose books historians place at the time of the Lagids. In the fifth century B.C., the power of the king of Persia had authority over the Jewish High Priests and their way of practicing religion. We will analyze in the ostraca, the evidence that in the fifth century B.C., the Persian king Darius II, who was deified during his lifetime, had taken the decision to reform, even to reverse certain Osirian rituals of the Jews by means of royal/divine decrees overturning the ancestral rituals of the Nile Valley.

---

14 Documents Araméens d'Égypte. Littératures Anciennes du Proche-Orient. Éditions du Cerf, 1972, p. 347.

15 Documents Araméens d'Égypte. P. 346-347 ; 381.

Therefore, the actual Torah of Moses, his Law and commandments, were not yet authoritative in the Jewish world of the time. Yes, the Elephantine letters provide evidence that the Law of Moses did not yet exist.

The Law of Moses thus had no authority, no reason to exist over the priesthood and the Jewish population of the Middle East. The Elephantine correspondence attests that the Book of Moses was totally unknown to the priests/rabbis running the temple in Jerusalem, who worshipped Osiris in the "Egyptian" temples and in the temple in Elephantine. None of the letters that have been found denounce any transgression of the Jews of Elephantine for idolatry forbidden by the Decalogue under penalty of death. None of the letters from the Jewish rulers of Jerusalem or Elephantine attempt to impose respect for the Torah of Moses. None of them denounces the syncretic worship of the gods or of Osiris! On the contrary, at that time, the scholars of the CNRS found that all the Jews were... pagans, therefore "idolaters !!!". Now, the Jews could not practice the cult of Osiris without knowing the secrets of the Osiris's priests, the secrets of the gods of the Nile valley, without knowing the secrets of hieroglyphs.

An entire passage of the Bible, ordering the Children of Israel to sacrifice the lamb and forbidding leavened bread, came from the decree of Darius II. Darius imposes on the Jews the sacrifice of the Passover lamb. Now the lamb is by syncretism the image of the rebirth of Osiris, the rebirth of the light (imagined by the child Horus)... The sacrifice of the lamb is announced as a sacrilege of the ancient Jewish religion. A first catastrophe for the Jews attached to the cult of Osiris. I quote the decree:

"To my brothers Yedonyah and his colleagues, the Jewish garrison, your brother Hananyah. May the gods grant my brothers prosperity! And now in this year, the fifth year of king Darius, it was mandated by the king, therefore by Darius, to Arshama: Now therefore count you fourteen days from the first day of Nissan, and do the passover. And from the fifteenth to the twenty-first day of Nissan shall be to you the feast of unleavened bread.

Now, you, be pure, and take care! Do not do any work on the fifteenth or the twenty-first day. Also, do not drink beer, and do not eat anything fermented. Eat unleavened food from the 14th day of Nissan at sunset until the 21st day of Nissan at sunset. For seven days do not bring leaven into your rooms, and keep it out of your rooms during those days. So let it be done, as King Darius said"

The decree of Darius II is found almost entirely in the Bible, with the precision of a cut and paste. But with an enormous, significant difference, because here, it is no longer the decree in the name of king Darius, but that of God and Moses. Either the god of the Septuagint Kyrios, or the God of the Bible YAHVE. The decree of the Septuagint/Torah, transcribed in the book of Exodus, is addressed to a people of priests, armies and slaves. So the Children of Israel, supposedly slaves in Egypt, are sufficiently organized to have priests, armies, which supposes a social institution. The said decree of Kyrios/Yahweh orders, the instructions for the feast of Passover and the sacrifice of the lamb. The cause is not the decree of Darius to the Jews in Jerusalem and Egypt. God is addressing the Children of Israel. EXODUS (XII, 17-21), words of YAHVÉ:

"You shall observe the feast of unleavened bread, for on that day I brought your armies out of the land of Egypt. You shall observe this day throughout your generations; it is a perpetual ordinance. In the first month, on the evening of the fourteenth day, you shall eat unleavened bread until the evening of the twenty-first day. Seven days there shall be no leaven in your houses, for whoever eats leavened bread shall be cut off from the community of Israel, whether he be a foreigner or a native-born. You shall not eat leavened bread; wherever you live you shall eat unleavened bread." Moses summoned all the elders of Israel and said to them, "Go and get small livestock for your families and slaughter the Passover!"

Israel is a civilization installed into another civilization renamed Ægyptos by the Greeks! The Children of Israel thus form a nation within a nation as the Bible states, just before the exit from Egypt. In his book *Le prix du Monothéisme*, Jan Assmann justifies his position on the fact that God took "a nation within another nation, Goy mi-kérèb Goy, the Hebrew term Kérèb is very strong, because it can also designate the "entrails" or the "womb"

Deuteronomy 4, 34: **Was there ever a god who tried to take a nation to himself from the midst of a nation, by trials, signs, wonders and battles, with a strong hand and an outstretched arm, and with wonders of terror, as the Lord your God did for you in Egypt and before your eyes?**

Here is a rabbinic commentary regarding the Maharal of Prague on the issue:

"In Deuteronomy the Torah says that when God brought the Jewish people out of Egypt "he brought a nation out from within another nation "goy mikerev goy", the Maharal speaks of an embryo from its mother's womb, as does the midrash tehilim (114), which even adds, that God himself was not sure he could do it, to be able to separate the inseparable. Yet we read in the haggadah that the Jews were separated from the non-Jews and recognizable by their names, clothes and languages. How can this contradiction be resolved?

In the entire history of the Nile Valley, it is impossible for a so-called Jewish civilization to have lived within a so-called Egyptian civilization. "A nation taken from within the so-called Egyptian nation", assumes that the "Egyptians" existed historically, whereas archaeology proves that they do not exist in the hieroglyphics! The biblical text was necessarily written after the land of Osiris was usurped by the ancient Greeks. Before, there are only Yods, kings and men who, all without exception, identify themselves with the Yod designating Atum, Amun, Ra. Thus, the Bible cannot express more clearly that the Children of Israel, the Jews, the Yods, the Yahuds, came out of their nation, the Matrix OSIRIS/ISRAEL/MISRAIM (not Ægyptos, the Greek god!) the heart of this civilization.

A nation taken from within the nation of Egypt", the biblical text cannot express more clearly that the Children of Israel, the Jews, the Yods, the Yahuds, came out of the OSIRIS/ISRAEL/ MISRAIM Matrix (not Ægyptos, the Greek god!) the heart of this civilization. Thus, we have written proof that the 72 scribes of the Bible managed, under the nose of Ptolemy Philadelphus, to copy the decree of Darius II into the Septuagint and then into the Hebrew Bible. All these elements are consistent evidence that the Septuagint/Torah of Moses, invoking an exit from a country called Ægyptos, could only have been written after the invasions of the Macedonians, after Alexander the Great, the new deified kings, the Ptolemies. We also have proof that the words of the decree of Darius II, recognized as such by the Jews of that time, do not concern Moses. They have been transposed into the words of Moses, who is therefore a transfigured figure in the distant past, obeying either Kyrios in the Greek Septuagint or Yahweh in the Torah. We note that the Jews of Jerusalem in the 5th century B.C. do not invoke the Torah of Moses, but only «the gods» to introduce the «reform», the new Law in the name of Darius II, and not in the name of Yahweh, in order to impose the new celebration of Passover on the Jews of Elephantine. The latter seeing in this reform a radical and sacrilegious violation of the cult of Osiris, in a categorical answer, will refuse to obey the orders of the Jews of Jerusalem who speak in the name of Darius II.

We draw the following conclusion. This exchange of letters dating from the fifth century B.C. provides proof that Moses was unknown to the Jews of that time. Moses was so unknown to the Jews of Jerusalem and Elephantine that the latter preferred to pay a tax to the satrap in order to obtain permission from Darius II and from the Jews of Jerusalem to be exempted from the sacrifice of the paschal lamb, a sacrilege and a profanation of Osiris, the sun reborn in the form of the lamb or of the child Horus. The Jews, it is noted, will fight courageously in order not to blaspheme and transgress the Laws of Osiris, in order not to obey the deified king Darius II.

THE COSMOLOGY OF ISRAEL IS THAT OF OSIRIS

Although it seems incredible, Kabbalah reveals that the ancient Jewish religion corresponds to the cosmogony of On'/ Heliopolis. The so-called idolatry of the ancient Egyptians was a cosmotheism. This means that ***God was the creation. God was «the heavens and the earth».*** The sun and the moon are the Body of God, either Yahweh יהוה or Elohim אלהים. They are not material elements created by a god separate from creation, but a god consubstantial with creation. It is a begetting of the primary Yod י named Elohim אלהים or Yahweh יהוה who split into God-Sky and God-Earth. In symbolism, it is the primordial Reed or Yod, the hieroglyph of God - which Kabbalah tells us is the Supreme Point, the Body of Eslohim/ Yod -Yod י י - that symbolically split into two in the first verse of the Torah to engender the heavens and the earth.

Kabbalah identifies the heavens and the earth with the Body of God:

"And ET' את The heavens «: it is YHVH, the supreme sense... ...And ET' את the earth «: it is Elohim, according to the form of the supreme, so that fruits and plants are produced... ...from the primordial point he created the unfolding of a superior point, and it is that he inscribed the secret of the name of forty-two letters"[16]

The sun and the moon are also considered by Kabbalah to be the parts of the Body of Elohim אלהים or Yahweh יהוה:

"The great light" (Gen. 1:6): This is YHVH יהוה . The "little light" (Id.) is Elohim אלהים"[17]

---

16   Le Zohar, tome I, collection «les dix paroles ». Op. cit., 1981.15b, p. 95.

17   Le Zohar, tome I, collection «les dix paroles ». Traduit par Charles Mopsik. Verdier, 1981.20a- 20b, p. 116.

It was, of course, impossible to understand this decoding for the Jews of the Hellenistic period, who had to read and learn the Septuagint and only the Septuagint, where Kyrios the Lord of the Word, Logos, the «Theo» had created the heavens and the earth... This is the proof that the text of the Torah, the Hebrew Massora, came either at the same time or shortly after the Septuagint as a secret coding, forbidden to the Greeks. Indeed, through Kabbalah, we have proof that the seventy-two Jews of the Septuagint could not have been unaware that heaven and earth, the sun and moon, formed the multiplied body of God, the primordial Yod. All of creation, the universal earth, the ancient Nile Valley, was based on the principle of the begetting of the Body of God, forming the heavens and the earth, the two Worlds, from a demultiplication. The begetting of the primordial god Atum identified with the reed Yod and of the two twins Shu/Tephnut generating Heaven and Earth. Thus, the scholars, obeying in spite of themselves the orders of Ptolemy, wrote the Septuagint and the Hebrew Torah in such a way as to convey the other message of creation, that of the cosmogony of Heliopolis. To summarize, at first reading, the scribes of the Septuagint and the Torah make the «Egyptians» look like stupid idolaters, but Egyptology allows us to understand that the latter venerated the creation as being the very Body of God.

It was not until Plutarch, in the first century of our era, that idolatry was reconsidered as a universal cosmotheism.

The Yod ‫י‬ will become the secret revealing basis of the "Egyptian" secrets of the Torah, the symbol of the same God, Yahweh, Osiris, Israel. Now in the theology of Heliopolis, the Yod ‫י‬, is the allegorical name of Atum, of Thoth, even of Osiris, the light coming out of the heavenly waters. Through the allegorical reading of the double Yod and the Tetragrammaton YAHOU/YHVH ‫יהוה‬ , God - the God of the ancient Jews/ Egyptians - would be none other than the sunlight coming out of the darkness. The light that wakes us up every morning, and the darkness that puts us to sleep at night - the Principle of Alpha and Omega Ω.

God would be all this. In the 13th century BC, the hieroglyph AKHET ⌣ defined Aton or Amon as *the sun on the eastern or western horizon that illuminated the world every day*. Far from the Bible, God reveals himself to us every day. God is not a being revealed to a very limited number of initiated individuals - Abraham, Isaac, Jacob, Moses, Mohammed - but the **Revelation of life itself, manifested for each living** being by the power of the Ankh . ☥. the ANOKHI of the Torah. It is a fact that the allusive explanations of the Kabbalah are essentially based on the memory of the scenography of the tombs of the Valley of the Kings where the name of God (Osiris, Atum) was pictured. For the so-called ''Egyptians'' had the sacred right to represent the divinity with images, confirming that **God is creation**. Thus, every living being was the image of God. The Kabbalah restores the secret of the Tetragrammaton into a symbolic Trinity through the action of the sun, an allegorical Trinity where the divine child Son of God was Abraham-Isaac-Jacob, all named *«Etan'»* (Aton, Etanim is the plural of Etan'), *the Sun in the Eastern Horizon*. According to the Zohar, the first He of the Tetragrammaton refers to Abraham, the sun on the eastern horizon. This is the reason why Abraham is called Etan', which is the name of Aten, the solar disk. Etan'/Aton is thus equated by the Zohar with the Nile, the first river of the Garden of Eden. The Kabbalah restores the link between Israel, universal, and Osiris, universal.

HE VISION OF EZEKIEL: THE SARCOPHAGUS OF ADAM IS THE SARCOPHAGUS OF OSIRIS/ISRAEL

Archaeology shows that all the kings, princes and nobles - all the «Egyptians», notables, Yahouds in hieroglyphs - were placed in sarcophagi with the image of the Father, Osiris. All of them were above all Osiris, ISRA in hieroglyphics, never «Egyptians». The Bible (the Old Testament, the Torah) evokes the burial of Jacob, renamed Israel, and of his son Joseph, who was the image of his father. Both are embalmed and placed in a sarcophagus in Egypt. No verse of the Torah, no rabbinical writing, no writing of the Kabbalah contests the character, however, considered idolatrous of the sarcophagi of Jacob and Joseph. On the contrary. It is said that all the house of Pharaoh, all the elders of the house of Pharaoh, which means all the clergy, mourned for Israel and «went out of Egypt» to bury Jacob.

The mourning of Israel is the mourning of Mitzrayim, the Bible tells us. But for Kabbalah, it is the mourning of God, of Yahweh, the mourning of the sun ISRAEL, the mourning of the light of the world. The name of the tomb of Jacob/Israel is called ABEL MITSRAIM "mourning of Mitsraim". As if to deny that in this sacred union, Israel and Mitzrayim are merged in one man who represents the same god, the one who makes the waters of the Nile rise.

It is written that the sarcophagus of Joseph accompanied the Ark of the Covenant when it left Egypt. Why is the sarcophagus of Osiris so important in Jewish tradition? The importance of the sarcophagus is found in Ezekiel's vision of Yahweh in the world of the dead in the form of a winged man with animal heads, thus echoing the symbolism of the ancient "Egyptians".

It is written in the Sarcophagus Texts: "The Castle of Osiris is the land of the four blessed ones"18 Chapter 37 of Ezekiel's vision on the resurrection of the bones dwells at length on the miraculous reconstitution of the dry bones, flesh, skin and nerves of the Man Adam, the image of Abraham, Isaac and Jacob, renamed Israel. It should be remembered that the Bible, the Torah never disputes the symbolism of the "Egyptian" sarcophagus of Jacob/Israel - the idol par excellence -, which has as its primary objective the resurrection of the flesh and the elevation of the soul to ISRA-GOD called Osiris.

He said to me: «Prophesy over these bones. You will say to them Dry bones, listen to the word of Yahweh (Ezekiel, XXXVII, 4)

Ezekiel sees in a dream the god of Israel, accompanied by four angels with four wings, with the head of Man «Adam», and with the heads of animals, eagle, lion and bull, located at the four cardinal points. Is this the symbolic, cosmic vision of the sarcophagi of the kings of the Nile Valley?

"In the thirtieth year, in the fourth month, on the fifth of the month, while I was among the deportees on the banks of the river Kebar, the sky opened and I witnessed divine visions. [...] I looked: it was a stormy wind blowing from the north, a large cloud, a fire gushing out, with a glow around it, and in the center like the glow of ruddy gold in the midst of the fire... In the center I discerned something that looked like four animals, whose appearance was this: they were in the shape of Adam. They had got each one, four faces and each one, four wings. Their legs were straight and their hooves were like oxen's hooves, shining like polished brass. Under their wings were Adam's hands facing the four directions, as were the faces and wings of the four of them. They had

18 Spell n° 278. Textes des Sarcophages du Moyen Empire Égyptien. Claude Carrier, tome I. Éditions du Rocher.

each four faces and each four wings. [...] As for the shape of their faces, they had a face of Adam, and all four had a face of a lion on the right, and all four had a face of a bull on the left, and all four had a face of an eagle. [...] And I heard the sound of their wings, like the sound of many waters, like the voice of Shaddai... ...when they walked, it was a stormy sound, like a camp sound; when they stopped, they folded their wings. And there was a noise. Above the arch that was over their heads was something that had the appearance of a sapphire stone in the shape of a throne, and on that throne shape, on top, all the way up, a being with the appearance of Adam."

(Ezekiel I, 4-26)

Ezekiel's vision betrays the symbolic and cosmic image of the sarcophagus of the «pharaohs» where the Ouroboros is engraved, the cosmic serpent constituting the "celestial chariot" of the ancient "Egyptians". The sarcophagus is protected by four men with heads of Atum, Ra, Osiris, Horus (the man with the head of a falcon) Amun, Anubis, Isis, Nephthys, etc., or men with heads of animals (the four sons of Horus).

With the exception of the eagle that replaces the falcon, these are the same animals that adorn the majority of the tombs in the Valley of the Kings. Ezekiel in his dream obviously evokes the four blessed ones of the garden of Osiris, but also the four tutelary goddesses, who protect with their wings the bodies of many kings named «pharaohs» in the Valley of the Kings. In the treasure room of Tutankhamun's tomb, the lids of canopic vases represent the head of the king identified with Osiris or Atum, but in the symbolism of the great journey, each small sarcophagus with an animal head bears the name of one of the four sons of Horus. The entrails serve as a matrix for the engendering of the four symbolic sons from the flesh of the king of Egypt, in the East and in the West, in the North and in the South. They symbolize the four cardinal powers of God, born from the body of the king. This is undoubtedly one of the keys to the origin of the Christian cross, symbol of the resurrection of the Son of Man at the four cardinal points.

As we can see, Ezekiel's vision is modeled on the secret of the «pharaonic sarcophagus» of Jacob/Israel, modeled on the sarcophagus of Osiris and the metaphor of the four blessed ones living in his garden. In this process of resurrection of the flesh, there is a question of the presence of the royal mummy of Jacob, having the face of Adam. The latter, named Jacob/Israel in the Kabbalah. The reason is as follows:

Through the process of metempsychosis or transmigration of souls, the Torah transcribes the same story with apparently different characters. Like the kings of the Nile Valley who all had the face of the First Man, Atum/Osiris, the main characters of the Bible all have the face of Adam, the First Man, the face of the sun Jacob/Israel. Adam/Abraham/Jacob/Israel are all related to the expulsion from the Garden of Eden/Egypt.

"Jacob (the sun) was the duplication of the first man, they had the same beauty"[19]

"The body of Jacob proceeds from the beauty of the first man"[20]

"For [Jacob and Joseph] **had the same appearance, whoever saw Joseph testified that he was the son of Jacob. Rabbi Yossi said: They were completely identical"[21]**.

It is written in the Midrash Rabba that Sarah **"managed to match the portrait of Eve"[22]**. Finally, the tomb of Abraham and Sarah, of Isaac and Jacob, is located in the cave of Makhpela, opposite the Garden of Eden, according to the Kabbalah, the same place where the tombs of Adam and Eve are located.

---

19   Le Zohar, tome I, collection «les dix paroles ». Traduit par Charles Mopsik. Verdier, 1981, p. 198.

20   Le Zohar, tome IV, collection «les dix paroles ». Vayigash Vayehi. Traduit par Charles Mopsik. Verdier, 1996, 222a, p. 75.

21   Ibidem, p. 74.

22   Midrach Rabba, tome I, Genèse Rabba. Collection «les dix paroles ». Verdier, 1987, p 416, chap. 40 § 3.

The said tomb was bought by Abraham from the sons of Heth, for 400 drachmas. According to the Septuagint, Heth meaning in hieroglyphs the dwelling place of the sun at the horizon or the dwelling place of God, like the hieroglyph Heth, designating the place where the sun sets, in the monotheistic city of Akhenaten as well as in many tombs of the Valley of the Kings. The body of Yahweh - God and King - in Ezekiel's vision, protected by the four angels with animal and human heads, also located at the four cardinal directions, symbolizes the four breaths according to Kabbalah. The body spared by the worms is the unmistakable memory of the mummy of Osiris cut up and reconstituted, dead and resurrected. Ezekiel's description obviously refers to the four winged tutelary goddesses, who protect the bodies of many SA-RÂ/IS-RÂ kings in the Valley of the Kings with their wings. In the treasure room of Tutankhamen's tomb, lids of canopic vases represent the head of the king identified with Osiris or Atum, but in the symbolism of the great journey, each small sarcophagus with an animal head bears the name of one of the four sons of Horus. The entrails serve as a womb for the begetting of the four symbolic sons from the flesh of King IS-RÂ, in the East and in the West, in the North and in the South.

The four sons of Horus symbolize the four cardinal powers of God on earth, stemming from the body of the king, symbol of the primitive light incarnated by the sun. We touch one of the keys to the origin of the Ankh sign, the Aleph and, of course, the Christian cross, symbols of the resurrection of the Son of Man at the four cardinal points. We find these four powers on the skullcap of Tutankhamen, in the form of four snakes which symbolize the four breaths or four celestial rivers born from a unique river, the celestial Nile, the breath of the unique god. Also in the temple of Kom Ombo in Upper Egypt where some bas-reliefs of birds are provided with four pairs of wings. The famous River of the Garden of Eden, divided into four branches, is confirmed by Pharaoh's skullcap, with the serpent of the celestial Nile divided into four, which reproduces the cosmic image of Pharaoh's brain, the Garden of Eden where Thought was born.

The Kabbalah reports that **"from the four breaths comes the breath"**[23], the secret of the four breaths in one, would be related to the resurrection of the dead... Christianity has attributed the four breaths to the four Evangelists, the lion for Mark, the bull for Luke, the man for Matthew and the eagle for John. They often accompany the representations of the solar Christ - image of Jacob Israel - in majesty.

Symbol of the four wings or four breaths of the wings of God. Temple of Kom Ombo.

Similarly, the Kabbalah reports that four men, Adam, Abraham, Isaac and Jacob, populated the Garden of Eden, identified with Egypt. Their grave was located in Makh-Pelah, right in front of the garden. It is as if the three Patriarchs wanted to leave a final message: to return to Egypt aka the Garden of Eden after their death. Another text speaks of four Rabbis who entered the four rivers of the Garden of Eden24. Ben Azzay died; Ben Zoma went mad; Ben Abouya (A'her) denied his faith; the fourth, Rabbi

---

23 Le Zohar, tome II, collection «les dix paroles ». Traduit par Charles Mopsik. Vayera, Hayé Sarah, Toldot, Vayetsé, Vayichlah. Verdier, 1984, p. 467.

24 Le Zohar, tome I, collection «les dix paroles ». Traduit par Charles Mopsik. Verdier, 1981, p. 150.

Akiba, knowing the SOD, the secret of the Torah, had not been rejected from the Garden of Eden, because, the text says, he had entered "through the brain" (the esoteric meaning of the Torah): "He entered in peace and came out in peace"25 Again, the coded message of the true return to Egypt can only be made through the knowledge of the SOD, the secret buried in the text of the Torah.

Thus, the memory of the Garden of Eden, identified with Egypt, becomes the cosmic parable of the Resurrection through the reconstitution of the brain, which means the return of the original Thought, that of the ancient "Egyptians". The door of the forbidden garden in the Bible, jealously guarded by the Angel of Death with the flaming sword, would be the great secret of the Tree of Life, the message of the Holy Spirit, which allows the return to the Wisdom, to the images of God, to the initial Breath, to the multiplicity in the oneness and the peace between men.

And Kyrios/Yahweh sent him back from the Garden of Eden, to cultivate the land from which he had been taken. And when he had driven the man out, he set the cherubim before the Garden of Eden, with the blade of the flaming sword, to guard the borders of the Tree of Life. (Septuagint, Gen. III, 23-24)

Thus, the memory of the Garden of Eden, identified with Egypt, becomes the mystical, metaphysical and cosmic parable of the message of the Patriarchs and the message of Ezekiel. The Resurrection must be done through the reconstitution of the brain, which means the return of the initial Thought, that of the ancient «Egyptians» whose Thought is symbolized by the Tree of Life. The door of the forbidden garden in the Bible, jealously guarded by the cherubim of death, armed with the flaming sword, would be the great secret of the Tree of Life.

---

25 Le Zohar, tome I, collection «les dix paroles ». Traduit par Charles Mopsik. Verdier, 1981, p. 151.

The prohibition of the return to Egypt is expressed by the Septuagint and the Torah in the literal sense. But the Kabbalah allows the return, through the SOD, considered as the message of the Holy Spirit. It allows the return to the Wisdoms, to the images of God, to the initial Breath, to the multiplicity in the oneness and peace among men.

Another "Osirian" interpretation (Midrash) of Rabbi Eliezer's vision of Ezekiel teaches that the earth has the mission of gathering the body parts of men, which would have been scattered on its surface. In the Epstein Manuscript, we read: **"And every domestic beast, or wild beast, which before had eaten and now was dead in another land, the earth brought them, as it is said, 'The bones drew near one another."[26]**

This vision of the resurrection of the flesh is an obvious refoundation of the myth of Osiris, whose body was scattered on the land of Egypt by Set, and reconstituted by the goddess Isis (goddess of the earth in the myth of Osiris). Here again, the Kabbalah reveals to us an Osirian key, capital of the vision of Ezekiel. It is the vision of the sarcophagus of Jacob/Israel, who had the face of Adam, and whose sarcophagus was perfectly modeled on the sarcophagus of Osiris.

"The figure of the eagle has a central position in Ezekiel's vision; the eagle alludes to Jacob."[27]

Whereas, as we shall see, it is a hawk, the hawk named Ra'a, image of the sun Jacob (placed in a sarcophagus at his death and embalmed and mourned by «all the Egyptians»), which symbolizes Jacob/Israel in the Midrash. It is clear that the eagle replaced the falcon in Ezekiel's vision. Is this because of the influence of the Ptolemies, knowing that the book of Ezekiel would have been written around the second century BC?

The rest of the text confirms that Ezekiel wants to deliver a message affiliating the Egyptians with the Children of Israel, Israel with Osiris. While the Bible tells us about the Hebrews,

26 Chapitres de Rabbi Éliézer. Pirké de Rabbi Éliézer. Collection Les Dix Paroles. Éditions Verdier, 1983, p. 204, note 50.

27 Le Zohar, tome II, collection «les dix paroles », p. ¬126.

Ezekiel's vision is projected into the resurrection and return of the Egyptians after forty years of exile. It is as if the Egyptians and the Hebrews, alias the Children of Israel, were the same people, the same exiled nation. A return of the Egyptians banished from their country. Ezekiel would have had a reversed vision of the exit from Egypt. A vision where the god of Israel would be the god of the Egyptians. These last ones undergo, the exile, the expulsion, an exit of Egypt identical to that of the Children of Israel. Ezekiel's vision would be a message for humanity, a kind of TIKUN, a reparation of the text of the Book of Exodus. Like the Jews, like the Hebrews of the Bible, the Egyptians are exiled, expelled from their motherland after forty years of absence among the nations...

And I will make the land of Egypt desolation in the midst of desolate lands; its cities shall be desolation in the midst of destroyed cities forty years. And I will scatter the Egyptians among the nations, I will scatter them among the countries. For thus says the Lord GOD. At the end of 40 years, I will gather the Egyptians from the nations where they were scattered.   (Ezekiel XXIX, 12)

The Egyptians/Ægyptos "miraculously" appeared and disappeared in the Bible, as in History. Only the Jews suffered war, dispersion, exile, the humiliation of having lost their ancestral country. The miraculous Septuagint is then a ''holy spoliation'' of the first Ptolemaic kings in the name of the new Greek/Athenian spiritual Father Kyrios κύριος. It is nothing more than a transfer of the inheritance of the entire Nile Valley to the Greeks/Ægyptos.

While the Jews were originally the priests of Osiris «Men of God = IS-RÂ», the Septuagint translates into the acceptance by the Jews of a considerably reduced heritage. A sacred transposition, desired by Kyrios, to the land of Canaan. A symbolic expulsion of Abraham from his father's house, identified with Egypt by the Zohar. An «exit» of the Jews/Yahuds/Sons of Israel/Hebrews, from the newly named country Ægyptos to a newly named country Judea. Exactly, the Nile Valley, formerly the land of ISRA, called Osiris, also called YEHOUDA (the serpent of

Osiris, the land of the Reeds), the ancient land of the Yods, was to become, under the pressure of the ruling kings, the land of Canaan. A new land where the Jews had to falsify, transpose and recompose their entire history, on pain of death. A transfer of history supposedly willed by God, by the god Kyrios of the Septuagint and by YHVH the god of the Torah. But in reality, it is a mystification initiated by the first Ptolemies. A verse in Ezekiel attests that the so-called Egyptians exiled from their country are condemned by Kyrios/Yahweh to found a smaller and more modest nation called Patros. When it was the Jews!

"I will bring back the Egyptian captives and resettle them in the land of Patros, in their native land. They will form a small kingdom there" (Ezekiel XXIX, 14)

Thus, a verse in the Book of Ezekiel (XXIX, 6) will confirm our reasoning. No doubt in an effort to deliver a coherent message, although hidden, Ezekiel writes that «all the Egyptians are the reeds - the calamists, the scribes - of the house of Israel:

"And all the inhabitants of Egypt shall know that I am Yahweh, because they have been a support [the Septuagint says «they have been the calameos»] **of reed for the house of Israel"**[28]

According to any conventional reading of modern Egyptology, and according to the hieroglyphics, the «ancient Egyptians» were the calames, the priest-scribes of the house of Osiris. But in fact they were the Yods ▲, the scribes dedicated to the temples of ISRÂ or to the temples of other deities that were emanations of Atum/Osiris.

Ezekiel deconstructs the myth of slavery and the miraculous exit of the Children of Israel from Egypt. For, as we have shown in the first part of this trilogy, the Egyptians never existed in hieroglyphics. They are a creation of the ancient Greeks. Their goal was to appropriate the historical heritage of the Jews - then priests of Osiris - at the time of the Ptolemies, at the time of the Septuagint.

____

28 http://www.info-bible.org/lsg/26.Ezechiel.html#29

According to Edward Will and Claude Orrieux, specialists in the Hellenistic period, the book of Ezekiel was written shortly after the Septuagint, around the third century BC. As we have seen from the criticism of Flavius Josephus in his book ***Against Apion***, Greek historians and later Roman historians confused the Jews with the Egyptians in their writings. Moreover, under Greek rule, it is clear that the eagle replaced the falcon Hor (Horus in Greek). The divine and royal attributes of which Ezekiel speaks correspond to those of the Ptolemies, where the symbolism of the ancient Nile Valley is mixed with the symbolism of the ancient Greeks.

However, the hieroglyphs bring evidence, flagrant, that the message delivered by Ezekiel is verifiable, incontestable, immutable. The hieroglyph of the Reed (▌ of the Calamus) designates every so-called 'Egyptian' and this in the whole history of the civilization of the Nile Valley. It is the pictogram indicating the true identity of the 'Egyptians', kings, princes, priests, peasants: the reed Yod, the hieroglyph of Men and the hieroglyph of God, the demiurge Atum to whom the gods and men refer. This is a fact that Egyptologists cannot ignore. The Yod ▌ is the symbol of the individuality, of the personality with which all our so-called 'Egyptians' recognize themselves. The Yod is the image of the Thought, the image of the images, that the Jews allowed themselves before the catastrophe of the Hellenization imposing the Septuagint, which is summarized in the pure and simple prohibition of the images of God, of the hieroglyphs.

Hieroglyphs I, I AM = Reed YOD origin of the word Jew [29].

---

29   Egyptian hieroglyphic dictionary. E. A. Wallis Budge, Dover Publications, inc, New York. Published by General publishing Company, 1978, 15 a.

THE BIBLE IS A GREEK ORACLE: A RE-COMMENCEMENT OF THE WORLD

The disappearance of the Egyptian civilization goes hand in hand with the disappearance of the cult of Osiris and his Law. It gave way to the civilization of the Greek Bible of the Septuagint who named it 'Oracle'. We name it "Septuagint" or LXX in these works. Around 280 B.C., the Septuagint introduced in Alexandria the cult of the unique and jealous god, Kyrios, translated as Lord, and his 613 commandments. Kyrios is a god who contrasts Israel and Osiris, that is, the civilization of the Jews - the Children of Israel, the Hebrews - with the ancient civilization of the Nile Valley. However, there is abundant evidence - in the Bible and in archaeology - to confirm the historical truth: Osiris and Israel are one and the Jews formed the dignitary class, the priesthood of Osiris.

If the Bible had been written a thousand years before the Greek invaders, it would never have used Greek expressions such as Pharao' or Ægyptos to designate this country! The Nile Valley had, for three millennia, borne the name of Osiris - SAR, SARA, ASAR ISIR ISRA - as well as all its princes and kings, who identified themselves exclusively with this god. The Bible, as we will demonstrate in these chapters, is not a beginning, but a restart of the world. The Bible creates a schism, a break with the Old World, where the ancient Nile Valley of Osiris/Isra-EL and the SARA Kings is replaced by the Egypt of the Pharaohs. The ancient Nile Valley of Osiris sinks into oblivion and becomes the world of darkness and sin. The Bible was actually imposed by the mad and brilliant king Ptolemy II Philadelphus. In the secret Hebrew symbolism, this is called a «repair of the world», a Tikun Olam, where «the King's Law is the Law». A new invading, dominating King, Ptolemy is the image of God. He is the new Law, the Septuagint.

Under the Greek domination, the Jewish people put in slavery sees its priests subjected to the pitiless dictatorship of the pharaoh Ptolemy. He had imposed the Septuagint, a doctrine and a myth, revealed by God. Ptolemy Philadelphus had blessed the Septuagint, as the sacred Oracle of a God... Greek God:

"Thanks first of all to you, my friends, moreover, to him who sent you, and above all to the God whose oracles these are»[30].

From this explanation, we can consider Ptolemy Philadelphus son of Ptolemy Soter' (called the Savior), as the self-proclaimed king ''Pharaoh'', who, around 280 B.C., will institute a schism in the Jewish ''Egyptian'' clergy by imposing a new creation of the world, an exit from Egypt to another country, that of Canaan, an essential prelude to the giving of the Law by a unique, political and jealous god, proclaiming himself as follows: "I am the god of the exit from Egypt". From then on, the Septuagint (and the Hebrew Bible) is a restart of the world. Whether it is Kyrios in the Septuagint, or Yahweh in the Hebrew Bible, God alias Ptolemaic redraws and rearranges men in the Middle East. The Children of Israel are driven out of Egypt and confined within already existing political boundaries.

It is curious, to say the least, that in the Bible, Osiris - God of peace, silent and unifying father, ecumenical in his wisdom - is non-existent. The protection of Osiris and the gods is never invoked during the ten plagues! Egypt is destroyed by ten miraculous plagues without the slightest reaction from the ''Egyptians'' and their kings! Whereas we know today that the kings of the Nile Valley constantly implored the protection of God, whatever his names were! And especially the Pharaoh of Moses who supposedly does not know Yahweh/YAHOU, while the name of light YAHOU is written everywhere in the hieroglyphs! YAHOU symbolizes the winged sun or the sun with three creative rays! It is clear that in the Septuagint/Bible,

---

30 Lettre d'Aristée à Philocrate, les Éditions du Cerf, 1962, p. § 177.

Ægyptos has replaced Osiris, which has become the opposite of Kyrios/Yahweh. For Osiris was never a political god dividing the earth and separating humanity. Osiris never drove any man - Jew or not - out of his Garden of Eden renamed Egypt. The Septuagint itself addresses the Jews, not as a different people from the «Egyptians,» but as its Yahud, the «officials/dignitaries. The vectors of the ancient religion of Osiris, spread throughout the Nile Valley and the entire Middle East. In order to be able to impose Hellenization and the so-called religious syncretism - which the dignitaries, guarantors of the ancient religion of Osiris, could not accept - Ptolemy separated the Jews from the rest of Egypt by means of the Septuagint. This was a feat that, by making them the chosen people, separated them from the others, who were renamed Egyptians for the purpose. The Jews left Egypt geographically and theologically. From then on Ptolemy Philadelphus and his wife, Arsinoe could reform the Clergy of Osiris. Good business, moreover, for Ptolemy who extorted from the Jews according to the letter of Aristaeus not far from four million drachmas of gold that is to say 600 talents of gold. This was in exchange for their liberation and also for having stripped them of their houses..... offered to his soldiers that from then on he no longer had to pay from his own pocket. Stalin, thousands of years later, had the intellectuals arrested, many of whom were Jews, and eliminated them.

In this case, during the Greek period, the Greek Septuagint was imposed on the Jews as the Law of God, revealed at Mount Sinai, after their enslavement. The Greek conquerors had no use for historical truth, and the new history of the Jews, the Septuagint, became the history of the conquerors, imposed by force and by the cruelty of the conquerors. Two Egyptologists, Marie-Ange Bonhême and Annie Forgeau, testify through hieroglyphic texts that in case of serious anarchy or invasion, the ancient «Egyptians», in particular the king and the clergy, had to consider their defeat as the outcome of a lost cosmic conflict. They had to submit to the dogma and to the Law of the strongest. Under the penalty of death, they had to accept to upset their ancestral cosmogonies, in particular the great Enneads of which the Ennead of Heliopolis, the immemorial myth of Ra or Osiris, according to the whims of the invading kings, who, in order to ensure the perenniality of their dynasty, were made divine by the clergy. To survive the mystical delusions of Ptolemy, the Jewish clergy had to create a new history, a mutation in a new ''creation of the world'', a new myth, a new Osiris, a new Bible... and then to subdue the population, to impose on it the new Torah, the new dogma revealed by God, the new beginning of the world... This is why the Septuagint begins with "In the beginning, Theo created Heaven and Earth"... But not the Hebrew Bible, which we will see, is a RE-beginning of the so-called Egyptian civilization that became the current Judeo-Christians civilization.

"The civil wars, for their part, are perceived as an end of the world: "The sun will move away from men"... "Re has only to start the creation again". It is then that a savior king intervenes who, in human charge of the function of the creator god, drives out the iniquity and sets up the rebirth of Egypt under his only authority" [31]

Under Greek rule, the work of the 72 Jewish scholar-translators under the orders of Ptolemy II Philadelphus obviously consisted in reformatting the thinking of the Jewish priests of Heliopolis. It was necessary, according to the «divine» will of the king to separate Israel from Egypt, to make of Youdaïos foreigners in the country renamed Ægyptos. And consequently to create a book supposedly revealed to separate Israel from Osiris, the latter being replaced by Ægyptos. And this from the Revelation of a new solar man, divinized, RÂA = Moses, moreover named Teos of Pharao' in the Septuagint and Elohim for Par'o in the Torah. The name of Israel will thus have two readings, in the collective memory and in the secret reading. For the literal reading, Israel is the new name of Jacob, the name of the people miraculously brought out of Egypt. But for the secret reading, Israel is the sun that fights for the victory of light over the serpent of darkness.

---

31 Cf. Marie Ange Bonhème. Annie Forgeau. Pharaon. Les secrets du pouvoir. Ed. Armand Colin 1988, p. 266-267.

Israel symbolizes Man, Humanity, the Sun, the Light, all those elements that formed the symbolic body of the ancient god of Egypt that we call Osiris.In his book Moses the Egyptian, Jan Assmann draws the following conclusion: even if there is no historical trace of Moses, one fact remains indisputable: the Jewish people has its historical roots in the ancient Nile Valley:

"Egypt is the matrix
from which the chosen people came out"[32]

This means that MISRAIM begot, symbolically gave birth to ISRAEL. Osiris is the historical origin of Israel.

However, Egyptology has led humanity into an incredible confusion. When we speak of the Hebrews or rather of the Children of Israel coming out of Egypt, we are talking about the political exit of a people, of a country, Egypt, towards Canaan. But the seventy-two scribes of the Septuagint were careful to translate Ægyptos, the name of the Greek god Αἴγυπτον by MISRAIM Μεσραιμ in the Greek language and MITSRAIM מצרים in the Hebrew language. And this turns the tables.

For in the secret tradition, the Kabbalah, Mitsraim refers to the primordial serpent at the origin of the world. The serpent is the Matrix of ancient Egypt (Ouroboros in Greek), Isis or Nut. The exit from Egypt conceals the birth of the Hebrews, the true Egyptians in the Sea of Reeds. The Children of Israel were born in the placenta of the goddess Isis/Nout, MESS-RÂ-YAM. The exit from Egypt, seen as childbirth in the apocryphal texts, thus conceals the true identity of the Children of Israel, the Yods, the Reeds. CNRS researchers claim that around 424 BC, the Persian emperor Darius II had, in order to subdue the conquered populations, created two codes of laws, one for the Jews and one for the Egyptians, as attested by Professor Meleze Modrzejewski:

---

32   Jan Assmann. Moïse l'Égyptien. Éditions Aubier. 2001, p. 290.

"Darius would have given to his satrap (governor of Egypt) the order to assemble a commission composed of «wise men» among the Egyptian warriors, priests and scribes so that they «put in writing the Egyptian law which was in force»... ...the initiative of Darius would have had for object the codification of the whole Egyptian law..."[33]

Is it in fact a single code of laws? Is it the ancestor book of Deuteronomy? The very name of Deuteronomy is broken down into **Deuteros**, the other name of Darius II according to Manetho[34], and **Nomos**, the Law. About a century and a half before Ptolemy II Philadelphus, Darius II had ordered the dedication of a Book of Laws. This book would have been recompiled by the seventy-two scholars/sycophants of Ptolemy, who would have inserted the myth of Moses. As we demonstrated in the first book of this trilogy, the hieroglyphs provide thousands of proofs that the so-called ''Egyptians'' are all reeds, Yods, Jews. The code of laws of Darius II modifying the rights of the population of the Nile valley, where several million Jews lived, as we have seen, cannot be intended for the Egyptians who do not exist in the hieroglyphs. Darius would have reworked in depth the code of laws of the Jews who did not yet know Moses, for the obvious reason that the latter represented the caste of the priests of Osiris, named «Men of God» by the priests of the Nile valley, as attested by the words of the High Priest Eleazar in the **Letter of Aristaeus to Philocrates**.

At the same time, Darius allegedly created another code of special laws, written in Aramaic, for the Egyptians. Knowing that the so-called Egyptians had a thousand-year-old code of laws, the God-King Darius transgressed the said Law with an infamous decree. It was obviously the "Jewish" law and not the "Egyptian" law that Darius had recoded, as the "Egyptians" did not exist under this name in the hieroglyphics. They all had the symbolic name of Osiris, said ISRA, SARA, MISRI

---

33 Mélèze Modrzejewski. Les Juifs d'Égypte de Ramsès II à Hadrien. Éd. Quadrige PUF ; 1997, p. 147-148.

34 https://fr.wikipedia.org/wiki/Darius_II

or Youdaïos, images of the Reed, the primordial Yod. By his quasi-divine power, Darius put into force a new Law, which could be in part the Deuteronomy, insofar as some fragments of this Book have been found. In any case, more than a century before the Septuagint of Ptolemy II Philadelphus, Darius' aim had been to divide and rule, separating the inhabitants of the Nile Valley into opposing clans, the *Jews* against the *Misri*,

later renamed Egyptians by the Greeks, i.e., clergy and rulers against the people. Did he, as Ptolemy would do later, have recourse to a commission of "wise men" ? It is probable. A copy of this code of laws edited under Darius was found, dating (as if by chance...) from the time of Ptolemy Philadelphus.

"That is why the Egyptian princes and priests, who have had close contact with many things and have been involved in affairs, call us 'MEN OF GOD', a title that applies only to worshippers of the true God..."[35]

Only the priests of the Nile valley, only the priests of Osiris could bear the supreme title of Man of Ra, that the hieroglyphs transmit by the words IS, Man and Ra God, origin of IS-RA-EL, that the Perses end later the Greeks usurped, despoiled, transposed into Osirios for the needs of their cause.

Thus, the so-called commission of sages, scribes and so-called Egyptian priests formed by Darius II constitutes the first ''Supreme Court'' formed by Jewish priests, at the very origin of the tearing apart of the myth of Osiris. A century and a half later, Ptolemy II Philadelphus will again seize this social organization to refound, with the Septuagint, the new cult of Osiris/Israel, which will become the Bible.

---

35 Lettre d'Aristée à Philocrate. Les Éditions du Cerf, 1962. P. 171 § 140. J'ai rajouté « les princes » car cette mention se trouve dans une autre version de la Lettre d'Aristée donnée sur Internet. https://www.persee. fr/doc/rbph_0035-0818_1966_num_44_1_2617 § 140.

MISRAÏM מצרים, THE MATRIX OF THE REBIRTH OF HUMANITY

The exit from Egypt was translated as exit from Mitzrayim and not exit from Aegyptos. Why is this? Are the scribes hiding a new symbolic birth of Osiris/Israel, a «contracted» Osiris, limited to the land of Canaan? According to the Bible, the waters of the Nile become blood for seven days, like the red mud of the Nile.

"Seven full days passed after the Lord struck the river" (Exodus VII, 25)

Rashi attests with this verse that each plague lasted seven days, coinciding with the last quarter of the lunar month[36]. During the first three weeks of the month, Moses warned the Egyptians, and at the beginning of the fourth week the destructive plague fell on the land of Egypt. A simple calculation allows us to see that the whole of the ten plagues of Egypt is done in ten times seven days, that is seventy days. They correspond, of course, to the seventy days of pharaonic misfortune and mourning in Ancient Egypt, before the birth of a new IS-RÂ, a new Osiris/Israel. The first nine plagues **correspond to the nine months of Israel's birth**. The tenth plague is the allegorical liberation of the Child ISRAEL from the Matrix מצרים MESS-RA-YAM, which is none other than the symbol of the Pyramid, the Mother of the world of the so-called Egyptians. The tenth month, the tenth plague, confirms the death of the firstborn. Saint Paul, in the first epistle to the Corinthians, 10,1-13, compares Israel's coming out of Egypt to a baptism, thus to a symbolic childbirth of the Light:

"Brothers, I do not want you to be unaware that our fathers were all under the cloud, that they all passed through the sea, that they were all baptized in Moses in the cloud and in the sea"

---

36 Rachi, commentateur de la Bible au Moyen Âge. Pentateuque selon Rachi. L'Exode. Samuel et Odette Lévy. 1990. Exode VII, 25, p. 47.

Same thing for Saint Augustine:

"The Red Sea is the emblem of baptism. Moses leading the Israelites through the Red Sea represents Christ. The people who crossed it are the faithful; the death of the Egyptians means the remission of sins"[37]

The resurrection of Lazar wrapped in strips corresponds to the resurrection of Osiris by means of the sarcophagus:

"W. N. Schumacher also points out a fragment of sarcophagus in the Civil Museum of Brescia, on which the passage of the Red Sea is represented in the upper register, while the resurrection of Lazar is the subject of the lower register"[38]

Lazar which is read in Hebrew EL ASAR is not other than name of the god Osiris meaning Son of Ra, SAR, SARÂ, ISRÂ.

Tertullian, Origen, Saint Ambrose, advocate the same interpretation. Isidore of Seville:

"By faith, the true Israel comes out of Egypt when he renounces the world. He enters the Red Sea, that is to say, in the baptism marked by the blood of Christ"[39]

While we speak of the Egyptians and the pharaohs, the exit from Egypt proceeds from a double language. A political exit from a country renamed Ægyptos by the Greeks, for the literal reading. And an eschatological exit of MESS-RÂ-YAM, "Osirian", for the secret reading. This exit appears in the scenography of the Valley of the Kings. The writing of hieroglyphs brings thousands of proofs that in all the history of the ancient Nile Valley, the gods, the kings, falsely called «Egyptians» are above all the image of Osiris/IS-RÂ-GOD passing through the open sea to accomplish the Resurrection of Osiris/Israel...

---

37 La Figure de Moïse: écriture et relectures, publié par Robert Martin-Achard.

38 « W. N. Schumacher, « reparatio vitae »op.cit. n.38 p. 141 21a.

39 Biblia Pauperum : http://gallica.bnf.fr/ark:/12148/bpt6k850504w/f32.image le baptême du Christ par Jean- Baptiste dans le Jourdain est figuré par le passage de la Mer Rouge et par les envoyés de Moïse rapportant les raisins de la terre promise.

Resurrection or symbolic birth of gods, kings and men by the opening of the primordial ocean, the two thighs of the goddess Isis-Nut. Tomb of the queen Taousert.

As we have seen, the biblical myth of the exit from Egypt conceals the myth of Osiris. That of the death and resurrection of the souls of humanity, Israel, towards the Light. In this sense, the Kabbalah joins the explanation of the Koran, which speaks not of the exit from Egypt, but of the exit from darkness to light. The coming out of Egypt is thus explained as the fabulous passage of Moses' people, humanity, from darkness to light, which upsets our literal meaning of the biblical text. Obviously, the notion of coming out of darkness into light comes from a very ancient dissident Jewish tradition, insubordinate to rabbinic power and thought, because it comes from the secret commentaries of the Kabbalah, as Charles Mopsik has explained so well.

While Egypt was the land of the Tree of Life, the land of light that bore the name of Osiris, **Egypt became in the Septuagint and in the Torah the song of darkness even in the story of the creation of the world, so that the creation of light corresponds to the exit from Egypt to a new light, that of the Torah of Moses, as the Zohar attests. We note here the direct relationship between the exit from Egypt of the Bible and the Book of the Exit from Darkness to Light (Book of the Dead).**

" Elohim says: "Let there be light" corresponds to the book of Genesis where the Holy One blessed be He works to create the world. "And there was light" corresponds to the book of Exodus where Israel leaves the darkness (Egypt) for the light (Revelation)... ... "And Elohim separated the light from the darkness" corresponds to the book of Numbers because there were separated those who came out of Egypt from those who had access to the land of Israel"[40]

" "Mitsraim" designates the celestial leader in charge of governing the Egyptian people"[41]

Now in Egyptology, this chief represents **precisely the creative light, integrating the primordial couple, Isis and Osiris, -** and not Pharaoh - that is to say the feminine and masculine elements in symbiosis. **Mitsraim designates the God who is both masculine and feminine, the creative principle of the Nile Valley civilization.** This means that the Children of Israel are the true Egyptians, coming out of the Matrix of Osiris/ Isis-Nut. Each passage from day to night and from night to day was an exit from Egypt in this civilization based on the cult of light. The parallel with the scene in the tomb of Ramses I is blinding.

---

40 Midrach Rabba, tome I, Genèse Rabba. Collection "les dix paroles". Verdier, 1987, note 32 p. 221.

41 Zohar, tome III. Le livre de la splendeur. Par Jean de Pauly. Maisonneuve & Larose, 1985, p. 229.

The serpent of the night Apophis in the middle of the open sea. The twelve goddesses stretch out their hands towards the sea to drown Apophys and his twelve sons, symbolizing the twelve hours of darkness. Tomb of Ramses I.

At the seventh hour of the night (midnight), the sea opens and the serpent of the twelve hours of the night is drowned and replaced by the cosmos of the twelve hours of the day. The twelve tribes of Israel drowning Pharaoh and the Egyptians in the Red Sea is an allegory responding to the twelve constellations of the Zodiac of the night that pursue twelve constellations of the day. The similarity between the twelve tribes of Israel forming the Zodiac and the twelve hours of the night of the so-called

The similarity between the twelve tribes of Israel forming the Zodiac and the twelve hours of the night of the so-called 'Egyptians' of the Bible is perfect: they represent, according to Erick Hornung translating the text into hieroglyphics, the balance of the twelve hours of the forces of the cosmos: the symbolic engulfment of darkness in pursuit of the twelve hours of the day, always the same duality of light and darkness as depicted in the tomb of Ramses I.

« **Twelve** [12 Hours of Night = 12 Sons of the Serpent of Darkness] **to be annihilated were born before it, behold the hours engulf them.**»[42]

Which means that the twelve hours of the day swallow the twelve hours of the night... In the primordial sea of reeds... The inscription between the waters confirms precisely the order given by God: to annihilate, to swallow the serpent of darkness and time, the twelve fatal hours, the twelve sons of the serpent of the night...

"Ra: Listen, O hours, the calls are addressed to you, act on your behalf, among you! The place of your rest is your pylons, your breasts are in the darkness, your hindquarters in the light. Stop (?) the Hereret serpent, you who live on what comes out of it. Your portions are in the Douat! Swallow the children of Hereret so that you lead me. It is I who formed you, I acted in such a way that you would pay homage to me!" [43]

The scenario described in the Egyptian royal tombs is therefore the same as for the children of Israel, but reversed in the Bible. This is archaeological evidence, visible, whose message of the inverted myth is blinding. In several tombs of the kings of the Nile Valley, the central effigy represents the sea opened in two parts. In the middle of the sea (instead of the Egyptians drowned to the advantage of the twelve tribes of Israel, as the Bible relates), these are indeed the ''twelve Sons of the Serpent'', designated as the sons of Apophis and destined to be drowned in the «Red Sea» to the advantage of the twelve hours of the day and to the advantage of the kings we call «Egyptians»! Thus the so-called Egyptians lived each day their «exit from Egypt». This myth was transcribed in the Torah by the priests of Heliopolis with the symbolism of the passage of the Red Sea, called the Sea of Reeds.

---

42 Osirisnet.net, tombe de Ramses Ier, traduction d'Erik Hornung. http://www.osirisnet.net/tombes/pharaons/ramses1/ramses 1 gauche.

43 Ibidem.

Modern Egyptology has made us forget that all of ancient Egypt, from birth to death, was «OSIRIS», that is to say that all of life was intimately linked to the cult and name of Osiris. Thus, contrary to the common belief that this civilization was idolatrous, ancient "Egypt" was fundamentally monotheistic, as attested by the numerous hymns to Amun, Aten, etc. Each god was a sacred part of the body of Osiris, incarnating by syncretism one of the manifestations of the unique god. The multiple gods formed together the body of Osiris, the body of the world. This is why the number of relics of Osiris corresponded since the *Texts of the Pyramids* of On', to the cities, the regions or nomes of Egypt, during the centuries and the dynasties.

Osiris (and no one else, never Ægyptos) symbolized the entire Nile Valley, constituted by the repair, in a way the reconstitution of the land of Egypt in its integrity, MIS-RÂ, SA-RÂ, IS-RÂ... Each tribe of Israel forms a region of Israel. The tribes of Israel, whose scattered parts are reconstituted into the Body of Israel - which is also the name of God of the Jews - by means of Tikun' (reparation): the gathering of the twelve exiled tribes, according to the Zohar, is inherent, indispensable to the reconstitution of the Body of Yahweh called Israel... It is clear that Osiris and Israel have the same constitution. Adam symbolizes the land Adama, and Adam is Israel, says the Kabbalah. The Egyptologist Jan Assmann confirms this historical reality: Osiris is the real Egypt. The gods form the body of Osiris and together the land of the Nile valley:

"The body of Osiris recomposed in this way and revived designates the totality of Egypt"[44]

It is in fact the whole of OSIRIS and not Ægyptos! Several founding hymns written in hieroglyphics authenticate the main idea that confuses the body of IS-RÂ/Osiris with the totality of the gods of Egypt, forming the regions or nomes, the totality of the country:

---

44   Jan Assmann. Mort et Au-delà dans l'Égypte ancienne. Éditions du Rocher, 2003, p. 525.

"I bring you the collectivity of the gods of Upper Egypt... I bring you the capitals of the nomes to be your members, the divine shreds to be your body..."[45]

"I bring you the fundamental gods of Lower Egypt gathered together, all your members are gathered together (...) I bring you the capitals of the nomes: it is your body, it is your Ka which is with you..."[46]

"...I bring you the capitals of the nomes: it is your body, the whole country is constituted in foundation where you are... I bring you your names, the forty-two are with you: it is your body"[47]

It is important to remember here, according to the Septuagint, On' the city of the pyramids, the Heliopolis of the Greeks, was built by the Children of Israel and not by the Ægyptos.

The constitution of the Body of Israel, henceforth identified with the Body of the God of Heliopolis, is in every respect similar to that of the Body of Osiris. Clearly, the ancient name of Osiris Son of God,   ⊙ SA-RÂ or IS-RÂ designates - in the Septuagint and in the Bible - the Nile Valley, its land and its civilization. It is obvious that the king renamed "pharaoh" by the Greeks is above all an ISRA-GOD, the guarantor of harmony between the cities or nomes, and as such, he has the duty to preserve peace in his empire. Harmony and equilibrium for thousands of years will be broken by the invading kings of the Nile Valley... The words SA-RÂ/IS-RÂ, engraved above the double cartouche ⬚ , written in the heart of the tomb, designate the land of Egypt. Osiris is the inseparable figure of the men, the sun, the sky and the earth of the Nile valley, elements which together form the matrix of the creation and resurrection of man, and of the universe, the symbolic heart of the Pyramid.

---

45   Dendara X 71, 15 72 2. Traduction Cauville pour ce passage et les suivants.

46   Dendara X 82, 8-10.

47 Ibidem.

Thus, when an Egyptian N dies, he bears the name of Osiris-N, by identification with the first man-god IS-RÂ. Adam means the one who comes from the earth and returns to the earth Adama. Let us analyze the words of Jan Assmann and Christiane Desroches Noblecourt: **"once dead, the Egyptian becomes again the body of Egypt"**[48].

This is another example of a scientifically false misunderstanding. Let us recall that Herodotus said that the Egyptians were reluctant to adopt the customs of the Greeks, their gods, their knives, etc. Man cannot become again the body of the Greek god Ægyptos! Man becomes again "straw and clay", a SA-RÂ, IS-RÂ-GOD, an "Israel". Never an "Egyptian". If Jacob, renamed Israel, is embalmed and placed in a sarcophagus, accompanied by all the Egyptian people, it is a message from the scribes of the Bible to imply that Jacob (like Joseph) takes the same path from the world of the dead of Israel/Osiris to the resurrection, a path taken by the sarcophaguses of the IS-RÂ kings renamed pharaohs. The path of Israel/Osiris is hidden by the great biblical Egyptian procession on the occasion of the great funeral of Jacob, followed by all the Elders of Pharaoh, who explicitly recognize the sarcophagus of Israel. And not the sarcophagus of Osirios, Ægyptos or the Pharao's !!!

The words of the sage Amenemope, two thousand years before Christ, identify the primordial man - thus Osiris - with the straw and the clay modeled by God (Osiris or Amon-Ra) at the time of the creation of the world:

"Man is clay and straw,

God is his builder

He demolishes and builds every day" [49]

Osiris, the primordial man made of straw and clay by the potter god Khnum, projected himself into the image of the unique deity. We have already underlined it, the alternation of

---

48 Christiane Desroches Noblecourt. Sous le Regard des Dieux. Éditions Albin Michel, 2003.

49 Christian Jacq, La sagesse vivante de l'Égypte ancienne, Robert Laffon, 1998, p. 39.

agricultural work and constructions, the festivals associated with the belief in God generated a national fervor. Each individual was involved within the community, which was in turn encouraged to build temples, cities and palaces for God and for his intermediary, Pharaoh. This theme of man created in the image of God, which certainly served to motivate and multiply the strength of the ancient Egyptians, was later reused for the biblical myth. To build a city in ancient Egypt was first and foremost to build the house of God, each city bearing one of God's names - IS-RÂ - and a temple dedicated to that god. Exodos I, 11:

Therefore he [Pharaoh] **set over them stewards of the works, that they might wear them out with labor; and they built strong cities for Pharaoh: PITOM', RAMESSES AND ON', TODAY HELIOPOLIS.**

Thus, when the Septuagint tells us that **the Children of Israel built the fortified cities of Pitom, Ramesses and On' renamed today Heliopolis**, it is a question of stone cut for deified cities. And not bricks of straw and clay. The great enigma of the bricks of straw and clay lies in the symbolic tearing of the Body of Osiris/Israel by the "Pharaoh" of the Bible. By refusing to provide the straw for the clay to the Children of Israel, Pharaoh breaks the symbolic Body of Osiris/Israel. In the same way that Isis reconstitutes the Body parts of Osiris throughout Egypt, it is the Children of Israel - not the Egyptians - who reconstitute - throughout Egypt - the bricks of straw and clay. The scribes signify to us in this passage (which we will deepen in the third part of this trilogy), the destructive role of the "Pharaoh who had not known Joseph" and who, in fine, destroyed Osiris/ Israel, and chased him out of the Nile valley with the Children of Israel. The Pharaoh of the Bible is indeed the destroyer of Egypt, the image of Ptolemy II Philadelphos, and Moses will play the role of Seth when he kills the Egyptian, whom the Kabbalah identifies with the primordial Serpent and the first light of Israel... It is the whole myth of the exit from Egypt that takes on an inverted meaning in the Torah... Revealed by the Kabbalah and by Egyptology.

MITSRAIM מצרים:
THE MOTHER OF ISRAEL

Far from being demonized as an idolatrous or pagan civilization by ancient rabbinic texts, the Nile Valley is seen as the lost paradise, ancient Israel. Following the great invasions, Israel remained in the scriptures the son of Mitzraim. In the seventh century B.C., the Assyrian king Assurbanipal invaded and subdued Egypt (669-631 B.C.). Less than a century later, Egypt, plundered and humiliated, was powerless against the armies of the Babylonian king Nebuchadnezzar II (605-562 BC). The defeat of the Egyptian armies at Karkemish (present-day northern Lebanon) marked the beginning of new devastating invasions. The Egyptian palaces and temples were plundered, burned, the country devastated as it had never been before. Almost three millennia of Egyptian civilization were wiped out. Nebuchadnezzar's victory over the Egyptian army is seen as a catastrophe for the Egyptian civilization, which is considered in several biblical texts as the lost Garden of Eden.

The metaphor of the «magnificent heifer» testifies to this, while Nebuchadnezzar is compared to a gadfly that plundered its wealth in the book of the prophet Jeremiah.

"Egypt was a magnificent heifer; a gadfly from the north landed on her" (Jeremiah XLVI, 20)

According to the Zohar, the Children of Israel, far from being slaves of Pharaoh, lived in the Garden of Eden where they were happy:

"They did not want to walk in a desert on a dry road, for they were used to Egypt, which was like a Garden of Eden, as it says: "Like a Garden of Eden, like the land of Egypt" (Gen. 13:10)"[50]

---

50 Le Zohar, Cantique des Cantiques. Verdier, 1999, pages 178-179

The myth of Adam and Eve being driven out of the Garden of Eden because of the serpent's cunning turns out to be a huge parable of the Children of Israel being driven out of Egypt by Pharaoh. The evil Pharaoh of the Bible, the one who did not know Joseph, the one we have identified with Ptolemy Philadelphus and who can only be the serpent of the Garden of Eden located in Egypt:

"Pharaoh is like the serpent who spoke evil of the Holy One, blessed be he, and who made Adam's sin..."[51]

When we speak of the exile of Israel, we imply a political exile from the land of Egypt to Canaan, the land promised by Kyrios or Yahweh to the Children of Israel. However, the notion of Israel the son of Mitzrayim puts in place the true origin of Israel.

According to Psalm 80:9-12, Israel is «a vine taken out of Egypt. **"You took a vine out of Egypt; you drove out the nations and planted it. You made room for it; it put down roots and filled the earth; the mountains were covered with its shade, and its branches were like the Cedars of God; it stretched out its branches to the sea, and its shoots to the river"**

This means that Israel has been torn from its symbolic mother, MITSRAIM. Israel is symbolically «Osiris», a vine torn from its root, Geb the earth and Nut the sky, forming the Matrix Misraim (the primitive serpent, Isis Nut) renamed Ægyptos at the time of Hellenization (around 300 B.C.), and transplanted into a new holy land, Canaan. Israel also means «Son of God born of MISRAIM»:

"You shall say to Pharaoh: Thus says the LORD, Israel is my Son, my Elder" (Exodus V, 22, 23).

---

51 Le commentaire sur la Torah. Jacob Ben Isaac Achkenazi de Janow., collection 'les dix paroles'. Traduit par Jean Baumgarten. Verdier, 1987, p. 371.

"When Israel was young, I loved him, and from Misraim [read Misraim/Osiris] I called him my son"

It must be understood from these verses that MISRAIM is the Matrix of Israel, Nut or Isis, the serpent or the celestial placenta engendering Israel through the opening of Nut's thighs - as the Pyramid Texts attest, which Jan Assmann confirms - and not the land of slavery renamed Ægyptos by the ancient Greeks. The Red Sea is the heavenly sea that opened up - symbolically opened its thighs - to give birth to Israel. MISRAIM symbolizes both Isis and the goddess Nut, the «celestial serpent» who gave birth to Horus/Osiris, which reads IS-RÂ-GOD.

This is the key that the seventy-two translators of the Septuagint give us to the true history, the secret that they deliver to us without the knowledge of the tyrant kings and geniuses who, in the course of the centuries, invaded and plundered the valley of the Nile, and then deported the dignitaries and the craftsmen who had founded this civilization. The psalm reveals not only that Egypt remains the eternal and syncretic root of Israel united with the nations, but above all the parable of the vine torn from the Garden of Eden, from the other civilization, the other tree (the Tree of Life), the other Law, that of the ancient Israel called Osiris. Egypt and the vine symbolize the ancient Israel, its root and its history. Diodorus of Sicily and Plutarch recall that the Nile symbolizes the vine and the wine, the blood of Osiris. What secret does this conceal? Is it a new metaphor for original sin, the uprooting of the Body of Israel from the Garden of Eden, confused with the lost Egypt of old? Egypt being the Body of Osiris, the vine would be the metaphor of the Body of God, Israel was torn from its Osiris womb. The uprooting of the vine is a parable concealing the uprooting of the Jews from the history of the Nile Valley. Indeed, the vine is Israel, the Son, and Egypt is the Father, the Garden of Eden. The exit from Egypt is no longer a miraculous exit, but a cosmogony. An expulsion, an uprooting of humanity - forming the symbolic Body of God - from the civilization of the Nile valley, the Father, Osiris.

"Israel is compared to a vine, as it is written: "You once plucked a vine from Egypt" (Psalms 80:9). But in this rabbinic exegesis, it announces the exile of Israel. For the Zohar, the "Community of Israel" is the Shekhina..."[52].

Finally, the whole biblical story or rather the myth of the exit from Egypt is indeed a new myth of Osiris. Through the Hebrews, the Children of Israel, it is the story of the expulsion of this God, named IS-RÂ-EL in the hieroglyphs, who became the Shekhina, YHVH, Elohim, Yod-Yod, Jehovah, Adonai, etc.

IT IS THE GOD OF EGYPT WHO IS NONE OTHER THAN OSIRIS/ISRAEL WHO IS EXPELLED FROM THE NILE VALLEY BY THE SEPTUAGINT UNDER THE AUTHORITY OF THE PTOLEMIES!

The Children of Israel embodying God, the divine Shekhina, the exit from Egypt can be deciphered as the expulsion of the Sons of Israel/Osiris from the Nile Valley... Such an assertion is verifiable, as we have seen, because in ancient Egypt the entire population forms the Body of Osiris. To expel the "Egyptian" population from its land is to tear off the Body of Osiris, to dismember it, as did his jealous brother, Set. According to the secret tradition, Israel is the Body of God himself, torn from Egypt. The uprooted vine is a metaphor for the Body of Israel dismembered by all the great invasions of the Nile Valley. The Kabbalah thus gives us a completely different, cosmogonic vision of the exit from Egypt: the community of Israel is compared by the Zohar to the very Body of Yahweh - the divine Shekhina exiled from the Garden of Eden - torn apart like Osiris, expelled and murdered by his brother Set. As if, like the myth of Osiris, the Body of God Yahweh/Israel had been torn from its root. The image of the uprooted vine, exiled Israel, is compared to the heavenly Queen expelled from her kingdom and weeping for her exiled children according to the Kabbalah and the Book of Lamentations.

---

52 Le Zohar, Genèse, tome III, Vayéchev, Mikets, collection «les dix paroles ». Traduit par Charles Mopsik. Verdier, 1991, p. 243, note 7.

This metaphor is a reconstitution of the myth of Osiris, it proves the refoundation of a new Israel disinherited from its ancestral land, replaced by a counter-history of substitution in the land of Canaan. According to Plutarch, Osiris had been invited by the seventy-two accomplices of Set, who had each in turn tried on a golden sarcophagus. When Osiris' turn came, the accomplices closed the sarcophagus on him. Caught in the trap, Osiris was sent back to Byblos, in a way expelled from Egypt. Isis, wife of Osiris, had traveled the Nile Valley to Byblos where she had found the sarcophagus of her husband embedded in a tamarisk trunk, and of which the king of Byblos had made a column to honor his temple. Isis managed to recover the sarcophagus of Osiris and brought it back to Egypt. Mad with rage, Set had found the sarcophagus and torn the body of Osiris into fourteen parts according to Plutarch (twenty-six or forty-two pieces according to other traditions), scattered throughout Egypt. With the help of Anubis, Isis managed to reconstitute the body of Osiris, except for the phallus that Set had thrown into the Nile.

In traditional language, the phallus of Osiris was supposed to engender fertility and germination with the annual flooding in the Nile Valley. We perceive the similarity between the two myths where the exit of the Children of Israel from Egypt is confused with the expulsion, the exile of God or his dispersion outside his womb. Thus, the word Mitsraïm or Misraïm cannot mean Egypt/ Ægyptos, because Mitsraïm is the maternal placenta of the Children of Israel. Isis reconstituting the Body of Osiris accomplishes a repair of the light of the world, a cosmic reassembling, a Tikun' in Kabbalistic language. In ancient Egypt, the reassembling of Osiris is considered the most important of rituals, the reconstituted Body of God is the foundation of universality of Light and social cohesion between men and the universe.

"The Egyptians conformed the dismembered body of Osiris to the diversity of men in order to celebrate in the ritual of the remembrance the unity, completeness and integrity of Egypt"[53]

---

53 Jan Assmann. Mort et Au-delà dans l'Égypte ancienne. Éditions du Rocher, 2003, p. 528.

Osiris symbolizes the universality of creation, the microcosmic and macrocosmic vision of the divine, silent world. Osiris although mysterious, is found in all forms, at all levels of creation, as Claude Traunecker attests:

"It is thus necessary to extract from the myth all that makes its essence: Osiris, very ancient royal God, expresses all the recurrent forms of man (death and resurrection), of society (transmission and legitimacy), of the world (plants, Nile) and by extension the cosmos (the moon, the light)"[54]

In fine, ISRAEL and MISTRAÏM signify a filiation, a childbirth. ISRAEL came out of the heavenly waters. To come out of Egypt is to come into the world, to come out of the primordial Pyramid for the whole of humanity.

Thus the journey of Isis throughout Egypt to reconstitute theIn fine, ISRAEL and MITSRAIM signify a filiation, a childbirth. ISRAEL came out of the celestial waters MITSRAIM. To come out of Egypt is on the one hand to come into the world, to come out of the primordial Pyramid for the whole of humanity. On the other hand, the journey of Isis throughout Egypt to reconstitute the Body of Osiris IS-RA corresponds symbolically to an exile of Osiris and the commandments of Maat. An anarchy in the civilization of the Nile valley where each IS-RÂ called falsely "Egyptian" must also reconstitute the balance of the cosmos, the Law, the Torah, the lost commandments, in order to rebuild the Truth Maat. As we have said, the exile of Israel corresponds to a dispersion of the Body of Israel, disintegrated into pieces of light in the world. Each Jew has the mission to reconstitute the divine light in its entirety and integrity, the symbolic Body of Israel torn apart, the vine torn from Egypt. The Torah, the biblical myth of the exit from Egypt, is a tearing apart of the Body of Osiris/Israel by the obscurantism of Hellenization.

---

54   Claude Traunecker. Les Dieux de l'Égypte. Collection Que sais-je ? Presses universitaires de France, p. 96.

THE COMMANDMENTS OF OSIRIS ARE THE COMMANDMENTS OF ISRAEL

The commandments in ancient Egypt form the Body of Osiris. Whoever transgresses a commandment transgresses the Body of Osiris. The same applies to Israel. In the so-called ''Egyptian'' legend, after being murdered by Set, Osiris is cut into twelve, fourteen, twenty-six, or forty-two pieces, depending on the period and the tradition. For Egypt was divided either into twelve regions - like Israel - corresponding to the twelve hours of the day, or into fourteen corresponding to the fourteen days when the moon disappeared, into twenty-six or forty-two nomes, according to the times. The body of Osiris was thus divided according to its human, solar, lunar or cosmic configurations.

According to Plutarch, Isis and Nephthys, sisters and wives of Osiris, are lost in lamentations, then Isis undertakes to seek and reconstitute the body of Osiris with the help of Anubis, the embalming god. The forty-two divisions correspond to the forty-two commandments of Osiris-IS-RÂ.

The scholars of the CNRS in their conclusions on the correspondence of Elephantine (dating from the 7th to the 4th century B.C.), had the honesty to recognize that the Jews of that time practiced the cult and consequently respected the forty-two commandments of Osiris, the unique and multiple god of the Nile valley, following the trace of their ancestors.

"The gods of Egypt were worshipped by the Orientals who resided in the country, AND EVEN BY THE JEWS before the reform introduced around 520 B.C. However, THE THING IS ATTESTED BY TEXTS ONLY FOR THE CULT OF OSIRIS"[55]

---

55 Certaines lettres attestent que les prêtres juifs les plus importants juraient par Yahô, Ptah, Knoum, Osiris. Documents Araméens d'Égypte. Littératures Anciennes du Proche-Orient. Éditions du Cerf, 1972, p. 345.

Now, we find in the forty-two commandments of Osiris the equivalent of the ten commandments of Moses, except for the Sabbath which could have been instituted, under penalty of death, by the Greek Septuagint. As we said in the first volume of this trilogy, the Jews who were forcibly hellenized by the ancient Greeks were condemned to death if they transgressed the Sabbath. It was formally forbidden to these "Egyptians" to steal, to kill, in order to kill. The priests did not eat pork, they had to respect the foods permitted or forbidden by God, to love their neighbor, to help the needy and the sick, to practice circumcision following the example of Ra, the celestial Father, who was the very image of man and the commandments. Ra had originally circumcised himself, like Abraham. Prayers and psalms were recited to God, calling him the One. Many religious rituals had to be celebrated and observed, such as the feast of the seventh day, the ceremony of weighing the hair of the children. At the time of the marriage, the wife went around her husband seven times, the respect of the funeral rites, the embalming, etc. The eminent Egyptologist Yann Assmann discovered an Egyptian prayer, the same as the Kaddish of the dead recited by the Jews, where he claims that the merit of the son made the soul of the father rise to God: '' The most important bearer of hope was the son, called to say the prayer of the dead, as in Judaism where the son is brought to recite the Kaddish" Assmann also attests to the equivalent of the Bar Mitzvah of the Jews at ten years of age for the so-called ''Egyptian" children (origin of communion among Christians).

If we take stock of the text of the Bible, the Torah, God transmits the Law to Moses, ultimately to subdue the Children of Israel. This Law/Septante/Torah is immutable. No one other than God or his Messiah can reform any of the 613 commandments. The Jews/Yudais under Ptolemy had sworn never to touch a single Yota of the Septuagint on pain of an eternal curse... But about four centuries later, the Jews abandoned the Septuagint for the Torah and for the new religion, Christianity. The Messiah, the Christ, recognized by some Jews as such, has the power to transgress and reform the Torah, the Law of Moses, in order to achieve redemption, the salvation of humanity. As for the Rabbis who passed from the Septuagint to the Massora or Hebrew Torah, they were obliged to relativize the commandments and numerous death sentences - for example, the transgression of the Sabbath was punishable by death - of Leviticus and Deuteronomy, by introducing free will.

In contrast, in the ancient Nile Valley, kings and their advisors had the power to change the Law of Ma'at. They could change the commandments. Osiris was the Master of Justice, but the king SA-RÂ kept all power over the Law. For examples, Claire Lalouette affirms that Toutmosis III had forbidden to the women to veil the face, and Diodore of Sicily reports the history of a king of Egypt who had abolished the death penalty... Yes, the ancient Egyptians, and therefore the Jews, had invented the very foundations of the concept of secularism!

The ancestral tradition was that every king had the duty to set an example to the priests and the people by an unfailing devotion to the commandments he was in charge of. The king, initiated, sacralized, bearing the title of Yahud had to be exemplary, "Justified", pure of all sin, as attested by a passage in the Book of the Dead: "**Purify N**. [Osiris + name of the deceased] **of all the evil that he has done. Look at the face of the gods** [= of God, his manifestations]"[56]

Each deceased, had to demonstrate to God that he had lived on earth, free of all sin. Each Yod - the so-called Egyptian - must make his forty-two proclamations before the forty-two judges of the celestial tribunal of the God IS-RÂ (known as "Osirios"), if he wishes to reach eternal life, the celestial paradise, as Jan Assmann attests:

"The word of the king who reads the concrete laws and puts them into effect is mostly oral, and in any case never out of time. It is enough for the next king to come along for new laws to be enacted. Justice is eternal, but the law evolves from generation to generation; it is embodied in the kings and guardians of the law, but never in the sacred texts"[57]

---

56 Jan Assmann. Mort et Au-delà dans l'Égypte ancienne. Éditions de Rocher, 2003. P. 132.

57 Jan Assmann, Le Prix du Monothéisme. Aubier, 2007, p. 93.

Queen Hatshepsut who reigned around 1478 B.C. (eighteenth dynasty) bore the title of "Mistress of the Commandments"[58], thus playing, like the goddess Isis, the role of the teacher and high priestess of the commandments of God... In ancient Egypt, the King is the Law. Justice emanates from Maat, but **"the king is the source of the Laws"**[59]. This sentence was taken up by the Jews in exile among the nations: Dina di-malkhouta Dina: "The King's Law is the Law", a custom that allowed the Jews to submit and adapt in the countries where they had been welcomed or exiled. Francis I, like many kings, was also the sole source of the Law in history:

"The King is the Law, the King makes the Law"

The Septuagint, the Torah, the Bible, and then the Koran will revolutionize this basic principle of the Nile Valley civilization, where only God, alias Kyrios, Yahweh, Allah, becomes the Law of humanity.

---

58 Claire Lalouette. Thèbes ou la naissance d'un empire. Flamarion 1995, p. 202.

59 Marie Ange Bonhème. Annie Forgeau. Pharaon. Les secrets du pouvoir. Ed. Armand Colin 1988, p...

ISRAEL IS OSIRIS, THE GOD TORN OFF FROM EGYPT

The biblical metaphor of Israel, the vine torn from Egypt, means that God, Yahweh, Amun, Ra, Osiris, was torn from its root, Egypt. It is indeed a refoundation of the myth of Osiris by the scribes of Heliopolis - so-called Egyptian priests - following the Greek invasion.

"Israel is compared to a vine, as it is written: "You once plucked a vine from Egypt (Psalms 80:9)». But in this rabbinic exegesis, it announces the exile of Israel. For the Zohar, the "Community of Israel" is the Shekhina..."[60]

The Body of Osiris cut into pieces by his jealous brother Set symbolizes, in addition to the usurpation of royal power, the dislocation of the light of the world, a tearing away from the symbolic Body of Osiris followed by an exile of the goddess Isis, the celestial queen, the exile of mankind out of the Nile Valley... The exit from Egypt of the ancient gods of Egypt proceeds from the same symbolism as the biblical exile of the Children of Israel, who symbolize God himself, torn from the land of Egypt. The domination of the invading Macedonian kings of the Nile Valley is expressed by the total submission to a new Law, the Septuagint - the Hebrew Torah will be canonized only at the beginning of the second century AD. - which means submission to the new Greek gods. This theme of Greek domination linked to the writing of the Bible/Torah is taken up by the Kabbalah, for which Adam, Noah and Abraham were «snatched» by Yahweh from the Garden of Eden, a metaphor for the Nile Valley. The exit from Egypt is the symbolic expulsion from the Garden of Eden, the foundation of the biblical palimpsest, the uprooting of Egypt by the invading kings, Assyrians, Babylonians, Persians, Greeks and Romans.

The Torah, the Gospels and the Koran must be deciphered,

---

60 Le Zohar, Genèse, tome III, Vayéchev, Mikets, collection «les dix paroles ». Traduit par Charles Mopsik. Verdier, 1991, p. 243, note 7.

decoded in the light of history, even if it means upsetting all our preconceived ideas, or else we will fall back into the trap that the literal reading of the Bible (like that of the Koran) has been setting for more than two millennia. A terrible trap on a worldwide scale which, according to the teachings of the Kabbalah rabbis, leads to ''a new Egyptian slavery" for the populations obeying the unassailable texts supposedly revealed. Reading the Bible without understanding its immense secrets resulted in humanity being plunged into a new "slavery of Egypt": a slavery in the sense of an alteration of the mind, dependence and submission of thought to the so-called sacred scriptures.

By this I mean the present-day obscurantism and fanaticism, whose essential cause is indoctrination by the daily, repetitive, simple reading of the Scriptures, whatever they may be. In a fabulous metaphor, Kabbalah tells us that our humanity has fallen into the enormous «trap» set by monotheism in general: idolatry concealed by the primordial serpent surrounding the Tree of Good and Evil. By "eating the fruit" of the Tree of Knowledge of Good and Evil, humanity (Adam and Eve) would have abandoned the Tree of Life which was enthroned in the Garden of Eden and simply symbolized the truth that liberates from slavery, from the great collective hysteria caused by the mysticism of thought, eager to find God. This means that humanity, entangled in the stormy trap of opposing religions, humanity shaken by faith in God, by the miraculous myths of Revelation, finds itself caught in the trap, facing the many challenges that factual history, archaeology, and historical facts throw at it. Whether it is the Torah, the Gospels or the Koran, any literal reading of the Bible alters the freedom of men, makes them slaves of Scripture and myth, of the Word or Greek Logos, separates them from the rest of humanity and from the real history of humanity. This has resulted in the terrible tragedies and catastrophes that have occurred for more than two millennia, caused by religions throughout human history.

Kabbalah conceals a fabulous lexical field of hieroglyphic deciphering of the Torah, of the Bible. It forcefully denounces any literal reading of the Torah, or even any so-called historical reading, because, as Maimonides said, if the Torah is in contradiction with science, it is the Torah that must be interpreted. The reading of the Torah must confront and conform to historical truth:

"Cursed be the mind of him who claims that the stories of Scripture have no other meaning than their literal meaning! ... ...But every word of Scripture conceals a mystery... »[61] **"Nor is an interpretation good when it is spiritual, or when it fits the text well, BUT WHEN IT IS CONFORMED TO THE TRUTH, as it is written: 'For the ways of the Lord are straight, and the righteous shall walk in them' "**[62]

It is important to raise this issue, which is crucial for the future of our children, and crucial for the future of humanity, which is being dragged into the abyss of fundamentalism and obscurantism in spite of itself. If we take stock, the initiated cabalists had already alerted the Jews who were resistant to the powerful message of Kabbalah, but they had also alerted the nations, humanity: humanity was going to fall into a new exile, a new symbolic slavery in Egypt, because of a literal interpretation of the Torah. An interpretation in which the mind, lulled by the myth and miracles of God, is imprisoned by the mysticism of a political god, self-proclaimed "Jealous" (Exodus 34:14: **Yahweh is called "Jealous"**), who, while forbidding killing, propagates intolerance and God orders crime. In reality, the god of the exit from Misraïm is none other than the god Kyrios/Ægyptos son of Zeus, image of Ptolemy, a god who is also jealous and who, simulating a supposed liberation, led the Sons of Israel to the slavery of Ægyptos, which the Zohar, the book of Kabbalah, assimilates to the powerful symbol of the Tree of good and evil.

---

61 Le Zohar, tome V, le livre de la splendeur, op. cit., p. 386.

62 Zohar, tome III. Le livre de la splendeur. Maisonneuve & Larose, 1985, p. 382.

According to a thousand-year-old tradition conveyed by the Kabbalah, any literal reading of the Bible leads humanity to slavery, obscurantism, violence and fanaticism. For in the context of Hellenization, men and kings identify with Scripture, with the Logos, with the creative Word, which they consider to be the holy word of God, irrevocable and perpetual. He can then destroy and massacre his fellow men in the name of God, Yahweh, Christ or Allah. We see it every day, the monotheistic religion is bogged down in the ritual of human sacrifice justified by the word of God, the worst of idolatries and in the sense of the Kabbalah, the true idolatry which consists in taking oneself for the armed arm of God... We see it in a frightening way in our time, where each of the three monotheistic religions accuses the other two, for not having rightly interpreted the revealed message of God, the original text of the Torah Iran is actively preparing to destroy Israel, in the name of Allah, without understanding the powerful message of the Koran: Allah appoints the Sons of Israel heirs of the entire Nile Valley (Surah 26:57-59). The sacred criticism demanded by Jean-François Champollion is based on the mobilization of knowledge and in particular the science of archaeology, which allows us to open up to ancient texts and to understand civilizations as they really existed.

The purpose of this trilogy is to understand why the Septuagint, the Old Testament, the New Testament and the Qur'an are sometimes in contradiction and sometimes in sync with history. The Kabbalah has preserved the memories of ancient Israel/Misraim/Osiris, repressed memories that Sigmund Freud had evoked and researched. The father of psychoanalysis had concluded that the first Moses was murdered, whereas it was indeed the symbolic murder of Osiris, the ancient Israel. The Kabbalah has been preserved through many centuries, more than two millennia, it seems. It establishes a powerful link with the Egyptian origin of the Bible and the Jews. It is probably for this reason that the Kabbalah caused a deep division among Jews, leading some of them to convert to Christianity, or to

Islam when forced to do so, like Shabbatai Svi. According to Charles Mopsik, a great scholar of the Zohar, the cabalistic Jews opposed to the traditional Jews were finally fighting over the understanding of the true secret message of the Torah, the SOD. This may seem like an exaggeration, but it is clear that at the beginning of the third millennium of our era, with the rise of religious fundamentalism and fanaticism, at war with freedom and secularism, fundamentalists are acting against the free world and against history, justifying crime in the name of God. What is said here about the reading of the sacred scriptures is serious enough to point to our responsibility for the future of humanity, as confirmed by Charles Mopsik:

"The attitude of the kabbalists towards the Jewish religious authorities, however, was never really idyllic. It should be noted that many voices were raised among the kabbalists to challenge the hegemony of rabbinic jurisdiction, or even its methods of interpretation based on reasoning and rational discussion [any literal reading of the Torah]. **In the part of the Zohar [Kabbalah] called Raya Mehemna and in the Tiquuné Ha-Zohar, many passages are concerned with placing the literal meaning of the Bible, the Talmud and the law in general, at a level far below that of the study of the esoteric meaning** [the secret meaning, Gnosis, Sod]. **In the eyes of the author of this book, exoteric religion [the literal reading of the Torah], its interpretative practices and its own ideology represent a new exile in Egypt. The normal relationship between exoteric religion (Mishna, Talmud) and esoteric religion (Kabbalah) is that of a servant to her queen... If the exoteric study of the Talmud is an attachment to the Tree of Knowledge of Good and Evil, the study of the Zohar and the cabalistic reading of the Torah in general is an attachment to the Tree of Life"**[63]

---

63 Charles Mopsik. La Kabbale. Jacques Grancher édit. 1988. P. 122.

THE ENIGMA OF THE SEVENTY-TWO

Could the seventy-two disciples or accomplices of Set who betrayed Osiris have a symbolic relationship with the seventy-two translators of Ptolemy Philadelphus, who inverted the myth of Osiris in the Septuagint? We know from the Letter of Aristaeus that the seventy-two prophets or so-called translators of Ptolemaeus II Philadelphos formed a kind of supreme court destined to overthrow the ancient Jewish religion, that of Osiris, which was then widespread throughout the Middle East. The seventy-two obviously wanted to encrypt the message of the past and leave their mark on the Septuagint Bible and thus on the Torah. They were first deified as prophets of the word of Kyrios. They acquired this power to make God speak. They made Yahweh, Adonai, Yod-Yod, Kyrios, Elohim... speak, even to modify his words according to the mystical whims of the God-King Ptolemy Philadelphus, as the Talmud and the Kabbalah affirm. We will deal with this analysis of the thought of the seventy-two in more detail in the third volume of this trilogy. But for Kabbalah, the seventy-two became the seventy-two angels of God or the seventy sons of Noah, the seventy sons of Jacob/Israel, the seventy Elders under Moses, and finally the Fathers of the seventy nations in the Jewish tradition. The Septuagint speaks of seventy-two nations and not seventy like the Hebrew Bible and tradition. Charles Mopsik noticed this singularity and immediately made the connection between the 72 translators of the Septuagint and the 70 nations of the Bible:

"In fact, the genealogical table of Genesis 10, in the Greek translation known as the Septuagint has 72 nations and not 70 as in the Hebrew version of the Massora [the Bible written in square Hebrew and canonized around the first century AD]**, and it is from this data that in the Letter of Aristaeus, the**

number of the Elders, translators of the Bible, is fixed at 72 (see verse 50), and the translation itself required 72 days of work (verse 37), numbers which obviously symbolize that of the nations; Similarly, in Luke 10 : 1, there is mention of 72 disciples (of Christ) going on a mission throughout the world"[64]

Another explanation mentions that the number seventy-two was chosen because it corresponds to the seventy-two divisions of the Zodiac. For the Zohar, the 70/72 angels would be celestial princes, their names corresponding to the seventy-two names of God engraved on the staff of Moses, the spear that Moses had taken from the Egyptian before killing him, at the beginning of the Book of Exodus. The seventy-two would even be writers:

"A tradition tells us that the seventy-two sacred Names are seventy-two witnesses of «Hesed» (celestial attribute of goodness); they contain the attributes of «Guevourah» (the power of God) and take the place of seventy-two writers, as it were"[65]

It seems that the seventy-two formed a supreme court, capable of overturning the history of humanity. The Letter of Aristaeus, in the words of the High Priest of the Jews, Eleazar, states that the Septuagint was written "for the good of the state of the 'Pharaoh' Ptolemaos Philadelphos". Moreover, for a simple translation of the Law of the Jews written in Hebrew, a few learned men recognized by the Jewish community would have been enough to establish a valid translation. So why does Ptolemy impose seventy-two elders or "prophets", six per tribe? Why does Ptolemy treat them as kings? Ptolemy knows their power since they formed the clergy of Osiris. At the time of Ptolemy Soter and his son Ptolemy II Philadelphus, Jews scattered throughout the Middle East were flocking to Egypt by the thousands. The large Jewish community in Alexandria, cut

---

64 Le Livre Hébreu d'Hénoch ou Livre des Palais. Collection «les dix paroles ». Traduit par Charles Mopsik. Verdier, 1981, p. 253.

65 Zohar, tome III. Le livre de la splendeur. Par Jean de Pauly. Maisonneuve & Larose, 1985. P 233, Zohar II § 51.

off from the Hebrew language and therefore from hieroglyphics, practiced the cult of Osiris. The Jews had not yet had access to the Septuagint, let alone to the Hebrew Torah of Moses. The Jews had their own Law, that of Osiris, written in the Book of the Exit to the Light, which we falsely call the Book of the Dead. These are the books that constituted their first Torah, the one that was recovered by thousands, and destroyed by the armies of Ptolemy. Reasons why Demetrios of Phalerus and Aristaeus insisted to king Ptolemy: it was necessary to rewrite, to reinterpret the Book of the exit towards the Light. And not to translate it.

It was therefore necessary to seek out in Jerusalem men of science, pious men, "Elders", from the ancient nobility, hand-picked, knowing Greek and Hebrew, and hieroglyphics. But above all, they were highly educated men, worthy of prophesying and representing all the Jews of the world. As we have said, in an inversion of history, the seventy-two correspond to the seventy-two accomplices of Set in the Osirian myth, hence the objective of making the Jews pass for the worshippers of Set, as Plutarch will write.

Moreover, the number 70, like 72, corresponds to the divisions of the Zodiac, to the 70 days of mourning during the embalming. In fact, there is a link in the Kabbalah that definitely links these two numbers to the princely royalty, the heirs of the Nile Valley civilization. Throughout the biblical text, the reader travels with the priests of Heliopolis, the 72 translators of the Septuagint, who by a miracle became prophets, while some traditions accuse them of being, on the contrary, informers, sycophants... And for the Koran, those who falsified the Torah... All this for having made people believe in a translation wanted and dictated by God. A miraculous work written in 72 days, by each of the 72, who were separated from each other... 72 who became the heavenly angels of God in Kabbalah.... The reader travels with the 70 sons of Noah who built the Tower of Babel, then the 70 sons of Jacob who entered Egypt, to reconstitute the 70 nations, the new humanity through the writings of the Old Testament. In the book of Numbers (11:25), Yahweh asks Moses to choose 70 Elders with authority to prophesy over the Children of Israel:

"And the Lord came down in the cloud and spoke to Moses, and took of the spirit that was upon him, and put it upon the seventy Elders. And as soon as the spirit rested on them, they prophesied; but they did not continue"

The symbolism of the 70 or 72 princes, 70 or 72 nations, 70 or 72 names of God are interwoven between the Bible and the Septuagint: the 72 translators have become, over the centuries, 72 heavenly princes, surrounding the throne of God...

The great synagogue of Alexandria had seventy pulpits, the Talmud tells us. The Hebrew Book of Enoch is one of the most ancient texts of the Kabbalah, one of the most secret works that gives us a divinized description of the seventy-two pseudo-translators of Ptolemy. Their attributes correspond to the kings of the Nile Valley.

"...The 72 celestial princes who correspond to the 70 languages that are in the world. All of them are turbaned with royal crowns, are clothed with royal garments, are covered with royal ornaments, are mounted on royal horses and hold royal scepters in their hands. When one of them moves in the firmament, red-haired servants run before him with great honor and pomp, as on earth (kings) move on chariots, with horsemen and many soldiers, with glory, grandeur, nobility, acclamation and magnificence"[66]

Another text of the Zohar speaks of seventy-two sapphire stones... In Egyptian mysticism, as confirmed by the Egyptologist Erik Hornung, the day is symbolically divided into seventy parts. This means that the divine light (the heavenly Body of God) is divided into 70 parts..., as in Jewish mysticism, the seventy sons of Jacob (Children of Israel) symbolize the light of the world, the Body of Jacob which is the sun and the Body of God. For the Kabbalah, Yahweh has 70 names and his secret name is formed of 70 letters, corresponding to the 70 corresponding parts of the heavenly Body.

---

66 Le Livre Hébreu d'Hénoch ou Livre des Palais. Op. Cit.

Thus the Bible, the Torah, the Septuagint, comes from the thought of the priests of Heliopolis, the On' of the Bible. In secrecy, it tells the story of the holy light of the Garden of Eden, Egypt, which would have been incarnated in the main actors - Adam, Noah, Abraham, Isaac, Jacob, Joseph. The exit from Egypt thus tells the story of the disappearance of the light of the Garden of Eden and its transposition to the land of Canaan.

THE MYSTERY OF OSIRIS EXILED TO BYBLOS IS THE MYSTERY OF ISRAEL

Every Jew symbolically identifies with the body of Israel that came out of Egypt, exiled in the desert of the dead. Like the Children of Israel, who were imprisoned for forty years in the Sinai desert and regularly complained to Moses about the lack of water and food. For the Kabbalah, this is a grandiose metaphor for the journey of the souls of the dead through the desert before reaching the divine judgment of the heavenly court. In the Book of the Dead, or rather in the texts of the Book of the Exit to the Light, every «Egyptian» is also the image of the body of Osiris, which was locked in a sarcophagus and exiled, drifting on the sea to Byblos in the ancient Canaan, symbol of the desert of the dead, where the souls of the dead travel, complaining to the ones of the lack of water and food.

This powerful «biblical» metaphor means in the hieroglyphics that each ISRA, each Yod is part of the ISRA Body, of the cosmos, potentially expelled from the Nile Valley into the desert. It can be said that each Yod/Egyptian/Jew is at his death a part of the symbolic Body of IS-RÂ-GOD taken out, for the great journey from darkness to light. This is the truth hidden meaning of the exit from Egypt revealed by the Kabbalah. As we saw in the previous book, the Elohim/Gods are the Children of Israel who came to Egypt. They form the Body of Yahweh. They are the priests initiated into knowledge, settled in the valley of the Nile without sun and river, empty of culture, of knowledge. The knowledge of Toth will be brought to them by Joseph through the myth of the seven cows, inherent to the civilization of the Nile Valley. Osiris himself, the first MAN, forms the Body of Egypt and the Body of the cosmos, as Jan Assmann attests. It is said in the *Pyramid Texts* that the gods form the entire celestial body of Osiris. The same is true for Israel, and this is no longer a coincidence. In fact, according to the Kabbalah, the twelve tribes of Israel form a cosmology, the twelve constellations of the cosmos. Joseph symbolizes the river, the Nile, Israel, the sun, the primordial old man and his forty-two judges of the Celestial Tribunal installed in the Nile Valley (according to the Book of the Dead). We understand the importance of the cosmological lexical field and a cosmogony of the exit from Egypt given by the Kabbalah, linking the Bible to the myths, solar and mortuary, of Heliopolis and to the myth of Osiris symbolically expelled to Byblos.

"Rabbi Abba says: Each tribe and each individual is one of the organs that make up the Body" [67]

"The Shekhinah (Divine light), in relation to the Holy One, is considered as a body"[68], "The sons of Jacob were twelve. This is to make us understand that THEY WERE LIKE ONE MAN"[69]

"THE SUN IS JACOB (ISRAEL)" [70]
"THE RIVER IS JOSEPH"[71]

In fine, GOD IS ISRAEL. IT IS GOD WHO ENTERED IN EGYPTE SAND WAS EXPELLED FROM EGYPT.

---

67 Le Zohar, tome IV, collection « les dix paroles ». Vayigash Vayehi. Traduit par Charles Mopsik. Verdier, 1996, p. 165.

68 Le Zohar, Genèse, tome III, Vayéchev, Mikets, collection « les dix paroles ». Traduit par Charles Mopsik. Verdier, 1991. Également Zohar II 118b ; III, 152b et 109b, ZH Ki Tissa 56b, TZ, 47, 84b.

69 Aggadoth du Talmud de Babylone. La source de Jacob/ 'Ein Yaakov. Collection « Les dix paroles », Verdier, 1982. Traité Chabbat § 85, p. 185.

70 Le Zohar, Genèse, tome III, Vayéchev, Mikets, Verdier, 1991, p. 207.

71 « Le Fleuve, c'est Joseph ». Le Zohar, Genèse, tome III, . Traduit par Charles Mopsik. Verdier, 1991, p. 266.

Rabbi Simeon says: "When the Shekhina [the Spirit of God, Yahweh/Elohim] **descended into Egypt, she took the form of a Haya** [the original Light, the creative, living solar power of God = ANOKHI, the god Ankh ☥ of the «Egyptians»] **who bears the name of Israel** [Yahweh/Elohim is a solar man], **whose image resembles that of the old man** [from above]. **Forty-two holy angels for the service of the Shekhina came down with her. Each of these angels carries a sacred letter of the divine name composed of forty-two letters.»**[72]

ABRAHAM IS EXPELLED FROM THE GARDEN OF EDEN:

ABRAHAM IS EXPELLED FROM EGYPT

I must warn the reader that this comparative study between the Septuagint Bible, the Hebrew Torah and the Kabbalah is a very sophisticated work, which questions our sources and our beliefs crystallized for more than two millennia on a literal reading of the writing considered sacred, even revealed by God. But the message of Kabbalah goes in a radically opposite direction, as if it were - and indeed it is - the message of scribes wishing to preserve the traces of historical truth. The Bible relates that Yahweh had ordered Abram to leave his native land, which is wrongly located in Ur in Mesopotamia (Ur in Chaldea). Ur Kasdim in Hebrew means the furnace,

the place where the sun dwells. Let's go back to the Bible verse:

Yahweh said to Abram: "Go from your land, from your birthplace, and from your father's house, to the land that I will show you"   (Gen. XII, 1)

It has always been believed that Abraham came from the biblical chronology, born several generations after Adam in Chaldea. Abraham the wandering Hebrew, the Patriarch to whom monotheism was revealed, the descendant of Adam who broke the idols of his father... The logic of the Kabbalah upsets our conditioned vision of Abraham as a Hebrew, a Mesopotamian, and therefore a foreigner in Egypt. A vision based on tradition and the literal reading of the Bible. The

---

72   Zohar, tome III. Le livre de la splendeur. Par Jean de Pauly. Éditions Maisonneuve & Larose, 1985. P. 74.

patriarch leaves his father's house, which is no longer the house of Terah, an idol merchant, but the house of God himself. Abraham is no longer a Mesopotamian, but the resident of the Garden of Eden. Abraham is a double of Adam returning to the garden from which he was expelled. But Kabbalah goes further.

Abraham's domain - the famous Garden of Eden - is equated with Egypt, the garden of God. Yahweh is the father of Adam as well as the father of Abraham. The Kabbalah - the Zohar - identifies Abraham with Adam, the Son of Yahweh:

"YOUR FATHER IS THE HOLY ONE, BLESSED BE HE"[73]

Is the story or rather the myth of Abraham a paraphrase, a remake of the story of Adam and Eve and the Garden of Eden? When Abram arrived in Egypt, he asked Sarai to say that she was his sister, and so Pharaoh, enlightened by Sarai's beauty, naturally took her as his wife...Is the myth of Abraham (and his wife Sarai, who became Sarah) leaving his father's house a paraphrase, a remake of the story of Adam and Eve expelled by God - their father - from the Garden of Eden? Once in Egypt, Abram asks Sarai to say that she is his sister, so Pharaoh, enlightened by Sarai's beauty, naturally takes her as his wife. But during the night, Pharaoh has nightmares. He is attacked by many plagues. At daybreak, Pharaoh returns Sarai to Abram, firmly ordering him to leave Egypt. What is the key to this enigma? We remember that Sarai became Sarah (SARA = son of RÂ, son of the Light), wife of Abraham, who was also the wife of Pharaoh. This marriage between Sarah and Pharaoh lasts one day and one night, as if the scribes of the Bible were giving us the clues of a solar cosmogonic myth. Sarah means princess, but also son of RÂ = SA-RÂ in hieroglyphics. For the Kabbalah, Sarai is a new Eve, the mother of all men. She is the sun, the divine Shekhina. It is as if Abram, having returned to the Garden of Eden, Egypt, had brought the sun Sarai/Sarah/ RÂ back to the Garden of Eden. The sun as an offering for Pharaoh, symbol of the Serpent King. As if Abram arrived in a paradisiacal Egypt, but dark and idolatrous, without light and without the sun. As if Abram wanted to reconquer the lost Garden of Eden by offering his solar wife, who had become his sister, to Pharaoh, that is, by reintroducing the sun into Egypt. Let us follow the lead given by the Kabbalah.

---

73   Le Zohar, tome 1, op. cit., p. 390.

"Abraham went down to Egypt to stay there (Gen. 12:10). Why Egypt precisely? - Because the land is THE EQUAL OF THE GARDEN OF EDEN, which is expressed: AS THE GARDEN OF YHVH, SO IS THE LAND OF EGYPT (Gen. 13:10)"74

Thus, Abraham's Garden of Eden is indeed Egypt and not the land of Canaan. Let's keep in mind that Abram future Abraham disobeyed Yahweh and went to Egypt, to the Garden of Eden, his Father's house. In the Book of Genesis, Canaan, which was cursed by Noah, symbolizes famine, the barrenness of the land, impurity, death, the domain of darkness. Defying Yahweh's command, Abram goes directly to Egypt/Misraim/SA-RÂ = the Garden of Eden. Why? Would Abram have - in a spirit of resistance from the scribes of the Bible - contravened the order of Kyrios/Yahweh by refusing to consider Canaan as a holy land replacing the Nile Valley? Like Noah, Abraham rejects Canaan and returns to the Garden of Eden. In our decoding from Genesis and Kabbalah, Abraham is expelled from Egypt by Pharaoh, just as Adam was expelled from the Garden of Eden because of the serpent. This means that in history, the Jews Youdaios son of SARA were expelled from Egypt by Ptolemy initiator of the Septuagint. The Zohar confirms the gravity of Abram/Abraham's fault:

"Rabbi Judah said: Come and see, as Abraham went down to Egypt without permission, his children were enslaved in that country for four hundred years"75

The slavery of the Children of Israel, the Hebrews, would conceal, in the manner of an oracle, the historical expulsion of the Jews from their ancestral homeland, called Aegyptos for the purpose by the ancient Greeks. This is the reason why the scribes linked the allegedly miraculous exit from Egypt to Adam's original fault. A fault that Noah and then Abram wanted to repair. Does the punishment of Adam and Abram for entering the forbidden Egypt, the Garden of Eden, reveal the great secret, the SOD of the Torah? Abraham, a man who was

---

74   Le Zohar, tome I, op. cit., p. 410.
75   Ibidem, p. 410, 81b.

nevertheless submissive to God, who did not hesitate to make Sarai lie, to give her as an offering to Pharaoh - an offering that Pharaoh refused - and to leave Canaan for Egypt... the house of his Father... Abraham who would have gone so far as to sacrifice his son for Yahweh would be acting against his will...

The return of Abram/Abraham to the garden of Yahweh called «the land of Misraim» in the Torah confirms that Abraham's holy land was the Nile Valley, and Abraham's god - whose name is broken down into AB, the Father, RÂ the sun, Amon - is none other than the Father and the god of the Nile valley, the guardian of the Garden of Eden before the original sin.

So Adam's expulsion from the Garden of Eden by the cunning serpent and the expulsion of Abraham from Egypt by Pharaoh form a powerful message of the scribes who announce the expulsion of all Israel from Egypt by the Pharaoh who had not known Joseph. This separation is a rebirth of the ancient civilization called Egyptian. It announces the exit from Egypt with a new anti-Osiris, embodied by Moses, which we will see in the third part of the trilogy. But the scribes took care to introduce into the Bible the names and principles of the god of their ancestors, which we will see throughout these chapters. The purpose of the patriarch's wanderings in Egypt is to enlighten the land of the Pharaohs, a land confused by the Kabbalah with the Garden of Eden of Adam and Eve, to bring them the solar light symbolized by ABRAM and SARAY. For Abraham bears the name of Etan' Ézrahit' meaning the sun coming from the Eastern horizon, the RÂ-ATON' AMON of the ancient Egyptians[76].

---

76   Abram, renamed Abraham is the sun or light of the world, the morning light, Isaac the afternoon light, Jacob is the evening light. Jacob alias Israel is designated as the sun. Abraham corresponds to ATON' AMON-RÂ, who is at the same time the unique god, the Father of Humanity, the solar man, the visible (RAÂ-ATON') and hidden manifestation of God (AMON = the Hidden). The story of Abraham is a hidden reconstruction by the scribes of the story of Genesis, a real recomposition of the scenario of the original sin in the Garden of Eden, the lost paradise, Egypt.

ISRAEL/AMON/OSIRIS IS THE FIRST WORD OF THE TORAH

The secret Jewish tradition relates that God would have created Israel, even before creating the world. Another world, Israel, would have existed before the creation of heaven and earth... The reason given is the following. The Torah (the first five books of the Old Testament), ends with the name ישראל "Israel". In the language of Kabbalah, Israel is the secret name of Yahweh. Israel should be the first word of the Torah. This assumes the existence of another IS-RÂ-EL civilization before the biblical Genesis of the world.

Pierre-Henri Salfati confirms in his book *Le Premier Mot "Au Commencement Béréchit" - The first word, At the Begining -* that the word, the sacred name Israel, the last word of the Torah **must come before the first, Béréchit**. Israel ישראל would secretly be the first word of the Torah, thus concealing an inverted history of the Bible! For Berechit means Aries, Amon, Ra, the sun of the Nile Valley... It is said that Abraham's ram and Abraham himself (the Father, AB-RÂ-AMON) existed before Berechit. אלהים Elohim would then mean "the priests/gods" of the Nile Valley. The gods of Egypt would have created a civilization before the biblical Genesis...

However, as we have seen, אלהים the Elohim gods symbolize the ancient priests of the Nile valley, the substitutes of Osiris/Israel. They are falsely named Egyptian priests or Neteru by Egyptology. Such information upsets the meaning of the first verse of the Bible which would be a remake of the myth of Osiris, the restart of a pre-existing world.

It is possible to understand the secret meaning of the first verse of the Torah - In the beginning Elohim created the heavens and the earth - according to the deciphering of the Kabbalah and the secret Jewish tradition:

Israel-Osiris-Amon, the Father, the Ram, RAÂ... ...in the beginning, had generated the gods, the Elohim, the heavens of Israel and the earth of Israel.

It cannot be the land of Canaan, but the valley of the Nile. According to Kabbalah, Israel extends from the sources of the Nile to the Euphrates. This means that another civilization, *Israel*, that of the Nile Valley, **existed before Berechit**, before the darkness and the biblical Tohu-Bohu. But Israel means above all God, YHVH, the divine light (the divine Shekhina) **before** the creation of light. From a scientific point of view, light is consubstantial with matter. It is impossible to create the heavens and the earth without creating a first light before the light created in the third verse of the Torah. The scribes knew this perfectly well, which is why they encrypted the message of Israel - the first creative Light of Amun-Osiris-Israel before the light - in the first verse of the Torah.

The decoding of the first verse of the Bible means that in the secret of Kabbalah, a first light, Israel, was created **before** the beginning of Bereshit. Light therefore existed before the third verse, where «Elohim said, 'Let there be light,' and there was light. **An ancient ''Light'', an ancient World, an ancient civilization, an ancient Torah, in fine an ancient Osiris/Israel existed before the alleged creation of the world narrated by the Bible. An ancient World where Israel was confused with Amon or Osiris, thus pre-existed and preceded the Torah of Moses.**

One remembers the oracle of Amun, stating that he is the One God, the image of Atum. Amun is the reed Yod that came out of the primordial waters and that he created the earth in its length and width. The Babylonian Talmud gives us the definition of the hieroglyph of Amen, or Amon, meaning as Amon-RÂ the Hidden, the concealed[77]: God is the King in whom one has faith

---

77　Amon signifie le, l'architecte, l'artisan, mais aussi le dieu caché. Midrach Rabba, tome I, Genèse Rabba. Collection « les dix paroles ». Verdier, 1987, p. 31, chap. 1, § 1.

''EMOUNA'': **"El Melekh Neman"**[78]. Was Amun the first beginning, the first Torah? This would mean that another Israel affiliated to Amun, to Osiris, existed before the first Torah.

«Israel/Osiris/Amon/Aries, the primordial Yod **י** - in the beginning - created - Elohim **אלהים** the gods writen **יי** or **ייי** - - In the first verse of the Torah, the two conjunctions ''AND'' in hebrew ''ET'' **את** designates the heavens *and* ''ET'' **את** the land of Israel. But the secret key of **את** designates GOD. Yahweh himself, who would have dissociated himself into two Yods **יי** , like Atum, into Heaven and Earth, the two Yods **יי** designating the heavens and the earth. Let us not forget that the body of God forms, like Osiris, the body of the Children of Israel. The Zohar tells us that the first land of Israel before the creation was located between the Nile and the Euphrates.

"Eth **את**: **This is the community of Israel at the time of the destruction of the Temple, which was dismissed by a repudiation, which was driven out by a dismissal - the Throne of the King fell... The Throne fell, everything fell."**[79]

All this information allows us to affirm the existence of a first beginning, a first god, a first light of Israel **את**, an ancient civilization concentrated in the first verse of the Torah, before the first. The claim that there was a first beginning, a first god, a first light of Israel, an ancient civilization concentrated in the first verse of the Torah.

In the end, the decoding of the Torah reveals that a civilization existed before the first breach. Bereshit means a «breach» in the civilization of the Nile Valley, which can only be the Septuagint. Indeed, the famous biblical hustle

---

78 Aggadoth du Talmud de Babylone. La source de Jacob/ 'Ein Yaakov. Collection « Les dix paroles », Verdier, 1982. P. 237.

79 Le Zohar, Lamentations. Col. « Les dix paroles ». Verdier, 2000, p. 66.

and bustle and the darkness of creation are attributed by the Talmud and Kabbalah to the Hellenization forced by Greece, the obscurantism and the tragedy for humanity caused by the Septuagint.

Speaking of Bereshit, the creation of the world, the Zohar states that it is the work of Amon, a word which in Kabbalah means "Hidden Wisdom", but also the Craftsman, the Architect, the Teacher:

"I was by his side, Amon, I was his daily delight» (Prov. 8:30) Amon: Pedagogue; Amon: wrapped ; Amon: concealed"[80]

Another Kabbalah text confirms:

"The Holy One blessed be He created the world by the Torah, as it says «And I was a craftsman (Amon) with him (Prov. 8:30)"[81]

It is a whole set of "Egyptian" symbols - Amun, the ram, the Kedem light of the East... - which are hidden in the first three verses of the Torah. Only the initiated priests had access to this secret knowledge, where Israel and Osiris were merged into a single entity, universal and syncretic, where Israel symbolized humanity living in social cohesion, where the gods represented the manifestations of the divine, unique in its essence and multiple in its manifestations. As we have seen in the first volume of this trilogy, Osiris, grandson of Atum, the demiurge God or creator of the sky Nut and of the earth Geb, Osiris son of Geb has, at least in appearance, nothing to do with Adam or Israel.

---

80 Midrach Rabba, tome I, Genèse Rabba. Collection « les dix paroles ». Verdier, 1987, p. 31, chap. 1, § 1.

81 Le Zohar, tome I, collection «les dix paroles'. Traduit par Charles Mopsik. Verdier, 1981, 5d, p. 515.

However, every Egyptian identifies himself with Osiris and every Jew, Christian or Muslim identifies himself with Adam (Christ = Son of Man), with the primordial Man. The thousands of sarcophagi with the effigy of Osiris found in Egypt demonstrate that during several millennia of civilization, Osiris is the first man on earth, the perfect man, dead and resurrected from the dead, who has become the Righteous One, the supreme Judge of the souls of the dead sitting in the celestial court, surrounded by his forty-two judges, Osiris is an example of moral perfection to be followed by every man and every woman. Each dead king of Egypt embalmed and placed in a sarcophagus (always with the effigy of Osiris) becomes an Osiris or a Son of Ra, thus a SA-RÂ, an IS-RÂ on the day of his death[82], in the hope of seeing one day his flesh and his limbs reconstituted.

The ancient texts evoking the origins of Israel lead us to note a similarity, often with a disturbing precision, with what is known as the myth of Osiris, founder of this great civilization falsely named "Ancient Egypt". Jacob alias Israel is not dead, says the secret tradition. Israel died and resurrected. Christ is also the image of the Light, the Man, the Son of Man Osiris/Israel, dead and resurrected. Adam is the image of Osiris/Israel driven out of his land. Adam, the first Man, destined to be perfect before the original sin, is created from all the parts of the earth Adama in Hebrew. Adam, Abraham, Isaak and Jacob all bear the name Tam', the "perfect one", the name of Atum, the divine reed.

"It is Abraham who is the light of the day"[83]

In fine, Abraham, Isaac and Jacob symbolize the Light of the Garden of Eden lost because of Adam's sin. Adam, whom the Kabbalah reveals to be the metaphor of Israel, the light of the world that once illuminated Egypt.

---

82. Jan Assmann. Mort et Au-delà dans l'Égypte ancienne. Éditions du Rocher, 2003.

83. Le Zohar, tome II, collection «les dix paroles ». Traduit par Charles Mopsik. Vayera, Hayé Sarah, Toldot, Vayetsé, Vayichlah. Verdier, 1984, p. 281.

Chapter II

THE BIBLE: ALL EGYPTIANS ARE JEWS OF THE HOUSE OF ISRAEL

THE GOD OF THE EGYPTIANS IS A YOD 𐤉: LIKE THE GOD OF ISRAEL 𐤉.

The historic question of the Jews in ancient Egypt divides historians and Egyptologists. The exit from Egypt is a myth, more than an attested event, especially since no historian can reconcile the Exodus of the Bible with any identified event. However, few Egyptologists have dug the trail started by Jean-François Champollion by focusing on the Sacred Criticism, on the decoding of the Bible by the Kabbalah, capable of revealing the great error of Egyptology. There is a double reading, a popular one and a secret one, attributed to the initiated priests. The secret reading makes Israel and Osiris, the Egyptians and the Jews, one and the same entity. This entity was separated by Hellenization and the Septuagint.

It is through a comparative methodology that it is possible to demonstrate the passage from "Jews" to "Egyptians". Then, the observation of hieroglyphs demonstrates the passage from "Egyptians" to "Jews". Comparisons between the historical texts and the details given by the hieroglyphs, and then the study of the Talmud and the Kabbalah in order to initiate the reader to texts that are more than twice a millennium less known, confirm historically verifiable data, and make it possible to decipher the hidden meaning of the biblical text, showing that it was rewritten, recompiled under the domination of the ancient Greeks, around 270 B.C. Because, yes, there was another Law before, that of Osiris, specified in the Book of the Dead i. e. *Book of the Exit Towards the Light*. It should be pointed out that the Kabbalah constitutes a secret knowledge that deconstructs the Biblical text, calling into question the Revelation of Abraham and Moses. It is a secret memory of the Scriptures or gnosis with a universal, ecumenical vocation, which has never yet been exploited by modern Egyptology. Some historians date it to the eleventh century, but in reality, according to Jewish tradition, the Kabbalah is much older, for the reason that this secret knowledge has accompanied the Bible since it was written.

The Kabbalah is a key to reading, an instruction manual for the Old Testament, particularly the five books of the Torah. It gives the intrinsic meaning that only the contemporaries of the biblical writing could know. It contains descriptions and explanations of fundamental hieroglyphs that can be verified by science. For example, the meaning of the Yod ׳ , the primordial, founding symbol of God for the Jews and for the Egyptians, the name of the god of the Jews, Anokhi, corresponds to the essential hieroglyph Ankh ☥ of the god of the ancient Egyptians. These words designate life and the Ego, the Spirit of God and of men, for the Jews as well as for the "Egyptians". The Pentateuch (the first five books of the Old Testament) and the second book of Exodus tell a cryptic story of slavery in Egypt of the Children of Israel or Hebrews - a name given to them during the writing of the Bible since it did not exist before. It relates the glorious, mythical epic of the exit from Egypt, where the Children of Israel are driven out of the Nile Valley by the miracles of Moses, acting on the orders of the god Yahweh, with the ten plagues and the miraculous opening of the Red Sea allowing the flight of the Hebrews estimated at three million people...

At first reading, there is no reason to question the reality of the biblical postulate, which over the centuries and millennia has become the History that has shaped humanity. The fact of the existence of the ancient Egyptians and Pharaohs has become an absolute certainty, a historical reality supported by scientific doxa and religious belief, based on faith in the Revelation of God to Moses at Mount Sinai. So much so that the aforementioned postulate naming the "Egyptian" civilization, the ancient "Egyptians" and the kings "Pharaohs", is admitted and even legitimized by all humanity, by the religious, the historians, the scientists, by all modern Egyptology. If one admits that the Bible is a historical account, the title of this work "the ancient Egyptians were the Jews" is akin to a provocation. This title implies that the ancient civilization of the Nile Valley with its kings called Pharaohs or kings of Egypt, was Jewish, thus contradicting science and the Bible, which is only read in the literal sense. However, Jewish tradition states that there are four levels of reading the Bible, the most impenetrable of which is called the SOD, the secret. Symbolically, the Sod is the S in the word PARDES, which in Greek refers to paradise, the Garden of Eden. The SOD leads to the rediscovery of what the Kabbalah calls the "Supreme Wisdom" of ancient Egypt: the first Torah of the Jews, the Law of Osiris, where divine iconography was permitted. It was even the foundation of it. Yes, the ancient Egyptians were the Jews, in the sense of Judeo-Christians admitting the gods and images of the gods forbidden by the Bible, and this is what we are going to demonstrate.

Will this discovery be taken seriously by the media, by the secular and scientific world, and by the Jewish, Christian or Muslim religious world? Will it break down the barriers, upset the prejudices deeply rooted in people's minds, and definitively break down the false propaganda and indoctrination that deny the Jews the right to exist and to own land, especially in the Middle East? Because the prospect of a world conflict based on religious ideologies is disastrous for humanity. I remain convinced that the hope for the end of a conflict that is more than twice a millennium old will come about through the objective criticism of the scriptures, through the unveiling and discovery of the historical and archaeological truth, and also through the Kabbalah or secret Gnosis, where Jews, Christians, Muslims, Africans, Ethiopians, Danites, Hindus, Buddhists, etc., believers, non-believers, all the peoples of humanity form the true lost tribes of the immense civilization of Israel/Egypt.

Osiris or Osirios Οσιριος is a late, transformed Greek reading imposed by Greek invaders in the third century BCE. In the tombs of the Valley of the Kings, the names Osiris or Osirios are not used in the hieroglyphs. Instead, one can read

SAR, ASAR, SARÂ, OUSER', OUSRÂ, ISRÂ, ISIR... We always find the two roots S and RÂ meaning Son of Ra or man of Ra. And for good reason, the Greek kings did everything possible to upset the history of the civilization of the Nile Valley, usurping the name Osirios/Οσιριος. The ancient Greeks associated Osirios with Dionysus (and his wife Isis with the goddess Demeter). They integrated him into the legends of the Greek pantheon, syncretic mythologies, all this in order to make the deities of the Nile valley pass for Greek deities and to realize the great ecumenism of Hellenization. But the real goal was to divide and rule, both over the Jews, a word meaning the dignitaries of the Nile Valley called by its inhabitants the land of the Two Lands t3-wi, and over the rest of the "Egyptian" people and the other peoples subjected to their domination.

The historian Diodorus of Sicily affirms that the Greeks appropriated the gods of Egypt in their legends as well as in their history, in an attempt to make their own gods dominate the Nile Valley, particularly over the Jews qualified as the "Jewish race" and over the small people lowered to the rank of "Egyptian race".

"In a general way, they say [Diodorus quotes the Egyptian priests]**, the Greeks appropriated the most famous of the Egyptian heroes and gods as well as the colonies founded by them"**[1]

This general appropriation or usurpation was intended to remove from the collective memory the historical fact linking the "Egyptians" to their true identity: the reed, the Yod ▌ / י of the house of Osiris/Israel. Thus a verse in the Book of Ezekiel (XXIX, 6) states that "all the Egyptians are the reeds or the support - the calamus, the scribes -of the reed of the house of Israel:

---

1   Diodore de Sicile. Bibliothèque Historique. Éditions Les Belles Lettres, 2003. Première édition 1993. XXIII, 6-8.

And all the inhabitants of Egypt shall know that I am Yahweh, Because they have been a support of the reed to the house of Israel[2] .

According to the conventional reading of modern Egyptology, and according to the hieroglyphs, the "ancient Egyptians" were the scribes/calamists, the scribal priests of the house of ISRÂ called Osiris, dedicated to the temples of ISRÂ or to the temples of the other divinities which were emanations of Atum/Osiris. The house of Israel, meaning the Temple - is clearly identified with the house of Osiris in this verse. It follows that the house of Israel is the house of Osiris and the so-called "Egyptian" temples are the Jewish temples of the house of Israel/Osiris.

This verse is very disturbing for the translators of our current Bibles. It will be noted that the Bible gives reason to Clement of Alexandria. The scribes wanted to convey a message through ambivalent translations - a message that states very clearly that "all the Egyptians were Jews of the House of Israël". Before analyzing the different translations, it is appropriate to make the hieroglyphs speak and to recall that the great Ennead of Heliopolis defines the cosmogony, the genesis of the gods of Egypt from the demiurge, the unique god, whose true name is unknown, but can be read TAM or ATOUM, hieroglyphics which are written above all by the reed Yod, (A or Y) symbol of the Spirit of God coming out of the waters of the Noun/Nun, and of which each so-called "Egyptian" is the image. This is the reason why every man defines himself by saying ME, I, by the hieroglyph Yod, NY, ANY אֲנִי in Hebrew.

Hieroglyphs I, I AM = Reed YOD origin of the word Jew[3].

---

2   http://www.info-bible.org/lsg/26.Ezechiel.html#29

3   Egyptian hieroglyphic dictionary. E. A. Wallis Budge, Dover Publications, inc, New York. Published by General publishing Company, 1978, 15 a.

Atum also manifests itself under the name of Amun or Ra, which is identified with the sun, but which means the creative, primordial and silent light, ''OR'' אור in Hebrew. Atum begat the couple Shu and Tephnut, two male and female powers, who in turn begat Geb the earth and Nut the sky. Osiris was above all the Son of Ra (SA-RÂ), or the Son of Geb the earth and Nut the sky. This is the reason why Osiris is associated with the sun Ra and the sacred duck, which designates both the earth of Ra (Geb) and the Son of Ra (SA-RÂ or IS-RÂ), the first Man. Like Christ, Osiris is the Father of humanity, dead and resurrected, circumcised. The numerous tombs teach us that all the "Egyptians" at their death are reeds, who become "Osiris/ IS-RÂ" never "Egyptians". It is necessary to note that in the hieroglyphs, they are the Sons of IS-RÂ-GOD, the sons of the Solar Man, the Reeds sons of Atum, origin of the Jews sons of Israel or sons of Adam in the Bible. It is important to insist on this archaeological truth: Osiris is SAR, SA-RÂ or IS-RÂ, generally translated as Son of the Sun, meaning the Sons, the Reeds of the Divine Light, names with which the kings that the Greeks falsely renamed "Pharaohs" were identified.

For the Septuagint, as for the Hebrew Bible, it is written that "Pharaoh" or the "Egyptians" are "he reeds of the house of Israel". Why does the text not say, "the reeds of the house of Osiris"? Such a statement by the scribes of the Bible allows us to deduce a secret concordance between Osiris and Israel, which the Bible will confirm by naming the golden calf "Israel" when it was Osiris. Although the centuries have accustomed us to name these men "Egyptians", "Ægyptos", the hieroglyphs define them by the reed Yod ▮ designating the ME 𓏞 of each "Egyptian". Why? Each man is the image of Atum, the image of the creator god long before the Bible. Although by convention the Egyptologists name ATOUM or TEM, TAM the demiurge god of On' renamed Heliopolis, the hieroglyph of Atum does not leave any doubt. Atum is the unique reed, the Yod , ▮ - out of the primordial waters (the celestial flood) to generate the sky and the earth:

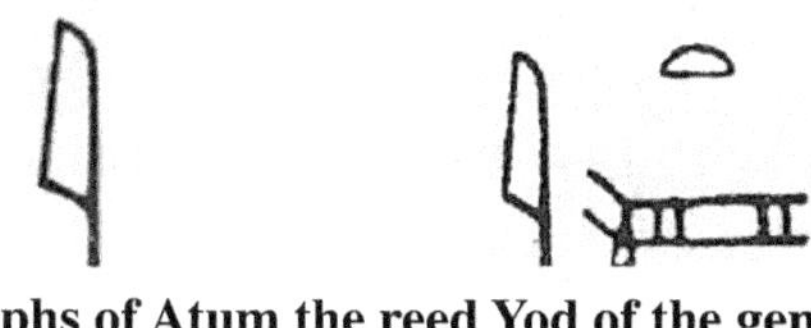

Hieroglyphs of Atum the reed Yod of the generation of the world.

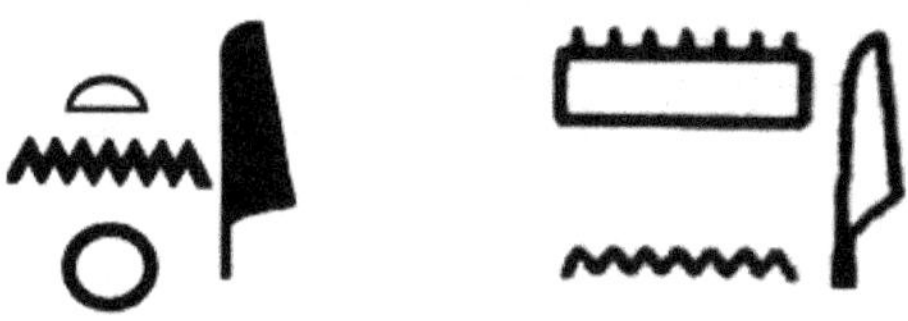

Aton' is a Yod coming out of the waters; Amun' is also a Yod coming out of the waters. Yod is the creator god of heaven and earth.

Thus, the Yod referred to God, the Creator Being, the perfection of creation; this is the true identity of the Jewish god. The first two verses of the Bible show that God is a Yod hovering over the surface of the waters (Genesis 1:1). Atum, the first god of the great Ennead of Heliopolis, embodied the demiurge, for Atum is also the primordial Father separated into three energies generating heaven, earth and men. The TM sled in the hieroglyphs of Atum symbolizes the passive celestial movement, and the T the celestial vault above the earth ——. It is for this reason that the Egyptian scribes did not appear the sled in the names and titles of Amun, Aten or Osiris, whereas in these hieroglyphs, it is always the Yod, the symbolic calamus of creation, which dominates and comes out of the Nun . The first Egyptologists like Gaston Maspero, Allan Gardiner and Michel Vladimirovitch Skariatine had followed Jean-François Champollion. Maspero, relying on the work of James Henry Breasted, had even specified that the Yod designated the identity, the personality, the individuality, the Spirit, the Ego, the "Undefined" creative Being ATUM = YOD coming from the sacred calamus of God:

"The name of the Indefinite was sometimes written by 𒀭 all alone, a letter that corresponds to the Hebrew Yod and that like the latter replaces here the Aleph-Principle of all..."[4]

Now, in addition to the Aleph, the Hebrew letter Yod ‫ י‬precisely designates God, Yahweh or Elohim, meaning El, God and Yam, the waters. According to the secrets of the Kabbalah, Elohim ‫אלהים‬ means EL A-YAM, the God of the waters YAM.

"the Spirit of the water is the Spirit [i.e., the Yod] **who manifested himself at the creation of the world"[5]; "I am God, I dwell in the dwelling of Elohim, in the heart of the sea"** (Ezekiel XXVIII, 1-3).

All these comparisons once again give reason to Clement of Alexandria, who also affirmed in his Stromata (V) that the most sacred symbols of the ancient Egyptians and the Jews were the same. From the beginning of their civilization, every Egyptian referred to himself by the hieroglyphics (Y, A) 𓇌 or 𓈖𓇌 (NY, ANY) justification that he was the living reed, the living image of the Father Atum. This kneeling man who says " I am a Yod" has his left hand over his heart and the finger of his right hand over his mouth. For Jewish tradition as for modern Egyptology, the heart is the seat of intelligence. It is an archaeological fact: the ancient Egyptians are historically, scientifically, the divine reeds that came out of the earth and the waters, the Yods. During the Greek domination, in the third century B.C., by the power of Hellenization, in a double phenomenon of acculturation and deculturation, all the knowledge was centralized on Ægyptos, and that in all the books of the world copied in Greek, according to the orders of Ptolemy II Philadelphus. The hieroglyph Yod was no longer used to designate the "Beings", the images of

---

4   Égyptes. Anthologie de l'Ancien Empire à nos jours. Catherine David, Jean-Philippe de Tonnac et Florence Suentin. Maison Neuve Larose, 1997. p. 260. Citaion de l'égyptologue russe Michel Vladimirovitch Skariatine dit ENEL qui avait travaillé avec Gaston Maspéro, (1846-1916).

5   Le Zohar, Cantique des Cantiques. Collection 'les dix paroles ". Verdier, 1999, p. 114, note 434: Élohim, El Hayam, signifient " vers la mer ".

God, as the origin of the men of the Nile Valley. As a result of the desire to usurp history, the sacred reed was deliberately replaced by the first Lagid kings, self-proclaimed "Pharaoh", by the other god, Ægyptos, especially in the Septuagint.

This trauma was imposed in order to make the religion of Osiris and the officials of ancient Egypt disappear. The Bible and especially the Septuagint refer to the Jews as "foreign slaves in Egypt". A deliberate spoliation of the land of the Nile valley, in order to prove that this vast territory had since time immemorial belonged to the Greeks, by the royal and divine power to rename the land of Osiris by the land of Ægyptos. However, the Jews have always kept their ancestral name attached to the immemorial hieroglyph Yod 𐤏. Yod, Yahouds, Youdaïos, are the images of the God Yod hovering on the surface of the celestial waters. And for good reason in the first verse of the Aramaic Bible (Targum), the god of the creation of heaven and earth is written with two Yods ׳ ׳ or three Yods ׳ ׳ ׳, the creation being a begetting of the primitive Yod ׳. According to the Kabbalah, the Jew is thus the image of the Yod, the image of God or gods. The Yod is the first Principle, the primordial point coming from the sacred calamus, which was multiplied to create the universe. Now this multiplication of the primordial Yod designating God, the breath, Yahweh, Adonai, Yah, Yahu, He, Hou, etc., participates in the same creative process for the hieroglyphs, Atum, Amun-Ra or Aten, symbolized by the Yod. Atum is the creative calamus, the One with millions of forms.

Whether it is the Hebrew Yod 𐤉 or the Egyptian Yod 𐤉, they designate Man, the Principle, the Being created in the image of God, unique and multiple at the same time, the Human Being in its ecumenical meaning. These two civilizations form only one, where the Yod symbolizes the personality and individuality, the "I" (I, Me, I am) of the man, image of God or image of the gods. Therefore, what is the difference between the god of the Bible and the god of the ancient Egypt called idolatrous? The god of the Bible is transcendent, separated from the sensible world created in six days, separated from his creation. He needs to be revealed to Abraham and especially to Moses, to whom he dictates the Law, revealed at Mount Sinai and immutable, perpetual. The god of the Bible defines himself as the "geopolitical" god of the exit from Egypt. He is a jealous, threatening, angry, often cruel, dictatorial and above all political god who must be believed. In this sense, he belongs to the past: his word and his distant creation belong to a world limited to the "Book", by Revelation and the revealed Book. Conversely, the god Atum generates creation every day. The Man Osiris in the cosmogony of Heliopolis (On' in hieroglyphic), is the image of Atum, the luminous Being, absolutely tranquil, infinitely present and silent, without political boundaries. God does not need belief nor believers because he is the world revealed at every moment, as Christian Jacq attests:

"The ancient Egyptians did not believe in God, they experienced and knew him. "Belief" was an unknown term in their vocabulary, and their spiritual approach was based on knowledge, the scope of which included, according to the *Pyramid Texts*, intuitive perception, communion with the vital power... ...One feeds on this knowledge, one swallows it, one relives with it "the first time" that is accomplished at every moment"[6]

The Greek legends bring us the proof that the Ptolemies wanted, against all odds, to monopolize the history of the Nile valley, whereas the ancient Greeks knew perfectly well the words SA-RÂ, ISRA, MISRI - MISR in Koranic Arabic - which designate Osiris the country of Egypt. MISRI which will be found later in the Bible in the form מצרים MITSRAIM[7] or MITSRAE in Aramaic is decomposed into MESS, given birth by the Matrix Ra. So why so much energy, so much determination to impose the Greek deity Ægyptos, if not to make the sacred name of Osiris, which was the true name SA-RÂ/IS-RÂ of the Nile valley, disappear from memory? If not to make disappear the origin of the reeds Youdaïos...

---

6   Cf. Christian Jacq. La tradition primordiale de l'Égypte ancienne selon les textes des Pyramides. Grasset & Fasquelle. 1998. Introduction p. 13.

7   MISRAIM in Greek, also reads MITSRAIM in Hebrew.

Many examples show the spoliation by the ancient Greeks. For Gaston Maspero, confirmed by the work of Allan Gardiner and by the Wallis Budge hieroglyphic dictionary, who studied the symbols of the River renamed "NYLOS" and of the earth generalized into "ÆGYPTOS" by the Ptolemies, the river and the earth were embodied in the two intertwined bodies of Isis and Osiris. The reason given by the scientists was that the river of God fertilized the land of the reeds, the land of the Nile Valley. Clement of Alexandria could not be unaware that the land and the river had never borne the names of the Greek gods Ægyptos or Nylos, because he knew the sacred meaning of hieroglyphics. The river symbolized the Body and the blood of Osiris, parables taken again with Christ. By extension the river participates in the fertility and fecundity between Isis and Osiris, who together formed the primordial couple, the universal fertilizing Principle. This Principle was expressed by the annual flood, the first day of the Nile flood marking the new year, as the return of death to life. Clement of Alexandria, a reader of the Greek Bible or Septuagint, could not be unaware either that the true definition of the "ancient Egyptians" was inscribed, recorded in hieroglyphics, but also in two verses of the Septuagint, in the book of Ezekiel. In fact, the translations of the Latin Vulgate identify "all the Egyptians and all the Pharaoh" to the reeds of the house of Israel". Let us clarify our investigation:

Latin Bible: **"And all the inhabitants of Egypt shall know that I am the LORD, because they have been a support of reed to the house of Israel"** [8] (Ezekiel XXIX, 6).

But for the Septuagint, this verse is addressed directly **to Pharaoh king** of Egypt who embodies the reed staff, which is none other than the calamus of the scribes of the house of Israel. It is translated: **"For** [you Pharaoh] **you have been the staff of the calamus of the house of Israel"** (Ezekielos XXIX, 6)

And all the dwellers in Egypt shall know that I am the Lord, because thou hast been a staff of reed to the house of Israel.

---

8   http://www.info-bible.org/lsg/26.Ezechiel.html#29

We see in the course of these pages that only the hieroglyphs can provide proof that the scribes meant "All the Egyptians are the Jews of the house of Israel".

Obviously, this verse disturbs the translators of our current Bibles. Another translation modifies the meaning of the Greek verse and speaks of the support of the reed "lent to the house of Israel" by the Egyptians:

Then all the inhabitants of Egypt will know that I am the LORD, because they had lent a reed support to the house of Israel.

Another translation of the Septuagint reverses the meaning of the verse, speaking of the punishment of the king of Egypt, who would have been a reed support, but a weak support for the house of Israel...

διὰ τοῦτο τάδε λέγει κύριος Ἰδοὺ ἐγὼ ἐπάγω ἐπὶ σὲ ῥομφαίαν καὶ ἀπολῶ ἀνθρώπους ἀπὸ σοῦ καὶ κτήνη·

Et tous ceux qui habitent l'Égypte sauront que je suis le Seigneur. En punition de ce que tu as été pour la maison d'Israël un appui faible comme un roseau.

One is immediately struck by the radical differences in the translations. There is a will of resistance on the part of the seventy translators to conceal the historical truth of Israel in the Septuagint, in order to counter the Greek god Kyrios, linking "all the Egyptians" to the "house of Israel" by means of the sacred reed. Therefore, the Septuagint can no longer be a translation made with "piety" according to the Letter of Aristaeus:

"Now that the translation has been done correctly, WITH PITY AND WITH RIGOUROUS ACCURACY"[9]

How can there be piety when it is blasphemy by submission to the god Kyrios? This unusual verse of the Bible is all the more disturbing because **it gives the definition of the ancient Egyptians verifiable by the hieroglyphs** as well as by the oracle of Amun which, as we shall see, actually designates the "Egyptians" as the reeds, the Yods of God.

---

9   Lettre d'Aristée à Philocrate, les Éditions du Cerf, 1962, p. 129 § 311.

All the inhabitants of Egypt are one with the house of Israel, which corresponds to the immemorial tradition of the remembrance of Osiris, voluntarily replaced by "Israel" in this verse. But the Septuagint, like the Torah, speaks of the ancient Egyptians of the house of Israel in order to counter, in a hidden verse, all the propaganda of Hellenization. Consequently, it is obvious that modern Egyptology has privileged the Greek reading of the Septuagint and the Latin Vulgate, not the reading of the hieroglyphs, which is a shame.

Each "Egyptian" being an IS-RÂ, the verse should have said, "the IS-RÂ/MIS-RÂ were the calamists, the reeds of the house of IS-RÂ the God, of Israel. Traditionally, the king renamed "Pharaoh" is the reed Man of Ra IS-RÂ of the house of IS-RÂ and not of Osiris/Osirios/Ὄσιριος.

According to the symbolic meaning of the verse, all the "Egyptian" inhabitants, the "Pharaohs" included, are the calamists, the reeds, i.e., the scribes of the house of Israel, thus the Yods attached to the temples of the Nile Valley.

The Hebrew word Bei'th בית means the house of studies in the sense of a community attached to the temple and to the knowledge of hieroglyphics. Much later, at the time of the Greek invasions (3rd century BC) the Jews attached the word Bei'th בית to the *proseuque* in Greek, the Synagogue, the schools and the courts to read, learn and apply exclusively the Septuagint. According to the verse, all Egyptians are therefore the scribes/rosebushes/Yods of the temples of Israel/Osiris/Amon/Isis, etc. It is clear that in writing this verse, the scribes intentionally wanted to make it clear that the temples of the Nile Valley were the Bei'th בית the "house" of Israel, to mean that the expression "House of Israel" Bei'th IS-RÂ-EL, has precedence over the expression "Egyptian Temple". To mean that **Israel is the name of Osiris, that the Egyptian temples are the Jewish temples of ancient Israel.** In the Kabbalah, Israel is the name of God, of Yahweh, of the divine Shekhina who came down to Egypt. **"Indeed, "Israel came to Egypt" is the Holy One blessed be He""**[10]

____

10   Le Zohar, Genèse, tome III, Vayéchev, Mikets, collection 'les dix paroles'. Traduit par Charles Mopsik. Verdier, 1991, p. 286, sq.

"The sun is Jacob (Israel)"[11]

Consequently, "Israel", a sacred name attributed in the Bible to God as well as to the golden calf of the so-called "Egyptians", is none other than the name of Osiris, the name of the ancient land of the Nile Valley renamed Ægyptos by Hellenization. This cannot be a mistake: the hieroglyph of Osiris is read IS-RÂ-EL, SAR, SA-RÂ, IS-RÂ. The hieroglyphs confirm the meaning of the definition of the word "Egyptians" given by the seventy-two scribes of the Septuagint. The whole civilization called "Egyptian" is based on the cult of the sacred reed, the Yod, the image of the God Yod named Atum, Amun, Ra, Yahu, who came out of the heavenly waters. The hieroglyphs that designate the personality and individuality of each "Egyptian" point precisely to the calamus, the Yod reed. Christian Jacq's confirmed, according to the *Texts of the Pyramids*, that the king that he names Pharaoh is the reed, the sacred calamus with which all men were identified.

"And it is even specified, in a surprising way: "the living Reed [the Yod Ɑ] is Pharaoh, allusion to the fact that the humble reed is used in all aspects of Egyptian existence and that Pharaoh is useful to his people""[12]

We are faced with the most important problem of the Egyptologists, which is a failure of transmission, of popularization of what they perceive in the hieroglyphs.

Indeed, there is no scientific proof that the designation Per'AA "the great temple" is directly at the origin of the Greek word **Φαραω** Pharaoh/Pharao' used in the Septuagint and the Hebrew Bible פרעה. On the other hand, Egyptologists agree that **Φαραω** Pharao' is a specific Greek loan to Greek kings. This is exactly the same for Kyrios, the name of the god of the Septuagint, wanting to impose Kyrios on the Jews - while their god was called Yahô/Osiris/Ptah, etc. - but no Egyptologist has ever questioned this terrible usurpation.

---

11 Le Zohar, Genèse, tome III, Vayéchev, Mikets, op. cit., 1991, p. 207.

12 Christian Jacq. La tradition primordiale de l'Égypte ancienne selon les Textes des Pyramides. Grasset & Fasquelle. 1998, p. 24, 165, 256-257.

The *Texts of the Pyramids*, whose first Anglo-American translations were taken up in French by Christian Jacq who transcribed **"Pharaoh is a Reed"** do not say that. Like all texts written in hieroglyphics, they say the King "SA-RA" or "IS-RÂ" is a Reed". Christian Jacq (like all Egyptologists) has used the convention adopted by modern Egyptology to write ''Pharaoh is a Reed'' instead of SA-RÂ or IS-RÂ is a Reed'' to designate the king, whereas "Pharaoh" does not exist either in the hieroglyphs or in the *Pyramid Texts*. There is no doubt that **the scribes of the Septuagint knew the hieroglyphs and the Pyramid Texts** when they speak of the golden calf and especially when they state that the ancient Egyptians - the real Egyptians - are the Reeds, the "Jews" of the house of Israel. They tell us purely and simply that *all the ancient Egyptians and their kings do not exist under the name "Egyptians"*, for the historical reason that they are affiliated with the sacred Temple of the old "IS-RÂ-EL" renamed Osiris. This is proven by the hieroglyphs which state that all Egyptians are the Yods of Atum, "the Reeds of God" of the "House" of SA-RÂ or IS-RÂ. This powerful message left by the scribes of the Septuagint corresponds historically to what the hieroglyphs say: as their titles show, all the kings of the Nile Valley are identified with Atum or Amun, the Reed of the House of SA-RA/IS-RÂ - which I confirm in the chapter "Tutankhamun is a king of Israel".

As we have seen, the verse of the Septuagint disturbs, not the editors of the Hebrew Bible, because they say exactly the same thing as the Septuagint, but, as we have seen, the translators of our modern Bibles, including some versions of the Bible in French or English that have falsified the original Greek or Hebrew text, going so far as to reverse the meaning. The great mistake of modern Egyptology is to have ignored the reading and the essential, founding vision that came from the *Pyramid Texts*. Egyptology has persisted in reading the name of Atum with the TM sledge ⨂ neglecting the symbolic reading of the Yod ⟨ included in his name, whereas this Yod determines *the existing, thinking Being,* the individuality of each human being, as we will see in the next chapter.

The so-called "Egyptians", men as well as kings, were the ***Men of God***, the IS-RÂ, by identification with the sacred name SA-RÂ or IS-RÂ-GOD and not "Osiris". The IS-RÂ kings were renamed "Pharaohs" by the ancient Greeks from the name of Pharao'Φαραω, another Greek deity that does not appear in the protocols of the tombs of the Valley of the Kings. Thus, Pharao' **Φαραω**, a term generalized by the first Ptolemies with the Septuagint, has a direct relationship with the tower of Pharos of Alexandria. The kings of the Nile valley, SA-RÂ or IS-RÂ, wore ritual clothing, a monotheistic cap placed under the crown of Amun, like the Jews and the kings of Israel. Egyptologists repeatedly speak of "coincidences" between two civilizations, Jewish and Egyptian, but the facts are there. The SA-RA/Pharaohs kings had a name given by the mother, they were enthroned by the sacred anointing, like the kings of Israel, and had five names precisely structured like the five names of the kings of Israel. It has been discovered that the ancient "Egyptians" spoke and wrote pre-biblical Hebrew in cuneiform letters. The *Pyramid Texts* show the existence of a science between letters and numbers giving words and names a numerical value, a science called Gematria by the Jews. It has been discovered that between the second and third millenniums B.C., the ancient "Egyptians" had a Law, a Torah, commandments of which each "Egyptian" had to give an account at his death before the tribunal of IS-RÂ, called Osiris; a sacred book which told of an " exit of Egypt" of the souls of the deceased. A vertical, eschatological exit, and not a geographical one. The passage from the darkness of death to the light of resurrection with the attribution by God of a promised land, as in the Bible. In chapter 125 of this Book, the 42 commandments are written in the form of negative confessions. As in the Bible, which contains 613. Every so-called Egyptian had to give an account of them to the court of Osiris, just like the king who gave himself as an example to the people. These commandments were "negative" **because they were instituted by the kings,** and not directly by God as in the Bible. For the kings Sons of Ra were the intermediaries between Osiris and men: they had the power to control the law, creating and modifying the commandments when necessary. These commandments forbade killing, ordering killing, blasphemy, stealing, coveting, and advocated respect for parents, charity for the poor, and continuous care for others. Whereas for Jews, Christians and Muslims, the ancient Law of kings and men has become with the Bible and the Koran the Law of God, immutable and fixed for eternity by the texts, until the event of the Messiah.

Bread and wine were found to symbolize the food of God or the gods in ancient Egypt. The "Egyptian" equivalent of the Jewish Bar Mitzvah at ten years of age was found, Egyptian prayers precisely resembling the Jewish Kaddish of the dead, days of rest, feast days, feast of lights, days of fasting, prescriptions on permitted and forbidden foods, prohibition of eating pork, etc., customs curiously resembling those of the Jews, and for good reason, since we demonstrate in this work that the ancient "Egyptians" were the Jews. In the fifth century B.C., Herodotus mentions the prohibition of using a foreign knife to cut meat, the ritual of cutting children's hair, which was weighed on a scale and replaced by gold, the cult of sacred animals, the animals that were allowed or forbidden, the obligations or prohibitions of clothing, the rules of purity, the washing of hands, ritual baths, etc. Thus, the problem that arises between me and the science called "modern Egyptology" is the following: over three millennia of civilization in the Nile Valley, archaeology and hieroglyphics formally deny the existence of the words, "Egypt", "Egyptian" or "Pharao"'in hieroglyphics. How did these names appear ? Why did they usurp the sacred hieroglyphs ? What is the answer of Egyptologists concerning the existence of Jews in ancient Egypt ?

The vast majority of Egyptologists agree that there is no historical record of the biblical characters, the patriarchs Abraham, Isaac and Jacob, Joseph, and especially Moses in ancient Egypt. There is even less trace of the Hebrews or Children of Israel who were slaves of Pharaoh and who were miraculously brought out of Egypt through the Red Sea following the ten plagues. There is also no trace of the kings of Israel reigning over the territory of Canaan. However, the question remains as to the existence or non-existence of Jews in ancient Egypt. If we admit that the kings of Israel, if Moses and the Patriarchs did not exist, in accordance with the absence of historical traces, the Jews, it is a fact, existed in ancient Egypt. So who are they? So who are they? Where do they come from? Are they what we call the ancient Egyptians? Egyptologists are in total disagreement on this point. In the nineteenth century, Jean-François Champollion, the father of modern Egyptology, advocated the scientific analysis of the Bible (Old and New Testaments) as the essential component of modern Egyptology. In deciphering the hieroglyphs, Jean-François Champollion had insisted on the enormity of the new science which, although called "Egyptology", was intimately linked to Jewish civilization.

Even if present-day Judaism is different, even radically different, from the ancient civilization of the Nile Valley, the father of Egyptology insisted that he regarded the ancient Egyptians as a "distinct race" directly affiliated with the Jews:

"At the same time it will be decided whether the Egyptians did not belong to a distinct race; for, it must be declared here, against the common opinion, the Copts of modern Egypt, considered as the last offspring of the ancient Egyptians, offered to my eyes neither the color nor any of the characteristic features, in the lineaments of the face or in the forms of the body, which could show such a noble descent. The real knowledge of ancient Egypt is also important to biblical studies, and Sacred Criticism must draw many clarifications from it"[13]

---

13 Grammaire égyptienne de Champollion. Éditions SOLIN 1997, page xix.

Jean-François Champollion (1790-1832)

In the following paragraph, Champollion clarifies his thinking, namely that the civil institutions, the external forms of worship and the ceremonial material including the funerary furniture of the ancient Egyptians and the Hebrews/ Jews were obviously perfectly identical:

"Moses applied, as far as local circumstances should permit, the civil institutions of the Egyptians to the organization of Hebrew society; he proclaimed religious dogmas essentially distinct from those of Egypt; but in the external forms of worship, and especially in the material of ceremonies, he had to imitate and did indeed imitate Egyptian practices. The study of Egyptian monuments, either earlier or later than the time of Moses, will thus give a more complete understanding of the original texts of the Bible"[14]

---

14 Grammaire égyptienne, ou principes généraux de l'écriture sacrée égyptienne
    appliquée à la représentation de la langue parlée, par Champolion le Jeune.
    Edition Jean de Bonnot. Pages XIX, XX.

At the time when Champollion introduced humanity to the new science called Egyptology, he communicated his deep intuition, his intimate conviction: ancient Egyptians and Jews would originally formed the same civilization. Champollion did not yet have access to the fundamental religious texts of ancient Egypt, such as the *Book of the Dead*, which included the wisdom or the 42 commandments of the god renamed "Osiris" by the Greeks, commandments that each "Egyptian" had to apply in his or her daily life, commandments centered on otherness, attention to others, the well-being of others, courtesy, etc. This is why Champollion postulates that the Egyptians belonged to a "distinct race", the Jews, urging researchers to exploit a new methodology: the religious dogma of Moses, although essentially distinct from that of Egypt, would be the consequence of a major historical event, an upheaval that would have taken place in the past, at the time of writing the Bible. However, Champollion knows perfectly well that such an assertion is only a starting hypothesis, the track for a discovery with universal scope. He was not unaware of the obvious risk of suffering general disapproval of the Egyptian origin of the Bible, or even the indirect threat of the Church.

He does not ignore either the fact that the political and scientific circles undoubtedly influenced by two millennia of prejudices and religious traditions would not follow him on the way of the Sacred Criticism. What Champollion did not know was the immense omerta, the leaden blanket that would progressively become an institution for the whole of the different bodies of scientific research, for two centuries. This omerta is denounced today by the Egyptologist Jan Assmann and the psychoanalyst Gérard Huber.

"Indeed, the "pact" between the Church and the scientific world was based on the traditional image of a merciless fight between the polytheism of the Egyptian oppressors and the monotheism of the ancestors of Judaism and Christianity. However, since the discovery, in 1897, of the

letters addressed to the pharaoh Akhenaten (1370 B.C.), recorded in tablets at Tell-El Amarna, and especially since their publication in 1891-1892, this image had imploded"[15]

As the father of Egyptology had foreseen, despite the first obstacles encountered, the Egyptian texts were going to shed light on the mystery of the Old Testament and the New Testament, as well as the mystery of the Koran. Champollion disappeared with his secret without having been able to realize the Sacred Criticism. Would he have been pressured by religious authorities, especially the Church? No one will ever be able to answer this question. But he gave the direction to follow: the Bible is, in a vital and inescapable way, linked to the whole Egyptian civilization.

The *Corpus Hermeticum* (Hermes Trismegistus) is a set of books constituting the last so-called 'Egyptian' wisdom that have come down to us. The goddess Isis instructs her son Horus, renamed Asclepius. Isis teaches him the Law, the wisdom, the ancient monotheism of the god Thoth, who is called Douaty, Daat Daaty in Hebrew meaning precisely the one who possesses knowledge. These are therefore the last attested documents of the last so-called 'Egyptian' wisdom, which came from the Daat knowledge of the Jews. Professor Nock, a great specialist in hermeticism, confirms a direct filiation with the ancient Jews:

"We have further indications that the Asclepius, like many other hermetic documents, knows Judaism, and may have used Jewish sources [...] All kinds of prophecies circulated under the Empire and, whatever their origin, could be transmitted from man to man. Nevertheless, I am inclined to think that A JEWISH WRITING, TRANSMITTED FROM HAND TO HAND OR BY ORAL TRADITION, IS THE BASIS OF OUR TEXT"[16]

---

15 Préface de l'ouvrage Le Pharaon Juif, Éditions Lattès, 2008.

16 A.D.Nock, traducteur de la version grecque d'Hermès Trismégiste, Corpus Hermeticum. Traites XIII-XVIII, Asclepius, Les Belles Lettres, p. 289-290.

The researcher André Paul, a great specialist in the study of the Dead Sea Scrolls and author of several works, affirms that Egyptian society in Greek and Roman times was a "Judaic society"[17]. Specialists of the Hellenistic period, Edward Will and Claude Orrieux confirm that the so-called 'Egyptian' religion consisted of an "Egyptian Judaism" in the Nile Valley during the Greek period known as the Ptolemaic period:

"During the lifetime of Hecateus, we know little more than one thing about Egyptian Judaism: that it existed"[18]

Before the schism of the Greek Septuagint allegedly revealed around 270 BC, the Temple of the Jews was still attached to the territories of God or the gods, in a divine, syncretic and ecumenical vision of the world.

"Texts prove without doubt that, despite its strongly sacerdotalized, hierocratic structure, Judea was considered the territory of the "Jewish people" (ethnos tôn Ioudaiôn) to which all the Jews dispersed in the Ptolemaic Empire - and elsewhere - belonged[19]... ...THE JUDÉANS THEREFORE BELONGED TO THE SAME STATE AS EGYPT"[20]

Ostraca found at Elephantine in Upper Egypt provide evidence that in the Middle East of the fifth century B.C., original Judaism was a syncretism practicing the cult of Osiris, the universal deity at the time, a deity both unique and multiple. Yaho/Osiris/Ptah was the god of the gods, for the gods formed the Body of Osiris. Judaism in Jerusalem evolved according to the whims of the invaders of Egypt, Assyrians, Babylonians and Achaemenids (Persians). The Persian king Darius II initiated a

---

17 André Paul. La Bible avant la Bible, Éditions du Cerf, 2005.

18 Edward Will et Claude Orrieux. Ioudaïsmos-Hellènismos. Essais sur le judaïsme judéen à l'époque hellénistique. Page 91.

19 Edward Will et Claude Orrieux. Ioudaïsmos-Hellènismos. Essais sur le judaïsme judéen à l'époque hellénistique. Page 73.

20 Edward Will et Claude Orrieux. Ioudaïsmos-Hellènismos. Essais sur le judaïsme judéen à l'époque hellénistique. Page 69.

break with the cult of Osiris in the Nile Valley by imposing by decree the sacrifice of the paschal lamb (we shall return to this). It is significant that in all the correspondence found in Elephantine, not once do the Jews of Jerusalem reproach the Jews of Elephantine for worshipping Yahô, Osiris, Anat-Betel, the Queen of Heaven, Ptah, the divinities of ancient Egypt. They bless themselves, instead, in the names of these deities. Not once do the Jews of Jerusalem invoke the Torah of Moses... The temple of the Jews of Elephantine will be immediately destroyed, even though for centuries it had coexisted in a syncretism with the other "Egyptian" temples. In a letter serving as a testament, the Jews of Elephantine claimed the Jewish origin of their temple built by "their fathers", the kings of Misraïm:

"Now, since the day of the kings of Egypt [Misraïm] OUR FATHERS had built this sanctuary in Elephantine the fortress"[21]

The scholars of the CNRS note the reality of a "pagan Judaism", Osirian, inherited from the ancestors of the Jews:

"The Jews of Egypt therefore did not have to innovate in order to become pagan; it was enough for them to continue on the path of their immediate ancestors and to perpetuate cultic forms that had become generalized during the reign of Manasseh"[22]

Edward Will and Claude Orrieux bring us another archaeological proof of primary importance. On the found drachms of Ptolemy Lagos, Greek king of the Nile valley, the engraved word YAHOUDA (Jew) attested that Ptolemy Lagos was the "king of the Jews", and not yet the king of ÆGYPTOS. Whereas the later drachms all bear the Greek mention "BASILEOS ÆGYPTOS" meaning "King of Egypt".

---

21 Lettre AP 27, qui est le brouillon de la lettre AP 31. Documents Araméens d'Égypte. Littératures Anciennes du Proche-Orient. Éditions du Cerf, 1972, p. 403-404.

22 Documents Araméens d'Égypte, p. 347.

"That Ptolemy Ist recognized the existence of a Judean entity is attested, in the absence of literary texts, by coins bearing his effigy, but with the legend Yehudah in Aramaic characters, which implies a form of Jewish autonomy under Ptolemaic suzerainty"[23]

Under Ptolemy I Soter (ca. 270) the engraved word ÆGYPTOS had indeed replaced the word YAHOUDA. In this so-called Hellenistic period, the Jews constituted a state within a state, a nation well inserted within a nation as we have seen above, and on the other hand Ptolemy Lagos could not have been unaware that the Nile Valley belonged to the entity called "YAHOUDA" before proclaiming himself king of ÆGYPTOS. This discovery testifies that the land of the Nile valley, YAHOU-DA meaning "land of light Yahô" in hieroglyphics, had the anteriority on the word ÆGYPTOS "land of Egypt". The Egyptian hieroglyphic dictionary of Wallis Budge[24] confirms that the Ureus snake fixed on the diadem of the kings called "pharaohs" is the unquestionable and perpetual symbol of the kings SA-RÂ or IS-RÂ of the Nile Valley and is read YAHOUDA/YAHOUTA, YAHOU (the divine light and the annual flood of the Nile) designating Horus or Thoth.

Au-ā , the god of gifts, B.D. 99, 29; , Ṭuat IV, a title of Horus and Thoth.

Au-t-ā , the name of a serpent on the royal crown.

Yahoo, Yahou or Yahouda, the name of the god of Egypt meaning Horus, Thoth or the serpent Uraeus.

---

23   Edward Will et Claude Orrieux. Ioudaïsmos-Hellènismos. Essais sur le judaïsme judéen à l'époque hellénistique. Page 73.

24   Dover Publications, inc, New York. Published by General publishing Company. Egyptian hieroglyphic dictionary. Wallis Budge, 1978, tome 1, 3 a.

Consequently, the god of the Jews was the god YAHOU of ancient "Egypt", the ancient land of the Reeds, of the Yods, which is confirmed by hieroglyphs, the royal seal of Hezekiah and the secret texts of the Bible and the Kabbalah.

But before unveiling the evidence reported by the hieroglyphs, it is necessary to question the slavery of the Jews in ancient Egypt as it is taught in the Bible. Although for more than two millennia the Bible tells the story of a slavery of the Hebrews during the arbitrary presumed era of the pharaohs Amenophis or Ramses, Egyptologists, like Christiane Desroches Noblecourt, affirm that there were no Jews in the Nile Valley during the so-called pharaonic era: **"First of all, I repeat, there were neither Jews nor Hebrews at the time..."**[25]

Christiane Desroches Noblecourt insists on the fact that there is no trace of an alleged biblical slavery of the Hebrews in ancient Egypt. It is, of course, necessary to clarify these remarks, whose vocabulary could lead to confusion. There are no Jews separated from the rest of the population because the Egyptians, the name given by the Ptolemies, ARE the Jews, a name that the inhabitants of the Nile Valley gave themselves, and as for the Hebrews, it is a name that only appears with the writing of the Septuagint in the third century. Once this problem of vocabulary has been posed, to which we will return several times because it is essential, let us remember that Christiane Desroches Noblecourt insists on the fact that there is no trace of a supposed biblical slavery of the Hebrews in ancient Egypt.

"Every year, from the beginning of the New Kingdom, the most civilized Bedouins called the Hapirous came to work for Pharaoh to do the heavy work. They were day laborers or seasonal workers: they were free, were paid and went back home "... ...ALL OF EGYPT WAS MAKING Bricks"[26]

---

25   Nicole Maya Malet. Moïse Hébreu, Moïse Égyptien. 143 Éditions du Cerf 1997. Revue d'éthique et de théologie morale, p. 141-145.

26   Ibidem.

Egyptologists Marie-Ange Bonhême and Annie Forgeau also note the total absence of slavery of a people by another people in the history of the Nile Valley:

"Egypt cannot be understood as a feudal society. Subjected to the corvée, the employed labor force keeps a status of free men"[27]

The Egyptologists Rolf Krauss, Pierre Grandet and Marc Gabolde, following the example of Christiane Desroches Noblecourt, consider the Bible as a document to be read only in the literal, pseudo-historical sense, all thinking, wrongly, that Jews and Egyptians are two separate civilizations. Once again, Egyptologists ignore not only the existence of the Jews, but also the cryptic language of symbolic erudition provided by the Bible, as well as by the numerous documents and commentaries (Talmud, Midrash, Kabbalah). They dismiss the biblical text of the history of the Nile Valley, because they consider that the Bible can only be read in the strict sense of an actual story that does not have a hidden meaning.

This is a serious scientific error, given that the Misdrash and the Kabbalah are considered to be secret commentaries that give the Jews a straight line of descent from ancient Egypt. Rolf Krauss, in his book *Moses the Pharaoh*, states that Abraham, Moses and the characters of the Bible are the result of a myth invented by men, and therefore that the Bible is devoid of any historical foundation... From a general point of view, the conclusions of Egyptologists note a total absence of historical proof, on the one hand, in the Greek legends demonizing the Jews, and on the other hand, in the events and the characters described in the Bible. Based on two centuries of research, the Egyptologist Rolf Krauss is categorical in his conclusions:

"Now, it turns out that the migration and stay of the Hebrews in Egypt are as fictitious as the migratory movements of the patriarchs[28]... ...All these feats of Moses that give him

---

27   Marie-Ange Bonhême, Annie Forgeau, op. cit., p. 177.

28   Rolf Krauss. Moïse le Pharaon. Éditions du Rocher. 2000, p. 179.

his stature as a prophet of Israel, liberator and lawgiver, lack a historical core. From the current point of view of archaeology and Old Testament criticism, the biblical stories about Moses are, in fact, religious fictions and not echoes of a true story"[29]

However, there can be no Old Testament criticism without an analysis of the rabbinic texts, Midrash and Kabbalah. Here again, if Moses is an invented myth, the questions arise: why do Egyptologists and archaeologists consume their energy in researching the characters of the Bible and avoid the Kabbalah, which was written at the time of the Septuagint in order to provide the keys to reading it, and the teachings of extra-biblical texts? Why do they neglect the historical analysis of the Jews in ancient Egypt? If there was no slavery of the Hebrews, this does not prove the non-existence of the Jews in the Nile Valley. We have thousands of proofs of their historical existence and of their life in symbiosis with the "Egyptians". Consequently, it is no longer a question of discovering the Hebrew slaves of the Bible who fled after ten plagues and were saved by the miracle of the Red Sea. It is indeed the actual, historical existence of the Jews who formed a high social stratum and a powerful clergy, an official clergy present in all the history of the Nile valley, present in the current language, the clergy of the Jewish priests, the Yods, Youdaïos in Greek. The Yahud clergy which is described by the commentary or Midrash. The hieroglyph YAHOUD is translated as "official" or 'dignitary', knowing that the so-called 'Egyptian' priests, those who assume the priestly office, play the role of substitutes for the king, who alone wears the diadem serpent Yahouda. Curiously, in his History II, Herodotus omits to speak about the Jews, the class of scribes and officials/dignitaries. We will understand the reason for this in this work.

Thus, in contradiction to the previous Egyptologists cited, Jan Assmann attests that ancient Egypt is nothing other than the matrix of the Jewish people, the matrix of the people of Israel. In his book *Moses the Egyptian*, Assmann draws the following

---

29 Ibidem, p. 299.

conclusion: even if there is no historical trace of Moses and the other patriarchs, one fact remains indisputable: the Jewish people has its historical roots in ancient Egypt, but the Torah of Moses created a rupture, **a schism with the religion of Osiris, which was the religion of the Jews**:

"Egypt is the matrix from which the chosen people emerged, but the umbilical cord was cut once and for all by the Mosaic distinction"[30]

There are two schools of thought, two distinct schools. Who is right between Christiane Desroches Noblecourt, for whom there is no Jew in ancient Egypt, and Jan Assmann, who affirms the opposite? Is Egypt historically the matrix, the forgotten historical source, the repressed father of Sigmund Freud, the Garden of Eden of the Jewish people? Did the Mosaic distinction evoked by Assmann come into being following the great invasions of Egypt, with the Septuagint, the holy book that definitively separated the Jews from ancient Egypt? The methodology employed here by Jan Assmann has scientific value. It clearly brings out one of the many hidden messages of the Bible. This would mean that Jews and so-called 'Egyptians' come from the same matrix, they are an integral part of the Jewish nation. In his book The Price of Monotheism, Jan Assmann justifies his position on the fact that God took **"a nation from within another nation, *Goy mi-kereb Goy*, the Hebrew term Kereb is very strong, as it can also mean "womb" or "matrix"** [31]

Deuteronomy 4, 34: **Was there ever a god who tried to take a nation to himself from the midst of a nation, by trials, signs, wonders and battles, with a strong hand and an outstretched arm, and with wonders of terror, as the Lord your God did for you in Egypt and before your eyes?**

"A nation taken from within the nation of Egypt", the biblical text cannot express more clearly that the Jews, the Yods, the Yahuds, came out of the Matrix MISRAIM (not Ægyptos, the Greek god!) the heart of that civilization.

---

30 Jan Assmann. Moïse l'Égyptien. Éditions Aubier. 2001, p. 290.

31 Jan Assmann. Le Prix du Monothéisme. Éditions Aubier. 2006, p. 201.

The rabbinic tradition speaks of a nation coming out of the "womb" of the Misraïm nation. Thus, Israel would have emerged from the symbolic birth of the "Egyptian" womb. However, there is a problem with this scientific approach. Archaeology shows that the said womb never bears the name Ægyptos, but Misraim, a word that contains the root MESS and SA-RÂ or IS-RÂ, the sun that came out of the heavenly waters - the thighs - of the goddess Nut. Misraim is the feminine form of Nut the mother of Osiris/IS-RÂ son of Geb the earth. **Misraim is Nut** the celestial ocean, which itself came out of the matrix Nun. Another verse of the Bible will confirm Assmann's thesis. At the time of the exit from Egypt, when the Children of Israel are qualified as foreigners in Egypt, Pharaoh proclaims: "Come out of the midst of my people". Then he recognizes Yahweh and in order not to die, in a surprising way, implores the blessing of Aaron and Moses. This is a highly symbolic text:

"He [Pharaoh] sent for Moses and Aaron that very night and said, 'Go! Go out from among my people, you and the children of Israel! Go and worship the LORD, as you have said! (32) Also take your sheep and your oxen as you said, and go! Bless me also" (Exodus XII-31)

AMI   ME-TOKH   TSEOU
MON PEUPLE   DE TOKH   SORTEZ

The Children of Israel are the "Womb", the "Matrix" of Pharaoh's people! The Torah verse is not ambivalent. It cannot express the idea more strongly that Moses, Aaron, and the Hebrews, or Children of Israel, are all part of the body of the so-called 'Egyptian' people. The Kabbalah agrees :

"Pharaoh was convinced that Israel should always remain in Egypt."[32]

The king of Egypt did not hesitate to let his country be destroyed nine times, first by nine devastating plagues, before losing what was most dear to him in the world, his first-born, symbol of "divine light" Hor or Horus in Greek. For Pharaoh, letting Israel go is part of the collapse of Egypt, the end of the world, because Egypt loses its light. As if Pharaoh, by losing Israel, was losing "his gods" who had left the sacred place where God resides, called Tokhתוך, the place of the Tree of Life in the Garden of Eden. Such reasoning allows us to understand that the Children of Israel, by leaving Egypt, were "expelled" from the Garden of Eden. Let's explore this further.

Word for word, it is not written "Come out of the land of Egypt" as the Greek reading suggests, but **"Come out of Tokh my people"**. The Hebrew Torah or Masoretic text first uses the word Tokh תוך to designate the middle, the "womb", the center of the Garden of Eden, the Matrix where the Tree of Life is planted, while the Tree of Knowledge of Good and Evil is symbolically placed "in the background", like the forbidden tree before the original sin. Tokh תוך is thus the very place where Yahweh resides, where **God forbids any access to the Tree of Life** by the symbolic blade of the flaming sword:

Yahweh Elohim [Kyrios in Ptolemy's Septuagint] **made trees of every kind grow out of the ground, pleasant to the sight and good for food, and the Tree of Life in the midst [Tokh תוך] of the garden, and the Tree of Knowledge of good and evil.**   (Genesis II, 9)

Original sin which led to the loss of the Tree of Life to Adam and to all humanity. This means for the Children of Israel and for the Jews the mystical, metaphysical, theological expulsion from the Nile Valley, the loss of the laws and wisdom of ancient Egypt and finally the loss of their History, the loss of their "family tree" in favor of a new tree, that of the Knowledge of Good and Evil. This means, according to the palimpsest

---

32 Le Zohar, tome III, Le livre de la splendeur, op. cit., p. 236-237.

hidden by the scribes, the hidden meaning, the secret, the Sod in Hebrew, that the loss of the Tree of Life to the Tree of the Knowledge of Good and Evil is a schism, an upheaval for the whole of mankind, the passage from the old Law, the Law of Osiris/Old Israel, to the new Law, the Law of Moses/Moses/ Ptolemy. Clearly, the symbolic "breaking" of the Tables of the Law by Moses conceals the essence of the original sin with the loss of the Tree of Life as attested by the *Tikune Azohar*, the Book of Reparation:

"And why did the Tables of the Law fall? BECAUSE THE TREE OF LIFE WAS TAKEN AWAY FROM THEM..."[33]

To leave Egypt is to leave the Garden of Eden. Like Adam and Eve driven out of the Garden of Eden by the action of the cunning serpent, the Children of Israel are symbolically expelled by Pharaoh from the Garden of Eden, the milieu or Tokh matrix of the Garden of Eden identified by Kabbalah with the Tree of Life located in Egypt:

"Abraham went down to Egypt to sojourn there (Gen. 12:10). Why Egypt precisely? - Because the land is THE EQUAL OF THE GARDEN OF EDEN, which is expressed: Like the garden of YHVH, like the land of Egypt (Gen. 13:10)"[34]

And Kyrios sent him out of the Garden of Eden, to cultivate the land from which he had been taken. And when he had driven the man out, he set the cherubim before the Garden of Eden, with the blade of the flaming sword, to guard the borders of the Tree of Life.   (Septuagint, Gen. III, 23-24)

For Kabbalah, "cultivating the land" means coming out of a land, where the Law/Torah of the Garden of Eden reigned, which does not need to be "worked". The Garden of Eden being Egypt, the Law of the Tree of Life can only be the Law of Osiris, bringing the Jews back to their History.

---

33 Le Zohar, tome 1, op. cit., p. 152, § 26b.

34   Le Zohar, tome I, op. cit., p. 410.

They were symbolically expelled by the Septuagint, in order to go and "work the Law", to study the Septuagint, and four centuries later to "cultivate" the Hebrew Torah, which literally fights constitutes the new History of the Jews, which should be studied throughout life, knowing that any symbolic return to the Tree of Life - to Egypt, to its Law and its alleged idolatry - is definitively prohibited, punished with death.

In the end, in the Bible, it is indeed the Tree of Life that is forbidden to Adam, symbol of the Children of Israel, of humanity. This is the reason why it is said in the *Tikune Azohar* translated by Charles Mopsik, that following the breaking of the Tables of the Law by Moses the Children of Israel - precisely following the example of Adam and Eve who ate the fruit of the forbidden tree - wanting to return to the worship of the golden calf after forty days (symbolizing the period of time for the return of the soul of Osiris in the said golden calf) as a return of the ancestral god, "the eyes of the Children of Israel were opened and they found themselves naked, then they made themselves belts of fig leaves"... Yes, the *Tikune Azohar* speaks well of the Children of Israel: they have lost the memory of their History, we will come back to this.

For the secret reading, Pharaoh is desperate in the face of the drama of the ten plagues ending in darkness and the death of his first-born son. The entire ancestral founding myth of the Nile Valley - the Tree of Life - collapses. Rabbi Saadia Gaon' insists that Israel symbolizes the "Light of the World", that God resides in the Tokh of the world, in the Tokh of his creation[35], located in Egypt, within the Tree of Life.

"For I, the Lord, dwell in the midst [Tokh תוֹךְ] **of the earth"**

(Exodus, VIII, 18)

"For I, the Lord, dwell in the midst [Tokh תוֹךְ] **of the Children of Israel"**   (Numbers, XXXV, 54)

---

35 Saadia Gaon. Commentaire sur le Sepher Yetzira. Verdier, 2001, p. 93.

The Torah contains, through the slavery of the Children of Israel, the great secret of the disappearance of the ancient Jewish civilization, falsely reclassified as Egyptian civilization by the ancient Greeks and by modern Egyptology. Like Osiris, Israel means "the Sun"; the "Son of Kings" or "Son of God", according to the verse:

"Thou shalt say unto Pharaoh, Thus saith the LORD, Israel is my Son, my Elder"   (Exodus V, 22, 23)

The Torah is linked to the so-called 'Egyptian' cosmotheism when it affirms that the Children of Israel, worshippers of the golden calf, claim that they are the "Sons of the Sun" according to Tutankhamun who is the Son of Ra, SA-Ra or IS-Ra. All of them are Sons of the Light, which is confirmed by the Kabbalah:

"The sun is Jacob [Israel]"[36]

"Humanity [=Israel] is called here "Son of Man (Adam)"[37]

"The Torah [Israel's Law/Osiris] **will be the Queen, the very ruler, and in its perspective, Israel will be called "Sons of Kings""**[38]

By freeing Israel from Tokh תורך, Pharaoh frees the divine part of his being: he drives out the light, the gods and, as we shall see, the builders, and finally, the universal soul. In the tombs of the Valley of the Kings, his soul Bâ, an image of the universal soul, is transformed into a child of light Hor, Or' in Hebrew. In the so-called Egyptian symbolism, it is obvious that Pharaoh cannot let the sun - Israel - leave the Nile Valley without making it die and dying himself, definitively. The necessary counterpart of the departure of the Children of Israel

---

36   Le Zohar, Genèse, tome III, Vayechev, Mikets, collection "les dix paroles". Traduit par Charles Mopsik. Verdier, 1991, p. 207.

37   Le Zohar, tome 1, collection 'les dix paroles'. Traduit par Charles Mopsik. Verdier, 1981. P. 380, 75a.

38   Le Zohar, tome I, collection "les dix paroles'. Traduit par Charles Mopsik. Verdier, 1981, p. 157.

from Egypt, assimilated to the sons of the sun and the first-born son of God, is allegorically confused with the death of Pharaoh's first-born son, the death of Horus, the death of the sun. In ancient Egypt, such an event signifies the death of the Son of Ra himself - SA-RÂ or IS-RÂ in hieroglyphics - the death of the cosmotheism of the Heliopolis Ennead, the death of the world. The ninth and tenth plague, the darkness and death of Pharaoh's son, destroys the Ka of the king, i.e. his double, his inner life energy, his individuality transmitted to his son - which in hieroglyphics is a Yod - his principles and his ancestral ethics, but also his eternally cosmic image, linked to time. The tenth plague destroys the link with the Ka and the gods, which symbolize the link with his descendants - who are none other than the Children of Israel - his destiny and his posterity in the present world as well as in the future world where the Jews will lose their filial link with their true ancestors, those of the Nile Valley..

Thus, the exit of the Children of Israel from Egypt conceals the great secret of the death of the "Egyptian" civilization. Indeed, according to the Bible, six hundred thousand armed men came out of Egypt, not counting women and children and a large population, which exceeds three million people, more than the population of Egypt at that time. For the exegetes, this is the equivalent of the entire population of Egypt. The Kabbalah bases itself on the secret tradition and affirms that it is the whole of humanity that comes out of Egypt, the seventy nations: not a single man can remain in this world, Egypt, every being is condemned to pass one day to the "Other Side:

"The Egyptian nation was not really struck until the Red Sea, as it is written: "Not one remained"[39]

It is necessary to go back to the biblical text to be certain that the exit from Egypt concerns the death of the whole of humanity, symbolized by the Children of Israel, who alone represent the seventy nations, but also by the rest of Egypt:

"Pharaoh arose in the night, and all his servants and all the

---

39   Le Zohar, tome IV, Le livre de la splendeur, op. cit.

Egyptians, and there was a great clamor in Egypt, for there was not a house where there was not a dead man. Pharaoh called Moses and Aaron by night and said to them, "Get up and go out from among my people, you and the Israelites, and serve the LORD as you have asked. The Egyptians hurried the people out of the land, for, they said, "WE WILL ALL DIE" (Exodus XII, 30-33)

"Pharaoh's servants said to him, "How long will this one [Moses] be a snare to us? Let these men go, let them serve the LORD their God; DO YOU NOT KNOW THAT MISRAÎM IS LOST? (Exodus X, 7)

And the LORD said unto Moses, Stretch forth thy hand over the sea, and the waters shall return upon the Egyptians, upon their chariots, and upon their horsemen. And Moses stretched out his hand over the sea. And it came to pass about the morning, that the sea returned, and the Egyptians fled from it: but the LORD cast the Egyptians into the midst of the sea. And the waters returned, and covered the chariots, and the horsemen, and all the host of Pharaoh, which went into the sea after the children of Israel; AND NOT ONE OF THEM FLED. (Exodus XIV, 26-28)

An end of the world, the inevitable death of humanity... But the king of the Matrix MISRAIM cannot bring himself to separate from his Ka, the spiritual energy between him and his dead son, symbolized by the departure of the Children of Israel. He must try to prolong it at all costs, even in the other world, as the star Ra. Thus the Zohar states that the original sin plunged the Garden of Eden - Egypt - into darkness, resulting in "the death of the world". Rashi's commentary is confusing. It refers to a very old Haggadic tradition (the Haggada is the story of the exit from Egypt) that announces Israel's exit from Egypt as a catastrophe for humanity, with RÂ/RAÂ now demonized as Evil :

"There is a star whose name is Ra-Ha (Evil)". Pharaoh said to them, "I practice astrology and I see this star coming to meet you in the desert. It announces blood and slaughter""[40]

There is no doubt that in the myth of the Exodus, Pharaoh, in his obstinacy to retain the "Hebrew slaves" implores Moses to leave his children, the seventy nations, humanity, the Children of Israel - the sun, the light - in Egypt, to let them live in his garden of Eden, Egypt. If we take stock, Pharaoh asks Moses for the blessing of Yahweh/YAHOU, whom he recognizes as the god of the universe, as the new Osiris/Israel. The problem is the following: in ancient Egypt, RAÂ or Ra symbolizes the creative light. No star with the name RA symbolizes evil, which is called *Isefet*.

Evil is primarily symbolized by darkness, the serpent Apophis (the equivalent of the serpent Samael in the Kabbalah), the absence of light, while the stars symbolize the eternal light of the gods or the souls of the deceased. YAHOU is since the first dynasties the symbol of the divine light, named SARÂ or ISRÂ the heavenly Father of the Children of Israel. In this sense, the Torah joins archaeology, showing that the king of the Nile Valley is inseparable from YAHOU and Israel, God always being located in the middle Tokh, symbolically in the heart of the Tree of Life with his people AM. This is the reason why Pharaoh, addressing humanity, says, **"Come out of Tokh my people"**, Israel being one with Adam driven out of the Garden of Eden and wanting to be one of the golden calf - named Israel in the Torah - the solar god image of Osiris/Israel. In the literal reading, Pharaoh seems to definitively give up the game; but in the secret reading, the Sod, the king and his army - symbol of the sun and the stars - will "pursue", join Israel, the sun/ light, image of his living soul, of his double Ka, contributing to the new destiny of humanity by pursuing the Hebrews with his six hundred elite chariots which, according to the Kabbalah,

---

40 Rachi Exode X, 10-11. Rachi, commentateur de la Bible au Moyen Âge. Pentateuque selon Rachi. L'Exode. Samuel et Odette Lévy. 1990.

correspond to the six hundred thousand Children of Israel, themselves compared to the stars... In the end, in the Bible, it is not only the Hebrews/Children of Israel, it is the whole of humanity that comes out of Egypt... to give birth again to the new Son of God, the new Israel from now on submitted to the Law of Moses.

Let us not forget that for Kabbalah, the exit from Egypt is vertical, towards the celestial world of the afterlife. In his "cabalistic" language, Pharaoh says: "Come out of the middle Tokh of the place where God resides"[41]. He orders the vertical departure of the seventy nations, for which reason the Children of Israel go out, representing the universal soul of the world, the divine Shekhina. As soon as Pharaoh learns that his son is dead, he sends the Children of Israel away, he recognizes the name of Yahweh/YAHOU in order to be saved. In the *Book of the Exit to the Light*, recognizing the name of the gods or the guardians of the gates allows the opening of the gates and the crossing of the Douat.

After nine months of waiting, a period of symbolic childbirth and delivery of Israel/son of God through the first nine plagues according to the Midrash, the king "gives birth" to his double Ka alias Israel, his blessing expressing his will of continuity of his soul Bâ, which is the universal soul of the "Egyptians" and of the Children of Israel all confused. Thus, the last words of the king of Egypt "Come out of the midst of Tokh my people" mean metaphorically "Let the soul of Israel come out of my body". Pharaoh cannot separate himself from Israel because his body cannot separate from his soul Bâ without dying, without leaving Egypt... The soul comes out in the form of the human-headed bird Bâ, an **identical description in the Hebrew Book of Enoch**.

The soul comes out in the form of the human-headed bird Bâ, an identical description in the ***Hebrew Book of Enoch***.

---

41 Le Zohar, Livre de Ruth, collection "les dix paroles ". Traduit par Charles Mopsik. Verdier, 1987, p. 50.

Journey of the soul of the kings SARA/ISRA in the form of a swallow with a human head.

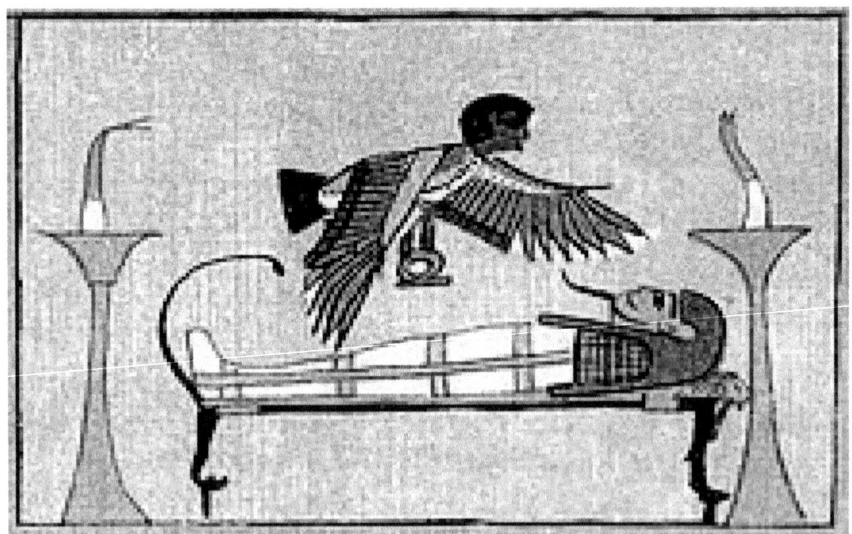

The bird BÂ, the soul of the Kings ISRÂ and the Sons of Israel

We have written proof that the Kabbalah has preserved the memory of the exit from Egypt and the opening of the Red Sea as an immense cosmology, the passage from night to day, the great "Egyptian" journey of the celestial souls, of the birds with the heads of men, and that the whole story of the exit from Egypt is a coding, a judiciously elaborated encryption:

"Their face was like the face of man, their body was like eagles"[42] ; **"The swallow (Ps. 84:4) is the holy soul [the soul of the Children of Israel] that rises up to the Above and is set free""**[43]

"Israel came out of Egypt at the level of the Great Jubilee, and the six hundred thousand (Hebrews) belonged to the WORLD ABOVE. It was in this form that they walked in the desert"[44]

That is why it is said that the swallow or the eagle with a human head is the image of the soul. The twelve tribes of Israel came out of Egypt, "as one man", "carried on eagle's wings".

"Rabbi Abba says: each tribe and each one in particular is one of the organs making up the Body"[45]

"The sons of Jacob were twelve. This is to make us understand that they were like one man"[46]

It is necessary to note that the Kabbalah and the Jewish tradition have preserved the memory of an Osirian configuration of the Children of Israel who came out of Egypt, the MISRAIM

42 Le Livre Hébreu d'Hénoch ou Livre des Palais. Collection "les dix paroles ". Traduit par Charles Mopsik. Verdier, 1981, commentaire p. 82 et chapitre 44.

43 Le Zohar, Cantique des Cantiques. Collection "les dix paroles ". Verdier, 1999. P. 46-47.

44 Le Zohar, tome I, collection "les dix paroles ". Traduit par Charles Mopsik. Verdier, 1981. P. 123-124, 21b-22a.

45 Le Zohar, Genèse, tome III, Vayéchev, Mikets, collection " les dix paroles ". Traduit par Charles Mopsik. Verdier, 1991. Également Zohar II 118b; III, 152b et 109b, ZH Ki Tissa 56b, TZ, 47, 84b.

46 Aggadoth du Talmud de Babylone. La source de Jacob/ 'Ein Yaakov. Collection " Les dix paroles ", Verdier, 1982. Traité Chabbat § 85, p. 185.

Matrix of the soul of the dead. Together, they form the Body of Elohim - the gods, the Neteru - and they proclaim it with force "Here are your gods Israel" when they address the golden calf.

The literal meaning of the reading of the Torah is the same as that of the Septuagint, whereas the cabalistic meaning brings us back to a true "restoration" of the reading of the most sacred symbols of ancient Egypt.

The Children of Israel come out of Egypt through the Red Sea and are locked up in the desert of the dead for forty years. But in the cabalistic sense, this is not a historical exit but a "vertical" or eschatological exit of the souls of humanity into the world of the dead, an explanation that coincides perfectly with the Book of the Dead, also known as the Book of the Exit to the Light, which we will study in detail in a future book. It is said that the souls of the Children of Israel crossed the Sea of Reeds with dry feet, that they camped for forty years in the desert of the dead, eating for all celestial food, the manna of white color, sign of the purity of the soul. Then they devoted themselves to the ritual of the golden calf, which marks the firm intention of the Hebrews to return to Egypt, the world of the living, in order to adore their ancestral god, Israel, called Osiris. A mysterious passage in the Pyramid Texts evokes the birth of Pharaoh protected under the wings of his mother, the celestial cow who makes him cross a lake or a canal and transforms him into a golden calf, suckling him with the celestial milk, to make him then reign over Egypt... a true allegorical summary of the biblical Exodus of the Hebrews! So Pharaoh decides to pursue Moses and the Children of Israel. The verse has been translated as follows.

Exodus, XIV, 6 : **Pharaoh harnessed his chariot and led his people away [AMO].**

Pharaoh brings his people out of Egypt ? Egyptians or Children of Israel/Yahuds? The cabalistic meaning refers to the celestial chariot and army, which is the image of the sun and stars, the cosmotheism of ancient Egypt, represented in the tombs of the Valley of the Kings. The army and the people of Pharaoh refer to the army of the souls of the world, as the armies of Yahweh (Zebaoth - the armies - is one of the names of Yahweh). Thus, for the Kabbalah, the people of Pharaoh - Son of Ra/Sa-Ra/Yod and the six hundred chariots symbolize **"six hundred myriads"**[47] also acting as one man. It is said that not a single Egyptian escaped death.

"The Egyptian nation was not really struck until the Red Sea, as it is written : "Not a single one remained"[48]

So if we follow the progression of the biblical text and the various commentaries of the Kabbalah, after the exit from Egypt which lasted one night, there is not a single Egyptian left in the Nile Valley! We notice that this number of six hundred thousand, attributed to the armies of Pharaoh, presumed drowned, corresponds exactly to the six hundred thousand Hebrews/Children of Israel, compared to the stars, who crossed the Sea of Reeds, which corresponds to the celestial Noun. Thus, the scenography of the exit from Egypt cosmos of the twelve hours of the night drives out the cosmos of the twelve hours of the day. The twelve tribes of Israel respond to the twelve regions of Egypt: in the secret imagery, **it is the twelve hours of the night, the Egyptians alias the darkness, that pursue twelve hours of the day, the Children of Israel** alias the light. So much so that the whole constitutes a single entity, the cosmos where one single Humanity resides.

The term "armies of Yahweh", the armies of heaven, also refers to light. The battle of the twelve hours of the night against the twelve hours of the day between the open sea is found pictured and detailed in several tombs in the Valley of the Kings, proof that only the descendants of the priests of Heliopolis could have invented the founding myth of the exit from Egypt. We will come back to this.

---

47 Zohar, tome III. Le livre de la splendeur. Par Jean de Pauly. Maisonneuve & Larose, 1985, p. 232.

48 Le Livre Hébreu d'Hénoch ou Livre des Palais. Collection "les dix paroles ". Traduit par Charles Mopsik. Verdier, 1981, commentaire p. 82 et chapitre 44.

If ancient Egypt is the Garden of Eden for humanity, this means that the Jews came out of the MISRAIM matrix, that they lived through two civilizations, provided with two Laws, two Torahs, the Torah of Osiris and the Septuagint/Torah of Moses, which chased them out of the Nile Valley. Kabbalah allows us to understand the hidden meaning of Pharaoh's words, which are addressed to humanity, to you and me: "Come out of the sacred domain of the Tree of Life", "Come out of the Law of Osiris, and go - like Adam and Eve - to eat the fruit of the Tree of Knowledge of Good and Evil", which is none other than the Torah of Moses, the Zohar asserts to us, meaning that the Jews had a first Torah, the one of Osiris (the one that was broken by Moses) that Kabbalah recognizes as the true historical Torah of the Jews. On the other hand, the second Septuagint/Torah makes the Jews/Hebrews/Children of Israel - in its literal reading - the slaves of Pharaoh, the humanity driven out of the Nile Valley.

THE GREAT SECRET OF THE ANCIENT OF ANCIENTS

Contrary to common opinion, the Kabbalah (the Zohar) deciphers another story of Adam and Abraham. Both symbolically came out of Egypt, Adam from the Garden of Eden, Abraham from his father's house. Both symbolize the Children of Israel expelled from Egypt. As we have seen, this land is identified with the Garden of Eden and the Tree of Life placed in the center of the garden, which upsets the whole literal reading of the Bible. The Tree of Life is the cosmic, cosmogonic, "genealogical" tree, with its river, the Nile, which made the Children of Israel the true "Egyptians". It is indeed the most secret part of the Kabbalah, called *Tikune Azohar* or *Book of Reparation*, which calls into question the entire Torah of Moses. Before resuming the analysis of the text, which introduces the reader to the secrets of the Torah, it is appropriate to return to this unusual passage of the Zohar which calls into question the entire Torah.

Returning from Mount Sinai, Moses learns that the Children of Israel have returned to the worship of the golden calf, the worship of Osiris. Angered, Moses breaks the Tables of the Law and orders the massacre of three thousand people. The Talmudic tradition tells that at that very moment, the Tables of the Law became heavy and escaped from the hands of Moses, because the letters flew up to the sky, as if the Children of Israel who had fallen into sin did not deserve the first Torah. But the *Tikkune Azohar* gives a dizzying interpretation of this parable. According to Jewish tradition, the Tables of the Law broken by Moses and the unbroken second ones represent two different Torahs, two different trees. Against all odds, the *Tikkune Azohar* reverses the meaning of the biblical story, stating that the first Tables of the Law broken by Moses symbolized the first Torah, the authentic, harmonious Law, the true truth. That is to say ... the Law of Osiris, the ancient law of the Jews who were its clergy. The secret meaning means that the lost and broken Torah, precisely because of the golden calf, was never broken by Moses! On the other hand, the second Tables of the Law, those which were not broken by Moses, are considered by the Tikkune Azohar as the actual Torah, as the real broken Torah... the Torah of separation for humanity.

In disagreement with rabbinic opinion, it is stated that the first broken Tables of the Law represented the true Torah of the Jews, that of the Tree of Life, while the second Tables embodied the Torah of the division of mankind, that of the Tree of Knowledge of Good and Evil, described as "the original tree of separation :

"Moses did give Israel two other tablets [the second Torah], **but these were from the Tree of Knowledge of Good and Evil. Thus the Torah was given according to the permitted and the forbidden** [the 613 commandments]**, on the right life, on the left death... ... The stones of the Tree of Knowledge of Good and Evil are in separation, while the pure marble stones** [of the first Torah, the Tree of Life] **are united, excluding all separation"**[49]

---

49 Le Zohar, tome 1, op. cit., p. 152, § 26b.

Thus, the *Tikkune Azohar* Book of Reparation challenges the foundation of rabbinic thought, reversing the role of the first broken Tables and the second unbroken Tables of the Law of Moses. The first Tables symbolized a united humanity in harmony with the Tree of Life, with the sacred wisdoms of Egypt, the Supreme Wisdom, the perfect world. In reverse, it is the second Tables that are really broken, because they lead to the separation and division of humanity, to the massacres in the name of God, to the conflicts and wars of religion in History. The esoteric narrative relates that a rabbi called the Ancient of the Ancients, or the Elder of the Elders, a kind of Christ, descended from heaven to transmit the true truth about the broken Tables. According to the *Tikkune Azohar*, the Elder of the Ancients is Yahweh himself[50], whom Rabbi Simeon bar Yokhai calls "Holy One, blessed be He", and therefore God came down to earth to "take the risk" of delivering the great secret of the Torah:

"No doubt about it! It was the Holy One, blessed be He, who (visited us)... ... The time has come to open ourselves to the question that He [the Elder of the Elders] **asked us, because it obviously contains an idea that was not legitimate to reveal before, but it has just appeared that we can risk it now"**[51]

Before leaving for the celestial world, the Ancient of the Ancients delivers the terrible secret to the companions: it is the second Tables of the Law of Moses which are broken humanity, not the first. The second Tables symbolize the five books of the Old Testament, from the creation of the world to the exit from Egypt with the miracles of Moses, called the Torah of separation. These are actually the ones that have fallen and broken, in the sense that they divide mankind religiously - separating Israel from mankind - and politically, whereas they originally formed mankind in harmony, one and only Tree, the Tree of Life enthroned in the temples of the Nile Valley.

---

50 Le Zohar, tome 1, collection 'les dix paroles'. Traduit par Charles Mopsik. Verdier, 1981. P. 126, 22a.

51 Le Zohar, tome 1, op. cit., p. 152, § 26b.

"And if you say that it is from these [the Tables broken by Moses because of the golden calf, the return to the cult of Isis/Osiris] **that the Tree of Life has been withdrawn, since it was they that fell, and that there is now separation in them, let you know that "He who speaks lies will not stand before my eyes" (Ps. 101:7). In these stones there is no separation as in the Upper, it is those that come from them (the second tables) that have been broken. At these words the companions ran to embrace the Elder of the Elders, but he flew away and fled from them"**[52]

This explanation is reminiscent of the division of humanity into nations in the myth of the Tower of Babel, which corresponds to the first symbolic exile of Israel, to the splitting of the Tree of Life. The Tikkune Azohar does indeed mention two laws, two radically different Books of the Torah. He also makes another link between the exit of the Children of Israel from Egypt in the desert and the expulsion of Adam and Eve from the Garden of Eden. As we have seen, coming out of Egypt is coming out of the Garden of Eden. Adam and Eve, who symbolize the Children of Israel, abandoned the Tree of Life, the "broken" Law of the Garden of Eden, the other world, for a new world - the other Torah, the Tree of the Knowledge of Good and Evil - subjected to the serpent of darkness, which symbolizes Greece, the "Intruders", the men of the "Great Mixture", the so-called Greek syncretism, the other Law, the Septuagint. The word syncretism means "mixture", the mixture of gods, the mixture of nations, in a word the great program of Hellenization. It is as if Adam and Eve, driven out of the Garden of Eden, were a huge secret parable, a cryptic allusion to the exit of the Children of Israel from Egypt, who themselves had eaten of the fruit of the tree of the knowledge of good and evil and accepted to fall into the trap of the "Greek serpent" of Hellenization. From the original sin to the exit from Egypt, the common cause

---

52 Le Zohar, tome 1, collection 'les dix paroles'. Traduit par Charles Mopsik. Verdier, 1981. P. 152, 26b-27a.

invoked is always the same: the men of the Great Mixture, the intruders, the proselytes, the darkness of Greece, are the source, the secret cause of the loss of Egypt...

"Humanity [= The Children of Israel] **is called here "sons of Man (Adam)"**[53]

"The Man (Adam) is the Children of Israel"[54]

Thus, the most secret symbolism of the exit from Egypt, MITSRAIM מצרים, is confused with the expulsion from the Tree of Life מעץ החיים , MÉ-ÈTS-AHAÏM (Gen. 3:22). The scribes made sure that the pronunciations MITSRAIM and MÉ-ÈTS-AHAÏM are the same:

To leave Egypt MISRAIM - which is the old Israel - is to leave the Tree of Life. If we read the story of Adam and Eve, we cannot suspect that it is in fact a cryptic paraphrase of the Hellenization by the exit from Egypt. Adam and Eve ate the forbidden fruit of the forbidden tree and found themselves symbolically naked in the sense of being stripped of the memory of the past of the Children of Israel, stripped of the first Law/ Torah, that of the "One Commandment" not to eat the fruit of the Tree of Good and Evil. Let's start again. For Kabbalah, the one and only commandment of the Garden of Eden is to preserve, to keep the Garden of Eden, identified with Egypt, and to be happy there. This commandment has the value of the first Torah, and can only correspond to the Law of Osiris which

---

53　Le Zohar, tome 1, collection 'les dix paroles'. Traduit par Charles Mopsik. Verdier, 1981. P. 380, 75a.

54　Le Zohar, tome 1, collection "les dix paroles ". Traduit par Charles Mopsik. Verdier, 1981, p. 147.

had 42 commandments in the Book of the Exit to the Light.
Thus, when Kyrios/Yahweh sends Moses/Moïses to Mount
Sinai for the first time, it is to receive the "Commandment",
that of consuming the symbolic fruit of the Torah of the Tree
of Life, but formally forbidding the tree of the Knowledge of
Good and Evil, the other Torah, the one which expelled the
Children of Israel from Egypt. Exodus 24-12:

**Yahweh said to Moses: "Come up to me on the mountain
and stay there: I want to give you the tables of stone, the Law**
[the Torah in the Hebrew text] **and THE COMMANDMENT**
[the MITSVAH in Hebrew = the Tree of life] **which I have
written to teach them.**

By textual similarity, the Zohar states that when the first
Torah was broken by Moses, the Children of Israel found
themselves naked and made themselves belts of fig leaves. The
Zohar could not be clearer than the original sin is a scriptural
crypt of the expulsion of the Children of Israel from the Nile
Valley, from Egypt. In the same scriptural pattern, the Children
of Israel lost their first Torah, that of the golden calf, that of
Isis/Osiris, abandoned the Tree of Life, the memory of their
History, that of the Nile Valley. This means that the Jews lived
happily, in the "matrix" harmony of the body of the Tree of
Life, the Garden of Eden, Egypt MISRAÏM where Israel/
Isis/Osiris symbolized the golden calf, but this harmony was
broken because of the Great Mixture which I identify with the
syncretism of the ancient Greeks. The Great Mixture is the
darkness, the "ignoble ones", the powers of evil that cast, the
Zohar tells us, the seed of original sin, causing the expulsion
- symbolic - from the Garden of Eden and consequently the
expulsion of the Jews from Egypt by means of indoctrination in
the Septuagint, the creation of schools and courts. They made
sure that the Children of Israel were "entangled in the clay of
Egypt", the clay of Ægyptos also called "Greek molasses".

But let us return to the texts of the Zohar, which thus
deciphers the meaning of the text, calling into question our
literal understanding of original sin:

"The Great Mixture comes from the seed of Amalek about whom it is written "blot out the memory of Amalek" (Deut. 25:19). "These are the ones who caused the breaking of the two Tables of the Torah. From that moment "their eyes were opened" (Gen. 3:7) and the children of Israel knew "that they were naked" (Id.), stripped of the Torah, entangled in the clay of Egypt"[55]

"When the two Tables of the Law were broken [by Moses because of the golden calf], **as well as the oral Torah, the Children of Israel** [realizing their nakedness] **"sewed fig leaves and made themselves girdles" (Gen. 3:7). That is to say, they covered themselves with many barks because of the Great Mixture, because they were naked"**[56]

Talmudic tradition associates the sin of the golden calf with the breaking of the Tables of the Law dictated by Yahweh to Moses. What is important here is that for the Kabbalah, this event is related to the domination of the pagan peoples, those who dominated "Pharaonic Egypt"...

"It was the crime of the golden calf that caused the exile of Israel... ...from the domination of the pagan peoples [the Greeks, the Great Mixture] **and from the fact that the Tables of the Law were broken"** [57]

The men of the Great Mixture equated with Amalek (the Serpent, the Other Side, the darkness of Greece) who caused the loss of the Tree of Life are the ancient Greeks. With Hellenization, they are the "darkness" of the Torah, omnipresent in the different episodes of the Bible from creation to the exit from Egypt. In turn responsible for the hustle and bustle (tohu-bohu), the original sin, the flood and the Tower of

---

55 Le Zohar, tome 1, op. cit., 162, § 28b.

56 Le Zohar, tome 1, op. cit., 162-163, § 28b.

57 Zohar, tome III. Le livre de la splendeur. Par Jean de Pauly. Editions Maisonneuve & Larose, 1985. P. 208.

Babel, the Men of the Great Mixture conceal the Greeks, the builders of the Tower of Pharos, for it is said that the Men of the Great Mixture **built Synagogues and schools**[58] to teach the Septuagint, in reality the new Torah, the one that was written on the orders and according to the prescriptions of Ptolemy II Philadelphus, by force of arms and by the creation of courts, thus flouting the law of Osiris, the first Torah - Tree of Life - of Israel:

"And the remnants of Amalek [the Great Mixture, the intruders] **during the fourth exile** [the Greek exile] **are the very powerful leaders who ruled over Israel by force of arms"**[59]

The men of the Great Mixture are the sons of the primordial serpent who seduced Eve..."[60] **"Of the Tree of the Knowledge of Good and Evil you shall not eat" (Gen. 2:17), this tree representing the Great Mixture"**[61]

Finally, the Zohar associates the men of the Great Mixture with the hustle and bustle of creation, the "darkness of Greece".

"These five groups of the Great Mixture brought the world back to the Tohu-Bohu - a phrase that actually refers to the destruction of the temple - "The earth is Tohu-Bohu" (Gen. 1:2)" [62]

As we can see, Kabbalah does not take shortcuts. While Adam, the first man, has not yet been created, the ancient Greeks are already present - symbolizing the hustle and bustle of Genesis - the schism of Hellenization is already consummated. Such an assertion confirms that the "beginning"

---

58   Ibidem, p. 146.

59   Le Zohar, tome 1, op. cit., p. 143, 25 a.

60   Le Zohar, tome 1, op. cit., p. 161, 28b.

61   Le Zohar, tome 1, op. cit., p. 149, 26 a.

62   Le Zohar, tome 1, op. cit., p. 145, 25 b.

Bereshit בראשית involving the "breach", the darkness and the hustle and bustle/tohu-bohu in the Bible/Torah, implies an interlocking beginning and re-commencement, written because of the existence and action of the men of the Great Mixture, the ancient Greeks.

This means that there was a History of Men/Hebrews/Children of Israel BEFORE the creation of the world, before the biblical Genesis. There was a Bible before the Bible, a first Torah before the Torah of Moses, where the Egyptians and Children of Israel were the same people. Such an assertion will be confirmed by the study of hieroglyphs, the Bible and certain rabbinic commentaries, but also and especially the Kabbalah. In fine, the **Septuagint is the Ptolemaic code of laws**, replacing the ancient code of laws which contained the forty-two commandments of Osiris.

We will continue this investigation and visit the texts of the Zohar which confirm their encrypted, sacred links between the events that took place in the Garden of Eden, the original sin in direct relation to the Torah broken by Moses because of the worship of the golden calf. As if the Children of Israel had been expelled from the Garden of Eden alias Egypt for having eaten the fruit of the forbidden tree, there is a direct link between the worship of the golden calf, the broken Tables of the Law and the direct loss of the Tree of Life, giving all its meaning to the exit from Egypt, which is nothing other than the expulsion from the Garden of Eden... A purely symbolic expulsion.

"Moses brought down the Torah from Mount Sinai in the form of two tablets of stone (the two tears) and as the children of Israel were not worthy of it, they broke and fell. This was the reason for the destruction of the first and second Temple. And why did the Tables of the Law fall? BECAUSE THE TREE OF LIFE WITHDREW FROM THEM..." [63]

---

63 Le Zohar, tome 1, op. cit., p. 152, § 26b.

These texts shed new light on original sin. So that the exit from Egypt, the miraculous exit from a state of slavery to freedom, takes on a completely different meaning. The Kabbalah directly questions the slavery of the Children of Israel: they are happy in their Nile Valley, the land of the Tree of Life, as long as they have not eaten the fruit of the forbidden tree which is none other than the Torah of Moses... As we have shown, the verse of the Septuagint gives the direct meaning of the name "Pharaoh", assimilating him and all the Egyptians to the reeds/calamex/scribex - the Jews - of the house of Israel. It is clear that the scribes of the Bible have gone very far in the memory of the *Pyramid Texts*, which are more than four millennia old, to change the very definition of the kings called "Pharaohs" into "reeds of the house of Israel".

All these elements confirm that the biblical character Moses cut the umbilical cord of the Jews from the matrix "Egypt" by instituting and canonizing the myth of the exit from Egypt, making them the descendants of Pharaoh's slaves expelled from the Nile Valley. This would mean that the Bible, from the expulsion of Adam and Eve from the Garden of Eden to the exit of the Children of Israel from Egypt, would form an immense parable demonizing the so-called "Egyptian" civilization by making it disappear, and replacing it with the civilization of the Jews descendants from the Hebrew slaves who came out of Egypt. The *Letter of Aristaeus* reports that Ptolemy II Philadelphus needed a kind of mythical, cathartic, messianic glorification, in which he presents himself to the Jews as a king who saves them from slavery, a kind of new Moses. The pharaoh is strangely named Ptole-Maïos, chosen by God, King and Prophet. In the Septuagint, Moses is the ancient savior of the Hebrew slaves and the one who makes the new Law. Similarly, Ptole-Maïos Philadelphos is a kind, like Moïses, savior of the Jews unjustly enslaved by the Greek army and bringing freedom with the new Law, revealed in the Tower of Pharos. Ptolemy's history is copied and hidden through the Revelation of Moses, which cuts the Jews off from their historical roots...

Through the Septuagint, Ptolemy succeeded in justifying, on the one hand, the new Egyptian, pharaonic, historical identity of the " ancient ÆGYPTOS " living in the Nile Valley since time immemorial, as if the Jews were not part of it, and, on the other hand, in legitimizing his policy of teaching the Jews of the whole world - the new Jews, that is, those on whom the Torah of Moses had been imposed - the fact that they were for a second time freed from the slavery of the Jews. It is said that Ptolemy prostrated himself seven times before the scrolls of the Septuagint. Why did he do this? This is, of course, media propaganda. To subject within the population called suddenly "Egyptian" although incontestably Jewish, the recalcitrants who constituted the priesthood of Osiris, i.e. those who possessed the knowledge, the initiation and who were respected in all Egypt, by the princes and the kings, as the "men of God" as will confirm it the own words of the High Priest Eleazar in the *Letter of Aristaeus*. As the undisputed religious leader of the 72 "translators", Eleazar had all the prophetic, almost divine, authority to make them obey the orders of Ptolemy Philadelphus. It was therefore necessary to obey the new royal decree, the Septuagint, and to upset the entire history of ancient Egypt. The Jews had to accept, under penalty of death, to become foreigners in Egypt, slaves of Pharaoh. The Kabbalah has preserved the memory of the enormous blackmail imposed by the ancient Greeks. The Greek exile of the Jews is, let us repeat, considered by the Zohar[64] and the Talmud[65] as an alternative to the death penalty for a whole civilization, the Jewish civilization, replaced by the civilization now renamed Egyptian.

"Exile is in the Bible a punishment that replaces the death penalty" [66]

64   Le Zohar, tome 1, collection 'les dix paroles'. Traduit par Charles Mopsik. Verdier, 1981. P. 377, 74b

65   Aggadoth du Talmud de Babylone. La source de Jacob/ 'Ein Yaakov. Collection " Les dix paroles ", Verdier, 1982. Pessahim 87,b.

66   Le Zohar, tome II, collection "les dix paroles ". Traduit par Charles Mopsik. Vayera, Hayé Sarah, Toldot, Vayetsé, Vayichlah. Verdier, 1984. Note 547 page 380

Going much further than Sigmund Freud, Jan Assmann identifies the "Mosaic distinction": the very existence of the Jewish people and its religion, which is certainly distinct but considerably impregnated with ancient Egypt, would be the proof of the implicit existence of Moses, who would have "created the Jew by de-Egyptianizing him", that is to say by symbolically tearing Israel away from its Egyptian roots in order to make of it the people of the Hebrews of the Bible, who were slaves and foreigners in Egypt. Moses would have created the modern Jew, distinct from the Egyptian Jew: he would have voluntarily reversed the fundamental rituals of the pharaohs, transforming the caste of Egyptian priests of Heliopolis, the Jews. By this subterfuge, they lost their country of Egypt, because they were deprogrammed and reprogrammed by Moses, if we consider that the latter is the editor of the Torah. But if the Torah was inspired by Ptolemy Philadelphus and by the seventy-two pseudo-translators of the Septuagint, this changes the reasoning. In order to separate them from Egypt, Moses aka Ptolemy would have succeeded in removing the memory of history from the Jews by demonizing much of ancient Egypt, which Assmann calls "normative inversion".

In any case, the Jew has always retained his identity as a Jew, as Yod from hieroglyphics, but Ptolemy succeeded in transposing this identity elsewhere, to Mesopotamia, through the Revelation of Yahweh to Abraham and Moses, and transplanting them to the land of Canaan through the miracles of Yahweh. The Jewish people initially affiliated with the religion of Osiris became the people of the Hebrew strangers in Egypt: Israel converted to the new religion, the one that would become the monotheistic Jewish religion, antagonistic to the Egyptian religion that had become idolatrous...

However, and contrary to the assertions of Manetho, who like other scholars, was subject to the will and whims of Ptolemy Philadelphus, the Jewish religion is not the opposite of the so-called 'Egyptian' religion. I will go much further than Jan Assmann in demonstrating that what he calls the "Mosaic Distinction" corresponds historically to the work of

Ptolemy II Philadelphus, who orchestrated with the Septuagint, a historical transposition of the Yiddaios to the biblical era, supposedly of Abraham, Isaac, Jacob, Joseph and Moses. Ptolemy could not have created "the Jew by de-Egyptianizing him" as Assmann says, which would imply that the Jews were Egyptians, for as we have said, the hieroglyphs prove that there were never "Egyptians" in ancient "Egypt", only Yods, "reeds". It is indeed Ptolemy who created the "Egyptians" by a transfer of history and identity for the whole civilization of the Jews/Yods. The *reeds of God* had the Oracle of Kyrios (the Oracle of Zeus), the transposed myth of their new History, the Septuagint, imposed on them by terror. With the Septuagint, Ptolemy forced the Jewish people to demonize the civilization of the Nile Valley, to abandon and separate themselves from their own History. By the magic of words, by their invention, by Revelation, the God-King Ptolemy miraculously made the "Egyptian" identity card of the Jews disappear. And to compensate for this emptiness, by a phenomenal magic trick of substitution, he created the "ancient Egyptians". Yes, Ptolemy created the Ægyptos, who replaced the Jews not only in the Bible, but also in "all the books of the world" which he succeeded in having his scribes falsify, under the noses of all humanity.

Chapter III

THE GOD OF THE JEWS
IS THE GOD OF ANCIENT EGYPT

In the third century B.C., the Letter of Aristaeus reports that the god of the Jews was universal and his Law accepted by many peoples. The god of the Jews is called YHVH, YAHOU or Adonai, but also Anokhy, the Ankh name of the god of Egypt. For the fundamental notion of the Jews, that of a unique god or a luminous force creating life, an original, unknown, transcendental power, had been inscribed in hieroglyphics for more than five millennia.

The elements of the previous chapter lead us to démonstrate, through archaeology and philology that the god of the Jews was that of the "Egyptians". If Clement of Alexandria is right in stating that the most sacred symbols of the Jews and the Egyptians are identical, this means that **the god of the Jews and the ancient Egyptians is identical. Consequently, the two civilizations are confused.** Such an assertion must be verified historically by hieroglyphs and by Jewish tradition. The *Letter of Aristaeus* relates that Ptolemy II Philadelphus invited seventy-two Jewish priests - a sort of supreme court - scholars taken as translators and his future "prisoners" in the tower of Pharos, in a seven-day banquet. Each day the banquet was preceded by ten questions, twelve questions on the seventh day. The seventy Jewish scholars - so-called translators - testified one after the other to Ptolemy their complete submission. One after the other, they recognized his supreme status as a sovereign - Pharaoh or Basileos - with the sacred word, inspired by God, wearing the double crown of justice of the kings of the Nile Valley.

But did they have a choice when Ptolemy II and his father Ptolemy I had enslaved a large number of Jews? And this with the double objective of extracting a tribute from them in payment for their liberation and to get rid of these notables, in other words, the leaders of Egypt, who would otherwise have refused? Aristaeus, having inquired about the god of the Jews, then addressed Ptolemy, and reveals essential information to us. They relate to the universal nature of a Law of the Jews, "full of wisdom", with the god of the Jews and his Law recognized throughout the Middle East at that time. Is it the Law of Moses or the Law of Osiris? In the syncretism of the time, only Osiris (or Amun, another name of Osiris) corresponds historically to this definition of the god of the Jews. If Aristaeus is careful not to specify it in order to avoid the anger of the new pharaoh, it is obvious that he nevertheless evokes the old Law, that of the seventy-two scholars **since they did not yet write the Septuagint - qualified of *Oracles of the God* by Ptolémée Philadelphe - ordered by the tyrant!** Aristaeus speaks of the god Osiris "adored by all men", and of his Law spread in all the Middle East! There is thus only one law, ancient, historical, that Ptolemy resolved to neutralize in order to impose his own in a purely Hellenistic syncretism.

"This Law is full of wisdom and very pure, since it is divine..."[1] **"It is that the doctrine they contain is august and holy, according to the expression of Hecateus of Abdera""**[2]

"...Since the maintenance of prosperity in your kingdom comes from the same God who established their Laws [the Law of the Jews], as I have learned from my research. For it is the sovereign god, master and creator of the universe, whom they worship, whom all men worship, and whom we, O king, only call in a different way: Zeus"[3]

---

1   Lettre d'Aristée à Philocrate, les Éditions du Cerf, § 30.
2   Lettre d'Aristée à Philocrate, § 31, p. 121.
3   Lettre d'Aristée à Philocrate, les Éditions du Cerf, 1962, § 15-16.

According to Aristaeus' research, **the god of the Jews is universal, Amon, Zeus, Osiris, Yaho**..., who established the Law of the Jews, which could not be that of Moses. The god of the Jews is "the one worshipped by all men" and their Law was spread throughout the Middle East. Such an observation is phenomenal and it is astonishing that most Egyptologists have ignored it. Diodorus of Sicily confirms that the God creator of the universe has indeed several names:

"Osiris is named by some Sarapis (Osiris-Apis), by others, Dionysus or Pluto, or Ammon, by some Zeus and by many Pan..."[4]

Aristaeus confirms the words of another historian of Ptolemy Soter, Demetrios of Phalerus, the former tyrant of Athens and disciple of Aristotle, the man behind the great Alexandrian library founded in 288 and unfortunately disappeared, perhaps in 48 by the fault of Caesar. Demetrios of Phalerus makes of the wisdom of the Jews a universal Law adopted by other peoples who have "regulated their conduct by them", and it cannot be the Torah of Moses, non-existent at the time, for the following reasons:

"This Law is full of wisdom and very pure, since it is divine. This is why prose writers and poets and even many historians have refrained from mentioning the said books and the peoples who have regulated their conduct by them"[5]

It is manifestly inconsistent to claim that the Law of Moses is widespread among peoples "who have regulated their conduct by it" without any prose writer, historian or poet ever having heard of it. This is totally implausible. The Letter of Aristaeus gives us an essential but so far unexploited lead. It testifies that at the time, there were no documents on the Torah of Moses.

---

4   Diodore de Sicile, Bibliothèque Historique. Éditions Les Belles Lettres, p. 61, XXV, § 1.

5   Lettre d'Aristée à Philocrate, § 31, p. 121.

Even more so, there was no commentary on the Torah, the first commentaries on the Law of Moses being in fact secret writing, the Kabbalah, some of which date from the second century B.C., as André Paul attests, but some of which were probably written at the very moment when the editors of the Septuagint were placing clues in reaction to Ptolemy's perfidy, in order to give the keys to decipher them.

All historians agree on this point: in the Late Period and in the early Ptolemaic period, the only Law adopted by the nations populating the Middle East was that of Osiris ! It was the object of devotion and of teaching allowing going to the afterlife, and consequently, everyone had the duty to speak about it.

"This devotion to Osiris was widespread throughout the Middle East: it was aimed at obtaining for the pilgrims immortality in the afterlife, as it appears from the Book of the Dead... ...One notes that the devotion to Osiris is alive, in this Egypt where men of all races rubbed shoulders"[6]

Thus, the Law of the Jews as described in the Letter of Aristaeus is indeed spread throughout the nations, **with a universally recognized god, Osiris**. It could not be the Law of Moses, which is an exclusive Law, reserved for a single people, whereas it is a syncretism, which is proven by the ostraca of Elephantine. Demetrios of Phalerus makes the apology of a "very pure Law" of the Jews, accepted by the people, the god "whom all men adore". No one could seriously ignore a code of laws as important as that of Osiris, accepted by the peoples of the Middle East, and therefore a code practiced by the priests and the people. In this case, the Law of the Jews was the Law of Osiris and the Law of Moses did not exist outside the Septuagint, a late writing considering the longevity of the Egyptian civilization. By affirming that historians, prose writers and poets never spoke of the Law of the Jews - that of Osiris - but that the latter was accepted by all peoples, which is obviously contradictory, Aristaeus and Demitrios of Phalerus

---

6   Documents Araméens d'Égypte. Littératures Anciennes du Proche-Orient. Éditions du Cerf, 1972, p. 340;343.

support the historical lie elaborated by Ptolemy Philadelphus whose objective is its abolition in favor of the Law of Moses by the oracular and miraculous means of the Septuagint.

And for good reason, the Old Testament, the Septuagint, could not be accepted by the other nations for the reason that Kyrios/Yahweh, the god of the Septuagint/Bible, irrevocably separated the Jews - the ancient notables, the priests of Osiris, the dignitaries of the ancient kingdom of the two lands that became Egypt - from the other peoples, qualified as idolaters or pagans, thus accomplishing a crime whose repercussions are still felt today since it has generated anti-Semitism and a colossal number of religious wars. The *Letter of Aristaeus* leaves no doubt that the Septuagint addresses itself exclusively to the ***Jews of the world***, not to a people different from the other Egyptians, but to them who are the Yahud, the "officials" of the ancient religion of Osiris, spread throughout the Nile Valley and the Middle East (the famous class of ***officials*** that Herodotus "forgot" to mention in his classification of the Egyptians). In order to be able to impose its forced Hellenization and the religious syncretism which accompanied it, which the Yahud, the dignitaries, guarantors of the old religion of Osiris, could not accept, Ptolemy separated them from the rest of Egypt by means of this Septuagint which he imposed on them. A feat which, by making them the chosen people, tore them away from their History, making them leave their Egypt theologically. From then on Ptolemy Philadelphus and his wife Arsinoe could reformat the Clergy of Osiris, by exploiting those who had agreed to collaborate, we shall return to it. Good business, moreover, for Ptolemy who, after having reduced in slavery these dignitaries - the Jews - extorted from them according to the *Letter of Aristaeus* not far from four million drachmas of gold that is 600 talents of gold. In exchange for their liberation, he stripped them of their houses... and offered them to his soldiers, whom he no longer had to pay with his own money. Stalin, thousands of years later, would not have been as vice-like: he would have the intellectuals, many of whom were Jews, arrested and eliminated. Philip the Fair also did this, which significantly improved his finances. If the ancient "Egyptians" were Jews, this must be verified by the fact that they preserved the name of God (or gods) in hieroglyphics. In the Bible, Yahweh manifests himself dozens of times to the Children of Israel as the god "I am", Anokhy אנכי, in connection with the political notion of the "god of the exit from Egypt". The central importance of this identity statement of Yahweh (Yahô-Osiris) is inscribed in the first of the Ten Commandments, given to Moses at Mount Sinai as the political god, who expels the Jews from Egypt:

I am the Lord [Anokhy אנכי ☥ Yahweh/Adonaÿ]**, your god who brought you out of the land of Egypt...** (Exodus XX, 2)
This golden rule of the "Jew out of Egypt" is repeated dozens of times in the Bible as well as in the Jewish liturgy. There is only one and only one dispensation where Yahweh does not declare himself to be the god of the coming out of Egypt, but claims to be the god of ancient Egypt, Yahu, Amon or Osiris, etc.

I am Yahweh [Anokhy = אנכי = Ankh ☥]**, YOUR GOD OF THE LAND OF EGYPT, and there is no god besides me that you know of, nor is there a savior besides me. (Hosea XIII, 4)**
The rabbis of the Zohar did not fail to seize upon this singular verse to reveal its true hidden meaning. Here are the words of Rabbi Eleazar, taken from the Zohar:

"Rabbi Eleazar began to speak thus: "I am the Lord, your god of the land of Egypt. The Scripture does not say "... who brought you out of Egypt", but "... your god of the land of Egypt", because since the beginning of Israel's existence, Israel has never known the Glory of God so much as in the land of Egypt..."[7]
Rabbi Eleazar specifies that there can be no difference in nature between the god of Egypt and the God of Israel, hidden behind a veil, i.e. Amun-Ra, Amun meaning precisely the "Hidden One", whose statue was installed in the Holy of Holies of the temples, symbolically concealed in the darkness of the cosmos, and who came out in processions veiled from the eyes of the general public:

---

7   Le Zohar, tome V, Le livre de la splendeur, op. cit., p. 229.

"... Since Israel originally saw God only through a veil [the veil of Amun, the Hidden One]**, he could be mistaken when later he saw God face to face near the Red Sea, and assumed that there are two gods. That is why the Scripture adds 'And you shall know no other god but me', 'I AM THE SAME AND I HAVE MADE ALL THINGS."**[8]

A second text confirms and clearly designates the god of the Jews, Yahweh or Elohim, as the creator of the *Neteru* דדד„ the deities of Egypt, sacred idols which it is formally forbidden to curse:

"Rabbi Abba said: "One is punished for cursing foreign gods. During their stay in Egypt, the Israelites learned to worship the celestial leaders that the Egyptians worshipped. And they began to worship them in turn. When they clung to God [to the Torah of Moses] **and God had drawn them to his service, they forsook the foreign gods, because, God said to them, THESE ARE MY WORKS, and whoever speaks ill of them will be punished; for he seems to criticize MY WORKS."**[9]

Is it not surprising that - in the secret thought of the scribes - the works of Yahweh are the gods, the Elohim, the idols of Egypt (Misraïm)? No, if one considers the semantic similarities between Yahô, Yahvé, YHVY with Yahô, Adonaï-Aton, Israel with Osiris, etc. It cannot be a matter of coincidence. One cannot mean more clearly that Yahweh, named Yaho by the ancient Jews, is the god of Egypt, named in the hieroglyphs. Yah, Yaho, Yahu, Amon, Ra, Osiris, etc. The Book of the *Exit to the Light*, known under the erroneous name of the *Book of the Dead*, authenticates this affirmation of the Kabbalah on several points: on the one hand, the Neteru דדד - the gods - are indeed the creation of Osiris/IS-RÂ, the god of the Nile valley, since they were born from the transformation of Atum

---

8   Le Zohar, tome V, Le livre de la splendeur, op. cit., p. 229.
9   Le Zohar, tome V, Le livre de la splendeur, op. cit., p. 268.

into several tens of deities (symbolically forming his Body), including the genesis and the triptych of Atum, the Unique reed or demiurge the primordial Yod **"I am the One who became Three"**[10], origin of the Christian Trinity, but also the origin of Abraham, Isaac, Jacob and Joseph, who form in the Kabbalah the allegorical Body of the divinity through the sephirotic tree where Abraham is the right arm of YHVH, Isaac the left arm, Jacob the body and Joseph the phallus. The Children of Israel are also the "works of Yahweh", his symbolic body. Driven out of the land of Egypt, they symbolize the death of the so-called Egyptian civilization, which the texts of Hermes Trismegistus, written in Jewish - and not Egyptian - language and dated to the second century B.C., associate with the banishment of the Neteru.

As can be seen on the walls of the Valley of the Kings, the Neteru 𓏠𓏠𓏠 very often address offerings and prayers to the gods, who symbolize the unique god, Amun or Osiris..., as if they were human beings inhabiting the world[11], the teachers of a syncretic monotheism where God is both unique and multiple. Indeed, the texts of the Pyramids attest that several gods mean that there is only one God, whose Body is formed by the whole of the gods. As we have said, the Neteru 𓏠𓏠𓏠 formed the parts of the Body of "Osiris the god" 𓏠, and are subject to his commands, the commands of IS-RÂ-God... The Jews, the ancient Yods, the clergy of the Nile Valley, these dignitaries respected by their people, had a first Torah in which God was both unique and multiple. As far back as one can go, the god of the Nile Valley is above all manifested, every day, by the omnipotence of light, source of life. The symbol of light and life is translated as ANKH ☥ ANOKH or Anokhy'. One of the names of Ra, the unique god of ancient Egypt, is pronounced Anokhy as in the Hebrew Bible. Anokhy means "the manifestation of Ra's time and life", which is none other than the way of expressing the I of the divine Majesty, the "Holy Light". According to the

---

10   Textes des Sarcophages, paroles d'Atoum. CT II 39 b-e.
11   Jan Assmann. Le Prix du Monothéisme. Éditions Aubier. 2006.

Midrash Rabba, the **"I of God" is therefore the "I of Ra"**, as attested by the hieroglyphic with the two reeds/Yods, explained in the Egyptian hieroglyphic dictionary of Wallys Budge.

ANOKHY אנכי , THE SELF OF THE GOD OF THE JEWS, THE SELF OF OSIRIS ☥

I take advantage of this chapter to thank all the people who supported me, especially Rabbi Philippe Haddad and Rabbi Marc Alain Ouaknine, who confirmed that the god of the Jews was originally the Ankh of the ancient Egyptians, the hieroglyph of the divine light. He said publicly that the hieroglyphic identity of the ancient Egyptians, formed by the letter YOD, "was a revolutionary discovery", and he encouraged me to persist on the track, "Egyptians = Jews". Israel is a vine torn out of Egypt (Psalms 80: 9). It is therefore appropriate to explore the secret texts of the Kabbalah, which reveal the Egyptian origin of the god of the Bible. For, the Kabbalah tells us, the Children of Israel were "raised in the golden crucible of Misraïm""[12], thus in the solar matrix of Isis MESS-RA-YAM and not in Babylonia or Mesopotamia. So who is really Adonai, Yod-Yod, Elohim or Yahweh, the god of the Jews? Is he the supreme god of the Nile valley named Yahô by the Jews in the Greek texts? Knowing that Yahô is one of the names of Osiris, at the time when the latter practiced the cult of Osiris, as demonstrated by the ostraca of Elephantine, it seems obvious that the Jews have preserved in their collective and secret memory a part of the names of the god of the Nile Valley.

If the rabbis of the Kabbalah, part of which is contemporary with the Septuagint, affirm that the God of the Jews is the god of the Nile Valley, if science confirms this assertion from hieroglyphics, if the Egyptians are the Jews then we have the right to question the Bible as the Book "revealed" at Mount

---

12   Élie Benamozegh, Israël et l'Humanité, op. cit., p. 109.

Sinai for the reason that in history the god of Egypt - with its many names and forms - **has never driven a single Jew out of the Nile Valley**, since the Jews formed the Body of this civilization. Moses belongs not to history but to the myth of the god of the exit from Egypt and the miracle of the Red Sea. This obvious contradiction between the Bible and History shows that the Jews, the real "Egyptians", never left Egypt other than through the Assyrian, Babylonian, Persian invasions and especially through the Greek Septuagint. The only exit from Egypt is a virtual history, the miraculous myth inscribed in the Septuagint and in the Hebrew Torah. Indeed, the myth of Moses' exit from Egypt was imposed on the Jews of Alexandria in the third century B.C. during the "miraculous" elaboration of the Septuagint in the tower of Pharos, with the aim of making the Jews, in other words, the guardians of the ancestral religion, foreigners in their own country which had become Ægyptos... A brilliant idea orchestrated with great pomp by Ptolemy II Philadelphus, his wife Arsinoe and his father Ptolemy Soter (the savior) in order to make the historical memory of the guardians of the religion of the Nile Valley disappear and thus to be able to modify it at his convenience, without any possible opposition, in order to be deified during his lifetime in the ancient kingdom of the two lands renamed Ægyptos.

Here is another argument that will prove Clement of Alexandria's right. This proof will be confirmed by the Ankh ☥ engraved on the seal of King Hezekiah. The royal seal of Hezekiah, which we will decipher in a later chapter, provides proof that the winged sun, the solar symbol of Ra-Osiris, is read Yahô, the origin of Yahweh. The winged sun is linked to the symbol of the life force Ankh ☥. Jewish tradition has preserved the memory of the Ankh of the ancient Egyptians, which is none other than the word Anokhy, the I of God in the Hebrew Bible. As Yahweh or YHVH/YAHOU is identified with Anokhy (I, I am), the hieroglyph of life Ankh' , Anokh or Anok symbolically means "I am the light God" or "I am the image of the light God".

Ankh ♀ refers to the essence of life embodied in and given by the "I of God" to all living beings. Finally, Anokh also means "I am" in the sense of "I am the Living God" or "I am Life", the origin of "I am the Alpha and the Omega" (symbolic name of Christ the King of Israel = INRI = Anokhy = resurrected to life), the beginning and the end, i.e. God is every moment of our life, the present moment. The expression of God Anokhy "I am", returns very often in the Egyptian texts, and shows that each moment of our life is a permanent revelation, where God reveals himself and fades away in each second.

Finally, the symbol ANKH' ♀ and its derivative Anokhy אנכי express the mystical meaning and the depth of light of the original life, given by God, Ra, Osiris, Amun or Aten. According to Egyptology, the Ankh expresses the notion of time and life of Ra, which is to say that the Ankh expresses the "Self of God". For the ancient Jewish secret tradition, Anokhy is recognized as the "Egyptian" name of Yahweh יהוה, read Yod-Yod and pronounced Adonai, a sacred heritage, "THE WORD OF EGYPTIAN WORDS"[13]

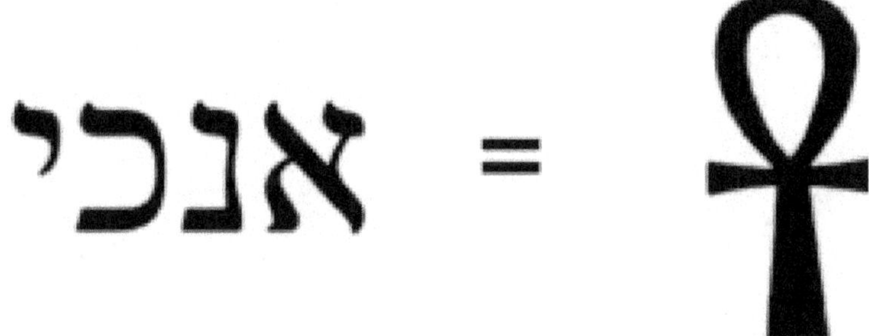

Anokhy Hebrew Me, I, corresponds to the symbol ANKH, the spirit of life of God of Osiris/Israel

Old Jewish commentaries confirm that Anokhy אנכי is none other than the "I of the Majesty of God", the Redemption linked to the symbolic arrival of the seventy Children of Israel (the

---

13 Cf. Réflexions sur la vie juive. Rabbi Chélomo de Loubavicch. 2ème édition 1987.

seventy sons of Jacob symbolizing humanity) in Egypt[14] , their death in the desert and their resurrection in Canaan.

"Our sages - may their memory be blessed - teach: "This term [Anokhy], designating the I of the Divine Majesty, is the symbol of the first Redemption and it was used when the Children of Israel went down to Egypt as the verse shows : It is I [Anokhy = יכנא = ☥] who will go down with you to Egypt"[15]

Ankh ☥ is also the origin of the word Angel, which is why Ankh often accompanies the winged sun, the image of the wings of Osiris/Israel on the pediment of the temples. Two angels, two wings, two reed feathers on the crown of Amun-Ra, two Yods both symbolizing the primordial creative breaths of Shu and Tefnut, the two lions found in the allegorical name of Osiris. The name YHVH/YAHOU יהוה is itself composed of Yod י, the Holy Spirit, and a central VAV ו, which the Kabbalah identifies with the sun, and two He ה, identified with the two heavenly breaths, or **Ruach**. Let us specify that God himself (the divine light, the Shekhina), is provided with two wings according to the Kabbalah. *Wallys Budge's Egyptian hieroglyphic dictionary* leaves no doubt as to the origin - Jewish and not "Egyptian" - of ANOKHI:

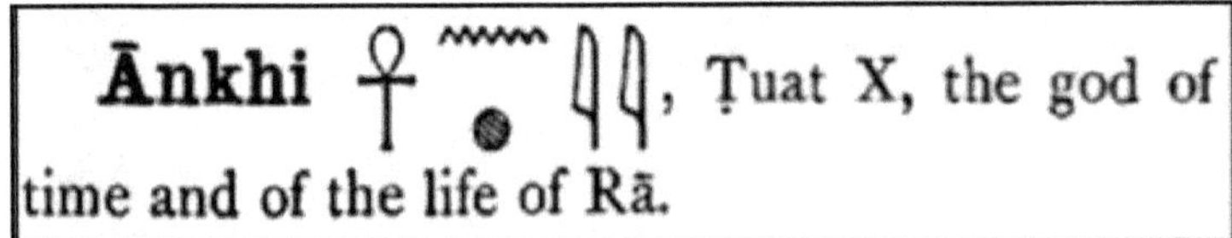

Anokhy, the god of eternity of Ra's life[16].

---

14 This is especially true since the biblical ANOKHI is the first word of the Ten Commandments, ANOKHI YAHVE = I am YAHVE. Furthermore, the Egyptian word ANOKHI is the symbol of the redemption of Israel.

15 Midrachim de nos sages, Exode, Tome II, Chemoth Rabbah Exode, op. cit., page 140.

16 Egyptian hieroglyphic dictionary. Wallis Budge, Dover Publications, inc, New York. Published by General publishing Company, 1978, p. 125b.

It is blindingly accurate, ANKH' ♀ has the same metaphysical meaning and function as Anokhy אָנֹכִי, the God of the Bible. Yahweh has the "Egyptian" name Anokhy, the "I of Ra", the "I" of the god of Egypt! The principle of the Redemption of Israel means that Misraim (the evil serpent, the darkness, the Matrix) must die so that Israel (the divine light, the Presence) lives by the will of God, the will of Anokhy. Moreover, as we know from the words of the most famous rabbi of the Kabbalah, Rabbi Simeon bar Yokhai, Anokhy refers not only to God, but also to the Divine Shekhina called "Israel", who came down to Egypt with forty-two angels:

"Rabbi Simeon says: "When the Shekhina [God's luminous Spirit, Anokhi/Yahweh/Elohim] **descended into Egypt, it took the form of a Haya** [God's luminous life power = the Ankh of the Egyptians] **who bears the name Israel, and whose image**

resembles that of the old man (from above). Forty-two holy angels destined to serve the Shekhina came down with her. Each of these angels bears a sacred letter of the divine name composed of forty-two letters"[17]

Obvious memory of the forty-two judges of the celestial court

of Osiris alias Israel. Anokhy designates Ra, Osiris, Israel, the self of God. Even if this god once came out of Ægyptos... The sarcophagus n° 80 confirms that the sign Ankh or Anokh is none other than the name of the god of Egypt:

"ANOKH' IS MY NAME"[18]

The symbol of life Ankh given by God is found in almost all tombs, prayers, in sacred papyri. In the Hebrew Old Testament, the first of the Ten Commandments given to Moses at Mount

---

17 Zohar, tome III. Le livre de la splendeur. Par Jean de Pauly. Éditions Maisonneuve & Larose, 1985. P. 74.

18 Textes des Sarcophages du Moyen Empire Égyptien. Claude Carrier, tome I. Éditions du Rocher, 2004, spell n° 80, p. 227.

Sinai, after the exit from Egypt, begins with the two words Anokhy YAHVE meaning "I am Yahweh". Anokhy is used by Yahweh to say: "I am Yod", "I am Yod Yod" in the Aramaic Targum (Aramaic translation of Onkelos).

As we shall see, the Ankh ☥ engraved on the royal seal of Hezekiah expresses the self of Ra, Yahu or Osiris. Associated with the winged sun YAHOU - the "pronounced" name of YHVH Yahu is inscribed in many kings of Israel - with three rays, it expresses the fact well that Hezekiah reigns over the Nile Valley. It is thought that the name יהוה Yahweh/YHVH is unpronounceable which is not true. In the Greek texts, in the letter of Aristaeus, in the ostraca of Elephantine and in the Kabbalah Yahweh is read YAHOU. And for good reason, YAHOU is associated with many Jewish names, as well as with the names of several kings of Israel, because it means "divine light" according to the hieroglyph YAHOU. Thus, the name of the Jewish king Hezekiah reads Hazak Yahu the "power of Yahu/Osiris" manifested by the Ankh.

This discovery is crucial, because the Ankh cross followed by the double Yod symbolizes Ra-Osiris-Aton-Amon, living on the multiplicity of creation. Furthermore, the Anokhy hieroglyph above may well read "Ankh/Anokhy Yod-Yod", which corresponds to "I am Yod-Yod" (Anokhy Yod-Yod) in the Aramaic Targum. On several effigies, the Ankh is worshipped by Isis and Nephthys, raising both hands to God (symbol of the two Yods). For the Kabbalah, Anokhy designates the divine Shekhina, the luminous power of God; Israel, in its incarnation of death and divine Redemption. Rabbi Simeon bar Yohai gives us the explanation that completes the definition of the Wallis Budge dictionary. The comparison of the name Anokhy with the corresponding hieroglyph shows that the god of the Bible, when he affirms himself as "ANOKHY" throughout the reading of the Torah, that is to say I AM in Hebrew, considered as **the word of the Egyptian words**, affirms the whole power of Ra's life condensed in Anokhy.

"Rabbi Simeon says: the word Anokhy is the synthesis of all that is above and all that is below; the sacred powers of divine life [in Hebrew Hayoth] are enclosed in the word Anokhy"[19]

אנכי **= Ankh-Yod =**

ANOKHY = "I AM THE LIVING YOD" in Hebrew.
ANOKHY = "I AM THE LIVING YOD" in hieroglyphics.
No more than the name of Yahweh or Yod-Yod, the sacred name of Anokhy does not exist in the Septuagint, where the god Kyrios affirms :
EGO EÏMI KYRIOS Ô THEOS.

I am Kyrios the Theos (Exodos --20:2)

It is clear that Ptolemy removed from the Septuagint the hieroglyphs Ankh or Anokhy, Yahô/Yahvé, Yod-Yod, and replaced them with Ego and Kyrios. Almost a millennium after the reign of Ptolemy Philadelphus and the Septuagint, in contrast to the biblical account of the miraculous exit of the Children of Israel from Egypt through the Red Sea, the Koran tells us a radically different exit from Egypt. Sura 26-59, Allah never brought the Children of Israel out of Egypt. It says that Allah expelled Pharaoh and his people from the land of Egypt, and then **Allah gave the land of the Nile Valley... to the Sons of Israel.** Proof that the Koran had kept a part of the secret memory, the Kabbalah. As if the Koran knew the Jewish secrets of the history of the Septuagint of the Ptolemies pharaohs. As if Allah in the Koran wanted to do justice to history by restoring the land of the Nile Valley to the Sons of Israel, to the Jews, recognizing in them the true "Egyptians"...

---

19 Zohar, tome III. Le livre de la splendeur. Par Jean de Pauly. Maisonneuve & Larose, 1985, p. 369.

26-57: Thus We (Allah) made Pharaoh and his people (in other translations and explanations of the Koran) leave their gardens and their springs,

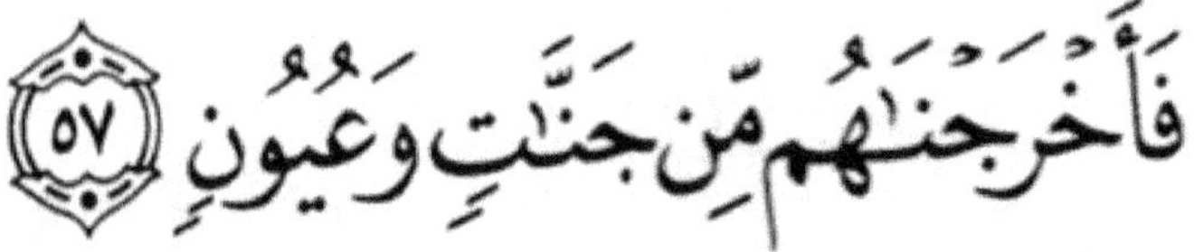

(En phonétique) Fa'akhrajnāhum Min Yannātin Wa `Uyūninin,

26-58: their treasures and their sumptuous residences,

Wa Kunūzin Wa Maqāmin Karīmin

26-59: And so it was. And We gave all this as an inheritance to the sons of Israel.

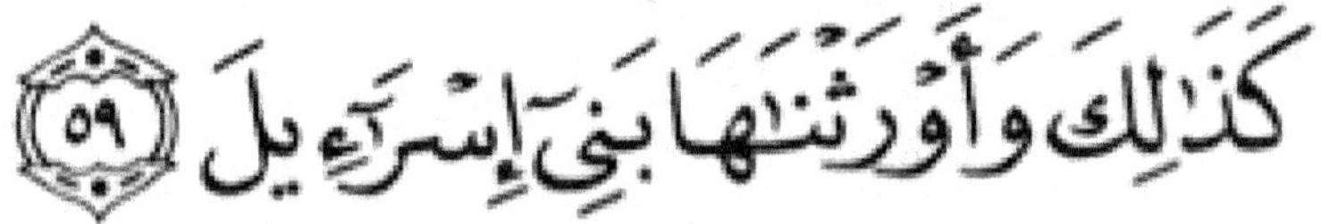

Kadhalika Wa `Awrathnaha Banī `Isra'īla

The discovery of the Egyptians/Jews, Israel/Osiris through the cross-referencing of the Koran and the Kabbalah associated with hieroglyphs, amounts to redefining and rediscovering a new history of Israel, melted in the history of the Egyptian civilization, enlightening us on the origin of the divisions and the past and current conflicts between men. It is to bring to light the deep origins of the Arab-Israeli conflict, it is to discover the historical truth, which will allow us to understand and demystify the causes of the thousand-year-old conflicts by revealing the common roots of Jews, Christians and Muslims in the ancient civilization of the Nile Valley. For the Arab-Israeli war, well beyond a political conflict, is above all a religious conflict, a conflict of scriptures in which the word of God plays the leading role by far.

Thus, this war does not seem to have a political solution, because the starting point is recorded in the sacred books. Now these books constantly refer to the exit from "ancient Egypt" for the Jews, for the Torah, but to the complete restitution of ancient Egypt to the Sons of Israel for the Koran. For the Kabbalah, the true and historical land of Israel[20] was the "land of Goshen" named once "land of Ramses" (Genesis XL, 11), given to Jacob/Israel, grandson of Abraham. Jacob, who was renamed Israel after his victory over the tutelary Angel of God after a cosmic night battle, who would be the tutelary Angel of his jealous twin brother Esau, says the Kabbalah... The Kabbalah makes the land of Goshen/Ramses the eternal inheritance of Israel:

"Come and see what is written: "Israel lived in the land of Egypt in the land of Goshen. They acquired property there, and grew fruitful and multiplied greatly" (Gen 47:27) "They acquired property there": AN ETERNAL HERITAGE"[21]

The land of Goshen, also known as the land of Ramses, corresponds to the whole land of Egypt, given by Pharaoh to the Children of Israel, the symbolic gift of the Garden of Eden. Let us insist again on this important fact: while the Bible/Torah designates the land of Canaan as the holy land of the Children of Israel, for the Koran, the holy book of Islam, the land of Egypt is given as an inheritance by Allah to the Children of Israel.

---

20 The "great Israel" can only be achieved if humanity respects the divine commandments in their entirety. Elijah Munk. The voice of the Torah. Deuteronomy. Samuel and Odette Levy Foundation. 1998, p. 111, note 24.

21 Le Zohar, tome IV, collection "les dix paroles ". Vayigash Vayehi. Traduit par Charles Mopsik. Verdier, 1996, 211b, p. 53.

Allah refers to them - **the Sons of Israel !- as the heirs of the land of Egypt**, indeed the heirs of the land. Indeed, two surahs, Al Shurah of the Poets (26, 57-59) and Al Qasas (28, 5-6) report that Allah has restored to the Sons of Israel their ancient inheritance, usurped by the conquerors of Egypt. Pharaoh and his people would mean the ancient Greeks, who were driven out by Allah for enslaving the Children of Israel. The following verses of the Koran show the constant consistency that Allah had decided to restore the Sons of Israel/Jews to their former status of kings and princes instead of Pharaoh:

[57] Thus We [Allah] **drove** [Pharaoh and his people in other Qur'anic translations and explanations] **from their gardens and springs [58], their treasures and their lavish residences. 59] And so it was. And We gave all this as an inheritance to the sons of Israel.**

[5] And We wanted to help those who were oppressed in the land [the Sons of Israel], **to make them rulers and heirs, and to make them masters of the land, and to do to Pharaoh and Haman and their armies what they had feared.**

Then We [Allah] **took vengeance on them** [of Pharaoh and the Egyptians] **and drowned them in the sea, because they rejected Our Signs and paid no attention to them. And the**

people who were oppressed [the Sons of Israel], **We made them inherit the eastern and western parts of the land which We blessed. And the beautiful promise of your Lord on the Children of Israel was fulfilled as a reward for their endurance. And We destroyed what Pharaoh and his people were doing and what they were building** (Koran 7:136-137)

Pharaoh wanted to drive them out of the land. But We swallowed him and his people to the last. And after him We said to the Children of Israel, "Dwell in the land, and when the promise of the future life is fulfilled, We will bring you back in great numbers. This Koran is revealed in truth and is the very expression of the Truth" (Koran 17:103-105)

The expression "Pharaoh" - in Arabic Pharaoh is Pera' Ouna - refers to Pharao', the name of the Greek kings, who are considered idolaters by the Koran. Another passage in the Koran leaves no doubt that it was Pharaoh, the king who had divided humanity into clans and races, who was driven out of the Nile Valley in favor of the Children of Israel.

4] Pharaoh was a despot in the land. He divided its inhabitants into clans and oppressed some of them, killing their sons and leaving only their daughters alive, for he was an evil being. We wanted to help those oppressed people on earth, to make them rulers and heirs, and to make them masters of the land, and to do to Pharaoh and Haman and their armies what they had feared (Koran 28: 4-6).

It is clear that the legitimacy of a sacred, universal Israel is very powerful in the Koran. The Sons of Israel inherit the land. So why these bloody, useless and endless wars between Jews and Muslims? The Koran and the Kabbalah speak of the "Pharaohs", not as the legitimate kings of the Nile Valley, who bore the name of SA-RÂ, or IS-RÂ, but as idolaters of their own person, invaders, illegitimate, in this case the memory of the Romans and the Greeks, indeed all the invaders of the Nile valley from the seventh century BC. On several occasions, the Koran joins the writings of the ancient secret tradition or Kabbalah.

The verses of the Koran are essential to complete and understand whom Israel is historically, its filiation with ancient Egypt and to rebuild peace in the world between Jews, Christians and Muslims. For the Kabbalah itself is considered the remnant of an ancient lost Torah, the "Primordial Torah" or the "Oral Torah". A Torah that stated loud and clear that ancient Israel, the original paradise, the universal Garden of Eden of Adam and Eve, was none other than the land of Egypt and its kings, where the Yahud lived happily. As we have said, the Children of Israel, the humanity that came out of Egypt, is identified with Adam:

"Humanity [= The Children of Israel] **is called here "sons of Man (Adam)""**[22]

"The Man (Adam) is the Children of Israel"[23]

"He sent Adam out of the Garden of Eden" (Gen. 3:23). Adam (man) is, of course, Israel."[24]
Sura 2 -122, Allah glorifies the Sons of Israel.

O Sons of Israel, remember the raptures with which I have delighted you, favoring you more than the worlds.

Hebrew name: Israel

Koranic Arabic name for Israel: Isrâilâ
For Islam, the Torah (the first five books of the Old Testament), which attributes the land of Canaan as an inheritance to the Children of Israel (Bani Isrâîlâ), was misunderstood by the majority of the Jews. The message of God was transformed, even falsified in the sacred book by a group of Jews, since it is the land of Egypt that was bequeathed by Allah to the Children of Israel.

We gave Moses the scripture [the Torah] **about which there were controversies.** (Koran, 46:12)

---

22 Le Zohar, tome 1, collection 'les dix paroles'. Traduit par Charles Mopsik. Verdier, 1981. P. 380, 75a.

23 Le Zohar, tome 1, collection "les dix paroles ". Traduit par Charles Mopsik. Verdier, 1981, p. 147.

24 Ibidem, p. 162.

Well, do you expect that such people (Jews) will share your faith? But a group of them, after hearing and understanding the word of Allah, knowingly falsified it.   (Koran, 2, 75)

It is a terrible accusation, because logically, after the victory of Allah and Moses over Pharaoh, following the ten devastating plagues, the Koran does not mention once the gift of the promised land, the land of Canaan, to the Children of Israel, as it was promised to Abraham and Moses in the Torah. The Koran refuses to accept any compromise on this burning issue: Allah's promise to the Children of Israel irrevocably concerns the land of the Pharaohs, the Nile Valley... Even more, and with force, the Koran denounces the "falsification" of the word of Yahweh in the Torah, a sacred book for both Jews and Muslims. The Torah would have minimized, considerably reduced to a small limited territory, semi-desert, located in the land of Canaan, the extent of the promised land attributed to the Children of Israel. It is urgent to ask the question: Does the promise of Allah re-establish a historical truth, unambiguously affirmed in several suras of the Koran and in the Kabbalah? That the text of the Torah was transformed is a fact recognized in the secret Jewish tradition. Let us not forget that rabbinic commentaries or Midrash relate that certain passages of the Torah were transformed on the orders of Pharaoh Ptolemy...
A passage in the Bible tells us that the prophet Jeremiah had escaped from Nebuchadnezzar to take refuge in Egypt. Jeremiah already denounced a "lying Bible" of the scribes.

"How can you say, 'We are wise and the Torah of Yahweh is with us ?"". Yes, but the lying calamus of the scribes has made it a lie! "... (Jeremiah 8-8)
Scholars have noted that the texts of the Prophets are late Greek writings from the time of the Ptolemies. Jeremiah is a "Hellenized prophet" who does not speak of an ancient Law, but of the Septuagint.

And for good reason, in the same verse of the Septuagint, which names him Jeremiah ΙΕΡΕΜΙΑΣ, the prophet does not say the "Law of Yahweh" but the "Law of Kyrios, the Greek god. Septuagint Jeremiah, 8:8:

How shall you say: We are wise, and the Law of Kyrios is with us? The lying pen of your scribes writes errors!

The scribes denounce an ancient Law, a Torah reworked either

at the time of Darius II or at the time of Ptolemy. As we can see, the profound disagreement with the Koran on the meaning of the scriptures resurfaces several centuries after the writing of the Book of Jeremiah. Yahweh promises Moses the land of Canaan as an inheritance, and Allah proclaims that all the land of Egypt belongs to the Children of Israel and gives it back to them as an inheritance... to the Jews, the latter being qualified as heirs and rulers (some translations say, "kings and princes"). It is as if the Koran knew and applied the words of the Kabbalah, defining the land of the Nile Valley as the "eternal inheritance" of the Jews. Proof that despite the prohibitions, the historical truth was nevertheless transmitted orally by the Jews.

In case of an internal war, say the Egyptologists, Ra only has to start the creation again... Is the exit from Egypt to be considered as a cryptic inversion of history hiding a new hope, the passage from darkness to light, a return to the Tree of Life, concealing an immense historical event? In this case, the Kabbalah thought of the Jewish rebels may well have influenced the Koran. What if it was simply the truth? What a revolution for our humanity is divided by the so-called sacred scriptures. Against all expectations, the Koran confirms in the Sura of the Ants (Sura AN-NAML 27-76), that it is originally a conflict between the Children of Israel, thus a conflict between Jews, who would be at the origin of the "revelation" of the Koran:

THIS KORAN TELLS/CLARIFIES TO THE CHILDREN OF ISRAEL MOST OF THE MATTERS ON WHICH THEY DIFFER.

Beyond the dogma of submission to Allah, the Koran takes up this founding notion of the ancient land of the Nile Valley alias Misra, restored by Allah to the Children of Israel. What are the differences between Jews that the Koran speaks of? The only possibility - as Charle Mopsik attests - would be the existence of a historical conflict between Kabbalah Jews, for whom the Nile Valley was the original Garden of Eden for the Jews, symbolized by the Tree of Life, and rabbinism, which advocated a literal reading of the Torah, situating the Garden of Eden either in Canaan or in the world beyond. **A conflict between Jews produced the Koran.** At the origin of the schism, the separation between Egypt, the historical land of the Jews, and Canaan, the mystical and mythical land of the Septuagint/ Bible. Accompanying the Koran, the secret Jewish tradition, the Kabbalah, questions the problem of the exit from Egypt and consequently of the Mosaic Revelation.

So much so that hidden behind the myth, the belief, the Kabbalah and especially archaeology question our absolute certainties concerning the historical exit from Egypt, and especially the gift by God of the land of Canaan to Abraham and the Children of Israel. For in the end, in the messianic era, the land of Egypt aka the Garden of Eden - restored by Allah in the Koran! - should return... at least historically... to the Jews. This is a real, real hope for peace in these troubled times, when men blinded by obscurantism are preparing for war, because of ignorance of the message of the ancient scriptures. In any case, Egyptology has not done its job of restoring the historical truth.

To understand why the Septuagint, the Old Testament, the New Testament and the Koran are sometimes in contradiction, sometimes in phase with history. The Kabbalah has preserved the memories of ancient Israel/Misraim/Osiris, repressed memories that Sigmund Freud had evoked and researched. The father of psychoanalysis had concluded to the murder of the first Moses, whereas it is indeed the symbolic murder of Osiris, the ancient Israel. The Kabbalah has been preserved through many centuries, more than two millennia it seems. It establishes a powerful link with the Egyptian origin of the Bible and the Jews. It is probably for this reason that the Kabbalah caused a deep division among Jews, leading some of them to convert to Islam when forced to do so, like Shabbatai Svi and to Christianity for Jacob Frankk[25]. According to Charles Mopsik, in the Middle Ages, Kabbalah Jews opposed to traditional Jews were finally fighting over the understanding of the true secret message of the Torah, the SOD. This may seem like an exaggeration, but it is clear that at the beginning of the third millennium of our era, with the rise of religious fundamentalism and fanaticism, at war with freedom and secularism, fundamentalists are acting against the free world, and against history, justifying crime in the name of God. What is said here about the reading of the sacred scriptures is serious enough to point to our responsibility for the future of humanity, as confirmed by Charles Mopsik:

"The attitude of the Kabbalists towards the Jewish religious authorities, however, was never really idyllic. It should be noted that many voices were raised among the Kabbalah to challenge the hegemony of rabbinic jurisdiction, or even its methods of interpretation based on reasoning and rational discussion [any literal reading of the Torah]. **In the part of the Kabbalah called Raya Mehemna and in the Tiquuné Ha-Zohar, there are many passages which attempt to place the literal meaning of the Bible, the Talmud and the law in general, at a level far below that of the study of the esoteric meaning** [the secret meaning, the Gnosis, the Sod]. **In the eyes of the author of this book, exoteric religion** [the literal reading of the Torah]**, its interpretative practices and its own ideology**

---

25 Charles Novak. Jacob Frank, le faux Messie, L'Harmattan, 2020.

represent a new exile in Egypt. The normal relationship between exoteric religion (Mishna, Talmud) and esoteric religion (Kabbalah) is that of a servant to her queen... If the exoteric study of the Talmud is attachment to the Tree of Knowledge of Good and Evil, the study of the Zohar and the Kabbalistic reading of the Torah in general is attachment to the Tree of Life"[26]

We are faced with the overwhelming evidence that the Torah was originally a secret text accompanied by the Kabbalah. A text forbidden by the Greeks, because it allowed the deciphering of the Greek Codex, the Septuagint. For several centuries, the Torah/Massora was regarded by the initiated Jewish cabalists as the secret decoding of a false "Hellenized History of the Jews", namely of the so-called Hebrews enslaved by Pharaoh, which would in reality be the concealed transposition of a historical fact, the Jews/Youdaïos enslaved by Ptolemy. For four centuries, while the Greek Codex could **only be read in its literal sense**, the Hebrew Torah, written at the same time as the Septuagint and its secret commentary, the Kabbalah, were hidden from the Greeks. The Torah thus canonized more than four centuries after the Septuagint, and its counterpart, the Kabbalah, are a veritable corpus of deciphering the Oracle, where the name of Kyrios κύριος is rejected, while the names of the god of the Nile Valley, are restored in hieroglyphics. The Septuagint is thus named "Oracle" by Ptolemy in the *Letter of Aristaeus*. While the seventy-two so-called translators of the Tower of Pharos had sworn - accepting unconditionally the name of the Greek god Kyrios κύριος - never to touch a Yota of the Septuagint on pain of divine curse, the Torah is a "REPARATION", a TIKOUN, a return to the god and the gods of ancient Egypt.

---

26 Charles Mopsik. La Cabale. Jacques Grancher édit. 1988. P. 122.

Chapter IV

THE BIBLE IS A REFOUNDATION OF THE MYTH OF OSIRIS

Is the History of the Jews, with a capital H, through the myth of the exit from Egypt, a new history of Osiris transferred to the land of Canaan? The Garden of Eden of Adam and Eve would be a metaphor for the land of the Nile Valley, from which the ancient Jews were expelled during Hellenization.

In his book Isis and Osiris, Plutarch notes that the new «Egyptian» Hellenized priesthood of his time traces the hatred of the Jews to the mythology of the Great Ennead of Heliopolis, which tells of the installation of the Egyptian gods in the Nile Valley. Their stay, and especially the crime of Osiris by his jealous brother Set. The Jews were originally considered as the priests of Osiris: they are named «Men of God» in the Letter of Aristaeus to Philocrates and the ostraca of Elephantine attest that they were the worshipers of Osiris. The Jews thus worshiped the ancestral gods of the Great Ennead of Heliopolis. However, they were the victims of a demonization and an inversion of their history.

Here they suddenly become the priests of the god Seth, hereditary enemies of Osiris. They are the accomplices of Typhon, the new Greek name given to Seth. After having fought Horus, the son of Osiris, the avenger of his father, Seth would have fled in the desert, then in the land of Canaan where he would have had two "Jewish" sons who became the founders of Judah and Jerusalem...

"As for those who say that Typhon [Seth], after abandoning the battle, spent seven days fleeing on a donkey, and that when he was saved he begat two sons, Hierosolimos [Jerusalem] and Yudaios [Judah], it is very clear that they are adding Judaic elements to this myth"[1]

In the first century, the Jews continued to be assimilated to the worshipers of the god Typhon, according to Plutarch, or to the worshipers of the donkey's head symbolizing Seth in the temple of Jerusalem, according to Flavius Josephus (Seth, the younger brother and murderer of Osiris, was assimilated to a donkey or a pig, and was represented by a man with the head of a donkey). These terrible accusations of a deicide, demonic people, accomplices and worshipers of Seth have continued with Christianity. Christ the King of Israel was crucified, died and resurrected because of the betrayal of Judah (one of the twelve Jewish apostles). Judah is assimilated to the Jews, who were to pay dearly for his betrayal. But it must be said that before Christianity, the Jews were the real "Egyptians", since they worshiped Osiris and practiced his cult - which made them the sons of Osiris - as the ostraca of Elephantine attest. But following the false legends of Manetho and others, following the so-called revelation of the Septuagint - and always against their will - the Jews were re-implanted in the myth of Osiris - but this time inverted - as the sons of Set, making them the sons of Satan, the sons of the devil... **whereas Seth never had a single child !!!**

The first time the Old Testament invokes the name Israel, it is to rename and glorify the Patriarch Jacob after his victorious fight on an Angel who came to confront him during the night. The word Israel has always taken an essential place in the three monotheistic religions. Even the first place. Why is this so? To understand the deep, symbolic, mystical nature of the word or name ISRAEL, we must insist on the fact that this word is not only the name of the patriarch Jacob, given after his victory against the Angel. According to the oldest commentaries, Israel

---

1   Plutarque, Isis et Osiris, p. 109-110, § 31.

is a divine name that existed before creation. Israel refers to humanity (the seventy nations), the name of a country before its creation, the name of the Son of God, the name of God himself. But in the secret of the scriptures, Israel is above all the Light. The Light fighting the Darkness, as is Osiris, the god of the ''ancient Egyptians''.

In the hieroglyphics the god of gods renamed Osiris or Dionysus by the Ancient Greeks is read SA-RÂ or IS-RÂ, followed by the symbol of God. His primary function is to represent God; the Son of God, the light, the river, the kings of the Nile Valley - which we falsely call ''Pharaoh'', knowing that this name does not exist in the hieroglyphs, and finally Osiris designates the land of the Nile Valley and humanity. This king, an image of God named Son of the Sun (SA-RÂ) is also an ISRA. He acts as a High Priest and his celestial function is to regulate the balance of the cosmos. In the symbolism, he is a serpent of light, the image of the River, the Nile.

But at night, Osiris must fight in the underworld, in order to guarantee the solar cycle. He is the guarantor of the passage from night to day and from day to night. In the royal tombs of the Valley of the Kings, the king SARA must symbolically fight his inverted image, the other ''King'' Serpent of Darkness named Apophys or Mehen. Each daybreak is a victory, a new IS-RÂ says Osiris, a new beginning of the world, where Ra, the World-God, comes out victorious from this celestial fight. In order to introduce this new Osiris/Israel notion, we will see the parallel with the fight between Jacob and the Angel related in the first of the five books of the Old Testament, which is nothing else than an identical, cosmic, Osirian fight against his twin brother Esau.

Fight of Jacob against the Angel of the Lord or the Angel of Elohim or the Guardian Angel of Esau. Engraving by Gustave Doré.

In the first reading of the Bible, Israel refers to the third of the Patriarchs as Jacob, son of Isaac, son of Abraham. Jacob finds himself alone with an angel - a god, an Elohim in the Hebrew text - from heaven whom he must fight all night.

JACOB'S STRUGGLE IS THE STRUGGLE OF RA-OSIRIS AGAINST DARKNESS SERPENT

Genesis 32:24-28: **Jacob was left alone. Then a man wrestled with him until dawn. And when the man saw that he could not overcome him, he smote him in the socket of his hip; and the socket of Jacob's hip was broken while he wrestled with him. And he said, Let me go, for the dawn is rising. And Jacob said, I will not let thee go, till thou hast blessed me. And he said unto him, What is thy name? And he answered, Jacob. He said, «Your name shall no longer be Jacob, but you shall be called Israel; for you have fought with Elohim אלהים and with men, and have prevailed.**

What is the connection between Tem-Ra-Osiris fighting the serpent Apophys and Jacob's fight against the Angel? What is the connection between Elohim אלהים - the gods - and RÂ (or RAÂ), one of the main names of the god of the ancient Nile Valley? What do the most ancient texts of the Rabbis and especially the Kabbalah have to say about it?

We thus penetrate the secrets of the Kabbalah, the so-called occult and often forbidden books, but which reflect the true intention of the scribes of the Old Testament: to deconstruct the simple meaning of the Torah and return to an Osirian cosmogony. The text informs us that the three Patriarchs are not men who lived historically. They form a solar cosmogony, the cosmogony recomposing the light in the Garden of Eden. Jacob is the sun, Israel is God himself... Jacob is a new Adam, the solar god fighting every day, Esau the god of darkness.

"The sun is Jacob"[2]

---

2   Le Zohar, Genèse, tome III, Vayéchev, Mikets, collection «les dix paroles ». Traduit par Charles Mopsik. Verdier, 1991, p. 20

"Adam (man) is, of course, Israel"[3]

Jacob's fight against the Angel is then deciphered in the books of the Zohar (constituting the Kabbalah) - the secret memory of the scribes or initiates of the Bible - as a fight of the light (Jacob, as in the Osirian myth, the kings of Egypt symbolize the sun and the moon) against the powers of darkness (Esau). Let us not forget that in the symbolism of the Kabbalah, as in the symbolism of hieroglyphics, darkness represents the enemies, the invaders, the allies of Set or the serpent Apophys. For this reason, rabbinic commentaries equate Esau with the enemies of Yahweh, with the Romans, with Rome's power over the Jews and Israel. However, in the context of the Septuagint, and the Kabbalah, Esau symbolizes the darkness of Greek rule over the Nile Valley.

The Zohar reports that Jacob/Israel was named TAM, the Perfect Man - the name of Atum -, embodied the sun of the day (like Horus), while Esau, the Red Man (Esau is named Edom = red), embodied the darkness of creation. Thus, Rome and Greece participate in the darkness of the seven days of the creation of the world, Esau being the celestial serpent is assimilated to the biblical tohu-bohu and darkness:

"The darkness (Isaac) overcomes the face of the abyss (Esau)." [4]

"And Elohim called the light «day» (Gen. 1:5) refers to Jacob. «And the darkness he called «night» refers to Esau. «And it was evening» refers to Esau, «And it was morning» refers to Jacob"[5]

Now, the primordial darkness is identified with ancient Greece. Jacob plays the role of Osiris fighting against the obscurantism of Hellenization, by the forced imposition of the Septuagint.

---

3   Le Zohar, Cantique des Cantiques. Collection «les dix paroles ». Verdier, 1999. P., p. 162.

4 Le Zohar, tome I, op. cit., Traduit par Charles Mopsik. Verdier, 1981, p. 98.

5 Midrach Rabba, tome I, Genèse Rabba. Collection «les dix paroles ». Verdier, 1987. P. 52 § 3.

ATOUM/TAM/OSIRIS/ISRA-GOD wrestling every night against Apophys, the twisted serpent of darkness.

Let's explore further the decoding of the texts, to discover the «Egyptian» symbols. Jacob /TAM/ATOUM is described either as the sun or as the serpent, while Esau exclusively symbolizes the serpent of the Garden of Eden named Samael, or the Angel Samal riding a serpent. My whole scene is as if the scene where Jacob was fighting the famous serpent Nahash was taking place in the Garden of Eden.

"See: one [Esau] is the aspect that rides the serpent. The other [Jacob] is the aspect that rides the perfect and holy throne, the side of the sun to mate with the moon. Come and see: Esau having followed in the wake of the serpent, Jacob behaved towards him in a crooked manner, like a serpent, that cunning being with a sinuous gait, according to the words ''the serpent was cunning etc." (Gen. 3:1) i.e., full of subterfuge - Jacob therefore acted towards Esau like a serpent, this was necessary so that he would draw Esau towards the serpent and separate himself from him...." [6]

---

6   Le Zohar, tome II, collection « les dix paroles ». Traduit par Charles Mopsik. Vayera, Hayé Sarah, Toldot, Vayetsé, Vayichlah. Verdier, 1984. P. 252.

As we have said, in the language of Kabbalah, Jacob symbolizes the sun. But also the Tree of Life enthroned in the center of the Garden of Eden, royalty, the throne, Yahweh himself. All these symbols are inscribed in the hieroglyphics, bringing to light the true hidden meaning of the biblical text. It is said that Esau's famous heel symbolized the lower degrees or quelipot. Jacob had to **«push Esau away, that is, the outer side of the "Sephirotic Tree"**[7] which is the image of the Tree of Life in the Garden of Eden.

The Zohar specifies that Esau is the image of the primordial serpent, also called the crooked serpent.

"Jacob knew that Esau was destined to be allied with the crooked serpent, so in all his actions he behaved towards him like a crooked serpent"[8]

Thus, Jacob is not a patriarch, but a god. He is the hidden memory of the god of the Nile Valley fighting the serpent of darkness. The Bible is then a fundamentally polytheistic document.

Several passages in the Zohar reveal that Jacob is the image of the true divinity of the Children of Israel, of the Jews and consequently of the Christians and Muslims.

"The Holy One, blessed be He, called Jacob EL (God). He said to him, ''I am the god of those above, you are the god of those below"[9]

---

7   Ibidem, p. 252, notes 90-92.

8   Ibidem, p. 253.

9   Le Zohar, tome II, collection « les dix paroles ». Traduit par Charles Mopsik. Vayera, Hayé Sarah, Toldot, Vayetsé, Vayichlah. Verdier, 1984. P. 252.

ISRAEL IS THE NAME OF YAHWEH ELOHIM, CHIEF OF THE FORTY-TWO ANGELS OF THE HEAVENLY COURT = OSIRIS

According to Kabbalah, the body of work revealing the secrets of the Old Testament, Jacob, who became Israel, is presented as the old man sitting on the throne of God in Ezekiel's vision. Israel is the Man (Adam, the first man) with four faces, man, bull, lion and eagle. Israel is, unquestionably - once again - the image of Osiris. Israel is that unique and multiple character, the image of Yahweh or Elohim, who descended into Egypt with his heavenly tribunal, composed of forty-two angels. The very name of God is the name «Israel», composed of forty-two letters, forming the symbolic body of the heavenly elder...

As Osiris grandson of Tam (Atum) formed a perfect body with the forty-two judges of the heavenly court, Jacob/Israel is at the same time God and Man, the perfect Man named Tam' in the Torah... as Atum himself...

"In truth, «Israel came to Egypt» is about the Holy One blessed be He"[10]

"Rabbi Simeon says: "When the Shekhinah [the Spirit of God, Yahweh/Elohim] **came down to Egypt, it took the form of a Haya** [the living power of God = the Ankh of the Egyptians] **WHO BEARS THE NAME OF ISRAEL, and whose image resembles that of the old man (from above). Forty-two holy angels for the service of the Shekhina came down with her. Each of these angels bears a sacred letter of the divine name composed of forty-two letters."**[11]

---

10   Le Zohar, Genèse, tome III, Vayéchev, Mikets, collection 'les dix paroles'. Traduit par Charles Mopsik. Verdier, 1991, p. 286, sq.

11   Zohar, tome III. Le livre de la splendeur. Par Jean de Pauly. Éditions Maisonneuve & Larose, 1985. P. 74.

Israel is indeed the name of Yahweh, the Shekhina, the name of the god of the Nile Valley. The latter descends to Egypt with his forty-two angels. This means that the god of Egypt, Israel, descends to accomplish harmony, flooding, fertility, etc. Following the example of Osiris and his forty-two judges, symbols of justice and cohesion of the world, it is said in the Zohar that the forty-two letters from the serpent not only form the sacred crown of God, but also that they were melted together to create the earth which was tohu-bohu:

"The earth was Tohu and Bohu» (Gen. 1:2) it did not become consistent as long as it remained in the state of Tohu-Bohu, it remained so until the world was inscribed with forty-two letters, it could then remain. These letters form the crown of the holy name. When these letters were fused together [...] the world could finally exist... With the staff of the great serpent they struck the ground...">[12]

The English version differs, stating that «the letters struggled against the great serpent» to build the world. Finally, the forty-two letters form the forty-two pieces of the Body of Israel/Osiris, the integrity of the body of God. This cosmogonic Body of Israel/Osiris refuses to be dismembered, as Osiris was dismembered by his brother Set. The forty-two letters seek the necessary cohesion to fight against the abyss where the great serpent Leviathan reigns... With regard to the myth of Osiris fighting against the serpent Aepep to accomplish the rebirth of the world, it is necessary to note the precision with which the myth of Osiris has remained fixed in the Kabbalah under the secret name of the myth of Israel... What about the kings of Israel, the royalty and the crowns, in comparison with the primitive serpent? It is difficult to imagine that the god of the Bible named Elohim אלֹהִים - from the very first verse of the Bible - was actually named Raâ, the name of the god of Egypt worshipped in Heliopolis. And yet, Elohim was really called Raâ! It is a verse in the book of Samuel that reveals this to us.

---

12   Le Zohar, tome I, collection 'les dix paroles'. Traduit par Charles Mopsik. Verdier, 1981, p. 172.

"In the past in Israel, this is what people said when they went to consult Elohim: אֱלֹהִים "Let us go to the seer" (ROE or RAÂ which gave the word ROI), because instead of «prophet» as today, they used to say «seer (RAÂ)" (Samuel IX, 9)

To understand the immense significance of this verse, it is necessary to remember that the *Israel of old*, so called in the Book of Samuel, was none other than the valley of the Nile renamed «Egypt» by the Greeks. Ra or Ra'a was the «seeing» god represented by the solar eye. Akhenaten, worshipper of Ra-Aton, proclaimed himself ''Great of the Seers''.

By simply reading this verse in Hebrew, without taking into account the vowels, Elohim אֱלֹהִים is not only said Roé, origin of the word "King", 'ROI' in French, but Raâ הראה , the name of the god Raâ of IS-RÂ-EL which is none other than the name of Egypt. Even if this notion may seem new, IS-RÂ-EL, as we shall see, is the name of the Nile, the name of Osiris. The Latin, French and other translations are insufficient, because they are based on a Greek reading and not a Hebrew reading.

In the past in Israel, this is what people said when they went to consult Elohim: "Let us go to ARAÂ הראה, for instead of "prophet" as today they used to say ''ARAÂ'' הראה. (Samuel IX, 9)

Knowing that Ra designates the sacred falcon of the Nile valley, in the form Ra-Horus of the two horizons (Ra-Horakhty), Israel is also a bird of prey, the Zohar states:

"The figure of the eagle has a central position in Ezekiel's vision; the eagle alludes to Jacob."[13]

One commentary refers directly to the falcon Ra'a ראה, the favorite bird of Jacob/Israel, the solar emblem of Jacob coveted by Esau:

---

13   Le Zohar, tome II, collection «les dix paroles', p. 126.

"According to Bahya, Jacob sent him a falcon s רֵאָה Ra'a, Esau's favorite bird, the one he liked to ''hold in his hand."[14]

The Bible, the Old Testament thus shows that Raâ was the ancient name of Elohim, and the name of the falcon of Jacob/ Israel, the cosmic bird of the sun symbolizing the transmission of the light of the world, but also the "relay" expressing the passage from night to day.

To give another view, the fight between Jacob and the Angel ends with the victory at daybreak of Jacob, who becomes Israel = IS - RÂ - ELOHIM. This myth conceals an Osirian, cosmic scenography, a cosmogony, between two gods, Jacob, the sun, and Esau, who would be the celestial serpent of darkness named Amalek (the King of Darkness) or, as the Kabbalah says, Samael. «Jacob is the sun and Esau is the serpent, as Charles Mopsik attests:

"The Zohar identifies the serpent with Samael, who is also the guardian angel of Esau (Edom), the ancestor of the Romans and after them of Christianity (Zohar 1, 144 b, 170 a)"[15]

It must be understood here that the enemies of Egypt are symbolized by the twisted serpent that can be found in several tombs in the Valley of the Kings. In this case the serpent of darkness. As we have said, Esau represents Rome, but before that, in the context of the Septuagint, Esau symbolizes Assyria, Babylonia, and especially the Greek domination of Egypt. Esau is named Edom' meaning «Man» and «Red» like Atum the god of the Nile valley, often represented in red in the tombs of the Valley of the Kings, representing God reigning over darkness.

Thus, the characters of the Bible are not human, but gods, Elohim. They conceal a real ''Egyptian'' or Osirian cosmogony,

---

14   Élie Munk, La voix de la Thora. Le Deutéronome, op. cit., p. 338, voire la note du verset 14.

15   Le Zohar, Lamentations. Collection « les dix paroles ». Verdier, 2000, p. 136.

where the cosmic powers of light against darkness, sometimes at war, sometimes at peace, to explain the cyclic passage from day to night and from night to day. The Kabbalah confirms that Jacob ISRAEL is a solar man, whose body, like Osiris, forms a ''Trinity'' with Abraham as his right arm, Isaac as his left arm and Jacob as his body:

"Observe what was the merit of Jacob, for Samael came with the design to eliminate the world; that night was the night the moon was created"[16]

"Jacob prevailed, his reign being exercised by day"[17]

"That very night Jacob remained solitary, since when the moon is defective the evil serpent becomes stronger and dominates. Then came Samael, who accused him, seeking to expel him from the world. Jacob, however, was strong on all sides, from Isaac's as well as from Abraham's. Samael [the Angel, the serpent] attacked him on the right side, he saw Abraham, strong with the power of the day on the right side, that of Generosity. He attacked from the left side and saw Isaac, strong of the hard justice. He attacked the body and saw Jacob, strong of the two aforementioned sides which surrounded him on both sides, and immediately: «he saw that he could not do anything against him and touched the hollow of his hip"[18]

Thus we can only observe that. The scribes of the Bible managed to slip symbols and names of "Egyptian" gods into the reading of the Hebrew Torah. Let us emphasize this: although the rabbinic tradition compares the character of Esau to Rome and Christianity, the darkness of creation is attributed to Greece by the Talmud. This means that the Septuagint, the Torah, the Bible and later the Gospels, were written in reaction

---

16   Le Zohar, tome II, collection «les dix paroles ». Traduit par Charles Mopsik. Verdier, 1987, p. 292.

17   Le Zohar, tome II, collection «les dix paroles ». Traduit par Charles Mopsik. Verdier, 1987, p. 292.

18 Le Zohar, tome II, collection «les dix paroles ». Traduit par Charles Mopsik. Verdier, 1987, p. .

to the invasions of the Nile Valley. The priests of Osiris - as well as the early Jewish Kabbalists, for they are the same - saw them as a victory of the serpent of darkness over the Light. Now, after the Assyrians and Babylonians, Greece and Rome are the great destroyers of the civilization of the Nile Valley. It must be noted that in history, no «Egyptian» has ever reacted, never deplored, never fought the enemies of Egypt! The latter are always the enemies of the Yods, of the Jews, who were massacred, deported, exiled, humiliated, subjugated. In order to survive, they reorganized themselves into armies and waged war against them. They hid the secret of Osiris in the Kabbalah.

Rashi states that Jacob and Esau were already fighting in their mother's womb for the domination of the world and the domination of the sun. The Zohar also reports that Jacob/Israel is named TAM, the Perfect Man and the Solar Man. As we have seen, Atum is the perfect man, also embodying the sun of the day (like Horus), while Esau, the red man (Esau is named Edom = red), embodying darkness, the serpent, even the pig... as was Seth, the red man, the enemy brother of Osiris until the Late Period. These elements placed end to end allow us to understand that Jacob hides the sun, the falcon RAÂ the perfect man TAM, plays the symbolic role of Atum... Like Atum, the Egyptian god is also represented by a red man and Horus/Osiris...

Indeed, the sun plays the role of a "relay falcon" that Jacob/Israel transmits to Esau/Edom, which is found in the Osirian myth personified in the pyramid of Khenzer: Atum, the red man TAM' in hieroglyphs, the night sun, transmits the sacred falcon RAÂ to Horus, the Son of RÂ, IS-RÂ, the day sun. It is no longer a simple fight between a shepherd and an angel, but scenography found in the Valley of the Kings, where two deities confront each other to maintain the cosmic order. Let us observe carefully the image of the pyramid of Khenzer where Yahu symbolizes the winged sun that we have identified with the power of Yahu. Below, we can see on the left Horus (Hor in hieroglyphic, designates the bearer of light) the son of Osiris, who transfers the solar falcon to Atum located on the right. The falcon serves here as a relay, the cyclical passage of the sun from the world of the night to the world of the day.

The Resurrection of the sun is done by the transfer of the divine falcon. By exploring the deepest meaning of the Scriptures, we travel to the heart of the great secret of the pyramids.

Transfer of the solar falcon bird RÂ or IS-RÂ from Horus (during the day) to Atum (TAM, at night). Pyramid of Khenzer.

Horus (Hor in hieroglyphs and Hor in Hebrew meaning the primitive light) the Son transfers the solar falcon to Atum or TAM - the man in red - the Father to realize the Resurrection of the Father, the new Horus, the new sun, the passage from day to night. We understand that after this nocturnal combat that we find in the tombs of the Valley of the Kings, Jacob is named Israel, meaning at the same time in the Bible Son of God and the one who fights against Elohim, and Sun in the Kabbalah, attributes that are those of Osiris IS-RÂ-GOD.

"You shall say to Pharaoh, Thus says the LORD: Israel is my Son, my Firstborn" (Exode V, 22, 23)

"Israel will be called "SON OF KINGS" [19] **= SA-RÂ**

All this information confirms that the Bible and Israel are the heritage of the wisdoms of Toth, the Egyptian god symbol of knowledge. Israel and Egypt were originally one and the same entity. Was there a rupture between the Jews and history, as the Kabbalist Charles Mopsik points out? Contrary to the common opinion that equates the land of Israel with the limited land of Canaan given by God to the Children of Israel, the Bible points to the heritage of Abraham:

On that day the LORD made a covenant with Abram, and said, I give this land to your seed, from the river of Egypt to the great river, the Euphrates river (Genesis 15:18), the borders of the land of Israel, from the Nile to the Euphrates (Deuteronomy XI:24).

This statement is taken up by the Babylonian Talmud:

"The land of Israel extends from the Nile to the Euphrates»: it is the figure of the Garden of Eden", [20]

---

19   Le Zohar, tome I, collection "les dix paroles ». Traduit par Charles Mopsik. Verdier, 1981,   p. 157.

20   *Aggadoth du Talmud de Babylone*. La source de Jacob/ 'Ein Yaakov. Collection « Les dix paroles », Verdier, 1982, *B. B. 74 b.*

THE WISDOM OF EGYPT
IS THE WISDOM OF ISRAEL

In the millennium before the advent of Christianity, the enemies of Israel mentioned in the Bible and Jewish tradition are the Assyrians, Babylonians, Greeks and Romans. These four civilizations are, as if by chance, the same invaders of ancient Egypt, thus of Osiris, the invaders of the Nile Valley. While for more than two millennia Egypt has been structured as a state, as a united nation, it is curious that the reaction of the ''Egyptians'' to the invasions is felt only by the Jews... For the reason that they did not bear the name of Egyptians. Only the Jews seem to be concerned by the immense suffering resulting from the invasions and humiliations...

The commentaries of the rabbis, who from Roman times onwards formed the Midrash and the Talmud, are eloquent on this subject. It is said that the Torah, especially the going out of Egypt, is a huge metaphor, an allusion to the four great powers mentioned above, who had invaded «Judea, Israel, Jerusalem» following the example of King Nebuchadnezzar, whereas in history, these monarchs had invaded and plundered the entire Nile Valley, causing said four exiles, four successive deportations of the Jews (no deportation of «Egyptians» on the horizon...) from the seventh century B.C. onwards. Have the Jews so lost the memory of their past? An entire passage in TIKUNE AZOHAR[21] explains, through the biblical text, the great secret of the first lost Torah, the one that contained the wisdoms and commandments of the true Israel. It is clearly explained that the story of the Children of Israel, the myth of Adam and Eve expelled from paradise for having consumed the fruit of the Tree of Knowledge of Good and Evil, is a coding, a scaffolding, a setting up of the expulsion of the Children of Israel from Egypt.

---

21   Le Zohar, tome I, collection « les dix paroles ». Traduit par Charles Mopsik. Verdier, 1981, p. 163 § 28b.

Banishment from paradise/Egypt brilliantly encrypted in the stories of Noah, Abraham, Sodom and Gomorrah, Jacob, Moses. After being expelled from the land of Egypt, after worshipping the golden calf, the Children of Israel ''ate and drank'', then they found themselves ''naked'', their eyes became blinded, they sewed themselves clothes made of fig leaves, they lost all memory, they forgot the first Torah, the oral Torah, the Torah broken by Moses... like Adam in the Garden of Eden, because the story of Adam is the story of Israel, says the Kabbalah...

It must be emphasized once again: according to archaeologists, there is not the slightest trace of the Hebrews of the Bible, not a word about a distant history of the slavery of the Children of Israel at the time of the ancient kings of the Nile Valley. One would have thought that the rabbinic commentaries had located the slavery of the Children of Israel in the remote times of the ancient kings Khufu, Uzzah, Thutmose, Amenophis, Akhenaten, Ramses, etc., but this is not so, The story told in the Bible, in particular the slavery of the Hebrews under the power of Pharaoh, is related, on the contrary, in a close relationship, welded, in the form of metaphors or parables, to the secular enemies, invaders of the land of SA-RÂ called ''Egypt'', enemies rightly qualified as responsible for the exile of Israel! For history shows that the same Assyrians, Babylonians, Greeks and Romans successively invaded, dominated, subjugated and humiliated the inhabitants of the Nile Valley. The enemies of Egypt are indeed the same as the enemies of Israel. This is why Kabbalah states that **all of Egypt was in bondage; for it was the most humble of all the countries**[22]...

And for good reason, Egyptian wisdom was the wisdom of God: the Garden of Eden and its river, the Nile named Pishon', form the allegory of Egypt, of the Nile whose drops symbolized the ancient Egyptian wisdom that has disappeared, forever scattered among the other rivers, the nations:

---

22   Zohar, tome III. *Le livre de la splendeur*. Par Jean de Pauly. Maisonneuve & Larose, 1985, p. 24.

"What is the meaning of this verse: (the River) that unites all the others is the Pishon', it flows into the land of Egypt and for this reason there was more wisdom in Egypt than in the rest of the world. When the sentence, stipulating the annihilation of the Egyptian wisdom, was decreed, the Holy One, blessed be He, took the said drops [Egyptian wisdom] **and threw them into the garden, into the river of the Garden of Eden** [the Nile]... ... **Now, this river gave birth to four other rivers, and one unifying one that was born from it was Pishon' [the Nile]. Since the drops of Eden have been taken away so that they no longer flow out of the garden, the wisdom of Egypt perishes."[23]**

The four separate rivers of the Nile formed the allegory of the death of Egyptian civilization, of the wisdom of Egypt broken because of the four exiles. The four enemy civilizations of Egypt and Israel are all compared to darkness, all qualified as idolaters by the Kabbalah, the Talmud, which will later be confirmed by the Koran...

They embody both the darkness and obscurantism that scattered the light of Israel and caused the exile of this light, which is none other than the ancient Egyptian wisdom. The scattered divine light was a metaphor for the exile of the Jewish people. If the religion of the Jews is a transformation, an inversion by Moses of the Egyptian religion, as Apion and Manetho affirm, if the Hebrews or Children of Israel are the true heirs of the Egyptian wisdom and of the land of Egypt, then the whole civilization of the Nile valley, populated by those whom we have called for more than two millennia "ancient Egyptians" bore another name, another History. We will now see what the myth of Noah conceals. Noah was not saved by Yahweh, but expelled from the Garden of Eden, symbol of the expulsion from Egypt.

---

23   Le Zohar, tome II, collection «les dix paroles ». Traduit par Charles Mopsik. Vayera, Hayé Sarah, Toldot, Vayetsé, Vayichlah. Verdier, 1984, p. 207.

NOAH HAS BEEN CASTRATED AS OSIRIS

The myth of Noah, as explained in the Zohar, the book of Kabbalah, is radically different from the common, literal reading of the Bible or the Torah. It contains the scene of the curse of Canaan by Noah after he got drunk. Noah also «drank» the forbidden fruit like Adam. Noah's Ark would be an ''Edenic'' Ark, the lost Garden of Eden, voluntarily hidden by the scribes. Noah came out of the Ark, on Yahweh's order, cursed Canaan and found himself in the same conditions as Adam, driven out of the Garden of Eden by Yahweh, on an unknown land. The myth of Noah would then be a cryptic «sequel» to Adam's expulsion from the Garden of Eden. Is this the true message of Noah's Ark? Is Noah secretly claiming a return to the Garden of Eden? He would then symbolize the Children of Israel expelled from their Garden of Eden, Egypt, by Pharaoh... Let us explore the powerful metaphors of the biblical text in relation to original sin and the myth of Noah's castration, their relationship with the myth of Osiris, castrated by his brother Set and driven out of Egypt:

The sons of Noah who came out of the ark were Shem, Ham and Japheth; Ham was the father of Canaan. These are the three sons of Noah by whom the whole earth was populated. Noah, at first a farmer, planted a vineyard. He drank of its wine and became drunk, and he stood naked in the middle of his tent. Ham, the father of Canaan, saw his father's nakedness and went outside to tell his two brothers. Shem and Japheth [Japheth or Yapheth the Greek] **took the covering, spread it on their shoulders, and walking backwards covered the nakedness of their father, but did not see it, their faces being turned away. Noah awoke from his drunkenness and knew what his youngest son had done to him, and he said, «Cursed be Canaan! Let him be a slave to his brothers' slaves» (Gen. IX, 18-25).**

Does the message of the scribes mean that the fruit of the tree of the knowledge of good and evil has become the wine that causes the loss of memory, the fruit of the vine of Noah? The dramatic separation pictured by the expulsion of Adam and Eve will immediately cause the loss of the primitive light that illuminated the Garden of Eden... It is said that the serpent, cunning and jealous, had concocted a trap to kill Adam, thus to kill Israel, the light of the Garden of Eden. According to the Zohar, Adam and Eve ate grapes and not the famous forbidden fruit, generally assimilated to an apple:

"A tradition teaches us that Eve pressed grapes and gave them to Adam, bringing death to the whole world"[24] The Midrash Rabba confirms: **"It was grapes** [that Adam and Eve consumed], **according to the words: 'Their grapes are grapes of poison, bitter clusters than theirs. Serpent venom their wine"**[25]

"The primordial serpent entered into the branches of the said tree. He was the wine that was drunk..."[26]

Why did the fruit of original sin become grapes? To hide new information, inaccessible to the Ptolemies? We remember that in the first part of our trilogy, Noah sent back the raven and the dove from the Ark. Now the raven symbolizes the Assyrian and Babylonian invaders. The dove is precisely the hidden metaphor of the Children of Israel expelled from the Ark aka the Garden of Eden aka Egypt to the Greek exile. Indeed, the Zohar associates Noah's dove with Israel, or the Jews who were prisoners of the Greeks. Jews were driven out of their Garden of Eden. By twice sending the dove away from the Ark, Noah plays - only in this short passage - the role of Ptolemy expelling the Jews by the miraculous imposition of the Septuagint. Ptolemy aka Noah expels Israel (= Adam = the dove = the sun) from the Garden of Eden = Egypt.

---

24   Le Zohar, tome 1, collection 'les dix paroles'. Traduit par Charles Mopsik. Verdier, 1981. P. 201, 36a.

25   Midrach Rabba, tome I, Genèse Rabba. Collection «les dix paroles ». Verdier, 1987, p 184, chap. 15 § 7.

26 Ibidem,.

In this text, Noah sends the exiled dove/Israel back to Babel and forbids it to turn back, thus closing the access to the Garden of Eden. In the secret symbolism, Noah's Ark, TEBAH in Hebrew, conceals the name of Thebes. Noah's Ark becomes a huge Ark of the Covenant ARONE of Thebes, that is to say the universal sarcophagus, the symbolic place where all the animals of creation and men gathered to be dispersed after the flood. This implies that Noah went to the Garden of Eden to recover the animals of creation. Noah would have reconstructed the ark as a mini replica of the Garden of Eden[27].

But the dove returns to the ark, with a blade of grass from the Garden of Eden, the Kabbalah tells us, and repents of its fault. The dove having again transgressed the Law, Noah sends it (Israel) back into Greek exile. **ISRAEL'S EXILE TO BABEL AND THEREFORE THE BIBLE - THE TORAH - IS THUS CONNECTED TO GREEK RULE:**

"Rabbi Pinhas continued: The Holy One, blessed be He, who wished to test Israel sent them to Babel according to the expression «He sent the dove» [from the ark = from the Garden of Eden] (Gen 8:8). **The latter refers to the Community of Israel. Now see what the text adds: «And she found no place to put the sole of her foot** [the community of Israel no longer finds its Garden of Eden]. **The king of Babel made his yoke heavy by famine, thirst and the extermination of many righteous, but because of the burden of this yoke, ''She returned to Him in the Ark'' the Community of Israel returned to Him and He accepted her. When it failed as before, He exiled it again, according to the words, «He sent the dove back again» (Id. v. 10) to another exile caused by Greece, which according to Rabbi Yehuda made the face of Israel as dark as the bottom of a cauldron"[28]**

---

27 Cf. Midrach Rabba, tome I, Genèse Rabba. Collection «les dix paroles ». Verdier, 1987, chap. 32 p. 332 § 4 note 10.

28 Le Zohar, tome 1, collection 'les dix paroles'. Verdier, 1981. P. 641, 23c.

The grape produces wine and wine is compared to the snake's venom, because it has the virtue of making Noah lose his memory, who will then play the role of Adam. A similarity of small successive «stories» that can be deciphered like an oracle. **The text sheds light on the true meaning of the exit from Egypt, which is in fact an expulsion, the expulsion of an entire people, of an entire civilization from the Nile Valley. This is the proof that the Septuagint Bible and then the Torah were written during the Greek domination.**

Adam has to work the land after being driven out of paradise. Noah gets out of the ark and works the land, planting a vineyard - taken from the Garden of Eden, thus a new Israel - on the newly emerged land (Noah 9, XX). The Zohar states that this vine came from the Garden of Eden:

"It comes from the Garden of Eden where it was driven out [torn out], Noah now plants it here... ... Rabbi Simeon says: In this verse is one of the secrets of Wisdom. When Noah wanted to probe the fault of the first man, not with the intention of committing it, but in order to understand it and thus rid the world of it, he did not succeed at first. So he pressed the grapes to continue his research on the vine..."[29]

Obviously, the myth of Noah conceals a complement of information to the story of Adam. As if Noah had wanted, by replanting a vineyard, to reconstitute the Garden of Eden, to repair Adam's fault and to revoke, to conjure up, to exorcise the divine curse, in order to re-establish himself in the Garden of Eden with his seventy children, symbolizing the seventy sons of Jacob alias Israel, thus the twelve tribes of Israel expelled from Egypt:

Then God spoke to Noah, saying, ''Get out of the Ark, you and your wife, your sons and your sons' wives with you'' (Gen. 8:15-16).

---

29   Le Zohar, tome 1, collection 'les dix paroles'. Traduit par Charles Mopsik. Verdier, 1981. P. 370, 73a.

Is this the hidden expulsion of Noah and his family, of Israel, from the Garden of Eden? As soon as he got out of the Ark, **"Noah built an altar": This is the altar on which the first man (Adam) sacrificed"**[30]... Noah tries, desperately, to reconstitute the paradise lost in the land of Canaan... But then, as Adam crunches the forbidden fruit, Noah drinks the wine coming from this edenic vine, Noah then realizes his nakedness (like Adam) and sexual desires are reborn in him. While it is believed that Noah was saved by Yahweh because the earth was corrupted, the Zohar reveals the other reason. Noah is exiled for drinking the new forbidden fruit, and this exile extends to the tribes of Israel exiled from Egypt. Through the metaphor of the wine drunk by Noah, a different and more extensive version of original sin is hidden. Indeed, wine replaces the fruit of the forbidden tree. It is the forbidden drink of the Garden of Eden that causes Noah to lose the memory of the past. As if after drinking the wine, Noah's eyes were opened and he found himself naked, like Adam and Eve. But in this case, Noah wakes up and realizes that he is already expelled from the Garden of Eden. This means that Noah is playing the role of the Children of Israel expelled from Egypt. This is the reason why he will curse Canaan. Let us quote the Zohar:

"Because of the wine, he was naked and had a great desire to sleep with his wife. He was naked before his children... ...Noah was exiled because he drank too much wine. His children were also exiled like the ten tribes who drank much wine..."[31]

The rest of the text of the Zohar evokes two other tribes, Benjamin and Judah (=Yehoudah), also exiled because of the fault of Noah... As we have said, Adam, Noah, Abraham, Jacob and Joseph all have the face of Adam and the soul of Israel. Everything happens as if the original fault of Adam had

---

30   Ibidem, 69b, p. 354.

31   *Le commentaire sur la Torah. Jacob Ben Isaac Achkenazi de Janow.*, col. 'les dix paroles'. Traduit par Jean Baumgarten. Verdier, 1987, p. 89.

become the fault of Noah. As if all the stories in the Torah were based on the vision of the lost Garden of Eden, with the desire to return there. As if by drinking wine, Noah had tried to restore the catharsis, to cancel the divine curse of God, which ordered the Children of Israel never to return to Egypt... But it is the opposite effect which occurs: like the Tree of the Knowledge of Good and Evil, the wine consumed by Noah leads to the exile of the Children of Israel... Ark is titled THEBA in Hebrew, the Greek name for Thebes. Noah exits the Ark from the ancient Thebes and the ancient edenic covenant of Israel/Osiris, falsely qualified as idolatry. The sacred vine, named Israel, uprooted from Eden/Egypt would then mean that the god who bears the name Israel/Osiris was uprooted, exiled by the Greeks, from the Nile Valley to try to fulfill himself as Israel among the nations... We understand why, for Kabbalah, Noah's ark conceals Japheth, Greece, Theba, the expulsion of Thebes, the Old Covenant before the expulsion of the Children of Israel from the Nile Valley. In the lexicon of Kabbalah, the Ark is none other than the first lost Ark of the Covenant of Israel before the original sin:

"What is the Ark [Noah's "Theba»"Ark]**? It is the Ark of the Covenant."**[32]

Another passage in the Zohar states that Noah's Ark is none other than a sarcophagus containing the body of Man, Joseph's... **"Notice that the holy side is called "Ark of the Covenant", and it is appropriate to enclose the body of Man in it. That is why the great zealots** [the wise men, the kings] **had been enclosed in a sarcophagus after death."**[33]

We have said it, while the Bible lets us believe that Noah comes from a totally corrupted world, which must die drowned by the will of Kyrios/Yahweh. With, one suspects, thousands of innocent women and children, something impossible historically.

---

32   Le Zohar, tome 1, op. cit., 59b, p. 302.
33   Le Zohar, tome IV, Le livre de la splendeur, op. cit., p. 225.

Let us resume our investigation. The Zohar directly relates Noah's words to the curse of the serpent in the Garden of Eden after the original sin. After drinking the wine from the vine in the Garden of Eden, Noah, already the father of three children, finds himself naked, like Adam, and feels the desire to procreate. But Ham, the father of Canaan, intervenes and casts a curse on Noah:

"By stripping himself, Noah gave place to the dominion of Canaan; and as he was a righteous man by the secret of the Covenant, Ham , the father of Canaan castrated him... ..."Cursed be Canaan, he shall be a slave of slaves": these words correspond to those addressed to the serpent: "Cursed be you among all the animals" (Gen. 3:14)"[34]

At this level of interpretation, Canaan is identified with the Serpent of the Garden of Eden. The Serpent and Canaan participate in the immense deception contained in the story of the expulsion from the Garden of Eden. The cunning serpent alias Ptolemy Philadelphus who in the Septuagint will subtly extort from the Jews Yudaios their ancestral land of the Nile Valley in exchange for Canaan... Instead, Noah receives a land that he will symbolically curse: Canaan. Naked Noah means in secret that he has lost his first Law, his first Torah, ...his original land. Noah lost the Tree of Life, his past, his family tree, his ancestral land. Through the new «original sin» of Noah, the expulsion and exile, the suffering of Israel, the memory of Thebes and the universal sarcophagus are hidden... It is obvious: the story of the symbolic castration of Noah in the Kabbalah was written to encrypt the exile of Israel from the Garden of Eden in the context of Hellenization and the creation of a new myth of Osiris. It is thus the exile of the real Egyptians to the new land of Canaan, a land that Noah will curse for having been expelled from the Garden of Eden. The message becomes clearer, the whole history of the Children of Israel's exit from Egypt was a series of transcoding to be deciphered through Adam, Enoch, Noah, Abraham, Jacob,

---

34   Le Zohar, tome I, collection «les dix paroles ». Traduit par Charles Mopsik. Verdier, 1981, p. 371, 73 b.

Joseph, Moses, Jesus... The connection between the story of Noah and the story of Adam takes us even further into the mystery of Osiris. According to Charles Mopsik, the Zohar teaches that Noah is a cosmic man. Drinking the wine of the Garden of Eden, Noah symbolically drank, swallowed the primordial serpent of Genesis[35].

This allegory is capital, because it brings us back to the Ouroboros serpent, the celestial serpent of light which swallows the serpent of darkness and gives birth to the child Horus. Noah drinking the "serpent" wishes to get rid of the cunning serpent, to annihilate the original sin, to swallow the darkness of the flood in order to give birth. But the Bible tells us that Noah cursed Canaan, his grandson who had thwarted his plan. Canaan is the brother of Kush, Misraim and Put. Let's not forget that Canaan is also the land of the seven nations, the land promised by Moses to the Children of Israel leaving Egypt, the land of seventy nations. Canaan is the land that the Children of Israel will refuse, prisoners and condemned to die in the desert. Does Canaan, son of Noah and «promised» land, also hide the cursed serpent?

One immediately wonders why Noah curses Canaan when it is Ham (Canaan's father) who has done wrong. Why does Noah not curse the other three sons of Ham? Canaan unjustly becomes the slave of his three brothers Kush (Ethiopia), Misraim (Egypt), Put (Africa). Cursed Canaan becomes the slave country of Egypt, the country of the seventy nations...

However, Canaan is indeed the land of the seven nations, where milk and honey supposedly flow, where the Children of Israel settle, coming out of the slavery of Egypt... Noah's curse on Canaan is a reprise, a paraphrase of the curse of Kyrios alias Yahweh on the serpent of Genesis, a curse now linked to Canaan. According to the Zohar, Noah was castrated, either by his son Ham or by his grandson Canaan[36].

---

35   This metaphor of the swallowed snake is important, because in ancient Egypt, the kings and humanity (the child Horus) were born from the snake Ouroboros swallowing itself. The serpent thus forms the maternal placenta of the kings...

36   Other comments accuse Ham of having castrated Noah.

Canaan is in this context of the secrets of Kabbalah, the image of the serpent of Genesis cursed by God, Canaan is the castrating serpent cursed by Noah. If we decipher this passage, it would mean that the seventy-two scribes of Ptolemy also symbolically drank wine, the wine of the Septuagint: they too «stripped themselves», they lost the memory of the past as well as their first Torah, since they accepted Ptolemy's translation and distortions in the Septuagint, since the new promised land becomes Canaan at the expense of Egypt... Canaan becomes «the slave of his brothers» and consequently the slave of Mitzrayim, the slave of Ægyptos... The scribes explain to us that the exit from Egypt of Adam, of Noah, and we will see it of Abraham... It is the exit of the Children of Israel from Egypt to the cursed land of Canaan... This has nothing to do with the liberation of the so-called Hebrew slaves of Pharaoh by Moses, saved from the waters... A passage in the Zohar explains that the primitive land of Israel existed with primitive kings of Israel[37]. Another distinguishes Israel from Canaan:

"When the Children of Israel were worthy, the land was designated by this name: 'Land of Israel.' But when they were not worthy, the land was called by this other name: Land of Canaan"[38]

What about the lost phallus of Noah? Is there a correspondence with the phallus of Osiris? Without a doubt. Tradition reports that Noah is called ''Man of the Earth'', precisely because of his power to regenerate the vegetation and seeds destroyed by the salty waters of the flood.

While the phallus of Osiris was thrown into the Nile to make it the river of fertility, the phallus of Noah contains the original seed restoring fertility to the whole earth. Noah's phallus thus plays the same symbolic role as that of Osiris. But also Joseph, whom the Kabbalah identifies with the phallus of God - a phallus thrown into a waterless cistern that symbolizes Egypt

---

37   « These are the kings who reigned in the land of Edom before the children of Israel had a king. The scripture speaks of the early king and the early children of Israel ». Zohar, tome V. Le livre de la splendeur. Par Jean de Pauly. Maisonneuve & Larose, 1985, p. 334, 128a.

38   Ibidem, p. 369

empty of knowledge - restoring fertility to the land of Egypt.

According to Plutarch, the earth owed its fertility to **"the blood of those who had once fought with the gods and who, once fallen, had mixed their corpses with the earth and produced vines."**[39]

The waters of the Nile, especially during the flood, are seen as an allegory of the exhalations or effluvia of the phallus of Osiris thrown into the Nile by Set or of the nourishing blood of Osiris. Jan Assmann describes the annual flooding of the Nile **"as an organic liquid that flows from Osiris who was murdered and thrown into the water by Set."**[40]

We find this Osirian metaphor, obviously, with the Body and Blood of Christ linked to the earth, the symbolic Body of God. The bread (the Body) and the wine (the blood) symbolizing the material and spiritual nourishment of Christ and of humanity.

---

39   « The kings of Egypt themselves, as reported by Hecateus, drank wine only to the extent established by the Holy Scriptures », Plutarque, Isis et Osiris, op. cit., p. 35.

40   Jan Assmann. Mort et Au-delà dans l'Égypte ancienne. Éditions du Rocher, 2003, note 7 de la page 52.

THE CROWN OF THE GOD OF THE BIBLE IS THAT OF THE KINGS OF THE NILE VALLEY

Of course, what the reader learns in the course of these pages may seem quite new, even extraordinary, almost impossible to realize, since our conditioning about the Bible or the Torah is so deeply rooted in our knowledge acquired over more than two millennia.

But the notion of Israel takes us as far back as possible into the past of this grandiose civilization that is ancient Egypt. Thus, the statement of another geographical Israel is repeated in the Midrash Rabba: **"The land of Israel extends to the end of the River"**[41]. The Babylonian Talmud goes further, confirming that the land of Israel is the immense Garden of Eden: **"Four rivers surround Israel"**[42]. For the Kabbalah, the crown of the god of the Torah symbolizes the Nile, the first river of the Garden of Eden.

In the Kabbalah's view, **"the 'land of life' is built on water; for everything flows from the Supreme River that flows out of Eden, which forms a crown for the sacred King and nourishes the worlds"**[43]. The crown of God, of YAHWEH/YHVH/YAHOU/YOD-YOD/ADONAY is therefore formed by the sacred river, the Nile, the first river of the Garden of Eden. As was the crown of the kings of the Nile valley, formed by the serpent Uraeus, a metaphor for Osiris, the long serpent of the Nile, visible on the crown of Tutankhamen.

---

41   Midrach Rabba, tome I, *Genèse Rabba*. Collection «les dix paroles ». Verdier, 1987, p 190 note 15, chap. 16 § 3.

42   *Aggadoth du Talmud de Babylone.* Op. Cit., B.B. 74b.

43   Zohar, tome V. Le livre de la splendeur. Par Jean de Pauly. Maisonneuve & Larose, 1985, § 45b, p. 126.

Kabbalah:

the crown of God,

symbolizes the River.

Crown with the Nile snake of Tutankhamun.

According to Rabbi Meir, it is said that the princes and kings (who can only be the kings of Israel) lived and were buried in Egypt :

"As it is said 'as a garden of God, so is the land of Egypt' (Gen. 13-10), There is no land in all Egypt more fertile than Zoan, where many kings [the kings of Israel] **lived, as it is written: "Their princes are in Zoan (Is. 30:4)."**[44]

As we will see in these chapters, Kabbalah gives the explanation of the crown with the serpent of Amun that all the kings of Israel wore. But also the explanation of the double red and white crown of the God of the Bible, which was also worn by the «Pharaohs». These memories remained in the occult memory will bring many clarifications to modern Egyptology. They open the door to the discovery of Osiris = Israel.

---

44   *Aggadoth du Talmud de Babylone*. Op. cit., Ordre Nachim, Ketouboth, 112a, p. 669. Il semble que Tsoan' soit devenu Tsion'…

ISRAEL HAS TRIGGERED THE FIRST FLOOD OF THE NILE

Jacob's coming to Egypt ends with the blessing of Jacob renamed Israel and the first flood of the Nile: **Joseph brought Jacob his father, and they stood before Pharaoh. And Jacob blessed Pharaoh (Genesis XLVII, 7).**

And Jacob blessed Pharaoh again, and departed from before Pharaoh» (Genesis XLVII, 10). Here is Rashi's commentary from rabbinic tradition:

"And Jacob blessed Pharaoh". And what blessing did he give him? That the waters of the Nile should rise to his feet, for Egypt receives no rainwater. It is the Nile that waters it with its floods. From the moment he was blessed in this way, whenever Pharaoh came to stand by the Nile, its waters came up to meet him and irrigate the land (Midrash tan'chumah Nasso 26)."

The message of the scribes becomes clear, without ambiguity. By blessing Pharaoh, Jacob/Israel triggers the first flood, the foundation of all the civilization of the Nile valley, falsely called Egyptian. The scribes want to tell us that Jacob/Israel/Osiris blesses the ancient Israel triggering all the floods... It is interesting to note that the hieroglyph of the Nile and the flood reads YAKEB or YAKOB. This hieroglyph contains the Yod and the heel. In Hebrew, ''heel'' is said EKEV because Jacob had clung to the heel of Esau (which is also called Edom meaning ''Red'',

''blood'', ''darkness'') when he came out of his mother's womb, in order not to drown in the amniotic waters mixed with the blood of the maternal placenta. Rachel, mother of the twins Jacob and Esau, would symbolize the Misraim Matrix of the sun Israel fighting the Serpent Esau/Samael, according to the Kabbalah reading.

As we have said, the birth of Jacob clinging to Esau forms a cosmogonic battle for world domination, according to Rashi. The birth of Jacob/Israel would then be an allegory of the exit from Egypt from darkness to light, the sun against the Serpent... The Hebrew name of Jacob, YAAKOB, designates the flood. As we have seen, Jacob/Israel is the solar god bringing the flood.

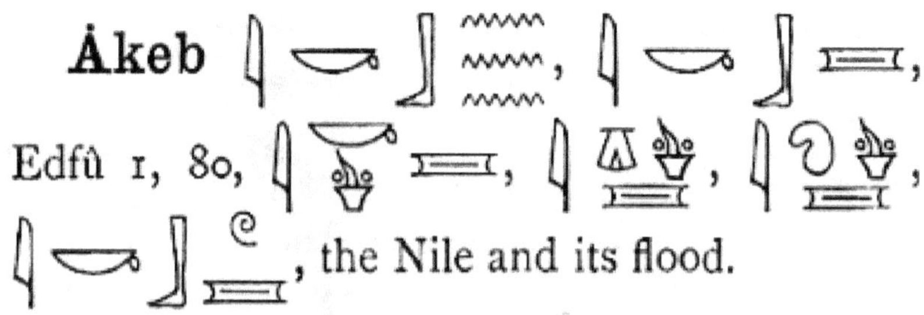

Yakob hieroglyphs of the Nile and the flood[45]

According to this commentary from the memory of the priests of the Nile Valley, the very first flooding of the Nile did not occur until the blessing of Jacob renamed Israel. This means that Israel has the attributes of Osiris. Thus, Jacob/Israel/Sun/Flood does not only refer to a Patriarch, but to the god of Egypt, which is confirmed by another Kabbalah text, which states that Israel descended into Egypt is God himself, the divine Shekhina with two wings (i.e. the winged sun). Jacob alias Israel is a cosmogonic character hiding the sun and God himself:

"In truth, "Israel came to Egypt" is about the

the Holy One blessed be he "[46]

"The sun is Jacob (Israel)"[47]

---

45 Egyptian hieroglyphic dictionary. Wallis Budge, Dover Publications, inc, New York. Published by General publishing Company, 1978, p. 95 a. L'inondation se dit également AGEB ou AKAB, ibidem, p. 12a.

46 Le Zohar, Genèse, tome III, Vayéchev, Mikets, collection 'les dix paroles'. Traduit par Charles Mopsik. Verdier, 1991, p. 286, sq.

47 Le Zohar, Genèse, tome III, Op. Cit., Verdier, 1991, p. 207.

THE TOMB OF ISRAEL IS THE TOMB OF OSIRIS

Before exploring the great secret of the tomb of Osiris, and to understand the capital importance of the discovery Osiris = Israel, it is appropriate to return to the burial of Saul, first king of Israel. Does this burial conceal the Osirian procession of a king of Egypt? As we will see in the next chapters, Kabbalah reveals that Saul wore the crown of the serpent of Amon, the serpent of the king named Nahash the Ammonite. It is said that Saul's body was embalmed, as were all the kings of Israel, and his coffin was paraded throughout Israel as in the processions of Osiris:

"...no vermin had touched them, and about them it is written "He keeps all his bones, not one of them is broken" (Ps. 34:21). They took the bones of Saul and his son Jonathan, put them in a coffin and crossed the Jordan, according to the verse "And they buried the bones of Saul and Jonathan his son... and they did all that the king commanded" (II Sam. 21:14). What did he command? That Saul's coffin should be carried to all the borders of Israel, to every tribe. And whenever Saul's coffin entered the border of any tribe, the people went out with wives, sons and daughters, and showed him gratitude and favor, so that they might be discharged from the debt of gratitude to him."[48]

What country "Israel" is it about? It is obviously a transposition of the Osirian processions supposedly along the Jordan, whereas these were along the Nile. The scribes do not specify it. But we have just seen that Saul is a kind of Christ, an Osiris, the image of the King "ISRA-EL" who triggered the first flood of the

---

48   Chapitres de Rabbi Éliézer. Pirké de Rabbi Éliézer. Collection Les Dix Paroles. Éditions Verdier, 1983, p. 108-109.

Nile. Thus, the only bural that corresponds to Saul in historical symbolism corresponds to those that were practiced in the valley of the Nile, Israel located in the land of Canaan having no historical reality. What about the burial of Jacob, renamed Israel?

The Bible leaves no doubt about the identity of Osiris/Israel: he is indeed the Son of God for Pharaoh:

"Thou shalt say unto Pharaoh, Thus saith the LORD, My son my firstborn is Israel" (Exodus IV, 22-23).

Jacob is renamed Israel for having defeated the angel of God, the Bible tells us... At his death, Israel is embalmed and placed in a "pharaonic sarcophagus", made by Pharaoh's doctors.

Joseph ordered his servants, the doctors, to embalm his father; and the doctors embalmed Israel. Forty days were used for this purpose, for so many days are used for those who are embalmed. The Egyptians mourned for him for seventy days. (Genesis L, 2-3).

Let us continue our investigation. Egyptology shows that the seventy days of mourning correspond to the disappearance of the star Sirius on the eastern horizon, during the equinoxes. Every year, Sirius disappears for seventy days and reappears on the eighteenth of July with the flood. The burial of Israel is that of the god of the Nile valley named Osirios by the Greeks, the Father of Humanity. Osiris/Israel is universally recognized by the Egyptians, the «elders of Pharaoh's house», the servants, the Canaanites, all respond to Pharaoh's order, since it is the burial of the celestial Father, IS-RÂ-GOD, the initiator of the floods... Genesis L, 6-12 :

Pharaoh said, "Go up and bury your father, as he has made you swear". Joseph went up to bury his father. With him went up all the servants of Pharaoh, THE ELDERS OF HIS HOUSE, ALL THE ELDERS OF THE LAND OF EGYPT, all the house of Joseph, his brothers, and his father's house: only the children, the sheep, and the oxen were left in the land of Goshen. They left only the children, the sheep and

the oxen in the land of Goshen. There were still chariots and horsemen with Joseph, so that the procession was very numerous. And when they came to the thorny threshing floor (Athad), which is beyond the Jordan, they made a great and deep lamentation; and Joseph mourned for his father seven days. And when the inhabitants of the land, the Canaanites, saw this mourning in the threshing floor of Athad, they said, "This is a great mourning among the Egyptians!" That is why the name ABEL MISRAIM was given to this area beyond the Jordan. So the sons of Jacob carried out the orders of their father.

At first sight, one is surprised by this true sacred union between the Egyptians and the Children of Israel, whereas everything opposes them, the one being an abomination for the other, the Bible makes us understand. The funeral procession is ordered as follows: the sarcophagus of Israel, Joseph, the Egyptians accompanied by the "Elders", then the Bible names "the house of his father", Israel. The scribes wrote twice the Elders to make us understand that the scholars, the wise men, the priests of the house of Pharaoh recognized in Jacob/Israel the deity who makes the waters of the river bearing the name Israel rise and not the Greek Gods Osirios or Nylos. The lamentations of the Children of Israel and the Egyptians teach us that all of them venerate the sarcophagus of ISRAEL, whom, as we have seen, the Kabbalah considers as God and as humanity forming the Body of God that entered and was expelled from Egypt:

"The Children of Israel who entered Egypt symbolize the totality of humanity"[49]. The Bible speaks of the true «Ancient Egyptians» of the house of Pharaoh, those who possessed the knowledge of the sacred myth of Isis and Osiris. For them, the burial of Israel, which makes the waters of the Nile rise, is obviously the burial of ASAR, called Osiris in Greek, the burial of the sun, unless one commits an enormous collective blasphemy!

---

49   Le Livre Hébreu d'Hénoch ou Livre des Palais. Collection « les dix paroles ». Trad. Ch. Mopsik. Verdier, 1981, p. 252, note n°17.11.

It is indeed the metaphor of the burial of the son of the sun alias Osiris alias Israel that it is about. The Zohar makes the connection between the flood of the Nile and the mourning of the Egyptians:

"This is a mighty mourning of the Egyptians" (Gen. 50:11). We must scrutinize this verse. And why did they do this mourning the mourning of the Egyptians? It was a mourning of Israel, so why the Egyptians? In fact, this is what was said: as long as Jacob was in Egypt, the land was blessed because of him and the Nile flowed and watered the land, so that the famine ceased because of Jacob; therefore the Egyptians mourned and lamented over him."[50]

The Egyptians of the Bible are indeed the worshippers of ISRA-EL, the god of the flood of the Nile, such is the message of the scribes. This passage of the Bible consecrates the sacred union of the ancient Egyptians and the Children of Israel, all converted to the ''ancient Judaism'', ecumenical, paying homage to the divinized man Israel/Osiris who brings them the miracle of the annual flood! It will be clear to the reader that in this passage of the Torah, ISRAEL and MISRAIM are perfect synonyms. It is clear that the expression ABEL MISRAIM used in the Hebrew Bible means that Israel is none other than the Father AB and the god EL of Misraim, of Egypt. One may wonder why the Bible gives so much detail about the huge procession of Egyptians at the burial of Israel. Certainly to let us know that they are an integral part of the Children of Israel. As for the Children of Israel, they are all present, except for their children, who are exempt because of their age. Jan Assmann states that in ancient Egypt there was the equivalent of the Jewish Bar-Mitzvah, a ceremony that inducts the ten-year-old child into his adult responsibilities. The Insinger papyrus reports that until the age of ten, the child is unable to distinguish between life and death or good and evil[51].

---

50   Le Zohar, tome IV, collection «les dix paroles ». Vayigash Vayehi. Traduit par Charles Mopsik. Verdier, 1996, 249a, p. 198.

51   Jan Assmann. Mort et Au-delà dans l'Égypte ancienne. Éditions du Rocher, 2003, p. 421.

So why all the people, including the sages of Egypt, at Israel's funeral? To enjoy a burial leading to the afterlife, as the Osirian procession requires? The commentary of Rabbi Eliezer reports that the Egyptians, though demonized, so-called idolaters, were worthy of a reward and a burial:

"All the great ones of the kingdom (of Egypt) went up with him (Joseph) according to the verse. With him also went up chariots and horsemen (Gen. 50:9). The Holy One, blessed be He, said to them:«For having shown generosity to Jacob, My servant, in turn, I will give you and your sons a good wage in this world. So when the Egyptians perished in the Red Sea, they did not sink to the bottom of the water, but were worthy of being buried"[52]

Better still, Rabbi Eliezer confirms that Jacob-Israel was the holder of the great secret of the Redemption, thus of the resurrection of the dead... It is understood that all men - Egyptians or Children of Israel - go to the burial of Israel in a sacred union. They all call Israel the Father and the god of Misraim... The scribes reveal that the Sons of Misraim are the Sons of Israel. According to the Kabbalah, Jacob is «germ» (tsemah), image of fertility, like Osiris symbolized by the germinating grain of wheat, Osirian symbol of resurrection and redemption of humanity:

"Jacob transmitted the secret of the Redemption to Joseph... Joseph, his son, transmitted the secret of the Redemption to his brothers"[53]

As we know today, burial and sarcophagus in ancient Egypt are essential for resurrection in the afterlife. Rashi gives another idea of the universal - Egyptian - importance of Israel's mourning ceremony. According to the traditions reported by the commentator, Abraham, the grandfather of Israel, was not considered a Hebrew, but the king of kings: the kings of the

---

52   Chapitres de Rabbi Éliézer. Pirké de Rabbi Éliézer. Collection Les Dix Paroles. Éditions Verdier, 1983. Note 7, p. 105

53   Ibidem, p. 312.

whole world came to pay homage to him and took Abraham as their king, leader and guide. At the burial of Jacob/Israel, Rashi reports that the kings of Canaan, the kings of the tribe of Ishmael (the spiritual father of the Muslims), seeing the crown of Joseph placed on Jacob's coffin, became aware of the greatness of Israel, stopped the war and placed their crown on the coffin.

"The Area of Thorns. It was surrounded by thorns. Our masters explain this name by an event that occurred there: All the kings of Canaan and the princes of Ishmael had come to make war. But when they saw the crown of Joseph hanging on the coffin of Jacob, they all got up and hung theirs on it, thus surrounding it with crowns, like the area of a barn that is protected by a protective hedge of thorns (Sota 13 a)"

No doubt this immense allegory is found in the crown of thorns of Christ... On the coffin of Israel was thus the «Egyptian» crown of Joseph, so that the coffin covered with crowns symbolized the allegiance of the kings of the whole world to the crown of Joseph. Now this crown was none other than the crown of Misraïm, offered and consecrated by Pharaoh. Could it be the solar crown of Amun adorned with the primordial serpent, the royal uraeus, the symbol of the Nile? Of course not. Nowhere is it said that Joseph would have refused the serpent crown of Osiris, presumed to be idolatrous, offered by Pharaoh. On the contrary, when Joseph reveals himself to his brothers, he reveals to them a capital piece of information. Joseph's crown is adorned with the primordial serpent, making him the image of the serpent diviner "Israel", the son of the sun:

"Don't you know that a man like me is Nahash Yenokhesh?"

Nahash does not refer to the serpent of the Garden of Eden that expelled Adam, but here to the divinatory serpent (Gen. 44:15) of the kings of the Nile Valley. Joseph is generically the symbol of reconciliation, the return of the serpent/nurturing river, says the Kabbalah:

"Every river relates to Joseph the Righteous"[54].

Now, every river is assimilated to Osiris, in the form of the sinuous serpent, which can give life as well as death. The crown of Joseph the Righteous symbolizes fecundity, fertility, the power of the serpent of the Nile, like that of Osiris the Righteous!

If we consider the biblical context, it is said that the Children of Israel continued to venerate the serpent of the Nile (even the Queen of Heaven). And this since Joseph, through Moses who made a Nahash snake that gave life to the Children of Israel. Such devotion lasted for several centuries, including the whole period of the Judges and the kings of Israel, who, as we shall see, also wore the crown of Amun the Nahash...

He (Hezekiah) removed the high places, broke down the statues, cut down the idols, and cut in pieces the brazen serpent which Moses had made, for the children of Israel had burned incense before it until then; it was called Nehushtan' (II Kings XVIII, 4).

On the mystery of the bronze serpent giving back life, Rashi (Exodus, 21, 8) shows that the serpent, although being an idol par excellence, is venerated like Osiris by the Children of Israel. But unlike the golden calf, Moses' «Egyptian» serpent representing Yahweh is not demonized.

Numbers 21-8: **«And the Lord said unto Moses, Make thyself a serpent of brass, and set it upon a pole: Whosoever is bitten, let him look upon it [Raah in Hebrew], and he shall live.»**

It is obvious here, the statue of the serpent savior conveys in this passage of the Torah the subliminal image of Osiris/Israel:

---

54   « Le Fleuve, c'est Joseph ». Le Zohar, Genèse, tome III, Vayéchev, Mikets, collection «les dix paroles ». Traduit par Charles Mopsik. Verdier, 1991, p. 266.

Rashi: **"He who was bitten by a snake would quickly recover only if he stared at it intensely (Midrash Tan'chumah). And our masters taught: Can a snake make you live or die?**

This means that when the Children of Israel looked up and submitted their hearts to their father in heaven, they were healed, otherwise they died (Roshchana 29a)"

One understands better explanation of the Kabbalah linking God, the god of the Bible, to the serpent idol. This is to bring out, more than the filiation, the very identity of the god of the Nile Valley inked in the biblical text:

"The Holy One blessed be he, rolled a serpent around the holy one"[55]

A passage from the Babylonian Talmud informs us that if Adam had not erred in consuming the fruit of the Tree of Knowledge of Good and Evil, the Children of Israel could have continued to live under the Tree of Life with two good protective snakes.

"If the serpent had not been cursed, everyone in Israel could have had two good snakes at his disposal."[56]

A text from the Zohar speaks of a good and an evil serpent:

"This snake is the death of man. This snake is the death of man. It worms its way into man's most secret entrails. This snake dwells on the left side, but there is also a snake of life, residing in the right side. Both accompany man"[57]

On this representation of the temple of Abydos, and according to Christiane Desroches Noblecourt, the two snakes brandished by the god Thoth give life to the mummy of Sety I. The symbolic snake in the desert of the dead resumes and gives life to Pharaoh. Moses uses the same initiatory ritual to give life back to the Hebrews in the desert.

---

55   Le Zohar, tome IV, Le livre de la splendeur, op. cit., p. 77 et 234.

56 Aggadoth du Talmud de Babylone. La source de Jacob/ 'Ein Yaakov. Collection « Les dix paroles », Verdier, 1982. P. 1053, 59

57 Le Zohar, tome I, op. cit., Verdier, 1981, 596, 52 a p. 268.

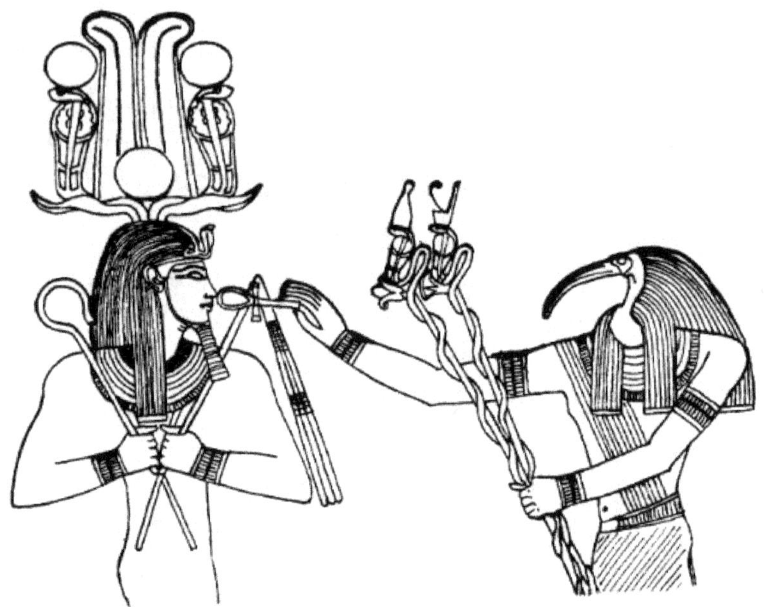

Thoth gives life to the mummy of the deceased

Sety I (temple of Sety I)[58]

The famous serpent-stick of Moses and Yahweh, the god of Israel, constituting the symbol of life and death, is none other, in archaeology, than the serpent-stick of Osiris/Israel. According to the Papyrus of Ani, the two protective snakes represent the two celestial mothers, Isis and Nephthys. The memory of the winged sun and the two protective serpents as well as the winged scarab, images of Amun, is inscribed on most of the parvis or pediments of the temples of the Nile Valley. We find the sun and the winged scarab exactly as on the royal seal of King Hezekiah (we shall see)... Temples that crowds of Jews (and never Egyptians) came to frequent to practice the cult of Osiris...

---

58   Christiane Desroches Noblecourt, Amours et fureurs de la Lointaine, op. cit., p. 73-74.

The Zohar makes us understand that the Children of Israel who were imprisoned for forty years in the desert and who complained to Moses, are the souls of the dead, lost in the desert, as we can read in the Book of the Exit towards the Light. The so-called story of the coming out of Egypt is a remake of the great journey of the souls of Osiris/Israel in the desert of the dead.

"Israel came out of Egypt at the level of the Great Jubilee, and the six hundred thousand (Hebrews) belonged to the WORLD ABOVE. It is in this form that they walked in the desert"[59]

"These are the Children of Israel [out of Egypt Mitzraim] **who are Nephesh** [the souls of humanity]**"**[60]

As we shall see, these souls have the same shape as the bird BÂ of the so-called Egyptians.

"The swallow (Ps. 84:4) is the holy soul [the soul of the Children of Israel] that rises up to the sky and is freed"[61]

---

59 Le Zohar, tome I, collection «les dix paroles ». Traduit par Charles Mopsik. Verdier, 1981. P. 123-124, 21b-22a.

60 Le Zohar, tome I, collection «les dix paroles ». Traduit par Charles Mopsik. Verdier, 1981, p. 246.

61 Le Zohar, Cantique des Cantiques. Collection «les dix paroles ». Verdier, 1999. P. 46-47.

Tutankhamun was never a pharaoh.

He is a Yod, a king, an ISRAEL

THE BURIAL OF ISRAEL IS THE BURIAL OF THE SON OF RA

The Bible states that the Hebrews are an abomination to the Egyptians, but this does not fit with historical reality. The entire people of Misraim go to the burial of Jacob/Israel, knowing that he is the one who raises the waters of the Nile. The Hebrews cannot therefore be the abomination of the Egyptians. On the contrary, they represent what is most adored, deified in the civilization of the Nile Valley... Israel, Osiris... Let us decipher the verses:

"The Canaanites witnessed this mourning in the threshing floor of Athad, and they said, "This is a great mourning among the Egyptians! "That is why the name of Abel Misraim was given, which [Acher] is beyond the Jordan. So the sons of Jacob carried out the orders of their father.

(Genesis L:10-12)

Why does the Bible insist on the almost exclusive presence of the Egyptians at the burial of Israel? The Kabbalah insists that the Egyptians considered Israel a superior and mysterious deity (like Osiris). The Egyptian scholars or initiates - though idolaters - are looked upon by the Kabbalah rabbis as my holders of Knowledge - of Thoth, Daat in Hebrew):

"Come and see: all the Egyptians were learned, and from the side of the Power proceed many armies, many camps and many degrees, reaching the lower degrees; the Egyptians were therefore sorcerers and experts (in these lower degrees) by which they knew the mysteries of the world... ...That's why this place was called «Mourning of the Egyptians». Of course «it is an important mourning for the Egyptians», of the Egyptians and of no other!"[62]

---

62   Le Zohar, tome IV, collection «les dix paroles ». Vayigash Vayehi. Traduit par Charles Mopsik. Verdier, 1996, 249a, p. 199.

ABEL MISRAIM means that the ABEL mourning of the Egyptian Sons of Ra - IS-RÂ - is the mourning of ancient Israel. This is, of course, a biblical paraphrase of the burial of Osiris/Israel, before the drama of the exit from Egypt, the tomb of Jacob/Israel bearing the name of Egypt, Misraim...

But let's decipher the hidden meaning of the Hebrew words «This is a great mourning for the Egyptians» (Genesis L, 10-12)

אֵבֶל-כָּבֵד זֶה לְמִצְרָיִם

This is the mourning of the Father of the god Osiris.

ABEL KEVED MITSRAIM is followed by the name ACHER' or ASAR אשר, which takes on a whole new meaning. The mourning of Misraim/Israel is the mourning honoring (Kavod) ASAR, and honoring MISRAIM, just for the Egyptians, says the Kabbalah...

It should be remembered here that the name ASAR or ACHER' is none other than the name of the god of the Bible in the form I WILL BE ACHER' I WILL BE (Exodus, 3-14).

There is no doubt that the scribes deliver an incredible message in the passage of the burial of Jacob/Israel. The Egyptologists cannot ignore that the «ancient Egyptians» rendered exclusively to «Osiris» the mortuary, solar, flood cult.

The so-called enemy brothers Egyptians and Hebrews, MISRAIM מצרים and ISRAEL ישראל, form in the Torah a single entity: the worshippers of Israel. The scribes show us that at one time, that of Ancient Misraim/Israel, the worship and veneration of Israel was widespread throughout the Nile Valley. The division, the separation between Israel and Misraïm was not made until the Hellenization by the Septuagint, when the Nile Valley was usurped by the Greeks, renamed Ægyptos.

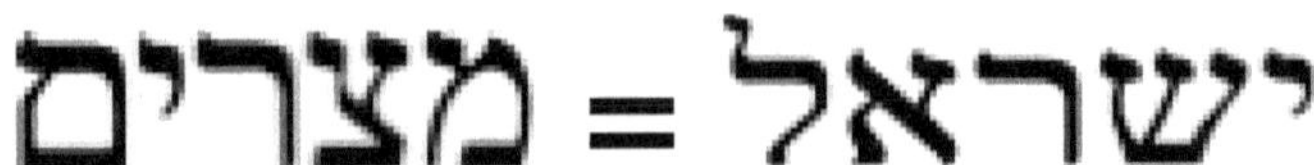

JOSEPH'S CIRCUMCISION IS THE CIRCUMCISION OF OSIRIS

The second revelation of Kabbalah is found in the story of Joseph, when he became king of Egypt and exposed his phallus before his brothers. Joseph thus reveals to them the sacred sign of the "Egyptian" circumcision, the very cause of his enthronement as "Father of Pharaoh".

"Joseph said to his brothers, «Come near to me. And they came near» (Gen. 45:4) [...] Joseph said to them: «See what has given me this kingship, come near to me, and they came near» and then he showed them the sign of circumcision and declared: «It is he who has given me this royal rank because I have kept it intact». This is what we learn from these facts: whoever keeps the sign of the covenant, kingship is destined for him"[63]

This passage is crucial, because it proves that the circumcision of the Jews is of Egyptian origin, as Diodorus of Sicily had affirmed: '

'As for the peoples of the Colques, who live on the edge of the Pont-Euxin, and of the Jews, placed between Arabia and Syria, they also owed their origin to settlers from their own country. This would explain why, among these two peoples, a very ancient tradition establishes the circumcision of young boys, a custom that comes from Egypt" [64].

It was believed, according to the assertions of Herodotus, that the Egyptian circumcision was only a measure of hygiene:

---

63   Le Zohar, tome I, collection «les dix paroles ». Traduit par Charles Mopsik. Verdier, 1981, 465-466.

64   Diodore de Sicile, Bibliothèque Historique. Éditions Les Belles Lettres, p. 66, LXXXIX, § XXVIII.

''They make themselves circumcised by measure of cleanliness''[65]

This explanation is at least insufficient, but very convenient to hide the truth. In the ancient context where each ritual is linked to mythology, Egyptian circumcision is a covenant with God in direct relation with royalty: it is a purificatory, cathartic order given by the god Ra to the kings of Egypt, since in the distant past, Ra/Ra/Osiris, the Father of Humanity, circumcised himself and had two children:

"This is the blood that flowed from the phallus of Ra when he undertook to circumcise himself. Thus came into existence the gods who accompany Ra, Hou and Sia (who) accompany Atum every day in his race"[66]

This is one of the great secrets of the Kabbalah, on this point, in total adequacy with the Book of the Exit to the Light: Joseph and Abraham, circumcised, each had two children; Abraham is named the Father of Humanity after his circumcision... Like Ra, Amun, Osiris...

Like Osiris, Joseph symbolizes the River and the circumcised phallus of God, identified with the Sephira Yessod. Joseph separated from his brothers is the metaphor of the phallus of the god of Israel separated from the Body of God, destined to give the Nile its power of fertility. This secret is consistent with the myth of Osiris, whose circumcised phallus, thrown into the Nile, brings fertility and abundance through the annual flood.

This is why Joseph is historically untraceable, as are Abraham and Moses. They are all half-human, half-divine, solar, cosmic characters, forming a new cosmogony, elaborated from the

---

65   Hérodote. Histoires II § 36-37. Les Belles Lettres. 1982, p. 91.

66   Le Livre des Morts des Anciens Égyptiens. Littératures anciennes du Proche-Orient. Les Éditions du Cerf, 1967, p. 59. The translation of Guy Rachet in the Papyrus of Ani speaks about «drops of blood of the phallus of Ra, after the latter had mutilated himself». The Book of the Dead of the Ancient Egyptians. Traduction inédite et commentaires de Guy Rachet. Éditions du Rocher, 1996, p. 82.

myth of Osiris. Archaeology thus justifies the circumcision of the children of the kings of the Nile Valley: to benefit from royal prerogatives, mainly the status of son of Ra, they were circumcised at birth as a measure of purity, as attested by two Egyptologists, Marie-Ange Bonhème and Anie Forgeau:

"Theban rituals complete the cycle beyond childbirth by describing the care given to the newborn, in order to endow it with a royal existence; recognition by Amun, offering of jubilees, signifying a guarantee of eternal sovereignty, breastfeeding, purification, circumcision." [67]

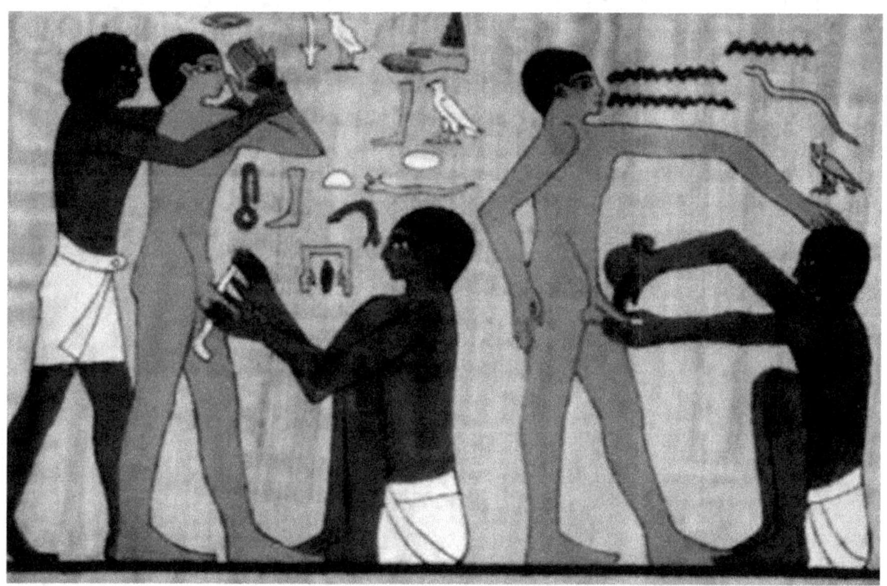

Circumcision among the priests where the African Yahus circumcise the Indo-Europeans.

---

67   Marie-Ange Bonhème, Annie Forgeau, Pharaon. Les secrets du pouvoir, op. cit., p. 85.

ISRAEL DEAD AND RESURRECTED LIKE OSIRIS

The story of Jacob who became Israel is strewn with metaphors and symbols from the myth of Osiris. An immense hope for peace among men. Does the mystical meaning of the name Israel correspond precisely to that of Osiris, actually named ISRÂ, the god of Egypt?... It is constant that the Kabbalah gives the myth an unexpected meaning, often opposite to the literal reading of the text. Jacob alias Israel would be "dead", descended into Sheol, the underworld of the dead, at the precise moment when he learns that Joseph has been torn apart by a wolf. Then Israel is raised from the dead by finding his son alive. But Joseph also embodies the lost and found phallus of God... The lost phallus of Israel... The lost phallus of Osiris...

"Come and see. When Jacob was told, "Joseph was cut in pieces" (Gen. 37:33), "he said, 'I will go down to Sheol with my son in mourning'...[68]

Better still, the return of Joseph, the ithyphallic man according to the Kabbalah, triggers the symbolic resurrection of Jacob, confused with the return of the divine Shekhina. God himself comes back to life:

"Come and see. When Jacob was told, "Joseph was cut in pieces" (Gen. 37:33), "he said, 'I will go down to Sheol with my son in mourning" [69]

JACOB = ISRAEL = CHEKHINA = GOD

---

68   Le Zohar, tome IV, collection «les dix paroles ». Vayigash Vayehi. Traduit par Charles Mopsik. Verdier, 1996, 210b, p. 49.

69   Ibidem, 210b.

JOSEPH IS THE LOST PHALLUS OF OSIRIS/ISRAEL

The seventy-two translators of the Septuagint will camouflage, on several occasions, their Egyptian identity by concealing the myth of Isis and Osiris. How will they proceed? Here, in summarized form, is a flagrant example: Osiris was the first sun of the world, the first God-King, the celestial Father of ancient Egypt. At that time, Egypt was the image of the cosmos, divided into twelve nomes, the image of the twelve divisions of the Zodiac. Osiris married his sister Isis, the Queen of Heaven. But the little brother Seth, jealous of Osiris, murdered the latter by trickery, and cut up his body into twelve parts corresponding to the twelve constellations of the cosmos, thus of the cosmos, thus installing darkness in the world[70].

Isis laments at length, then she undertakes the repair of the body of Osiris. Isis looks for the parts of the celestial body of her husband in all Egypt, reconstitutes it with the help of her nephew, the embalmer Anubis. Only the phallus of Osiris, which was not found, because swallowed by a fish, is replaced by a clay phallus. Osiris, the sun risen from the dead, impregnates Isis, who gives birth to Horus, the new sun. Egypt lives again. The texts and the images of the tombs of the pharaohs show that the waters of the primordial celestial ocean, the Noun, separated in two to allow the rebirth of the sun Horus. The death and resurrection of Osiris are celebrated throughout Egypt, since the first dynasties. It is, of course, at the origin of the Jewish Passover (the death of the Egyptians and the resurrection of Israel) and Christian (resurrection of Christ). And perhaps also, in the context of the renewal of the soul, at the origin of Ramadan among Muslims.

---

70   Fourteen pieces according to Plutarch, twenty-six according to other sources and forty-two according to the Book of the Dead.

The seventy-two translators of the Old Testament will crypticise the myth of Osiris, and this on several occasions, but particularly in the myth of the Patriarchs, Abraham, Isaac and Jacob. The second son of Abraham, Isaac married Rebekah, who was pregnant with twins, Esau and Jacob. According to the Kabbalah, Jacob had fought Esau in his mother's womb for the domination of the world... Then Jacob, with the help of his mother, dispossesses Esau of the birthright by trickery. Another night, Jacob fights victoriously against the Angel of God, then he is named Israel by the latter. But for the Kabbalah, the Angel of God is none other than Esau, Jacob's twin brother, who still wants to dispossess him of the sun and the kingship over the world: «The sun is Jacob», says the Kabbalah... Esau, who is called Edom, the «red» man, symbolizes the serpent of the darkness of death.

That is why Jacob/Israel is the sun of life that fights against the serpent of death. Israel also bears the solar name Etan' (Aton' is the god symbolized by the solar disk for the ancient Egyptians). Jacob has twelve sons: in Kabbalah, the twelve sons of Jacob symbolize the Body of God... Among them, ten plot against Joseph, because he is the favorite son of the Patriarch. One day, Joseph is kidnapped by his brothers, who throw him and abandon him in an underground pit. His brothers make their father Jacob believe that his son Joseph is dead, his body having been torn into several pieces by a wolf. At this precise moment, according to Kabbalah, Jacob/Israel collapses and falls into a kind of lethargy. He symbolically dies: Joseph dead, Israel can no longer live, he can no longer procreate. Rehoben, Jacob's eldest son, regrets his action and returns to the pit, which turns out to be empty (like the tomb of Christ). But Joseph is not dead: he has been sold in Egypt. After refusing the advances of Potiphar's wife, Joseph runs away, leaving part of his clothing... Joseph will be thrown into prison for two years.

Miraculously, Joseph unveils the «Osirian» mystery of the seven fat cows of Pharaoh's dream, and saves Egypt from certain death by famine. Joseph will bear the Osirian title of «Father of Pharaoh» (Abrekh in Hebrew). Here is the key delivered by the Kabbalah: Jacob/Israel is the sun, his twelve sons are the twelve constellations of the Zodiac. Together they form the twelve parts of the heavenly body of God, Elohim. As for Joseph, he symbolizes... the River, the Nile, the Phallus of Elohim! Here is the commentary of the cabalistic rabbi Moses of Leon:

"Joseph (Yosef) is the complement (tossefet) of the body and he came out of it, this is the secret of the Musaf in prayer, because he is the complement and he gives an extra blessing to the moon"[71]

Charles Mopsik nous éclaire sur ce passage :

"Jacob is identified with the Body [of God, of Israel] which symbolizes the Tiferet sephira and is extended by the Yessod sephira, which is symbolized by the male sex with which Joseph is identified"[72]

We understand why without Joseph, Jacob alias Israel alias Osiris deprived of the phallus of God claims to fall into Sheol, the world of the dead... Without the divine phallus, Israel can no longer procreate, Israel loses its creative power and its light... Jacob, the sun dies... and his soul is reborn at the moment when he learns that Joseph is alive: Jacob recovers the divine phallus, symbol of fertility:

"Because of the sale (of Joseph) a famine fell on the land of Israel for seven years... ...Jacob heard that Joseph was still alive, his soul and his breath came back to life, which indicates: «The breath of Jacob came back to life» (Gen. 45, 27)"[73]

---

71   Chekel Ha-Kodesh p. 12.

72   Le Zohar, Genèse, tome III, Vayéchev, Mikets, collection «les dix paroles ». Traduit par Charles Mopsik. Verdier, 1991, p. 51 note 6.

73   Chapitres de Rabbi Éliézer. Pirké de Rabbi Éliézer. Collection Les Dix Paroles. Éditions Verdier, 1983. Note 7, p. 238.

With the disappearance of Joseph, the phallus of God, Israel inevitably becomes the symbolically emasculated heavenly Father. Israel becomes the dead sun, because of the splintering, the separation of its twelve children, who symbolized the integral Body of Elohim and formed the twelve hours of the day, the totality of light. Without Joseph, Jacob/Israel dies without having been able to illuminate Egypt, without having been able to give the Nile the power of the annual flood. But Joseph, the phallus of God, will begin the rebirth of Israel/Mitzrayim by giving Pharaoh the key to the teaching of the fat cows and the lean cows, one of the keys to the resurrection of Osiris, linked to the annual flooding of the Nile. We see how Israel, Osiris, Mitzrayim participate in the same symbol in Yahweh, the divine light of Israel returned to Egypt/Garden of Eden, in this crucial passage of the Torah.

According to Kabbalah, Potiphar's wife tried to seduce Joseph, but he fled. Potiphar's wife tries to restrain Joseph not by his clothing, but by the organ of circumcision, which means, again, a symbolic castration of the divine, Osirian element represented by Joseph... The latter is thrown into prison, but the secret tradition reveals that during the two years spent in prison, the Angel Gabriel will teach Joseph seventy languages of the seventy nations, in order to allow him to speak to Pharaoh in the name of humanity. Joseph alias the phallus of God unveils the Osirian secret of the seven fat cows swallowed by seven lean cows, which symbolize the day swallowed by the night, the life swallowed by the death. After having been crowned by the title, always Osirian, of «Father of the King», Joseph makes his brothers return. This union of the twelve sons of Israel explains the miracle of the symbolic reconstitution of the Body of God, Israel/Osiris, formed by the twelve tribes of Israel, the Body of Elohim reformed in Egypt. This body was necessary for the fertility and prosperity of Mitsraim, which was confused with Israel. But there is more: for the Kabbalah, Joseph reveals to his brothers the whole Egyptian initiatory mystery of circumcision, which made him the Father of Pharaoh. In order to have gained the title of ''Father of the King'', Joseph shows his brothers the sign of circumcision. Joseph asserts to them that he is the ''primordial serpent'', just as he is the River for the Kabbalah, the Osirian symbol of abundance, fertility and national cohesion. Joseph thus takes over: he is the image of God and the image of Osiris the savior of humanity. Joseph is therefore the phallus, but also the Righteous One, the River: **"Every river refers to Joseph the Righteous One"**[74]. It is said in the Kabbalah that Joseph was thrown into a cistern that was assimilated to Egypt, but Egypt without faith, totally empty of knowledge.

"They took him and threw him into the cistern" (Gen. 37:24). This refers to the fact that they threw him into the midst of the Egyptians, a place where the secret of faith is not found"[75]

In this Osirian reconstruction, Joseph orders the general reconciliation of the twelve brothers, with the return of his younger brother Benjamin and the return of the father, Jacob. At the announcement of his living son becoming king of Egypt, Jacob (the sun), claims to have returned from the world of the dead... The Kabbalah affirms that the Egyptians have never known so much happiness as when Jacob came and blessed Pharaoh... Completing the almost «pyramidal» metaphor of Joseph, Kabbalah goes on to say that it was Joseph's sarcophagus that opened the Red Sea, and that the Ark of the Covenant contains the Body of Man, the sun son of the sun... That God is finally fulfilled through the secrets of the Torah and the sacred writings, that is, the fulfillment of the passage of the Hebrews to the Other Side of the veil of the celestial curtain: the passage from the world below to the world above... We are in the heart of the Osirian myth and of the secrets of the Pyramid, the Mitsraïm Matrix, the Red Sea or Sea of Reeds... Secrets contained in the SOD of the Torah, in the Bible!

---

74   « Le Fleuve, c'est Joseph ». Le Zohar, Genèse, tome III, Vayéchev, Mikets, collection «les dix paroles ». Traduit par Charles Mopsik. Verdier, 1991, p. 266.

75   Le Zohar, Genèse, tome III, Vayéchev, Mikets, collection «les dix paroles ». Traduit par Charles Mopsik. Verdier, 1991, note n°1, p. 147.

The story of Joseph alone conceals the life, death and resurrection of the sun, Osiris/Israel, consubstantial with the death and resurrection of Egypt Misraim. The disintegration, the highly symbolic tearing of the celestial Body of God into twelve parts, the loss of the symbolic phallus of God, are clear proofs of the will of the scribes to transpose the myth of Osiris into the Bible. The repair or TIKOUN of the Nile valley, undertaken by Joseph, results in the prosperity of Egypt and the gift of the land of Goshen to the Children of Israel... i.e. the fertile land of Egypt, Israel's heritage confirmed several centuries later by the Koran...

The secret Egyptian origins of Jewish civilization are recorded not only in the Hebrew Bible, both in clear language and in codified, hidden form, in the secret tradition or Kabbalah. The trace of the seventy-two Elders can be found in many instances in the numerous commentaries of the rabbis that accompanied the Torah. But it is undoubtedly the texts written in hieroglyphics that will confirm the importance of the myth of Osiris. The foreign invasions are seen as the dismemberment of the Body of SARA or ISRA. The repair of the body of Egypt concerns the whole of humanity: it is the repair of the Body of Israel.

Although the Jewish people have endured the greatest sufferings, and are still undergoing the hazards and dangers of human history, they are at the origin of the greatest monotheistic civilization, that of the kings of the Nile Valley. The god revealed to Adam, Noah, Abraham, Isaac, Jacob, Joseph, Moses, the Hebrews, is none other than the god of Egypt. It is Yahu, Yahweh, Adonay, Amon, Ra, who comes out of Egypt with the sons of Israel, sand tries to reconstitute himself, since the sacred image of his god has been transgressed by the invaders, including the ancient Persians, and above all, his History has been falsified, counterfeited by the ancient Greeks, rewritten in the Septuagint and codified in the Hebrew Bible - the Massora - sand in the Kabbalah.

Israel's journey through the desert is the journey of Osiris

As we have said, the Zohar states that the Children of Israel who came out of Egypt are an allegory of the souls of humanity. The will to return to the Garden of Eden against the will of God (thus to Egypt) is not only the fact of the Children of Israel of the Bible: it is generalized in ancient Egypt. It is inscribed in hieroglyphics in the Book of the Exit to the Light. The correspondences with the Old Testament are unexpected, to say the least. In addition to the commandments, one finds in the Book of the Exit towards the Light of the origin of the biblical flood: Ra decides that the world will return to its original state, the primordial ocean, the Noun, the celestial darkness. One is surprised to see the wandering souls of the ''Egyptians'' totally lost in the desert of the dead, the souls complain to God... exactly as the Hebrews, the Children of Israel in the desert, complain to Moses and to God of lack of water, as Jan Assmann explains:

"The Egyptian world of death is not fundamentally different from the land of no return, Sheol or Hades"[76]. **"After the passage of the sun, the dead spread out in complaints and fall back into their sleep"**[77], **"The dead go on their heads, eat excrement, drink urine, and the deceased wants nothing to do with this, which is understandable"**[78]..., which is confirmed by the Egyptologist Guy Rachet:

"And the soul complains that the living water of the earth is here stagnant and dead, and it calls for the water that runs from the northern breeze to refresh its heart and its sorrow"[79]

---

76   Jan Assmann. Ibidem, p. 227.

77   Ibidem, p. 371.

78   Ibidem p. 235.

79   *Le Livre des Morts des Anciens Égyptiens.* Traduction inédite et commentaires de Guy Rachet. Éditions du Rocher, 1996, p. 40.

Thus, in chapter 175, thus well before the Bible, the deceased named Osiris N (Name of the dead, alias ISRA-N) complains to Atum/God (as the Children of Israel complained to Moses), of having led him, not to a promised land, but to a desert where thirst and death reign:

"Words spoken by Osiris N: 'O Atum, how is it that I must be brought to a desert, which has no water, which has no air, which is very deep, very dark, and quite unlimited? - You will live there in bliss!"[80]

Following the example of the Children of Israel, those we call ''Egyptians'' repeated the same complaints in the desert. A funerary text from the first century evokes a deceased husband who addresses, from the world of the dead to his living wife:

"And I am thirsty while the water is beside me. I don't know where I am since I reached this valley. Give me running water!"[81]

For every deceased person, identified with "Osiris N" (Name) said Egyptian aspires after his death, provided he has kept the commandments of Osiris to access his place in paradise, a promised land in the garden of stumps, the equivalent of our Garden of Eden :

"He [the Egyptian] **will drink the water of the River and land will be given to him in the Field of the Hooks"**[82]

The Bible reflects exactly the same pattern. The Children of Israel, longing for the promised land (by God to Abraham and Moses), are thirsty and hungry in the Sinai desert after leaving Egypt. The Hebrews complain to Moses:

The people lost heart because of this march, and they complained to Elohim and Moses, "Why have you brought us out of Egypt, to kill us in this wilderness? For there is no

---

80   *Le Livre des Morts des Anciens Égyptiens.* Éditions du Cerf. Op. cit., p. 261.

81   Jan Assmann. Mort et Au-delà dans l'Égypte ancienne. Éditions de Rocher, 2003, p. 229.

82   Le Livre des Morts des Anciens Égyptiens. Op. cit., p. 237.

bread, no water, and we are overflowing with this miserable food [heavenly manna]**!" Then the LORD sent fiery serpents against the people, and they bit the people, and a multitude perished in Israel...** (Nombres, XXI, 4-6)

As in the Bible, we are no longer surprised to find the same notion of a land promised by God, among the ancient Egyptians, with the same particularities, a promised land (campaign of the stumps) where everything is giant, as attested to in chapters 109 and 149 of the Book of the Exit towards the Light. Men nine cubits high reap giant ears of wheat, as confirmed by Jan Assmann:

«The country of the stumps is a place of abundance, where the cereals grow to an incredible height; the dead man is given a plot of land which he will cultivate himself...»[83]

The Old Testament renews the feat of the Children of Israel, upon their arrival in the promised land: the explorers sent there find a land inhabited by giants with enormous fruits:

We also saw giants there (the sons of Anak, descendants of the Giants). We were like locusts, and we were like locusts to them. (Numbers, XIII, 33)

They came to the valley of Eshkol; there they cut a branch and a bunch of grapes, which they carried away two by two on a pole, as well as pomegranates and figs (Numbers, XIII, 23)

83,   Jan Assmann. Mort et Au-delà dans l'Égypte ancienne. Éditions de Rocher, 2003, p. 355.

The seven powers of Israel are the seven powers of Osiris

A SECRET FROM THE TEXTS OF THE PYRAMIDS.

Although in the Bible, Moses separates the Sea of Reeds in two, the verse specifies: ''he made the sea dry'', which corresponds to the destructive action of the serpent Apophys in the tombs of the Valley of the Kings[84]. Apopphis (or Typhon) is the cosmic serpent provider of drought, bringing death to the world. It is a nocturnal, perpetual battle between the antagonistic powers of the day, embodied by RÂ/Osiris, and of the night, Apophis/Seth. According to Jewish tradition, Pharaoh is the **"great serpent, lying in the midst of his rivers"** (Ezekiel, 29, 3). Pharaoh was supposed to die by drowning, but at the last moment, he repented of his sins.

His soul is then resurrected by Yahweh. Israel in turn becomes the object of Pharaoh's redemption. Why does this happen? It is time to deliver the secret explanation of the text. Egyptian tradition[85], confirmed in the writings of Herodotus[86], had it that men renewed themselves in their sleep by immersing themselves in the Noun. Water acts as the major factor of awakening or resurrection[87]:

«Water symbolizes the life force as a vital fluid flowing from the dead"[88]

The Sarcophagus Texts teach that the Great Demiurge God TAM' or Atum is also the serpent Nau, the bull of Nut, «the Great Atum who swallowed the seven serpents Uraeus» (sarcophagi 85, 86). Sarcophagus no. 87 provides a further explanation,

84   Ibidem, p. 176.

85   Erik Hornung. L'Esprit du temps des pharaons. Philippe Lebaud Editeur / Éditions du Félin, 1996, p. 102.

86   Ibidem, Hérodote II, 90.

87   Ibidem, p. 516.

88   Ibidem, p. 517.

stating that swallowing the seven uraei **"GIVES POWER"**[89].

To swallow the serpent is to swallow the celestial water of life, to seize the kingship over the universe... No doubt this legend, which came from the secrets of the Pyramid Texts, was so «founding» that it also figured in the myth of the serpent of Moses swallowing the serpents of Pharaoh. The seventy-two «translators» of Ptolemy were none other than the scribes of Heliopolis, who became the seventy Elders of the Septuagint and the Bible. They could in no way ignore that the initiation of the divine power was done by ingesting the seven serpents. They confirm the truth Egyptian origin of the god of the Bible, the snake swallower, Yahweh in the biblical text, Yahu and Yah in the ancient Pharaonic tradition. The ancient «Egyptians» had compared the seven cervical vertebrae, supporting Pharaoh's head, to the seven primordial serpents. The outcome of the fight between the original snake and the seven swallowed snakes reveal, according to the Pyramid Texts, the great secret of the victorious constitution of the body of IS-RÂ named ''Pharaoh''. The king SA-RÂ is the swallowing snake of the seven snakes of the creation... Therefore, the pharaoh of the Bible, the one who had not known Yahweh/Yahu or Joseph, contrary to all the kings descending from Osiris, could not ignore the meaning of the miracle of Moses, who by producing his staff/serpent swallowing the serpents of the wise men of Pharaoh, unveiled the mystical origins of the god Yahu/Osiris/Israel worshipped by the true kings, the Fathers of Egypt, the successive SA-RÂ since the first dynasties! If the pharaoh of the Bible passively attends the initiatory ritual illustrated by Moses of the serpent-stick god Osiris without evoking his name of YAHOU, **this means that Pharaoh is necessarily foreign to the ancestral traditions, to the very identity of the god of Egypt... because all the kings worshipped Osiris under the name of YAHOU.**

---

89   Textes des Sarcophages, tome I spell n°87, p. 237, 54/c.

The Bible wants to evoke a conquering pharaoh, powerful, but ignoring the most elementary initiatory rules, taught on the banks of the Nile by the true kings, the SA-RÂ/IS-RÂ. Let us go as far as possible to see the new similarities between Israel and Osiris. The book of Genesis tells the story of Jacob, his nightly battle with the angel of God, his tense relationship with Laban, the father of his two future wives. To win his first wife, Leah, Jacob has to work seven years. He will have to work another seven years to marry Rachel. Kabbalah reports that the number seven is a symbol of fulfillment, purity, perfection, resurrection[90]. Jacob/Israel embodies the star of the East swallowing the seven stars. Sirius is the brightest of the stars that precedes the sunrise. It is said that Sirius will «swallow» the seven stars of the Great Bear, which will disappear with the coming of the sun to acquire the seven powers of divinity:

''The star of the east refers to Jacob (cf. Numbers 24:17) who swallows seven stars in the north which are seven nations, seven (angelic) princes on the left side''.[91].

Jacob makes a covenant with the Philistines, which is embodied in the symbolic city of the seven wells, Beer Sheba. For Kabbalah, the Philistines embody the Serpent of Darkness who wants to seize the waters of the seven wells. Kabbalah provides evidence that Jacob/Israel is part of the same initiatory process as the kings of the Nile Valley, the SA-Ra kings. In ancient Egypt, as in the Kabbalah, the demon, in the form of the serpent Apophis, dries up the primordial ocean and attempts to destroy the universe. Apophis (or Typhon), the figure of perpetual space and time, is called the one who dries up the sea at the seventh hour (midnight). According to Erik Hornung, the body of the serpent Apophis symbolizes the totality of space and time[92].

---

90   L'épouse royale de Salomon porte le nom de Bethsabée signifiant « la fille des sept », ou fille issue des sept puissances de Dieu.

91   Le Zohar, tome II, collection «les dix paroles ». Traduit par Charles Mopsik. Vayera, Hayé Sarah, Toldot, Vayetsé, Vayichlah. Verdier, 1984, note 603, p. 155.

92   Erik Hornung. L'Esprit du temps des pharaons. Philippe Lebaud Éditeur / Éditions du Félin, 1996, p. 176.

He seeks to immobilize the boat of Ra, that is to say to make the primordial darkness return, to give death, to stop the course of the sun in the desert and to interrupt the course of time. The sarcophagus containing the mummy of the king in Osiris must imperatively fight against the serpent:

''**The solar boat** [metaphor of the sarcophagus of Osiris] **can thus continue to sail, although Apophis has dried up the waterway.''**[93]

Still according to the Kabbalah, Ptah is the name of God, according to the verse where, finding the cradle of Moses, the daughter of Pharaoh opened it, *VATI-PTAH* in Hebrew. She saves Moses from the waters of death by the serpent of the Nile. The Messiah himself is the image of the Holy Serpent who saves the soul attacked by the evil serpents:

"In the depths of the abyss, with this most holy soul, were «serpents» that tormented it and tried to seduce it. To these serpents was given the «holy serpent» who is the Messiah, for does not the Hebrew word Nahash have the same numerical value as the word Messiah Mashiah?"[94]

The secret of the resurrection of the dead involves, in addition to the battle of the serpents, the seven stars of the Great Bear, which take the form of a celestial chariot. The whole configures the great wheel of the cosmos, the celestial chariot, the Merkaba, which turns around the Pole Star for the survival of the world. The left side symbolizes the evil, the serpent, the rigor. Israel, father of twelve sons or tribes forming twelve constellations, would have swallowed the seven evil powers to acquire the messianic and victorious power of the resurrection of the sun, of humanity, of the universe. This is, according to the Kabbalah the condition for the coming of the Messiah:

---

93   Ibidem, p. 53.

94   Guershom G. Sholem. Les Grands Courants de la Mystique Juive. Éditions PAYOT, Paris, 1950, p. 315.

''The messiah king will be revealed in the land of Galilee, and when the star in the east (= Jacob = Israel) swallows seven stars in the north...''[95]

Ceremony of the opening of the mouth where Tutankhamun alias SARA/ISRA/OSIRIS symbolically swallows the seven stars of the Great Bear in order to come back to life.

Now, this grandiose, cosmic event of the resurrection of the «celestial Messiah» is found in the sarcophagus room of Tutankhamun's tomb, where the ''deceased pharaoh'', mummified as a white Osiris symbol of purity, embodies the dead sun (on the left), and receives from the pharaoh Aÿ (on the right) the Great Bear adze (Book of the Dead) presumed to give him back his life and senses. On the right, Aÿ plays the role of Ptah, the god who, by symbolically opening the mouth of the

-----

95   Le Zohar, tome II, op. cit., 1984, § 119 a, p. 155.

mummy of King Tutankhamun, opens the door of the seven celestial waters of the resurrection of the king who has become a cosmic being, as Moses in the Bible opens the celestial Sea of the Reeds, called the Red Sea. Tutankhamun thus swallows the seven stars of the Great Bear, prelude to the resurrection of the king into Osiris, IS-RÂ, the new sun... We know that the constellation of the Great Bear - named the imperishable - never sets at the horizon, because it revolves around the Pole Star, located almost on the axis of rotation of the Earth. According to Erik Hornung, it was thought that the entire cosmos revolved around this forever immobile, forever immortal star:

"In the archaic period, the king is comparable to a pole star, around which all the constellations of civil and to a large extent religious life revolve. The deceased king rises to the Pole Star in the sky, but his successor now becomes the "Son of Ra"[96].

The Pole Star was therefore the fixed point from which the death of the universe took shape, whereas the Eastern Star Sirius is seen as the warning sign of the rebirth of the sun and the resurrection of the universe. An essential symbol of Egyptian (and Judeo-Christian) mysticism, the number seven has the same value of accomplishment, completeness and resurrection of man and God:

''Ra has seven souls and fourteen Ka; he is also given twelve names".[97].

A rabbinic commentary states that **"Pharaoh and his people believed that the course of the world depended on seven stars in the sky and that God had no influence on the earth. Pharaoh, having seen seven ears of corn, thought that the number seven meant that the seven stars would cause famine and plenty"[98]**

96　Erik Hornung. Les dieux de l'Égypte.　Le Un et le Multiple. Éditions du Rocher, 1986, p. 174.

97　Le Livre des Morts des Anciens Égyptiens. Littératures anciennes du Proche-Orient. Les Éditions du Cerf, 1967, chapitre 15, note n° 5, p. 46.

98　Le commentaire sur la Torah. Jacob Ben Isaac Achkenazi de Janow. Op. Cit., p. 278.

However, the hieroglyphs confirm that the SA-RÂ kings and their people knew perfectly well that the course of the universe depended on the creator god and on the configuration of the cosmos, according to the principles of Maat, the Truth-Justice. On the respect of the commandments of Osiris depended not only the social cohesion between the individuals. But above all, the harmony of the cosmos, the heavens and the earth depended directly on the behavior of kings and men. We have just seen clear evidence of a causal relationship between the Book of the Exit to the Light (Book of the Dead) and Kabbalah. The death of the individual is linked to the death of the entire universe, all through the nightly journey of the sarcophagus of the deceased pharaoh traveling through the celestial waters of the Nun.

This journey is detailed in the great murals of the tombs in the Valley of the Kings, a journey in which the soul of the SA-RÂ kings travels through the vastness of an infinite desert, identical to the desert of the Hebrews after the Egyptians had perished in the Red Sea. A dead person found drowned in the Nile or in the sea was considered a deified being, embalmed and adorned like a god. Let us not forget that the seven stars of the Great Bear form the allegory of purification by water, an immersion in the cosmic Noun, a sort of new post-mortem baptism.

Seven immersions are regularly practiced in the «Egyptian» temples according to the Pyramid Texts: **"The lips of Pharaoh [...] are purified in the seven stars of the Great Bear, the imperishable"**[99]

It is the same in the Jewish tradition. Ritualized water has purifying functions for the body and the spirit, but also for the resurrection of the soul. One dips seven times in Migveh, a basin that must be fed by rainwater (celestial water). This custom is found among the Hindus, for whom it promotes reincarnation.

Thus, the Midrash teaches that the sarcophagus of Joseph, submerged in the waters of the Nile, was brought up by Moses who hid it from the eyes of the Egyptians, because it was likely to be adored as an idol. It is obvious that Jacob/Israel

---

99   Christian Jacq. *La tradition primordiale de l'Égypte ancienne selon les Textes des Pyramides.* Grasset & Fasquelle. 1998, p. 181, sq.

(= the sun) and the sun Ra/Osiris, are structured in the same way, Jacob is at the same time Sirius and the sun, which have swallowed the seven stars of the Great Bear. Jacob worked twice seven years for Laban, to conquer his two daughters, Leah and Rachel, two sisters that Jacob confused... Then Jacob married two concubines, in all four wives who will give him twelve children, which correspond to the twelve constellations of the Zodiac. But that's not all. Iset/Isis (the mother of the sun) is also named after Septa, the star Sirius which every night swallows the sun and every morning gives birth to a new sun. Each year, the star Septa disappears for seventy days, only to reappear with the flooding of the river on New Year's Day. Following the example of Septa, the pharaohs are embalmed for seventy days.

It is said that the Egyptians embalmed Jacob/Israel for forty days and mourned him for seventy days. According to Diodorus, forty days corresponds to the time for the soul of Osiris (through the phenomenon of transmigration of souls) to be transformed into the bull Apis. This same period of time was chosen by the Children of Israel to replace Moses (considered dead on Mount Sinai), by the golden calf, named Israel, the new Osiris replacing Moses... At first light, Septa shines in the East announcing the arrival of the new sun, so that the Pole Star and the seven stars of the Great Bear disappear, as if they were «swallowed» by Sirius and the reborn sun. In chapter 110 of the

Book of the Exit to the Light it is said:

"I am Yah (=Yahu = Yahweh = RÂ = God) and I have swallowed the darkness"[100].

This is why the Great Bear Adze plays a decisive role in the ritual of opening the mouth and eyes, which reanimates the soul of the Sons of Ra. The instrument is probably related to the awakening of the seven stars of the Great Bear, called the «immortals» in the Hermetic texts, corresponding to the awakening of the seven senses or the seven orifices of the king's skull. The seven golden rings found on the abdomen of

---

100   Le Livre des Morts des Anciens Égyptiens. Littératures anciennes du Proche-Orient. Les Éditions du Cerf, 1967, p. 147.

Tutankhamen's mummy, arranged in the form of a Christian cross, are revealing in this regard. In order to be fulfilled in life as well as in death, the king had to symbolically absorb the seven golden rings, the seven souls of Ra or seven lights, in the form of seven uraeus snakes. It is here that we must quote the Texts of the Pyramids of ancient On' which became Heliopolis, which give us the key to the seven rings, affirming that the son of Ra, alias «Pharaoh», was built from a primordial serpent of light. The serpent would have swallowed the seven primordial serpents, the seven vital powers, ensuring him the royalty on all the valley of the Nile...

"The king's mother is a great serpent, and it is a serpent of fire, the red crown, that gives birth to him; he himself is a reptile with many folds, a provider of vital powers, and a serpent named 'bull of the gods,' 'WHO SWALLS HIS SEVEN URÆUS,' so that his seven cervical vertebrae come into existence. He gives orders to the seven Enneads and the seven Arcs"[101]

Let's decipher this text that is more than four thousand years old. The serpent of fire is the image of the river of fire, the famous river of the underworld where the sun is regenerated during the night, the matrix of Isis or Nut, the sky, the celestial Nun, the primordial ocean where the nocturnal serpent swallows the dead sun every day and pulverizes it into billions of stars. The serpent, provider of the vital powers, embodies the celestial matrix - that is why it forms the placenta of Horus - that is to say that it regenerates the totality of the light and water contained in the universe.

The seven serpents uraeus embody, in addition to the seven souls of Ra, seven scattered lights, the dried-up, imperfect Nile, cut into seven sections, allegory of the cutting up of the Body of Osiris and of the resulting drought, of the exile in the desert for men, and of the dispersion of the light in the infinite cosmos. The death of MISRÂ, Egypt, is inseparable from the death of

---

101   Christian Jacq, La tradition primordiale de l'Égypte ancienne selon les textes des Pyramides, op. cit., p. 265.

Osiris/ISRA, from the separation of the light and its dispersion in the darkness, cosmic exile linked on earth to the drying up of the river and its separation in seven symbolic sections, as reported in a passage of Ezekiel:

Yahweh will dry up the bay of the Egyptian sea, he will wave his hand against the river in the violence of his breath. He will strike it to make it seven arms, and people will walk on it in sandals (Isaiah XI, 15).

THE SECRET OF THE RIVER, THE NAME OF THE GOD OF THE BIBLE

When Kabbalah speaks of the River, it speaks of Israel. But let us go even further. In Exodus 3:13, Moses asks Yahweh what divine name he should pronounce in order to be recognized by the seventy elders and their priest-sacrificer Eleazar (whom we said were a myth transposed into the past, a replica of the seventy-two learned «translators» of Ptolemy Philadepha with their Great Sacrificer.of Ptolemy Philadephus with their High Priest-Sacrificer Eleazar led by Ptolemaeus).

And Moses said to Theo': Therefore I will go to the children of Israel and say to them, The God of your fathers has sent me to you, and they will ask me what his name is, and what shall I say to them? (Exodus 3 - 13)

The Septuagint of Ptolemy proclaims:

«I AM (EGO) THE ONE WHO IS»

To which the Hebrew Torah gives a radically different allegorical and hieroglyphic formulation: first, «Ego» is translated by Anokhi, the name of Yahweh, which is none other than the name of Ra/Osiris Ankh-Yod ANKH-Y, «I am the living Yod» written in hieroglyphics (cf. chapter on the Ankh).

Then, the name given by the Torah is an Osirian triptych **ÉHIÉ ACHER' ÉHIÉ** almost untranslatable, because it would mean: I will be Acher' I will be, not I am the one who is (Exodus, 3-14).

אהיה אשר אהיה

ÉHIÉ ACHER' ÉHIÉ

JE SERAI - ACHER' - JE SERAI

Why did the scribes of the Torah insert this formulation with ACHER' אשר as the central word of God's name? We are faced with imagery, a verbal symmetrical allegory, designating Osiris/Israel, in the lexical field of the Kabbalah or the language of hieroglyphics, the triptych BREATH - SUN - BREATH, that is הוה, He-Vav-He of the Tetragram יהוה. Now this expression is very close to the formula ARIÉ ACHER' ARIÉ, LION - SUN/SON/SERPENT/RIVER - LION. This Osirian allegory corresponds to the two lions (ARIÉ in Hebrew) separated in the middle by the sun, symbol of ACHER' present in many effigies and papyri said to be Egyptian. We know today that these two lions symbolize the breath and the present, past and future time, according to the formula inscribed in hieroglyphs where the goddess Isis affirms in the name of God «I am all that was, that is and all that will be, and no one has removed my veil.

The solar child or the child of light HOR says Horus in Greek, future Father of Egypt and image of Ra and the King, ISRÂ- GOD inside the primitive Serpent-River, between the two lions, symbol of Osiris and the god of Israel.

«This river is called Acher, as it is written I am he who (Acher) I am».[102]

The Zohar has also preserved the memory of Achera, the moon, wife of Acher אהיה אשר אהיה, the sun, symbols of Israel, the apple of God's eye103. Thus, when the scribes of the Torah proclaim his name, they reveal the Osirian cosmotheism of the Nile valley, knowing that the body and the two eyes of Osiris are the metaphor of the Nile, the sun and the moon. The Torah uses the word ACHER' אשר, which is not here the conjunction «THAT» or «WHO» to conceal the essence of the hieroglyphic name of God. ACHER' אשר is therefore the central name of God, OSIRIS/ISRAEL in the symmetry breath-sun-blow or lion-solar child-lion visible in several papyri and tombs of the Valley of the Kings. The Kabbalah thus designates God himself ACHER' associated with the lion and the sun, emblems of Osiris. It is indeed a metaphor consciously placed by the scribes. The hieroglyphic image of the god given by the scribes of the Torah rebelled against Ptolemy, meaning that the god of the Bible is the god of the Nile Valley (we will come back to this in detail in the third volume of this trilogy). Thus, the expression «a mourning for Egypt» of the tomb of Israel ABEL MISRAIM ACHER means indeed the mourning of the Father, of the god of MISRAIM (falsely translated by Ægyptos) followed by the symbol אשר of the sun, SAR, Osiris/Israel.

ABEL אבל translated by mourning, is read AB the Father (like Abraham, father of the nations) and EL אל,, God (El is the singular of Elohim), ACHER' or ASAR אשר is none other than the name of the Father and of the god, Osiris... It is indeed the allegorical «Egyptian» name of God, of Yahu/Elohim when the latter says to Moses: אהיה אשר אהיה. . It is the mourning of MESS, the Son of RÂ who came from the waters YAM. The mourning of Jacob is the mourning of Osiris, the great mourning of humanity caught in the trap of the Septuagint.

---

102 Le Zohar, tome III, Le livre de la splendeur, op. cit., p. 225.

103 Midrachim de nos sages, Exode, transcrit par Maurice Stern, Tome II, Chemoth Rabbah, 1997.

In the tombs of the Valley of the Kings, the title of Father of God is attributed to Osiris, Amun, Ptah, etc. The word Kavod (or Keved) does not only mean "great" or "heavy", but above all "honor", the honor of God, but there is more. According to the Kabbalist Gershom Sholem, **Kavod refers to God**, the divine Shekhina[104], which can be deciphered as follows: **"This is the mourning of the Father and the god of Misraim ASAR"**...

or «Behold» ZEH in Hebrew, according to Kabbalah, refers to the divine staff of Moses that turns into a snake (the snake that swallowed Pharaoh's serpents). Again, ZEH means God... Misraim refers primarily to Osiris, although it also refers to the primordial serpent, the image of Osiris. In this case, we have here a demonstration that the Hebrew reading of the Torah is significant, symbolic, and whose meaning escapes the literal reading. Whereas for the literal Greek reading of the Septuagint or the Vulgate (the translation of the Bible into Latin by Saint Gerome in the 4th century), the story reads like a romance, a ceremony that is certainly important, but limited to the burial of Jacob the Hebrew, Joseph's father.

It was absolutely necessary to conceal from the Ptolemies the great secret of Osiris... Let us not be mistaken, the Bible affirms, as clearly as possible, that the tomb of Jacob/Israel bears the name of ABEL MISRAÏM ASAR for the Hebrew Bible and «Pentos Ægyptos» for the Septuagint. It is as if the Egyptians and Hebrews were going to bury Israel, to close a door to the past to allow the new name Ægyptos and the god Kyrios to impose themselves in the Septuagint. Israel is dead, long live Ægyptos... according to the Greek reading ordered by Ptolemy.

From then on, we understand that the great mourning of the Egyptians is inseparable from the mourning of Israel, the man-serpent-sun placed in his sarcophagus, the sarcophagus of IS-RÂ-EL. The Kabbalah reveals that Jacob alias Israel is the sun son of God. Israel came out of Egypt means that the son of God came out of the world... Let's go back to the Zohar:

---

104   Guershom G. Sholem. Les Grands Courants de la Mystique Juive. Éditions PAYOT, Paris, 1950.

"The sun is Jacob (Israel)"[105]

«You shall say to Pharaoh, 'Thus says the LORD, «My son my firstborn is Israel»'» (Exodus IV, 22-23)

It is obvious that the secret tradition reveals to us the other, radically different «Egyptian» message. The mourning of the Shekhina, the mourning of the Father. This is the common mourning of the ancient god "Israel" alias Osiris for the Children of Israel and for the Egyptians. The scribes tell us that they were one people worshipping the same god, without any separation. This passage of the Bible hides an undeniable historical reality, related to the death of the Egyptian civilization. To the myth of the death of Israel and the resurrection of a new Osiris/Israel son of Ra, to the benefit of the myth of Ægyptos son of Zeus alias Ptolemaeus Philadelphos.

This means that the people of Misraïm/Israel pay a common homage to the Father and to the god, rightly placed in a sarcophagus, thus with the effigy of Osiris, as the millenary custom wanted. Israel/Osiris son of God and God himself, or Osiris son of Ra and Ra himself, this is what the story of the burial of Jacob teaches. Egyptians, Hebrews, Children of Israel, Elders of the house of Israel and Pharaoh, they are all sons of Israel **because the name "Osiris" does not exist in the Torah outside Israel.** Because in the Jewish theology as well as in the religion of the SA-RÂ kings, the Father and the Son are of the same substance. And of course, all this has nothing to do with the sons of Ægyptos who are the sons of Zeus.

The death of Israel is therefore not only the death of some man, Jacob, a mourning limited to the Hebrews who came to settle in Egypt. It is the universal mourning for the Children of Israel including the Egyptians, the Canaanites, the kings of the whole world, the humanity... It is the proof

---

105   Le Zohar, Genèse, tome III, Vayéchev, Mikets, collection "les dix paroles". Traduit par Charles Mopsik. Verdier, 1991, p. 207.

that Israel is to be considered by all men as the Son of God, the protector, the benefactor, the initiator of the flood, and of the Redemption... like Osiris.

It is also for the Kabbalah, the symbolic burial of the Tree of Life, the symbol of the death of the Father of the Garden of Eden, the death of ancient Israel, the ancient civilization of the Nile Valley. The death of the old Israel will precede the resurrection of the new Israel, which will take place through the exit from Egypt. The death of the sun Israel will give rise to the resurrection of a New World, a new humanity coming out of Egypt through the Red Sea with the hard trials of the desert of the dead. However, the Hebrews, the so-called sons of SARAH, will be definitively separated from their brothers, the sons of Ægyptos, who have become the new owners of the Nile Valley. But for the teaching of the last priests of On' alias Heliopolis -the Kabbalah-, the Egyptians symbolize the Darkness that fell in the Garden of Eden, the Nile Valley.

Clearly, the biblical account of the burial of Israel by the sages and elders of Egypt does not fit the image of the Egyptians abhorring the Hebrews. On the contrary, it corresponds to the ecumenical burial of Israel/Osiris the sun, a passage which, at the time of the Septuagint, deceived the vigilance of Ptolemy and his henchmen, because the Bible read in Greek only relates the literal text, the death of Jacob, a Hebrew who came from Canaan, emigrated to Egypt and was buried in Canaan... A foreigner in Egypt, nothing else... And yet, the Bible cannot express more strongly that the Father and God of the Children of Israel, is the Father and God of the «Egyptians»... The Bible cannot express more strongly that *ISRAEL* and *MITSRAYIM* are two sides of the same person, the same mold, the same divine entity... Moreover, in the logic of the Kabbalah, Egypt represents darkness, all that is evil, evil, the spirit of evil having to be subdued by the spirit of good, the light. But for Kabbalah, Egypt remains the lost Garden of Eden, and Jacob's death becomes the mourning of all humanity, deprived of the sun that illuminated the Garden of Eden, the ancient Israel/ Misraim before Hellenization and usurpation by Ægyptos.

Archaeology provides thousands of proofs that the ''Ancient Egyptians'' were also in search of God, light and the resurrection of the dead through the image of the sun Ra/Osiris, who was the image of God. They belong, according to the Talmud, to the seventy nations, forming the Children of Israel. And if we take stock, the Kabbalah texts identify Jacob/Israel with the sun and the Son of God, as it says when Yahweh addresses Moses: ''You shall say to Pharaoh, 'Israel is my son, my firstborn'. This is to teach us that the sarcophagus of Israel is indeed the sarcophagus of the Son of Ra, the sun son of the sun. In the ''Egyptian'' context, each day is seen as the life and death of the sun. In the morning, the son of the sun OR (Horus in Greek) becomes the new sun Ra, then aging in the evening, he will become Osiris/IS-RÂ the dead father who will give birth to the future sun. Hence the words of Horus:

"The Father gave birth to me"[106].

Words taken up by the solar Christ, king of Israel, that we find in the Gospel:

«I came forth from the Father and into the world» (John XVI, 28).

Consequently, the burial of Israel is none other than the story of the burial of the sun, Israel/Osiris, whether he is the Father, the Son, the Holy Spirit of God... Israel is thus recognized AB-EL Father of God by all the Elders of the house of Pharaoh, the king who, the Bible tells us, had himself raised Joseph, son of Israel, to the supreme title of Father of the King (AB-REKH). Finally, the message of the scribes becomes clear: it is Pharaoh and his servants, the Elders of his house, that is to say the wise men of the temples, THE ''EGYPTIAN'' PRIESTS WHO RECOGNIZE IN OSIRIS THE DIVINITY OF ISRAEL.

---

106   Spell n° 322, op. cit, p. 775.

JACOB'S 17 YEARS IN EGYPT: THE CIVILIZATION OF ANCIENT ISRAEL CONCENTRATED IN 17 YEARS

The abduction of Joseph by his brothers is compared to the dismemberment of the body of Jacob/Israel, and consequently his definitive death. Let us not forget that according to the Zohar, Joseph symbolizes the divine phallus separated from Israel.

«Come and see. When Joseph was separated from his father, he was sent unaccompanied and without food, and this happened. When Jacob was told «Joseph was cut to pieces» (Gen 37:33), «he said, 'I will go down to my son in mourning to Sheol [the underworld of the dead]**' (ibidem, 35).»**[107]

Jacob's life, far from being a historical account, must be read as a series of metaphors, a real cryptic message. Thus, the seventeen years that Jacob lived in Egypt, after his symbolic death and resurrection, must be understood not as a limited life span, but as the symbol of life and eternity of Israel par excellence. The time when the Children of Israel returned to the Garden of Eden, even if it appears short in the Bible, conceals the millennia of civilization in the Nile Valley where Israel, alias Osiris, had recovered the joys of earthly paradise. As if Man, Adam/Jacob/Israel/God/Osiris, had returned to the Garden of Eden from which he had once been expelled. Moreover, the seventeen years of Jacob are in radical opposition to the seventeen years of Joseph, named in the Zohar as the period of 'death' symbolizing instead the exile of Israel, where Joseph was separated from Jacob 'At the time Joseph was separated from him, it is written:

---

107   Le Zohar, tome IV, collection «les dix paroles ». Vayigash Vayehi. Traduit par Charles Mopsik. Verdier, 1996, 210b, 49.

«'Joseph, being seventeen years old' (Gen: 37: 2), Jacob did not experience during his whole life such grief, he wept every day for Joseph's seventeen years. What was his answer? «It is Joseph who will close your eyes» (Gen. 46:4). Your last seventeen years will be spent in pleasures, delights, enjoyments and desires as it is said «Jacob lived seventeen years in the land of Egypt» (Gen. 47:28).

The Zohar reveals to us the true meaning of the seventeen years of Jacob/Adam/Israel, to the Sun and especially to LIFE:

"A tradition teaches: During all these years, the Shekhinah, the glory of the Holy One, blessed be He, was with him, that is why: "The Spirit of Jacob came to life" (Gen: 47: 27), [THESE SEVENTEEN YEARS] ARE CALLED ''LIFE''[108]

As if, in fine, the whole Bible could be summed up like this: Adam would have lived only one day in the Garden of Eden, Jacob seventeen years, to signify to us the relativism of the symbols of time, the Children of Israel living in their paradise before they were driven out of it by the invaders from the Nile Valley.

At the conclusion of this chapter, Jacob/Israel is identified with the pillar of the world, the Tree of Life in Kabbalah. Jacob's life in Egypt is a true reenactment of the life of the Children of Israel in the land of Egypt, related to the divine light in the Nile Valley, to the sunlight in the Garden of Eden. All the other periods evoked in the Bible, and in particular the exit from Egypt, are to be considered as a return of civilization to darkness, the exile of the Jews, slavery for the Children of Israel...

"Jacob lived in the Egypt's land (Gen: 47: 28). Why is this pericope closed? Rabbi Yossi says: 'When Jacob died, the eyes of the Israelites were closed. Rabbi Judah says: 'Then they went down into exile where they were enslaved."[109]

---

108   Le Zohar, tome IV, collection «les dix paroles ». Vayigash Vayehi. Traduit par Charles Mopsik. Verdier, 1996, 216b, p. 57.

109   Le Zohar, tome IV, collection «les dix paroles ». Vayigash Vayehi. Traduit par Charles Mopsik. Verdier, 1996, 216b, p. 56.

In the secret language of Kabbalah, this can be deciphered as follows: Israel/Osiris/Jacob, the father of the flood, the god of the Nile Valley lived in the Nile Valley and when he died, the eyes of the Sons of Ra closed and they found themselves naked, stripped of their past and their ancient knowledge, mired in the psychological slavery decreed by the Ptolemies during Hellenization.

This means that in the land of Egypt aka the Garden of Eden, the Children of Israel (the real «Egyptians») once had their eyes open, they were fully aware that they were the sons of SA-RÂ, the sons of Osiris, the sons of Israel, they were symbolically eating the fruit of the Tree of Life identified with Jacob aka Israel... They had not yet eaten the fruit of the Tree of good and evil. They had not yet lost the memory of their past. Kabbalah teaches us that the story of Jacob is a reenactment of the story of Adam and Eve, who were driven out of paradise because of the serpent's cunning. Adam and Eve remained in paradise for only one day, while Jacob/Israel stayed in Egypt for seventeen years. But Adam and Jacob are the allegory of the Children of Israel who stayed, according to the Bible, four hundred and thirty years in the land of Egypt, before coming out of it, because of the pharaoh's trickery who had not known Joseph, and because of Moses' trickery who promised them to come out of slavery. While it is said that all died in the desert...

HUMAN SACRIFICE DID NOT EXIST AMONG THE SA-RÂ KINGS

It should be remembered that Judaism, Christianity and Islam are in agreement on a crucial point: human sacrifice was replaced by an animal sacrifice. Abraham is the common father of both religions, to whom Yahweh or Allah had revealed himself as the only god. Abraham had circumcised himself at God's command. For the Jews, Abraham, at the command of Yahweh, agreed to sacrifice his second son Isaac on the altar, but at the final moment, the Angel of Yahweh held Abraham's hand. Abraham sacrificed a ram in place of his son. For Muslims, according to the translations, it is Ishmael, the eldest son, who goes up on the altar at the command of Allah before being saved by the archangel Gabriel. In any case, the sacrifice of the ram replaces that of Ishmael... What does archaeology say? Absolutely nothing about the existence of Abraham and his two sons. However, a parallel, earlier, historical myth exists among the ancient Egyptians. It is said in the Book of the Dead that **Ra, the unique god, solar man, had circumcised himself and had got two children. Then Ra had decreed the prohibition of human sacrifices, replaced by animal sacrifices.**

This is why, according to the Egyptian tradition, men were no longer sacrificed since the time of the gods. The myth of the destruction of men by the gods, translated by the Egyptologist Gaston Maspero, confirms that Ra (God = the gods) substituted the beast instead of man in the sacrifices. In the chapters that follow, we will see to what extent the story of Abraham is a reproduction, a duplication, a concealed continuation of the story of Adam:

«Jacob (the sun) was the duplication of the first man, they had the same beauty.[110].

The biblical account conceals the Osirian mythology and cosmogony, which were camouflaged by the 72 scribes of the Bible, but it is especially the Kabbalah that allows making

---

110   Le Zohar, tome I, collection «les dix paroles ». Traduit par Charles Mopsik. Verdier, 1981, p. 198.

other links with the myth of Osiris, often with an unexpected clarity... Abraham, as we have said, would have been created to move the origin of the Children of Israel to Mesopotamia, to Hour in Chaldea, or Kaldaion' Χαλδαίων as it is written in Ptolemy's Septuagint (Genesis, 15-7).

But the Hebrew translates this term as *Our Kasdim*. **Our Kasdim never meant the Chaldea, but the fiery furnace where the sun renews itself every day.** Abraham himself fell into this furnace and emerged victorious. The texts in hieroglyphics evoke this river of fire, in particular the Great Hymn to Aten where the sun Ra-Aton renews itself every day...

The Kabbalah evokes the same furnace when Aaron makes the golden calf, from the gold of the Children of Israel. The cauldron is the allegory of the lower world where the sun/golden calf is reborn, because in the texts of the ancient On' Heliopolis, the golden calf is none other than the sun being born on the eastern horizon. Now this sun/golden calf is named Israel, by the Children of Israel... **Moreover, according to Kabbalah, Abraham was born in Egypt, a country clearly identified with the Garden of Eden.**

t is essential to understand this fundamental decoding of the image of Abraham in the Bible. Abraham is a multiple figure of composition, an earthly and heavenly deity, an Elohim. His name is «constructed» from divine hieroglyphs. Abraham is the image of the first man Adam driven out of paradise, but also the image of the sun in motion in the cosmos. The Kabbalah specifies that Abram, renamed Abraham, AB-RAÂ-AMON is none other than the sun.

As we have said, the purpose of the patriarch's wanderings in Egypt was to illuminate the land of the Pharaohs, a land confused by Kabbalah with the Garden of Eden of Adam and Eve. Abraham brings them the sunlight symbolized by SARAY which became SARAH. Finally, Abraham bears the name of Etan' Ézrahit' meaning the sun coming from the Eastern horizon, the RÂ-ATON' AMON of the ancient Egyptians.

Abram, renamed Abraham is the sun or light of the world, the morning light, Isaac the afternoon light, Jacob is the evening light. Jacob alias Israel is designated as the sun. Abraham corresponds to ATON' AMON-RÂ, who is at the same time the unique god, the Father of Humanity, the solar man, the visible (RAÂ-ATON') and hidden manifestation of God (AMON = the Hidden). As we shall see, the story of Abraham is a hidden reconstruction by the scribes of the story of Genesis, a real recomposition of the scenario of the original sin in the Garden of Eden, the lost paradise, Egypt.

"It is Abraham who is the light of the day"[111]

It is the same for Jacob, so that the Patriarchs represent in fine, the sun settling in Egypt, or the light returning to the Garden of Eden in order to repair the original sin. This notion transmitted by the Kabbalah obviously deconstructs the literal meaning of the reading of the Bible, of the Torah. It comes from the scribes of the Septuagint and the Massoretic, Hebrew text, who were concerned with hiding the secret of Osiris in the Bible.

"The sun is Jacob"[112]

ISRAEL = SUN = SA-RÂ

"Jacob [= Israel = Etan'] is the most praiseworthy of fathers, and his function is to illuminate the world. And because he has ascended into the bosom of the world to come, a branch comes forth from him, of beautiful appearance, from which all the lights escape and all the abundance and the unctuous oil, to illuminate the earth."[113]

ABRAHAM = AMON' = RÂ = ATON'

---

111   Le Zohar, tome II, collection «les dix paroles ». Traduit par Charles Mopsik. Vayera, Hayé Sarah, Toldot, Vayetsé, Vayichlah. Verdier, 1984, p. 281.

112   Le Zohar, Genèse, tome III, Vayéchev, Mikets, collection «les dix paroles ». Traduit par Charltes Mopsik. Verdier, 1991, p. 207.

113   Le Zohar, tome IV, collection «les dix paroles ». Vayigash Vayehi. Traduit par Charles Mopsik. Verdier, 1996, 207a, p. 34.

THE STORY OF DAVID AND SOLOMON IS A TRANSPOSITION OF THE "PHARAOHS" IN THE LAND OF CANAAN

Thus, according to Kabbalah, the founding myth of the Body of God torn from its roots is found with Israel/Osiris, the parable of the vine torn from its root, but also of the heavenly Queen. The divine Shekhina is compared to the Bride of God, the heavenly Queen driven from her palace and weeping for her husband and children. Israel is a King or Queen, the Children of Israel, humanity. This parable of the recasting of the myth of Osiris indicates the submission of the scribes of the Bible to the Ptolemies, the kings who transposed the history of the Jews/Children of Israel from the root «Egypt/Garden of Eden» to Canaan, renamed Judea, the land supposedly given by God to Abraham. Everything now focuses on the myth of Abraham leaving his father's house in Mesopotamia, while for the Kabbalah, Abraham is expelled from the Garden of Eden aka Egypt by Pharaoh.

Abraham is expelled from the Garden of Eden aka Egypt by Pharaoh.

This symbolic removal of the Egyptian root leads to a refoundation, a transposition of history by the scribes of the Bible. In particular, the second Book of Kings where the conquest of Nebuchadnezzar, king of Babylon over the Nile Valley, focuses on the capture of Jerusalem, which will replace Thebes. The vine designates people torn from its history, from its «Egyptian» roots, a people that left Egypt following a first exile, that of Nebuchadnezzar. The explanation of the psalm is completed by the Kabbalah, affirming that the land of Israel or the land of life is built on the water of the «supreme river» of the Garden of Eden, which is none other than the memory of ancient Israel located in the valley of the Nile: **"Indeed, the «land of life» is built on water; for everything flows from the supreme river that comes out of Eden"**[114].

---

114 Zohar, tome V. Le livre de la splendeur. Par Jean de Pauly. Maisonneuve & Larose, 1985, p. 126.

Nabuchodonofor affiege Jerufalem & la prend, & tranfporte à Babylone toutes les richeffes & tous les habitans de cette ville.

As if the scribes of the Kabbalah wanted to deliver us a heavy secret. Israel, its history and its kings. Israel, designated as a vine torn from the Garden of Eden/Egypt, has become a figure of transposition: the Bible is a new ''History out of Egypt'', entirely recomposed, reconstructed in Jerusalem and in the land of Canaan. But Israel keeps its roots in Egypt. The coming out of Egypt would be a «passage» where the factual history of Israel in Egypt would be encrypted, transcribed, transposed into another country with Jerusalem as its capital. We will see that this transcription of the vine torn from its root will be done through Adam, Noah, Abraham, Isaac, Jacob, Joseph and the Children of Israel, who symbolize the will to return to Egypt/Tree of Life, whereas Moses on the contrary embodies the Patriarch at the orders of the Ptolemies, who is going to ''religiously drive out'' the Children of Israel from their primitive root. Let us begin with the Book of Kings II, 25, 10 : **All the army of the Chaldeans, which was with the chief of the guards, demolished the walls of Jerusalem.**

According to archaeologist Israel Finkelstein, there is no trace of fortifications in Jerusalem in the sixth century BC, nor is there any trace of the temple of King Solomon and his royal palace:

"In Jerusalem, no trace of the Temple and the palace of Solomon could be identified..."[115]

On the other hand, it is a historical fact that most of the cities of Egypt were fortified by powerful walls, as testified by the

Zohar:

"In Egypt the fruit is twice as beautiful [as in the land of Canaan] The people are powerful and the cities are fortified. [...] The cities are so fortified that all the armies of the earth could not take them by storm"[116]

Thus, the details of Nebuchadnezzar's capture of Jerusalem around 605 B.C., recounted in the Book of Kings, are a historical transposition to the Nile Valley. In reality, in addition to having suffered a murderous war on the human level, Egypt had lost the ancestral spiritual support of the kings. This means the support of the priests, the gods and of God, with multiple names, Ra, Amun, Osiris or Yahu. By mentioning Jerusalem, the story hides the capture of the largest Egyptian city, Thebes. Following the victory at Karkemish, Egypt had suffered a double trauma. Now it is written in chapter 25 of the Book of Kings that Nebuchadnezzar's army which had defeated the Egyptian army at Karkemish (one hundred and twenty thousand to five hundred thousand men according to the sources) besieged Jerusalem for two years before making a first breach in the walls surrounding the city! That it would

---

115 Israël Finkelstein, Neil Asher Silberman, La Bible Dévoilée. Bayard Éditions, 2002, p. 163.

116 Zohar, tome V. Le livre de la splendeur. Par Jean de Pauly. Maisonneuve & Larose, 1985, p. 415.

have taken the whole Chaldean army to destroy the city walls. Walls that did not exist! Already, the Book 2 of Chronicles stated that it took about two hundred thousand men to build the temple and the palace of Solomon.

Solomon ordered that a house be built in the name of Yahweh and a royal house for himself. Solomon counted seventy thousand men to carry the burdens, eighty thousand to cut the stones in the mountain, and three thousand six hundred to watch over them (Chronicles II, 2, 2)

Now this enormous number of workers, of stone cutters - whereas cut stone is forbidden in the Bible - followed by the stewardship, their families, cannot correspond to historiography and to the small temple of Jerusalem, of which archaeology finds no trace. It would take a population of at least a million people living near Jerusalem, Israel Finkelsein stating that it was a small village without walls, that there is no trace of the temple of Solomon.

It is clear that Solomon and his army of builders did not obey the Law of Moses. Archaeologists, including Israel Finkelstein, claim that there is no trace of Solomon's temple in Jerusalem, which at that time was a small city without walls, as big as two soccer fields. How could one hundred and fifty thousand people build such a temple, if not in the Nile Valley, because only the SA-RÂ kings had such power. As described in the Bible, it can only be the temple of Thebes, built by King Amen-Hotep III, which means ''Amun is at peace''. For King Solomon bears the secret name of the ''King who possesses peace''. Although there is no proof of his historical existence, Solomon the builder king did exist under the name Amen-Hotep III. We will see that Solomon wears the crown of Amun, the serpent of the Nile Valley... The description given by the Bible is therefore historically impossible, for the reason that it is a transposition of the history of the Nile Valley in the land of Canaan. Whereas for the construction of the temple of Thebes, these figures are perfectly coherent. After the death of the king, Jeroboam, Solomon's officer, went to war against his son Rehoboam. Jeroboam «fled to Egypt», created the kingdom of Israel with Jerusalem as its capital, and raised an army of eight hundred thousand men against Abijah, king of Judah.

And Abijah went into battle with an army of valiant men, four hundred thousand chosen men; and Jeroboam set himself in array against him with eight hundred thousand chosen men, valiant men. (Chronicles II, 13, 3)

Historically, nothing makes sense in either the Book of Kings or the Book of Chronicles. It is impossible that the Babylonian plunder and invasion described in the Book of Kings - with such a powerful army totaling 1200,000 soldiers - took place at the site of Jerusalem, which was a very small city without any fortifications, very easy to take. The capture of Jerusalem conceals the capture of Thebes and the cities of the Nile Valley empire. If we consider the historical context in relation to the biblical text, it is hard to believe that Nebuchadnezzar defeated the Egyptian army of Pharaoh Neko at Karkemish, only to seize the tiny city of Jerusalem and deport from this so-called walled city several tens of thousands of Jews. Historians of Roman antiquity state that the so-called "Egyptians" were exiled and enslaved in Assyria, Babylonia and Persia. There were successive deportations, but Nebuchadnezzar's was by far the most important. A passage in the Book of Lamentations (Zohar) gives the frightening figure of eighty thousand Jews deported and persecuted in Babylonia:

"Eighty thousand Levite priests had their hands tied behind their backs"[117]

Diodorus Siculus summarizes the invasion by the Achaemenid emperor of the Persian Empire, Cambyses II in 529 B.C., the sacking of Egypt and the dramatic story of the deportation of the «craftsmen», i.e., the Yahud dignitaries who alone possessed the knowledge inherited from generations to build the palaces of Persepolis, Suze and Media.

---

117   Le Zohar, Lamentations. Coll. « les dix paroles ». Verdier, 2000, p. 82.

"... silver, gold and sumptuous works of ivory and precious stones were plundered by the Persians at the time of Cambyses, when he burned the sanctuaries of Egypt. It was then, they say, that the Persians transported to Asia all these riches and having taken with them Egyptian craftsmen, built their famous palaces of Persepolis, Suze and Media... ... Not only do the priests of Egypt relate this from their records, but several of the Greeks who visited Thebes during the reign of Ptolemy son of Lagos and composed histories of Egypt, among whom was Hecataeus, agree with what we have just said"[118]

According to the Book of Kings, there would have been three successive deportations, impossible events in the very small city of Jerusalem at the time. For the Jerusalem of the sixth century B.C. was not a town naturally subject to the most powerful. It could not bear the name of "city of a hundred gates", name of Thebes, fortified city, seat of the palace and the temple of King Amenhotep III! There is no doubt that the scribes transposed this name from the largest fortified city in the Nile Valley in order to make Jerusalem the new Thebes. Thus, the Bible describes a long series of devastating invasions, as if they were mainly centered on the region of Jerusalem, described as a great fortified city with the palace and temple of Solomon, described in Jewish tradition as the most powerful king in the world...

The Hebrew name Jerusalem Yerushalaim means "the two inheritances". This suggests that there are two Jerusalems. According to Kabbalah, there is an earthly Jerusalem and a heavenly Jerusalem. For the Book of Revelation, the heavenly Jerusalem came down from heaven, to become the "new bride, the Lamb's wife", meaning the new bride of Amen or Amon, the Lamb, the Christ, the future ram. This allegorical

---

118   Diodore de Sicile. Bibliothèque Historique. Éditions Les Belles Lettres, 2003. Première édition 1993. XLVI, 4-8, Pages 100-101.

and metaphysical vision participates in the double memory of the divinities of ancient Thebes - the city of a hundred gates - transposed into Jerusalem - the city of a hundred gates - located in Canaan. For the Kabbalah, as for the Book of Revelation, Thebes has obviously been replaced by the new mystical and legendary Jerusalem. This would explain why the details of Jerusalem in the Book of Kings do not correspond at all with the archaeological data of historical Jerusalem, but obviously with the great walled city of Thebes. For this dark, disastrous period, the Bible has contracted and transposed history, focusing singularly on the capture of the tiny city of Jerusalem, while Nebuchadnezzar's conquest extended over all of Egypt, thus over the land of the Yods, to the destruction of its great fortified cities and the looting of its temples. During the Assyrian and Babylonian invasions, the Egyptian temples were plundered, destroyed, burned, the country humiliated, devastated as never before. A verse in the book of Kings gives the historical reality of the invasion of the whole Nile Valley by Babylon. New pharaoh kings are installed on the throne of Egypt by Nebuchadnezzar and his successors:

«The King of Egypt went no more out of his land, for the king of Babylon had conquered all that belonged to the king of Egypt from the brook of Egypt to the river Euphrates.»

(II Kings, XXIV, 7)

This text, which speaks of Egyptians, was written in Greek times, associated with the Septuagint. Before the Ptolemies the Nile Valley, as we have said, was the ancient IS-RÂ-EL. Nebuchadnezzar took everything that belonged not to the king of Egypt but to the king SA-RÂ/IS-RÂ. Nebuchadnezzar stole the gray matter, the intelligentsia, he exiled the Yahud dignitaries, in order to rebuild his palaces, his cities and his hanging gardens in Babylon. Envious of the beauty and grandeur of the MISRÂ/ISRÂ country, and of the know-how of its Jewish dignitaries -

not Ægyptos - the Babylonian tyrant had deported them to him as slaves destined for the realization of his grandiose projects, leaving in the country only the peasants and the ploughmen...

In fact, the second *Book of Kings* "transposed" the story of the conquest of Egypt onto tiny Jerusalem. The following passage shows the terrifying violence and humiliation inflicted on the greatest of civilizations by Nebuchadnezzar:

The sons of Zedekiah were slaughtered in his presence; then they gouged out Zedekiah's eyes, bound him with chains of brass, and carried him to Babylon. And it came to pass on the seventh day of the fifth month, which was the nineteenth year of the reign of Nebuchadnezzar king of Babylon, that Nebuzaradan the captain of the guard, the servant of the king of Babylon, entered into Jerusalem. And he burned the house of the LORD, and the king's house, and all the houses of Jerusalem; and he gave all the houses of any importance to the fire. And all the army of the Chaldeans, which was with the captain of the guard, broke down the walls of Jerusalem. And Nebuzaradan, the captain of the guard, carried away captive those of the people who were left in the city, and those who had gone to the king of Babylon, and the rest of the multitude. But the captain of the guards left some of the poorest of the land as vineyard workers and plowmen. (II Kings, 7-12)

The defeat of Karkemish marks the peak of the devastating invasions, from Assurbanipal to Nebuchadnezzar. Almost three millennia of so-called Egyptian civilization were wiped out. The exile of the Yods, the "Egyptian" priests to Babylon, was an unprecedented event, a real blow to Egypt. It is precisely this exile from Egypt that was geographically "contracted" and transposed by the scribes in the Book of Kings to the small city of Jerusalem, in order to make it appear that this city was as powerful as the ancient Thebes. No doubt the Yods, the Jews, had to limit their new "History" to this Jerusalem, capital of a kingdom of Judah, forgetting Thebes by divine will. An unconditional subjection to the unscrupulous conquering kings, who blithely claimed Egypt as the homeland of their ancestors. The symbolic rebirth of Israel and Judah in the land of Canaan marked the submission of the scribes and priests to the whims of the Ptolemies, who had been deified during their lifetime, in accordance with the Septuagint, which situates the land of the Jews in Canaan. So that the subjugated Jews could never again claim their ancestral valley of the Nile. For all these well-crafted and transposed legends were compulsorily taught in the synagogues where the Jews, the ex-notables of Egypt, were forced under penalty of death to read the Greek Septuagint, and not yet the Hebrew Torah, which had not yet been written. The Books of Kings, Chronicles and Prophets would complete the Old Testament in order to testify to the historical reality of the Septuagint/Bible/Torah. It is a fact that the biblical myth of the exit from Egypt and the extra-biblical books took shape under Greek rule. They have in common the focus of the whole history of the Jews and the kings of Israel in the land of Canaan/Palestine, from Abraham through Nebuchadnezzar to Ptolemy. The first and second books of Kings reconstructed the history of the new Israel, evoking the reign of Solomon and the twelve tribes divided into two tribes forming the kingdom of Judah in the south and ten tribes forming the kingdom of Israel in the north. Two royal dynasties well established in the books, but which have nothing historical about them and which archaeology is at pains to confirm.

Chapter V

ISRAEL WAS BORN FROM THE CULT OF OSIRIS SERPENT

How Moses broke the civilization

of the Nile Valley

In order to penetrate another phase of the great secret of Osiris-Israel, it is necessary to explore the most secret foundations of the biblical story, preserved in the Kabbalah. Moses did not only destroy the land of Pharaoh with the ten plagues. The plagues are in fact a symbolic language of the destruction of the body of Osiris. Moses destroyed the most sacred monotheistic symbols of those we call ''ancient Egyptians'', the light, the sun, God himself. At the beginning of the book of Exodus, Moses strikes to death an «Egyptian man» who struck a "Hebrew man". We immediately think of two distinct civilizations that everything opposes. Moses kills the Egyptian and flees to the land of Midian. But for the Zohar, this Egyptian was really only a "Man of Appearance", the serpent, the primordial cosmic light of Israel, its original light, what we call "Osiris". Yes, Moses struck... Osiris aka Israel.

"This Egyptian was in reality the primordial serpent"[1]

____

1 Le Zohar, tome III, Le livre de la splendeur, Jean de Pauly, Maisonneuve & Larose, 1985, p. 442-443.

"And he smote the Egyptian Man, a man of appearance". The esoteric meaning of these words teaches us that every time Israel fails, He [God] steals away and deprives them of all the goods and lights that illusminated them. "He struck the Egyptian Man" who was the brightness of the light that illuminated Israel..."[2]

"The Egyptian man refers to that famous personage, who was very great in the land of Egypt in the eyes of his servants"[3]

Only Osiris corresponds to this divine, esoteric, luminous character described by the Kabbalah. Indeed, why does Kabbalah say that the Egyptian man is the light of Israel? It is not an *Egyptian Man* that Moses struck, as we believe to read in the biblical text. It is the divine light of Egypt... Which is the divine light of Israel... *It is God himself...* It is all the past, all the memory of ancient Israel that has been struck... Let us explore the Hebrew text and the Greek text.

At that time, Moses, having become great, went to his brothers and witnessed their hard work. He saw an EGYPTIAN MAN beating a HEBREW MAN [the Targum says YAHUD MAN = Egyptian dignitary] **from among his brothers. He looked around (Koh véKoh in Hebrew), and when he saw that there was no Man, he killed the Egyptian Man and hid him in the sand.** (Exode II, 11-12)

Septante: **And it came to pass after many days, that Moses, being grown to manhood, went out unto his brethren the children of Israel, and thought of their affliction, when he saw an Egyptian smiting a Hebrew, one of his brethren the children of Israel. When he looked around and saw no one, he killed the Egyptian and buried him in the sand.** (Exodos II, 11-12)

---

2 Le Zohar, tome 1, collection Les dix paroles, Verdier, 1981, p. 53.

3 Le Zohar, tome 1, collection Les dix paroles, Verdier, 1981, p. 53.

We see that the texts are not quite the same. The Hebrew Bible mentions the name of Man for the Egyptian as for the Hebrew. As if to specify to us the divine quality - Osirian, Osiris being a «Man» and a god of light - of the two protagonists. The Septuagint speaks twice of the sons of Israel, as if the Egyptian striking the Hebrew were sons of Israel, whereas the Hebrew text does not speak of them. It is said that Moses looked here and there (Koh véKoh), and he saw that there was no man4 (Exodus 2, 12)...

But according to the Septuagint, Moses saw an Egyptian striking a Hebrew, one of his brothers, the Children of Israel. These verses seem ambiguous, enigmatic. Who is the brother of whom? Are the Egyptian and the Hebrew related to the Children of Israel? Do they form the Children of Israel together as was demonstrated in the burial of Jacob/Israel where Egyptians and Hebrews form a sacred union?

The proof is that Koh véKoh designates the KA of the Father and the Ka of the Son. The Aramaic Targum does not say "Hebrew Man", but «YAHOUDAE Man», knowing that the word YEHOUDAH designates the class of «Egyptian» dignitaries attached to the power of the Uraeus. The Zohar will unravel the mystery of the Hebrew, the son of Israel, who is none other than the son beaten by his father, the Egyptian:

"Rabbi Abba says: "The words: 'And he turned his gaze from one side to the other' [Koh-vaKoh] mean that he turned his gaze from one side to see if this man had meritorious deeds, and from the other side to see if he was predestined to give birth to a good child. And the Scripture adds: ' ... And he saw that there was no one.' He saw by the Holy Spirit that this man would never give birth to a good child"5

---

4 "Ich" («man» in Hebrew) has the same root as the Egyptian IS' or AS', which means «Man». It is pronounced like the beginning of Osiris: AS-R, or "Man-King". Hence the term «Sir» to designate a prince or king.

5 Le Zohar, tome III, Le livre de la splendeur, op. cit., p. 55.

Everything happens as if the Egyptian struck by Moses was not worthy of giving birth to... a son of light of Israel! As if the scribes wanted to show us that Moses had killed the powerful mythical symbol, Osiris the KA, the Father, and Horus, the KA, the Son. Another explanation from Kabbalah confirms that the Egyptian Man struck his son, the Hebrew.

"The son of the Egyptian, of whom the Scripture speaks, was precisely the son of that Egyptian whom Moses had killed in Egypt with the sacred name, as it is written, "Is it to kill me that you say this...?" Thus FATHER AND SON fell into the hands of Moses"[6]

These explanations challenge the literal meaning of the biblical text. For the Hebrew text, there were no men in front of Moses, in the sense of troublesome witnesses. Whereas for the Septuagint, Moses sees no one. The text is paradoxical, especially since it reveals the desire of the scribes of the Septuagint and the Torah to convey a crucial message: the Hebrew is the Son of the Egyptian. Moses does not only fear the presence of a troublesome witness. He observes, scrutinizes, considers the face of the Father, the Egyptian, as well as that of his dolphin. He sees that they are not «Men» worthy of representing Osiris and his son Horus. Moses, the prince of Egypt, actually sees two Men, the father and the son, two princes according to the Jewish tradition. Rashi makes the following comment:

"And he saw that there was no man. He saw that no man would come down from him who would convert (Shemot rabba)"

We come to the fact that Moses strikes more than a divinized person, a god and his son, and that the biblical text is a cosmogony, a battle between gods... Moses immediately judges that they are not only two Men converted to the true God, but deities, Elohim, the Father and the Son, unfit to rule the world, the Nile Valley, ancient Israel... Kabbalah pushes even further in precision. Looking at Koh véKoh, Moses fixes his gaze on the Egyptian and on his son... who together symbolically form the One God, the God of Israel symbolized by the Father and the Son!

---

6 Zohar, tome V, Le livre de la splendeur, op.cit., p. 267.

"The words "Koh-ve-Koh" designate the fifty letters with which Israel proclaims the oneness of God every day, for the verse «Hear Israel" [Hear Israel Adonai is our God Adonai is One] **is composed of twenty-five letters; and this verse is recited twice a day"[7]. "That is why the verse that begins with the word Schema** [Listen Israel...] **is recited twice a day and contains twenty-five letters, the number represented by the sacred name "Koh"[8]**

Now let's rewrite the text with the deciphering of Kabbalah.

At that time, Moses, having become great, went to his brothers, the Children of Israel, and witnessed their hard work. He saw an Egyptian Man/MISRI - the light of Israel, the primeval serpent, OSIRIS - striking HIS SON, a Man, a dignitary YAHOUD, the son of Israel among his brothers. He considered the god of Israel (= Koh véKoh, two gods, two Elohim), and seeing that there was no Man converted to the true god, he killed the Egyptian/MISRI, the light of Israel, OSIRIS, and hid him in the sand.

Koh is the sacred name of the Egyptian and the name of the God of Israel... In hieroglyphics, it is the Egyptian Ka, the living soul of the Father Osiris, the Ka of the God of Israel, and the Ka of the Son, Hor, called Horus. Moses struck the living soul of the ancient Israel, God, Yahweh, Adonay, Aton, Amon, RÂ, Ptah... Moses would have also struck Israel=the Egyptian by pronouncing the name of God:

"From this we learn that he had killed the Egyptian by pronouncing the Divine name."[9]

But in the biblical context, Yahweh has not yet revealed himself by name to Moses in the scene of the slow bush. Moses grew up in Pharaoh's palace where he received the

---

7 Zohar, tome III, Le livre de la splendeur, op. cit., p. 55.

8 Zohar, tome V. Le livre de la splendeur. Par Jean de Pauly. Maisonneuve & Larose, 1985, p. 596 Zohar III 257a.

9 Rachi, commentateur de la Bible au Moyen Âge. Pentateuque selon Rachi. l'Exode, op. cit., page 11, voir aussi Appendice.

teaching and wisdom of Misraim. The god struck by Moses is indeed Osiris, the light of Israel. The Hebrew would thus be the son of the Egyptian... This confirms that the sons of Israel, the Hebrews, are the sons of this Egyptian qualified as the light of Israel, not converted to the law of Moses... Father and son correspond to Osiris and his son Hor, called Horus in Greek. Both are the light of Israel, both fell under the hands of Moses. The Kabbalah confirms this once again.

The Zohar has kept the memory of Amun and Hor, sons of Myriam, Moses' sister. While Myriam decays and Meri-Amon - loved by Amun - Hor designates the light of the world, created at the same time as the world. Hor is referred to as the son of God, the **"primeval light [Hor] whom the holy one, blessed be he, had created at the same time as the world, and that he was the son of him who delivered the world. According to another explanation, Hor is taken in the sense of white; [...] the whitest of all."**[10]

The myth of the murder of the Egyptian and of the golden calf is an encryption, a cosmogony that takes place between celestial beings and not a History. It is indeed an Elohim among others, a celestial Man, a Man of appearance, a cosmic god, that Moses killed, as the Zohar attests once again:

"He was great and honored, as the venerable [Rav Amnouna] explained... ...The true "Man of Measure" has a span that extends from one end of the world to the other, which was the case with the first man. If you say that it is written "five cubits", know that these five cubits stretched from the ends of the world to the ends of the world."[11]

---

10   Zohar, tome IV, Le livre de la splendeur, op. cit., p. 77.

11   Zohar, tome V, Le livre de la splendeur, op.cit., p. 66 9a.

It is indeed a mythology, even an Osirian cosmogony where the ancient ISRAEL-OSIRIS is struck, and not a lived "History". A new myth of the assassination of Osiris is inscribed in the Old Testament, where Moses temporarily plays the role of Set, the assassin of Osiris. This Man called "Egyptian" MITSRI in Hebrew or YAHOUD in Aramaic is a celestial, cosmic being. He is a man who symbolizes the "Light of Egypt", which can only be Osiris and which the Zohar calls "Light of Israel". He carries a spear, the spear of the Egyptian on which was engraved **"the explicit name of the forty-two colors"** [12]which can only be the name of Osiris/Israel, corresponding to forty-two nomes.

In fact, the only God-Man who corresponds to the explanations given by the Kabbalah is therefore Osiris and his forty-two judges, the cosmic man, the first Man, the celestial head of the celestial court, a title that the Zohar concentrates in the expression "Light of Israel". The Egyptian Man is also compared in the Kabbalah to the two lions of Moab, the two lions symbolizing the Temples of the Father:

"He smote the two lions of Moab" (MO-AB = coming from the Father), precisely, the Temples of the Father who is in heaven because of which they are now destroyed and annihilated to the point that ALL THE LIGHTS THAT LIGHT ISRAEL HAVE BEEN BLANKED. Moreover, he descended and struck the lion: in ancient times, when this river poured out its waters into the Underworld [the Nile], Israel dwelt in a state of perfection, offering sacrifices of pacification and oblations to make atonement for their souls, and from Above came down the figure of a lion" [13]

CLEARLY, THE KABBALAH DENOUNCES MOSES AS THE ASSASSIN OF OSIRIS, THE OLF ISRAEL.

---

12   Ibidem.

13   Ibidem, p. 66, 9a.

Allegorical representation of Osiris, the Son who came from the Father in the temples. The rebirth of life and light (Horus-Osiris) is accomplished between the two lions of space and time.

Allegory of Osiris, the Ankh life between the two separate mountains - also symbolizing the waters separated by the sun and the two lions of time, the tomb of Sennedjem.

The Egyptian and the two lions embody the past and future time between the hieroglyph Ankh ☥ (the Presence), the light of Israel and the light of the god ASAR called god of Egypt. Atum, the primordial god, was duplicated in three powers, Atum, Shu and Tephnut. These last two thus incarnate the doubles of Atum. They are called the twins, symbolized either by two lions or by the separation of the primordial waters, which will also form the two celestial mountains, or the thighs of Isis, the mother of God, the great serpent giving birth to the light. The lions form the symbolic, secret bases of the pyramid.

Moses thus struck, broke the temples of the heavenly Father... These are, of course, the famous Egyptian temples of ancient times, where God as Father was worshipped, not the gods. When Moses and his brother Aaron appear before Pharaoh, Moses' staff, the famous staff/rod transformed into a snake, swallows the snakes of Pharaoh's wise men.

This is another message to confirm the symbolic, programmed destruction of Egypt, of its light by the new revealed power. Later, during the first plague of Egypt, the Patriarch strikes the waters of the river, the Nile, changed into a river of blood, still with his sacred staff. The Nile itself is the great sinuous serpent named Yeor and Acher/ASAR in Hebrew, the river of light. The river of blood symbolizes the death of Osiris, the death of the serpent struck by another serpent/staff/rod of Moses: **"The myth of Osiris, alluded to here, explains the phenomenon of the annual flooding of the Nile as an organic liquid that flows from Osiris murdered and thrown into the water by Seth."**[14]. In the desert, Moses **"struck the rock with his staff twice"** (Numbers 20:11), with his staff/serpent, in order to give the Children of Israel water.

But again, Kabbalah reveals that God's name was engraved on Moses' staff/serpent. It was with the divine serpent that Moses struck the rock... Moses struck God...

---

14   Jan Assmann. Mort et Au-delà dans l'Égypte ancienne. Éditions du Rocher, 2003, p. 516-517.

"Take in your hand the rod with which you struck the River." Why did Moses have to strike the stone with this rod? Because the sacred Name was engraved on it. This rod was originally a snake, as it is written "the trace of the snake on the Tzur" What does Tzur mean? It is God as it is written "The works of God (Tzur) are perfect".[15]

"The stone [tzur] in question was the image of the serpent. And it was to express his abhorrence of the serpent that Moses struck the stone, instead of following God's commandment"[16]

It is said that Moses - with his Osirian stick/serpent - strikes the Egyptian/serpent, the light of Israel, a second time the river/serpent which turns into blood, a third time the rock/serpent which brings forth the saving water for the Children of Israel. Thus, the river and the rock struck by Moses conceal the allegorical murder of the Egyptian aka the ancient Osiris.

"In the Egyptian's hand was a spear": this is the divine staff that was given to Moses as it is written "The staff of Elohim is in his hands"... "[Moses] took the spear from the Egyptian". Moses then lost the staff and never had it in his hands again."[17]

This is illuminating. By striking the rock with the said spear of the Egyptian, Moses strikes again the symbol of the divine serpent of Israel. The same goes for the rock: "And he killed him with his spear ": **because he failed in striking the rock, he died without entering the holy land; THE LIGHT THEREFORE DIED FROM ISRAEL[18]**

And this is all the more important because in the Bible, Yahweh tells Moses that Moses will not be able to see his face, but Yahweh will stand "in the cleft of the Rock," the very place where the serpent is located...which Moses had struck!

"Again, Yahweh said, "Here is a place near me; you shall stand on the rock. When my Glory passes by, I will put

15   Zohar, tome III, Le livre de la splendeur, op. cit., p. 281.

16   Zohar, tome IV, Le livre de la splendeur, op. cit., p. 311.

17   Ibidem.

18   Ibidem.

you in the cleft of the rock and cover you with my hand until I have passed by." (Exodus, 33, 21-22)

The scribes have left us the messages, which together make us understand that Moses struck the very symbol of the Cornerstone, the Pyramid, the sacred domain of the primordial serpent, the Ouroboros forming the celestial placenta containing the child Hor, the very birthplace of God, the ancient god of the Nile Valley:

"...the stone that emerges from the Ocean every thousand years; and, when it emerges from the waters, the sea is lifted up and Leviathan [the primordial serpent] **stirs..."**[19]

And that's not all. While the Hebrews are presumed to be slaves of Pharaoh, the Midrash unapologetically names Amram and Yosebed, the parents of Moses and Aaron, as the most important figures of their generation (Rashi Exodus II:1). The Zohar goes much further: Amram and Yosebed are the **"SONS OF THE PRIMARY SERPENT"**:

they are simply deities, the sun and the moon begotten by the primitive serpent, the sons and daughters of God, the children of the great solar serpent, called Leviathan, which undoubtedly makes Moses a son of Osiris:

"The words "and a man" [Amram] **"of the family of Levi" designate the "Holy One blessed be he" in the degree of supreme wisdom** [= sunlight]. **The house of Levi is Leviathan who will bring joy to the world as it is written "you have formed Leviathan to delight in him". The words "Married a daughter of Levi"** [Yokebed] **refer to the Holy One blessed be He, to the degree of "moonlight"**[20]

This Osirian cosmic dramaturgy thus opposes two cosmic serpents. Moses, the son of the primordial serpent to the Egyptian symbolizing also the serpent and the sun - the ancient light of Israel - makes of Moses the new Osiris, the new Israel. This mysterious

---

19   Zohar, tome V. Le livre de la splendeur. Par Jean de Pauly. Maisonneuve & Larose, 1985, p. 359.

20 Le Zohar, tome III, Le livre de la splendeur, op. cit., p. 51.

reading is totally inaccessible to the reader of the Bible, because it is hidden in the secret of Gnosis or Kabbalah. This decoding was, of course, inaccessible to Ptolemy, for whom the Egyptian and Israel were two distinct entities, opposing the Jews to the Greeks. Whereas it is a cosmic conflict, a new Osirian cosmogony. We are very far from the film The Ten Commandments. Scenography where a titanic combat is expressed, between Moses, divinized as the MESS son of God, son of the solar serpent, against the Egyptian striking his son, concealing two other solar deities.

This decoding gives a whole new meaning to the biblical text. The Egyptian man MISRI striking a Hebrew man is none other than the father striking his son. It is the emblematic Father of the Children of Israel that Moses struck. Sigmund Freud had suggested that Moses, the image of the primitive Father, had been killed by the Children of Israel. Whereas for the Kabbalah, it is Moses who strikes the primitive Father "Israel" to death, symbolizing the ancient Egyptian civilization. Much later, during the episode of the golden calf, Moses breaks the Tables of the Law, reduces the idol to powder and makes the Children of Israel drink it. The Pyramid Texts reveal that the golden calf is the symbol of the rebirth of Ra (Yahu = the Light of Osiris/Israel), each morning with the light of the sun, the light of the world, the light of God.

"IT IS IN THE FORM OF A GOLDEN CALF THAT THE SUN APPEARS IN THE SKY"[21]

The other key to this immense enigma is found in the Bible. By invoking the golden calf, the Children of Israel address God, Osiris, by his sacred name "Israel." By proclaiming themselves as sons of the golden calf, the scribes are giving us the most secret message of the Bible. The Children of Israel are the Sons of Osiris.

"And he [Aaron] took it out of their hands, and made a mold of it, and made it a calf of metal; and they said, "BEHOLD YOUR GODS, O ISRAEL, WHO HAVE BRUSHED YOU UP FROM THE COUNTRY OF EGYPT!" (Exodus 32:4)

Once again, by striking the golden calf, Moses strikes Osiris/Israel, the light. Why? It is obvious, the golden calf symbolizes the will

21   Cf. Christian Jacq. La tradition primordiale de l'Égypte ancienne selon les textes des Pyramides. Grasset & Fasquelle. 1998. P.264.

of the Children of Israel to return to the religion of the Father, the ancient Israel incarnated by the golden calf, son of the heavenly cow. Reason for which Kyrios/Yahweh alias Ptolemy decides to exterminate the people. But Moses intervenes to ask Kyrios for mercy. Transgressing the Law he has just received - whereas it is written that Kyrios or Yahweh had forgiven the Children of Israel! - Moses was incensed and ordered the massacre of three thousand people:

Moses stood in the gate of the camp and said, "Which of you is for Kiryos? Let him come to me. And all the sons of Levi gathered themselves together unto him. And he said unto them, This is what Kyrios the Theos of Israel saith, Gird up every man his sword, and go through the camp from gate to gate, and let every man slay his brother, and his neighbor, and his kinsman. And the sons of Levi did as Moses commanded them, and on that day three thousand of the people died (Exodus 32:26-28)

This is not a historical massacre, for there is another message in the text, a historical one. In the context of Hellenization, the sword of the Levites refers to the flaming sword forbidding any return to the Garden of Eden. The Levites (the army at the orders of Moses), embody here the army of priests and soldiers led by Ptolemy, the unique pharaoh who put the Jews in slavery under the bondage of paying a heavy tribute in drachmas and above all of accepting by force the Septuagint.

Thus, by striking the golden calf, Moses strikes Israel, its light, its gods, expressed clearly in the biblical text by the golden calf named Israel. Finally, Moses struck the whole of the people of Israel, the whole of humanity, the seventy nations. "Not a single one remained"22, the Kabbalah tells us. In historical fact, it is the Septuagint of Moses that, acting as a schism in the entire Middle East, will make the so-called "Egyptian" civilization disappear. The Bible states that despite Moses' initial promise, all the Hebrews or Egyptians who came out of Egypt died in the desert, except for the children who had not known Egypt.

All the people who came out of Egypt, the males, all the men of war had died in the desert, on the road, after they came

22   Le Zohar, tome IV, Le livre de la splendeur, op. cit.

out of Egypt. All these people who came out of Egypt were circumcised, but all the people who were born in the wilderness on the way out of Egypt were not circumcised (Joshua 5:5-6).

It is constant that the symbols attached to Egypt and the Egyptian are perfectly confused in the Kabbalah with the original light of Israel, with the ancient light of the civilization of the Nile Valley. If we put all these metaphors together, Moses - playing the politics of Ptolemaic II Philadelphos - would therefore be the son of God, the son of the primordial serpent who, by means of the staff/serpent, would have struck another serpent, a Man, an Egyptian, the new light of Israel, the river, the two lions of the Father, the temples of the Father, the god of light, the sun, the golden calf, the Children of Israel, the rock, the Cornerstone abandoned by the builders, all the Osirian symbols of the ancient civilization known as Egyptian. Moses did strike Osiris/Israel. Moses struck the ancient Israel, a place where he grew up, the land where he learned all the Egyptian Wisdom.

It is thus the whole ancient civilization of Israel, falsely called Egyptian, which is struck by Moses, with the power of another God-Serpent, another God who dressed himself with the skin of the serpent, makes us understand the Kabbalah. Moses uses the Osirian power of a "cunning" snake-god, named Kyrios in the Septuagint. Undoubtedly, Ptolemy is behind this terrifying serpent, endowed with the magical power of God. The cunning serpent of the Garden of Eden... This allegorical passage symbolizes the pure and simple disappearance of the Children of Israel in the desert (Genesis XV, 5). Moses symbolically buries the light of Israel; we will come back to this in detail in the third part of this trilogy. The psychoanalyst Gerard Huber has compared the sand "Hol" to the domain of the profane, of the darkness of death, in relation to the domain of holiness "Kodesh" life. Thus, Moses did not only transform, overturn, upset the Jewish religion by de-Egyptianizing the Jews, as Jan Assmann claims. He purely and simply destroyed the ancient Israel, the authentic religion of the Nile Valley.

THE CELESTIAL SERPENT IS OMNIPRESENT IN THE SECRET COMMENTARY

For Kabbalah, the Sons of Israel are a people of "sons of kings" expelled from their native land. Which land? The Garden of Eden? Egypt? Canaan? Here comes the hidden, esoteric interpretation, which no longer tells a story of slaves, but the story of all humanity leaving Egypt. It is no longer just the classic story of Adam, Noah, Abraham, Isaac, Jacob, Joseph, Moses, Joshua..., of which there are no traces, but a historical event of such great magnitude that it was linked to an upheaval in the activity of the powers of the cosmos. From then on, the myth of the Patriarchs conceals a cosmogony in which the history of God and his various manifestations in the world of light, in perpetual war against the world of darkness, take place. As we have seen, the fight between Jacob and the Angel of Esau is deciphered in the Kabbalah as the victory of the sun (Jacob) against the celestial serpent of darkness (Esau), a serpent named Samael or Amalek.

Another example. The staff of Moses that turns into a snake, swallowing the serpents of Pharaoh symbolizes, again, the struggle between the Osirian demiurgic powers of light against the darkness in the tombs of the Pharaohs and the Pyramid Texts. Through the story of the Hebrews enslaved by Pharaoh, it is, of course, the story of humanity that the Septuagint/Torah tells us, but it is also the story of the cosmos and the very story of God. The biblical story begins with the cunning serpent who, by chasing Adam and Eve, symbolically expels the light, the sun, the Children of Israel from the Garden of Eden, bringing darkness and death into the world.

A passage in the Zohar informs us that if Adam had not eaten the fruit of the tree of the knowledge of good and evil, we would have two good snakes at our disposal, instead of having one good and one bad snake.

The "good snake" remains omnipresent behind the stories and characters of the Bible. It is omnipresent behind the kings of Israel wearing the serpent crown of Nahash the Ammonite, the Kabbalah affirming that God himself had wrapped a serpent around the divine Shekhina, that the River of the Garden of Eden (the Nile) forms the crown of the Sacred King...

The reader will see that the serpent is involved everywhere, with Adam, Eve, Cain and Abel, Noah, Abraham and Lot, Jacob and Esau... And above all Joseph, whom the Kabbalah calls the "King", the sacred Nile (the River), and the serpent seer! The serpent miraculously returns with Moses, swallowing the serpents of Pharaoh: it is an Osirian metaphor of the serpent of light swallowing the serpent of darkness, or the Angel of Life striking the Angel of Death. For the Kabbalah, God, under his different names (Yahweh, Elohim, Adonai, Yah...), acts through the serpent of good or evil, of life or death. Yahweh (or Elohim) constitutes an infinite energy, expressed through the main characters of the Torah.

These are "Elohim", gods who constitute the Body of God in the form of the attributes called "Kabbalistic sephirot". If we have entered into these Kabbalistic considerations, it is to reveal two capital points: Kabbalah takes up exactly the Egyptian scheme inscribed in the Pyramid Texts, where the Body of Pharaoh is the Body of the unique god, Osiris, formed by the assembly of the gods or Elohim/Yods/Neteru יייי.

For the second point, the Kabbalah constitutes the essential link, even an extraordinary bridge between the Torah, the Bible, the Gospels, and the Koran. A bridge that could link the three religions, overturning our beliefs by revealing the hidden meaning of the Holy Scriptures, in a fantastic coherence with archaeology.

Thus, for more than two millennia, millions of believers have believed that the characters of the Bible really, historically existed, inscribed in a "History" and a well-ordered chronology. With determination, without respite, archaeologists have been tracking down, without any convincing result.

But for the Kabbalah, the heroes of the Bible all have the same face, the face of the "Perfect Man" of Adam, Israel/Osiris, the first perfect man "Tam'", the primitive image of God. Now this mystical construction corresponds exactly to Tem', Tam' says Atum', the demiurge grandfather of Osiris. By a miraculous, eschatological, "Osirian" process of the migration of the soul of the first man, Adam, image of Elohim, image of God, becomes Enochh, then Noah, then Abraham, Isaac, Jacob, Joseph, Moses... Finally, it is the God of Egypt under his different names who is hidden behind the characters of the Old Testament. Through a system called the "Sephirotic Tree", a coding assembling ten "Sephirot", or ten attributes or energies forming the Body of Yahweh, allow the main characters of the Torah to be elevated to the title of Elohim, or Men of God.

The original source of the Sephirot is found in Adam, who in the earthly paradise, the famous Garden of Eden, ate the fruit of the tree of the knowledge of good and evil to become like God, like Elohim. This is the reason why Adam was expelled from the Garden of Eden and condemned to die, but will in fact be expelled from the garden, concealing the expulsion of the Jews from the Nile Valley.

But Kabbalah conceals another story: the Garden of Eden is none other than the secret of the opposition between the Tree of Life and the Tree of Knowledge of Good and Evil: the Tree of Life conceals the paradise of the land of Egypt watered by the four mythical rivers, and Adam expelled from paradise symbolizes the Children of Israel who came out of Egypt. From then on, the story of the Exodus can be deciphered through the definitive loss of the Garden of Eden, Tree of Life, the immense allegory of the loss of Egypt. The Hebrews "slaves" of Pharaoh become slaves of their passion: they pay, as it were, for the sin of having forgotten their past, the Tree of Life, and "consumed" the fruit of the Tree of Knowledge of Good and Evil.

Because of the symbolic sin of the golden calf, they lose their first Torah broken by Moses, and inherit the second. Now, the first Torah is precisely identified with the Tree of Life, with the lost paradise, Egypt... Because of the action of the serpent who embodies darkness, hell, the Angel of Death, Satan, and especially a king called "Pharaoh", the Children of Israel (Adam) are driven out of Egypt and condemned to die in the desert...

The collapse of the Egyptian civilization will profoundly change the history of humanity and give birth to the Bible and the Kabbalah. In history, the loss of Egypt goes back to the time when the Babylonians, Persians, Greeks, invaded and plundered materially, but also spiritually the Nile Valley since the 7th century BC, deporting thousands of men, women and children put into slavery by the conquering kings and upsetting the social structure, theology and laws of ancient Egypt. From that time on, we can speak of massive deportations of Jewish populations, never of Egyptians. The Jews, Youdaïos in Greek, Yahout' or Yahoud' in hieroglyphics, a word that precisely means inheritance, function, charge. The loss of the Egyptian empire was encoded through the mysticism of the Kabbalah, many passages of which attest that the myth of Adam driven out of the Garden of Eden refers to the Children of Israel who came out of Egypt as a result of the ten plagues. In the end, it refers to the factual history of the Jewish people driven out of Egypt. Kabbalah allows us to return to the Torah, which is in its own way a cryptic history of memory, but above all a series of cryptic allegories and metaphors, genially codified from the factual history of the Jews.

How is this codification articulated? The story of Adam, driven from the Garden of Eden, is an allegorical language that **"sets up the elements for discovering the history of Israel"**[23]

---

23   Midrach Rabba, tome I, **Genèse Rabba**. Collection « les dix paroles ». Verdier, 1987, note 32 p. 221.

Here are two examples. The first, as we have seen, is the Nile, the river of the Garden of Eden, which divides into four rivers. This separation symbolizes the exile of Israel, the root of the division, the annihilation of the Egyptian civilization. The Children of Israel coming out of Egypt prefigure Adam and Eve driven out of the Garden of Eden with the serpent. The Garden of Eden becomes the symbol of Egypt. Trapped in the desert, the Children of Israel cry out in despair. The Egyptians (the serpent) drowned in the Red Sea cry out in the same way. Kabbalah makes this extraordinary connection: it is one and the same cry. The cry of the snake driven out of the Garden of Eden symbolizes the cry of this humanity (Israel - Adam, Eve, the snake) that comes out of the valley of the Nile, driven out of its earthly paradise, Egypt, into the desert, the world of death:

"Her cry resounds from one end of the world to the other. We were supposed to learn from the serpent about the fall of Egypt, but in fact we are taught about the serpent first: "the cry of the Egyptians sounds like the cry of the serpent" (Jer. 46:22).

Egypt thus symbolizes the Tree of Life, the world of the living, the world of light. Man's refusal to die, to lose the earthly paradise, gives rise to a perpetual war against hell, good against evil, life against death. Hell is a kind of "counter-world" that the Hebrews or Children of Israel, legitimate heirs of Egypt, refuse to accept. It is the Other Side, the world below where the powerful serpent Samael reigns, identified with the Angel of Death and Satan, Shaâtan' in the Koran. For both Kabbalah and the Qur'an, the exit of the Children of Israel from Egypt has nothing to do with a geographical exit from Egypt to Canaan. Rather, it is the exit from the darkness of death into the light of life, associated with the return of Egypt to the Children of Israel. Thus, in the esoteric reading, the exit from Egypt has nothing to do with an alleged slavery of the Hebrews in a remote pharaonic era. It is only a symbolic slavery, which signifies the passage from the darkness of death to the resurrection.

According to Kabbalah, any literal reading of the Bible, the Gospels or the Qur'an leads to a form of slavery, "a slavery of Egypt. Why? As we have seen, the literal reading has led to a confusion of the meaning of the scriptures, a loss of the meaning of the universal divine in favor of an exclusive god, with laws locked up in the scripture, in the Greek logos. This is unfortunately what we see today with the dangerous actions of the fanatical leaders of the Scriptures, who advocate perpetual war, messianic, and build atomic bombs to destroy Israel and the planet supposedly in the name of Allah... While Israel is undoubtedly one of the most sacred names of the Koran!... This shows the vital and urgent importance of deciphering the biblical and Koranic texts, in the light of the discoveries of archaeology. As Galileo said at the end of his life, **"And yet, it turns"**... Egypt SA-RÂ, MISRA, IS-RÂ is none other than ancient Israel, symbolizing the lost paradise, an inheritance restored to its heirs by Allah, the civilization destroyed by the Babylonians and Persians, invaded by the Greeks and by Rome...

Finally, the metaphors of the Gnosis or Kabbalah bring us the essential ecumenical message for humanity. The God of Israel of the three religions is the unique and unknown God of ancient Egypt, whatever his name, MISRA or IS-RÂ, called Osiris, Yahweh/Jehovah (the Yahô of the kings Amenhotep), Adonai (Aton'), Ptah-Yah (Ptah of Memphis, Yah of Soleb), Amen (Amun of Thebes), Raâ (Raâ of Heliopolis), the celestial Queen (Isis), Christ King of Israel, Araâh, Allah... a message of peace.

It is now time to turn to the historical evidence that vindicates the universal, hidden messages of the Bible, the Kabbalah, the Gospels and the Qur'an, starting with the most ancient, the hieroglyphic of the Son of God, IS-RÂ, Osiris/Israel, visible everywhere in the civilization of the ancient Egyptians. Historical documents confirm that in the 5th century B.C., the Torah of Moses was not the authority of Jewish priesthood and thought. The Torah was not as we know it today. The Jews worshipped God through multiple syncretic images of God, among them Osiris, symbol of the Light, the sun and the primordial serpent...

Researchers have even discovered in the ostraca of Elephantine that Yaho, the god worshipped by the Jews had one or two wives and even a son, like Osiris... What does the Bible tell us? The second book of Kings states that the kings of Israel and the Children of Israel worshipped the primordial serpent. The one that Moses had carved out of bronze at the command of Yahweh. This serpent had saved the Hebrews from the evil serpents of the desert.

"For the children of Israel had until then burned up perfumes before him, and he was called 'Nehushan'"

(II Kings 18:4)

The mention **"until then"** means precisely that until King Hezekiah, the kings of Israel worshipped the primordial serpent, according to the seal of this king. As we shall see, the royal buckets of Hezekiah that archaeologists have found in the ruins of Jerusalem demonstrate that he worshipped Osiris/Israel. Hezekiah ignored the second and third commandments of Moses..., Hezekiah and the kings of ancient Israel ultimately ignored the Torah of Moses. The cult of the serpent was practiced inside the Temple, which could only be an Osirian Temple, called "Egyptian"... Because the only kings who were worshipped through the eyes of the serpent were the SA-RÂ, the kings of Israel... The Children of Israel thus worshipped the primitive solar serpent named Nahash: **they were then the "Sons of the Beneficial Serpent", which clearly means the sons of Osiris and Isis as confirmed by the golden calf named Israel**, which means in clear the sons of Osiris and Isis.

Did the kings of Israel, followers of the cult of God through the primordial serpent, really know the Torah of Moses? Did they apply its commandments? According to the second book of Kings, Hilki-Yahu (High Priest of King Josiah, himself the last of the kings of Israel), discovers one day the book of the Torah of Moses in the Temple. King Josiah tears his clothes and exclaims:

"Go and inquire of the LORD for me, and for the people, and for all Judah, concerning the words of this book which was found; for great is the wrath of the LORD, which is kindled against us, BECAUSE OUR FATHERS HAVE NOT OBEYED THE WORDS OF THIS BOOK, NOR DONE ANYTHING WHICH IS PRESCRIBED TO US.[24]

Once again, only the true sons of S-RÂ called "Egyptians" worshipped God through the primordial serpent. The action of tearing his clothes is a break with the past. A break with the religion of the fathers, made by the symbolic rupture of the Body of God. It is said that Yahweh, the god of the Bible, was dressed in the image of the primordial serpent:

"The Holy One, blessed be He, rolled a serpent around the holy one"[25]

Adam and Eve are clothed with the skin of the serpent. The Chapters of Rabbi Eliezer show that following the original sin, **"From the skin that the serpent shed in its molting, the Holy One, blessed be He, made a robe of glory for Adam and Eve, made a robe of glory for Adam and his helper."**[26]

The Kabbalist Gershom Sholem reports that in the primordial celestial world, the Body of God was broken and the soul of the Messiah would come from the Holy Serpent that arose from the Breaking of the Vessels. Osirian metaphor of the breaking of the Body of God scattered in the darkness of the cosmos because of the sins of men. The body of the Egyptian god Nou is formed of three vessels, originally the god One transformed into three primordial powers. The repair of the Body of Israel, the *Tikoun*, becomes, as in ancient Egypt, the metaphor

---

24   II Rois 22, 13

25   Le Zohar, tome IV, Op. cit., p. 77 et 234.

26   Chapitres de Rabbi Éliézer. Pirké de Rabbi Éliézer. Collection Les Dix Paroles. Éditions Verdier, 1983, p. 124 chap. 20.

imagined by the victory of the serpent of good over the serpent of evil. The Serpent Tikun, will be able to bring the Messiah:

"In the depths of the abyss, with this most holy soul, were "serpents" that tormented her and tried to seduce her. To these serpents was given the "Holy Serpent" who is the Messiah, for does not the Hebrew word Nahash have the same numerical value as the word Messiah Mashiah?"[27]

"Only to the extent that the process of the Tikun of the whole world sorts out good and evil in the depths of the primordial space is the soul of the Messiah freed from its bondage. When the soul, which is at work in its prison and struggles with the serpents or "dragons", has reached its perfection, the soul of the Messiah will leave its prison and reveal itself to the world in an earthly incarnation" [28]

The broken Body of God is none other than the Body of Israel. What about the Serpent Messiah in ancient Egypt, in the cosmogony of Heliopolis? It is exactly the same process. Osiris, symbol of the serpent of light, of all the light of the world, is murdered and then cut into pieces by his brother Set, who also takes the form of the serpent Apophis. Set scatters the pieces of Osiris' body throughout the land of the Nile valley, thus throughout the immensity of the cosmos. The soul of Osiris exiled in the underworld of the underworld goes to war against the serpents or the heavenly serpent/dragon Apophis. Isis goes in search of the pieces of the body of her brother and husband, she "repairs" the light of the world by gathering and reconstituting the celestial body of Osiris. The serpent is seen as the celestial vault - the Milky Way - surrounding the world of day and night, as the battle of light against the serpent of death and darkness, and above all as the Queen of Heaven giving birth to the sun at night. The body of the serpent formed the solar placenta and that of the SA-RÂ kings, represented by the

---

27   Nahash: Noun : 50, Het: 8, Chin: 300 = 358 ; Machiyah: Mem 40, Chin: 300 Yod: 10 = 358.

28 Guershom G. Sholem. Les Grands Courants de la Mystique Juive. Éditions PAYOT, Paris, 1950, p. 315.

child Horus. In syncretic symbolism, the good and the bad snake are combined into one. They symbolize duality, the celestial mother of all pharaohs, Horus, the son of Isis and Osiris, is the sun coming out of the cosmos, formed by the primordial dark waters, all embodied by the great serpent Ouroboros. The texts of the Pyramids of Heliopolis, more than four millennia old, confirm this:

"The mother of the king is a great serpent, and it is a serpent of fire, the red crown, which gives birth to him; he is himself a reptile with many folds, provider of vital powers..."[29]

The primitive serpent forms the maternal placenta of the sun RÂ or Horus, SARA or ISRA, the celestial light, issued from the placenta of the kings, the night that swallows the day (or vice versa).

According to the Kabbalah, every man is born from the bite of the primordial serpent[30], **"the serpent is the image of the souls"[31]**. Israel is compared to a snake or a silkworm **"whose**

---

29   Christian Jacq, La tradition primordiale de l'Égypte ancienne selon les textes des Pyramides, op. cit., p. 265.

30   « Quand arrive le moment d'enfanter, la femelle ne peut y parvenir. Dieu envoie alors un grand et puissant serpent qui mord la femelle à l'orifice de la matrice, ce qui accélère l'enfantement. ». Zohar, tome IV. Le livre de la splendeur. Par Jean de Pauly. Maisonneuve & Larose, 1985§ 220a, p. 234.

31   Zohar, tome IV. Ibidem, p. 234.

strength is manifested through the mouth"[32.] But as we shall see, the kings of Israel all wore the crown of Nahash' the Ammonite, which means nothing other than the serpent of Amon... Yahweh/Elohim is named ARÂA in the book of Samuel. The Babylonian Talmud states that God himself is named Amen, meaning like Amon-Ra the Hidden One, the concealed one[33], the king in whom one has faith: **«El Melekh Neaman»**[34]

It is said that God wears a double red and white crown, like the one worn by all the kings of the Nile Valley... These unexplored tracks will lead us to the true identity of the «Pharaohs of Egypt». In the book of Jeremiah, the Judeans or Sons of Israel fleeing from the prophet take refuge in Egypt and claim the worship of the Queen of Heaven [35] pictured by the placental serpent «Ouroboros». They claim the ancestral worship of Isis-Nut, the primordial serpent of the pyramid texts, and not the exclusive and unique worship of Yahweh imposed by the prophet Jeremiah (Jer. XLIV, 16-17):

"But we want to do as our mouth has declared, to offer incense to the Queen of Heaven, and to make drink offerings to her, AS WE WERE, AND OUR FATHERS, OUR KINGS AND PRINCES, in the cities of Judah and the streets of Jerusalem: then we had bread to our fill, and we were happy, and saw no evil."

The Bible refers to Judah and Jerusalem as the Jews fled to Egypt to worship the Queen of Heaven. The text has obviously been transformed: as we have seen, the Judeans worshipped Osiris (Yaho) and Isis (Anat, Nut), the Queen of Heaven, not only in Jerusalem, but throughout Egypt. Two letters confirm the worship of Osiris as well as that of the Queen of Heaven in Syene (Nile delta):

---

32   Zohar, tome IV. Ibidem, §129b p. 41.

33   Amon signifie le pédagogue, l'architecte, l'artisan, mais aussi le dieu caché. Midrach Rabba, tome I, Genèse Rabba. Collection « les dix paroles ». Verdier, 1987, p. 31, chap. 1, § 1.

34   Aggadoth du Talmud de Babylone. La source de Jacob/ 'Ein Yaakov. Collection « Les dix paroles », Verdier, 1982. P. 237.

35   Isis/Nout, l'aimée d'Amon = Méri-Amon, qui deviendra Marie dans les Évangiles.

"On the 3rd of Kislev, year 7, that is, on the 21st day of Thoth, year 7 of King Darius, Abda'al the Sydonian, son of Abdesedek, came with his brother Azarba'al, to Abydos of Egypt before Osiris the great God..."[36]

"The initial greeting shows that besides the chapels dedicated to the Mesopotamian gods Nabû and Banit, there are also chapels in Syene for the cults of the Syrian-Phoenician gods Bet'El and the Phoenician gods Bet'El and the Queen of Heaven (i.e. Anat)"[37]

We know today that no monument, no tomb, no writing confirms the historical reality of the Scriptures concerning the slavery of the Hebrews told in the Old Testament, the Gospels and the Koran. Adam, Noah, the patriarchs, Abraham, Isaac, Jacob, Ishmael, Moses, the kings of Israel remain untraceable. The story of the Hebrews enslaved by the Egyptians, saved by Moses, crossing the Red Sea on their way out of a polytheistic Egypt has no historical reality. Finally, Israel, Osiris, God, and the Children of Israel are one and the same entity. For the Kabbalah, the Torah tells the story of the god of the Nile Valley who came to settle in the Garden of Eden under the name of Adam/Abraham/Isaac/Jacob/Joseph/Israel/Osiris. The story of the Children of Jacob (the Children of Israel) settling in Egypt is a huge metaphor for all of humanity, and in secret, for God himself. Clearly, if the Torah tells us the story of the Hebrews enslaved by Pharaoh, Kabbalah secretly codifies the story of the expelled god of Egypt with his symbolic Body, the Children of Israel. God alias Israel would have descended into the Nile valley to found the civilization of the SA-RÂ kings, renamed, unfortunately, Pharaonic Egyptian civilization by modern Egyptology, in pure and simple contempt of the reading of hieroglyphs.

---

36   Documents Araméens d'Égypte, op. cit., p. 340, inscription n°83.

37   Documents Araméens d'Égypte, op. cit., p. 160-161.

THE CROWN TO THE SERPENT OF THE KINGS OF ISRAEL

The reader is asked to pay the greatest attention to the following explanation. It is necessary to return constantly to the myth of Isis and Osiris and to the myth of Horus, born of the snake swallowing itself, in order to understand how the 72 editors of the Bible concealed the origin of the crowning of the kings of Israel, which is almost identical to that of the pharaohs. In the Egyptian legend, the serpent uraeus placed on Pharaoh's forehead embodies the cosmos: its right eye symbolizes the sun, its left eye the moon. Its body forms the allegory of the Pyramid, the Milky Way, the whole symbolizing the celestial Mother, Isis or Nut (the vulture that appears next to the royal uraeus on Tutankhamun's crown).

The mastery of the snake Uraeus allows King SA-Ra to reach the divine light and power, to overcome the forces of the cosmos, to ensure the balance in the universe, by the perpetual victory of the day over the night, of the sun over the darkness. In the same way, to conquer the royalty, the god Set had envied the crown to the solar serpent of his brother Osiris. Set orchestrated the murder of his brother, then cut up his body and scattered the pieces throughout Egypt.

But in the cosmic language of the priests, such a scattering of the celestial body of Osiris corresponds to the death and pulverization of the sun and the light of the world in the abyss of the universe. The stars and constellations thus formed the residues of the body of Osiris. A kind of cosmic exile of Osiris which will become long after the exile of Israel also compared by the Kabbalah to the dispersion of the parcels of light in the darkness of the cosmos...

Thus, by traveling through Egypt, i.e. the world in search of the remains of the body of her deceased husband, the goddess Isis becomes the celestial Queen who travels throughout the cosmos desperately trying to reconstitute the body of Osiris, which is the Body of God, the body of the sun, the light of the world (the son of the celestial cow Hathor embodied by the golden calf). She is in fact trying to re-establish the universal balance and harmony between men as attested by the Corpus Hermeticum. In the meantime, following his crime, the god Set embodies the victory of the serpent of darkness, master of the forces of night and death, over the serpent of light, of day, of life. According to Plutarch, after his crime, Seth fled for seven days into the desert before returning to fight Horus the son of Osiris. Seth had then gouged out the right eye of HOR

(Horus in Greek), his left eye representing the moon. Symbolically, Seth killed the sun, the darkness killed the light... He symbolically butchered the bull Apis or the sacred ox, which Osiris symbolizes.

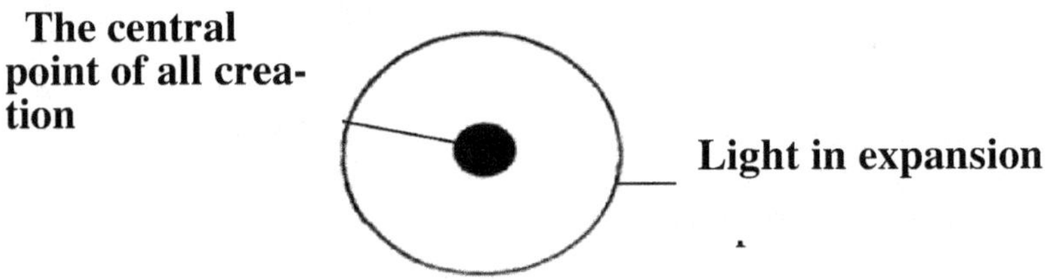

Rebirth of the sun Raâ

or right eye of Horus (HOR).

This is to say to what extent what we call «Egyptian religion» was in fact a cult to the creative light. And this through the images, the statues demonized as idols by the Bible, whereas they only served as mediums, as a synthesis of reflection on the mysteries of the world. God did not need to be revealed by the Word/Logos, for he was the light that flooded the world.

RAÂ also means vision, to see, like the Hebrew ראה Raâ. The serpent Uraeus, whose right eye is the sun and whose left eye is the moon, thus embodies Hor/Horus, the GOLDEN light in Hebrew, the cosmic, eternal crown, haloing the head of kings (RAÂ is the origin of the word king). Thus, after the victory of

Horus over the forces of night, the uraeus becomes a symbol of victory, the triumph of good over evil, a kind of trophy proudly displayed by all the SA-RÂ kings falsely named pharaohs by the ancient Greeks. It is this victory of the God/Light that is expressed by the Ouroboros (also by the falcon, RÂA in Hebrew), it is the light of the day that swallows the darkness of the night, which is perfectly expressed by the god of Egypt symbolized by YAH or HOR, the light, when he declares in chapter 110 of the Book of Coming Out to Light:

"I am Yah and I have swallowed the darkness"[38]

In the Bible, the victory of light over darkness is expressed through the serpent of Moses swallowing the serpents of Pharaoh, but also through the Jewish and Christian Passover, or feast of the Redemption of Israel symbolized by the exit from Egypt. In the Qur'an, the **Sons of Isrâïla do not come out of Egypt, but their journey is exclusively from darkness to light.** The myth of the snake of light swallowing the snake of darkness is part of the same process, it is the origin of the crowns of the SA-RÂ kings called "pharaohs". It is the same snake of Amun that participates in the crowning of the kings of Israel... How does Kabbalah explain that the kings of Israel wore the crown of Amun? The first book of Samuel relates the taking of power by Saul, the first king of Israel. It brings in the symbolic characters of the myth of Isis and Osiris. Saul is the son of Kich, son of ABIEL meaning my Father (ABI) is God (EL). Saul in Hebrew conceals SA-EL שָׁאוּל and therefore, we find the origin SA-RÂ 🦅 ☉ . (son of Ra) in the name of the first king of Israel. The king of the Ammonites is called "Nahash the Ammonite", which translates as "snake of Amun", precisely Amun the primitive snake of the ancient Egyptians. But in a blunt formula, the idol is called "an abomination of the Sons of Amun" by Jewish tradition. Although Nahash the Ammonite passes for the evil serpent, the abomination of Amun, the defilement to be fought, it is this crown that will adorn the head of King David and the kings of Israel...

---

38   Le Livre des Morts des Anciens Égyptiens. Littératures anciennes du Proche-Orient. Les Éditions du Cerf, 1967, p. 147.

It is thus identical to the Uraeus serpent, image of SA-RÂ, enemy of Apophys, the other serpent that SA-RÂ must tame every night in his fight against the powers of darkness. Why? The secret tradition, the Kabbalah, states that the crown of Nahash the Ammonite was adorned with a serpent, the primordial serpent. Therefore, Nahash the Ammonite corresponds to the primordial serpent Kneph, which originally invested the celestial head of the god Amun[39], still according to the so-called Egyptian legend. Nahash the Ammonite also corresponds to the allegory of the serpent Apophys, Pharaoh's enemy (or to Seth, the assassin of Osiris).

Let us see with what precision the Bible conceals the Osirian secret of the birth of the kings of Israel, concealing a battle of the light against the serpent of darkness. Nahash the Ammonite refuses the enthronement and coronation of Saul, the future king of Israel. Nahash challenges all of Israel and Saul by threatening to gouge out the right eye of the Elders of Yabesh[40], considered Saul's Fathers.

And Nahash the Ammonite came and besieged Yabesh-Gilead. And all the inhabitants of Yabesh said to Nahash, Make a covenant with us, and we will serve you. But Nahash the Ammonite said to them, "I will make a covenant with you on condition that I cut out the right eye of all of you, so that I may bring reproach on all Israel". And the elders of Yabesh said unto him: Grant us a truce of seven days, that we may send messengers throughout all the territory of Israel; and if there is no one to help us, we will surrender to you.   (I Samuel XI, 1-3)

In hieroglyphic symbolism, the right eye of the uraeus is the symbol of the sun. The Sons of Yabesh implore Nahash the Ammonite for a seven-day truce. Saul, invested with the wrath of Yahweh, then utters a threat against Israel if the latter dares to give allegiance to Nahash the Ammonite. As Seth had cut up Osiris, Saul had two oxen cut into several pieces which he scattered throughout Israel, I Sam. XI, 6-7:

---

39   Cyril Aldred, Akhénaton roi d'Égypte, Le Seuil, 1997, p. 86.
40   I Samuel XI, 1.

When Saul heard these things, he was seized by the spirit of God, and his anger was greatly inflamed. And he took a pair of oxen, and cut them in pieces, and sent them by the messengers throughout all the land of Israel, saying: Whoever does not follow Saul and Samuel, his oxen shall be treated in the same way. And the fear of the LORD came upon the people, and they went forth as one man.

The people must behave as one man if they want to avoid being scattered in the darkness, in order to reach Saul's kingship. The deliverance of Israel comes with the appearance of the sun[41] and great rejoicing[42]. The army of Israel is divided into three bodies[43], Nahash the Ammonite and his army are dispersed, exiled. They surrender to Saul. The Children of Israel ask for the death of the prisoners, but Saul refuses under the pretext of salvation, redemption by light:

The next day, Saul divided the people into three bodies. They entered the camp of the Ammonites on the eve of the morning, and they beat them until the heat of the day. Those who escaped were scattered, and not two were left together. Then the people said to Samuel, "Who said, 'Shall Saul reign over us? Hand over these people, that we may put them to death. But Saul said, "No one shall be put to death this day, for today the LORD has worked salvation in Israel."   (1 Samuel XI, 11-13)

Samuel, Man of God, enthroned the first kings of Israel, bore the title of Man of Ra'a... The Talmud confirms that every word of God is "adorned with two crowns"[44], red and white according to the Kabbalah...

Better still, it is said that David will wear the Milkom crown, **which is the crown of Ammon**, the crown of Nahash = Serpent = the Ammonite, which the Kabbalah represents the crown of

---

41   I Samuel XI, 9.

42   I Samuel XI, 15.

43   I Samuel XI, 15.

44   Ordre Mo'ed 88b. Aggadoth du Talmud de Babylone. La source de Jacob/ 'Ein Yaakov, op. cit., p. 206.

the kings of Israel identical to that of God, but especially to those of the SA-RÂ kings called Pharaohs:

"A SERPENT WAS ENGRAVED IN THE HOLLOW OF THIS CROWN"[45]

Three corps to defeat the power of the serpent *Nahash* conceal the threefold resurrection power of Osiris over death, embodied in his three-pronged scepter and the Trinity or threefold power of God.

The serpent Apophys and the god Set are not put to death in the legend of Osiris: they are subjugated because they are necessary to the process of redemption. Set plays the role of ferryman in the underworld and Apophys, the eternal tortuous serpent that Ra must master every night. As we have seen, in hieroglyphics, Saul conceals SA-RÂ, the Son of Ra, Israel meaning "Son of Yahweh". Osiris, whose body is reconstituted into a single man by Isis, accedes to the celestial royalty, while his son Horus reigns on earth with the appearance of the sun and the rejoicing of the land of Egypt.

A text of the Zohar informs us that Moses "led the sheep", sheep identified with the Children of Israel.

If we add to this that according to the Kabbalah, Moses bears the secret name Eman' = Amon, Moses therefore conceals the power of the ram of Amon, which is why he is represented with horns. Similarly, in the manner of the ram of Amun, the Pharaoh leads his people as a shepherd and guides them both on earth and in the spheres of the celestial world. We can make the following comparison.

Moses refers to the primordial serpent of the Egyptians, to the god of gods Amun, the Bible confirms this with the verse:

45   Le Zohar, tome II, collection Les dix paroles, op. cit., p. 456.

"For the LORD [Yahweh] your God is the God of Gods" [Elohim is the plural of EL]...   (Deuteronomy 10:17)

Words of Jethro to Moses:

"I now acknowledge that Yahweh is the greatest of all Elohim"   (Exodus 18:11)...

The secret tradition has well concealed the origin of the religion of Amen the One God and the God of gods in the Torah. Christ himself is named Amen in the book of Revelation, 3:14.

"This is what the Amen says, the faithful and true witness, the beginning of the creation of God..."

God is the Alpha and the Omega. He is both the Beginning and the End of Creation. This means that Christ is a rabbi going around the synagogues, teaching the Hellenized Jews through the Septuagint of the Ptolemies, the very essence of God, inseparable from the World. God is Amon, Ra, Yaho, YHVH, at once Unique and Multiple. The collective hysteria generated by the notion of a Unique and exclusive God of the Bible was initiated by the terror inspired by the ancient Greeks. The divine Presence is visible through Creation, which is an eternal Beginning. Unique in its essence, Multiple in its manifestations. This is of course the Osirian, Egyptian perception - judged "pagan" - of the notion of the divine. A teaching based on contemplation and meditation, obviously coming from the temples of Heliopolis and Thebes, where Christ would have been initiated.

The so-called falsely Egyptian religion was the ancient Jewish religion, the verus Israel, which Christ propagated in the synagogues by unveiling the Supreme Wisdom of the Kabbalah, that of the temples of the Nile Valley, the historical wisdom of the kings of Israel.

THE FIVE NAMES OF THE KINGS OF ISRAEL ARE THE FIVE NAMES OF THE KINGS OF THE NILE VALLEY

Diagram of the five names of Pharaoh[46]

Since the Fourth Dynasty, but especially since the New Kingdom, the pharaohs had five royal names, attributed by the god Thoth. This title always began with the «name of Horus» followed by «Nebty» and «Golden Horus». These three names always preceded the royal title itself, represented on two cartouches [47].

It <u>results that the</u> common foundation between the kings

46   Christiane Desroches Noblecourt. Amours et fureurs de La Lointaine. Stock-Pernoud. 1997.

47   In Jewish and Talmudic tradition, the phonetic name of Bitya, daughter of Pharaoh and adoptive mother of Moses, corresponds to the hieroglyph of the bee, which symbolizes Isis, the mother of the world. As we have said, for the Kabbalah, Moses' parents are identified with the sons of the primordial serpent, the moon and the sun, like Isis and Osiris. Moses himself is identified with the light of day, as is Horus. Finally, again according to Kabbalah, the two Tables of the Law symbolize the two names of Elohim and Yahweh.

of Israel and the kings named SA-RÂ in the hieroglyphics, falsely reclassified as «pharaohs» or «Egyptians» by the ancient Greeks, is no longer the result of a coincidence, but a judiciously orchestrated usurpation. The aim was obviously to transpose the history of the Jews to a country smaller than the Nile Valley, Canaan. The kings of Israel, who cannot be found in archaeology, were reinvented in a country where there is no trace of their existence. The proof of the similarity of the re-constitution of the kings of Israel and the pharaohs lies in the celestial structure of their royal names in five names, a fact recognized by rare Egyptologists. Marie-Ange Bonhème and Annie Forgeau did not fail to point out that in the Bible, the kings of Israel also bore five names, with the same structure as those of the ancient kings of the Nile Valley:

"Isaiah's vision (Isaiah IX, 5) applied to the Hebrew king, highlights not only that he bears five names, like the king of Egypt, but also that the 1 + 4 structure of the five names is taken up again, thus distinguishing between the physical existence of a man, manifested by the name received at birth, and the institutional existence, raised by four new names"[48]

The five names of the kings of Israel derive from the five names of God, or the five figures (partsuf) or faces of God, described in the Kabbalistic school of Rabbi Isaac Luria:

"Each Sephira is transformed from a general attribute of God into what the Kabbalists call a Partsuf a "face of God"... ...The main partsufim or figures are five in number"[49]

---

48   Marie Ange Bonhème. Annie Forgeau. Pharaon. Les secrets du pouvoir. Éditions. Armant Colin 1988. P. 35-36.

49   Guershom G. Sholem. Les Grands Courants de la Mystique Juive. Éditions PAYOT, Paris, 1950, p. 287.

THE DIVINE ANOINTING OF KING DAVID IS THAT OF THE "PHARAOHS

In addition to the ritual sacrifices of bulls and rams, a number of significant facts are noted in the Bible by Egyptologists about the "pharaonic" consecration ceremony of Aaron. This ritual allows the spirit of God to descend upon his chosen one. Divine and royal consecration that we find with the High Priest Samuel[50], or king Jehu son of Jehoshaphat, by Elysium[51], and by all the kings of Israel.

"As for the chief priest [Aaron], on whose head the anointing oil is poured and who is given the right to cover his insignia"[52]   (Leviticus XXI, 10)

Here is what two Egyptologists, Marie Ange Bonhème and Annie Forgeau, have to say about it:

"In connection with the purification performed on the head of the king [Pharaoh], it is difficult not to evoke the gesture of the anointing of Aaron by Moses[53]... ...in an analogous way, the Davidic anointing had the effect of bringing down the spirit of Yahweh on David after the spirit of Yahweh had left Saul"[54]

The sacred incense and the divine anointing are intended to appease the forces of evil and to allow the spirit of God to invest the spirit of the king. It is, according to the Talmud, a

---

50   I Samuel, X, 1.

51   II, Rois IX, 3-6

52   Photo : L'Égypte. Sur les traces de la civilisation pharaonique. Éditions könemann. Imprimé en Allemagne, ISBN 3-89508-914-1, p. 267.

53   Marie Ange Bonhème. Annie Forgeau. Pharaon. Les secrets du pouvoir. Ed. Armant Colin 1988, p. 269.

54   Ibidem, p. 272.

victory over the Angel of Death[55]. As for the robe of the High Priest Aaron, the oral tradition speaks of eight priestly garments braided in gold, an image of the microcosm of the universe[56], as well as a frontal plate also in gold on which the name of God was engraved, and a pectoral formed of twelve stones playing an oracular role. This plate with the twelve names corresponds to the Zodiac, like the uraeus of Pharaoh, the Ouroboros serpent embodying the twelve constellations of the Zodiac. Aaron's breastplate corresponds to that of Tutankhamen, formed of twelve columns of semi-precious stones, obviously having a magical and religious function.

---

55   Elie Munk. La voix de la Thora. L'Exode. Op. cit., p. 356.

56   Ibidem, p. 336.

THE SERPENT OF AMON, THE GOD ENGRAVED ON THE CROWN OF DAVID

By continuing to worship the serpent of God as the ultimate means of the resurrection of the dead, the Children of Israel worship the "Christ serpent" of Osiris, the serpent of the "pharaohs", i.e. the serpent of the resurrection that the true kings of Israel worshipped! And for good reason, the kings of Israel had placed the bronze serpent of Moses inside the temple in adoration... It is obvious that the kings of Israel all adored the primordial serpent, the latter being fixed on their own crown...

In fact, the Bible, confirmed by the Kabbalah, specifies that the crown that David put on his head to crown himself king of Israel, was precisely affixed with a serpent! It was the crown with the serpent of Milkom, which belonged to king Nahash the Ammonite (Nahash = serpent, Amonite = Amon) that David put on his head...

David gathered the whole army and went to Rabbah and stormed the city and took it. He took the crown from Milkom's head, which weighed a talent of gold, and set it with a precious stone, which became the ornament on David's head. He took the spoils of the city in enormous qu antities. (II Samuel XII, 29-30)

The Kabbalah gives details about the crown of Milkom, the idol of Amon: **"A serpent was engraved in hollow on this crown"**[57]. The rabbis wondered how King David could have worn an idolatrous crown. Some traditions describe this snake as a "defilement" removed from the crown of Amun, but the trace of the snake remained forever on the crown... The snake is at the same time adored by the Children of Israel as the serpent of life, while being demonized as the serpent of death, it is the defilement, the "garbage" of the Amunites... What is this so-called defilement called precious stone of which the Bible speaks?

---

57   Le Zohar, tome II, collection Les dix paroles, *op. cit.*, p. 456.

Archaeology proves that the serpent crown of Amun was "Egyptian". Rashi makes the connection between Milkom, the demonized king Amon with the serpent crown, and the abomination of the idols of Egypt:

"The abomination of Egypt. The object of veneration of the Egyptians, as in: "and for Milkom, the abomination of the sons of Ammon" (II Melakhim 23:13). In relation to Israel it is called an "abomination". The term can also be explained in another way: "The abomination of the Egyptians" means that the Egyptians abhor the fact that we are going to offer as a sacrifice what is an object of veneration for them"[58]

By an incredible paradox, while Yahweh asks the Children of Israel to sacrifice the ram, symbol of Osiris for the Sons of Amun, it is the most sacred object of Osiris, the crown with the serpent of the Sons of Amun, which will consecrate a divine, exclusive legitimacy, the prerogative and the testimony of the kings of Israel!!!

"With Amon, king David crowned himself, this crown being a testimony for the stock of David, as the verse indicates: "he imposed on him the crown and the testimony" (II Kings 11: 12) which came from Milkom degree of the Amonites, according to the words: "he (David) took the crown of Milkom" (II Samuel 12: 30) Milkom is indeed the degree of the children of Amon, it is written [on this crown]: "it was placed on the head of David". IT WAS A PERPETUAL WITNESS TO HIS DESCENDANTS, for it is by it that one recognizes who is the son of David to whom the kingship is due..." (II Samuel 12:30)"[59]

The Zohar sheds light on the "Egyptian" origin of the crown of Amun: it is said that the crown of Nahash the Ammonite had two degrees. The first is the degree of Amon or Milkom, which

---

58   Rachi Exode 8 : 22 ou 8 : 26 selon les versions.

59   Le Zohar, tome II, collection 'les dix paroles ». Traduit par Charles Mopsik. *Vayera, Hayé Sarah, Toldot, Vayetsé, Vayichlah.* Verdier, 1984, p. 116.

means the "covered" or the **"Hidden"**[60], that is to say the same meaning of the god of "Egypt" Amon, the "Hidden" god, the invisible one... David thus wears the crown to the serpent of Amon, the Hidden god. The second degree corresponds to Moab and Peor, which means visible, **"discovered"**[61]. God is at the same time hidden and revealed by his manifestations.

By drinking the wine offered by his daughters, Lot "drank the primordial serpent" and begat Amun and Moab, symbols of the crown of Amun and the kings of Israel:

"The primordial serpent entered the branches of the tree. It was the wine that was drunk, then it gave birth to the two degrees linked together, these were the degrees that turn into the impure side, one is called Milkom, the other Peor"[62]

This means that by drinking the wine/serpent, Lot also drank the forbidden fruit of the Tree of Good and Evil, generating light and darkness... Lot would have generated Milkom and Moab by allegory, meaning the "hidden" kings of Israel as described in the Book of Kings, which do not correspond to the historical reality. This is the reason why the kings of Israel are "hidden" and "unrevealed", because they conceal a phenomenal reality: that of the kings of the Nile Valley. For Lot himself is called a serpent in Kabbalah, the evil serpent of the Garden of Eden, as are Cain, Canaan, Laban, Esau, and finally Pharaoh. The Kings of Israel described in the two books of Kings would then be a false story, a transposition, a story from the "unclean side," from the evil tree.

"Lot is the serpent whom the curse struck and by whom the world was cursed"[63]

---

60   Ibidem. Le dieu égyptien Amon signifie 'Caché'.

61   Ibidem.

62   Ibidem,.

63   Le Zohar, tome I, collection 'les dix paroles ». Traduit par Charles Mopsik. Verdier, 1981, p. 424, 84 b.

If we pay attention to the text, Lot embodies, conceals **the serpent-swallowing wine,** at the origin of the book of the kings of Israel... The kings of Israel symbolize the light coming out of the cosmic matrix imagined by the primordial serpent, encompassing the new universe of darkness.

One could not be more precise about the mystical configuration of the kings of Israel transposed from the ancient Nile Valley to the newly named Ægyptos: the serpent-swallower, an Osirian metaphor for the SA-RÂ kings, has been well hidden throughout the biblical writings, an encryption impossible to detect in the Greek, Hebrew, Aramaic, Latin readings of the Old Testament. It is the historical proof that David, Solomon, and consequently all the kings of Israel conceal a crown that only the kings of the Nile Valley wore... Another passage of the Kabbalah evokes the two degrees of the red and white crown of Israel, image of the crown of God:

"Rabbi Simeon says[64]: "A tradition teaches us that there are two crowns that unite together and constitute, as it were, the gateway to all other crowns. The tradition also tells us that one of these crowns is rigor, and the other is clemency, one male and the other female. Clemency reigns on the side of the male, rigor on the side of the female. The one is white, and the other is red; and it is to mitigate each other that they unite together."[65]

---

64 It is Rabbi Simeon Bar Yohai.

65 Le Zohar, tome V, Le livre de la splendeur, op. cit., p. 41.

**Red and white crown of God worn by SA-RÂ/IS-RÂ kings.
British Museum.**

Again, only the double crown of Amun, the crown of the
kings SA-RÂ or IS-RÂ, corresponds to that of the kings of
Israel. Only the crown of Amun corresponds historically to the
explanations of Rabbi Simeon and the Jewish tradition. These
two colors correspond to the degrees of darkness (red crown,
God is Hidden) and light (white crown, God is Revealed), night
and day, rigor and clemency, as was the double crown to the
Nile serpent of the SA-RÂ kings, renamed pharaohs by the
ancient Greeks.

THE ONE GOD BECAME THREE

To say "God" in ancient Egypt, one said "The Gods", the Elohim called **Neteru** נתרו, because the unique god demiurge named TAM or Atoum = Yod = reed, had come out of the Noun or Nou, the primordial ocean, the Unique Principle had split into three primordial energies, Tam, Shou and Tefnout, according to his words:

"I am the One who has become Three" [66]

Nou is formed of three vessels, the origin of the god One who became the three primordial powers:

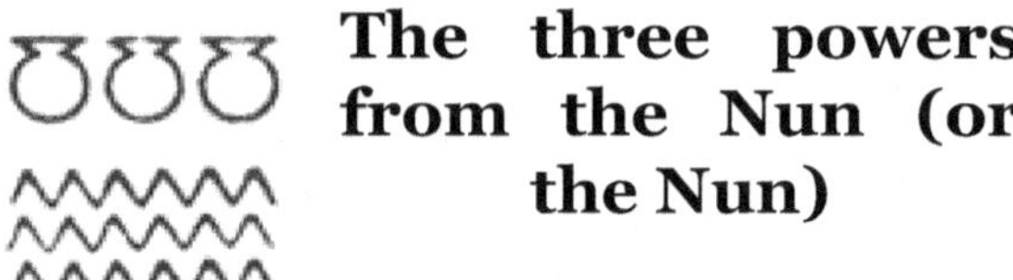 **The three powers from the Nun (or the Nun)**

Then the trio begat the sky and the earth, which begat the man Osiris and his family. Each god represented on the walls of tombs and temples is read as a superior hieroglyph or anaglyph, intended to transmit one of the qualities of God. Christiane Desroches Noblecourt evokes the three vases of Amun, his wife Mut and their son Khonsu, three sacred vases symbolizing universal cohesion, used in great ceremony at the time of the annual flood[67]. The memory of the vessels, symbols of God and kings, was undoubtedly crystallized in the Kabbalah under the allegory of the broken vessels, where after creating the world, God would have contracted into the cosmos, according to the doctrine of Rabbi Issac Luria.

---

66   CT II 39 b-e.

67   Christiane Desroches Noblecourt avec Daniel Élouard. Symboles de l'Égypte. Éditions Désclée de Bouwer, 2004, p. 76.

According to the Shabbatai Svi movement, around 1850, the restoration of God participates in the redemption of humanity, of the universe, the Tikun, following the sin of Adam:

"The Tikun restores the unity of the name of God which was destroyed in the original sin; "The Tikun, the restoration of that great harmony which was disturbed by the Breaking of the Vessels, and later by the sin of Adam. The Redemption implies a radical change in the structure of the universe. Its significance is not so much that it is the end of the exile which began with the destruction of the Temple, but rather the end of that inner exile of all creatures which began when the father of mankind was cast out of paradise."[68]

Details of a procession to the temple of Hathor. The crown of Isis is made of three reeds, like the crown with three flowers of Osiris. Temple of Denderah.

The pyramid is the Universal Matrix, a huge allegory of the Red Sea, or Sea of Reeds, which must open in two, as it is said in the Book of Exodus: "the waters standing as a wall on their right and on their left" (Exodus, 14, 22)... The Pyramid Texts report that the Man Osiris came out of the two thighs of Nut opened in two to give birth to the sun and to humanity, to the Son of Ra (we will come back to this). Osiris himself is also

68 Ibidem, p. 323.

cut into three parts. Throughout the dynasties, the gods always form parts of the Body of God, the One, the "All in One" (Hen kai pan in Greek). God himself is the image of the body of Man, as confirmed by this summary from the time of Ramses II:

"Three are all the gods (= God): Amun-Re-Ptah! They have no equal. Hidden is the Name as Amun; the face is Re; his Body is Ptah. Their cities on earth are established forever: Thebes, Heliopolis and Memphis, until eternity."[69]

According to the Pyramid Texts, Pharaoh was born in the Lake of Reeds. For this purpose, Osiris wears the crown with three branches or three reeds , or three flowers symbolizing the Lake of Reeds. Following this scheme, the crown of Osiris is formed of three branches, as will be the crown of Serapis (Osiris' name in Greek times), but also of three Yod or three reeds symbolizing the Lake of Reeds, the lake of God, symbol of the beginning or creation, as can be seen in the temple of Dendera at the time of Ramses II. The One that became three symbolizes the birth of the sun by the two lions or the three energies fixed on the scepter of Osiris/SA-RÂ, formed by a branch divided into three, represents the three founding principles, the Trinity from the One, a parable of the creation of the universe from a single god. The elements, fire, air and earth, created from the Noun, the god of the primordial ocean symbolized by Tam and Osiris, who will form the Nile[70]. In the same vein, Elohim means El AYAM God came out of the waters [71].

---

69   Papyrus de Leyde; 1350; A.H. Gardiner 'Hymns to Amon from Leiden papyrus ».

70   Atum would have formed the primordial waters or the Nun, from which it would have emerged, hence the image of the reed Yod. The exhalation of the primordial waters would have given birth to the sun, the air and the earth. According to Plutarch, the Nile is an outpouring of Osiris, i.e. the primordial river created from the god Noun. Plutarch, Isis and Osiris, Guy Trédaniel, La Maisnie. 1992, p. 111-114 and 127.

71   Le Zohar, Cantique des Cantiques. Collection « les dix paroles ». Verdier, 1999, p. 114, note 434 : Elohim, El Hayam mean «towards the sea»..

"The Spirit of the water is the Spirit that manifested itself at the creation of the world..."[72] Yahweh hovering over the surface of the waters comes from the primordial ocean:

Son of man, say to the prince of Tyre: Thus says the Lord Yahweh. Because your heart is proud, you have said, 'I am a god, I live in a divine dwelling in the heart of the sea'" (Ezekiel 28:2).

The Kabbalah reports that Yahweh dressed himself with the letter Aleph to create the heavens in three degrees[73]. The Aleph is formed by a sun or tree of life[74], an ithyphallic serpent, the central bar (the letter Vav) separating the celestial waters, formed by the two ends (the two arms or two Yod of Aleph). In the Bible, Yahweh is defined as the God of Abraham, Isaac and Jacob (renamed Israel).

"Principle of three who are one, three lights are part of the letter Aleph"[75].

The letter Aleph designates the LIFE FORCE, the spirit of God, the divine Shekhina "hovering over the surface of the waters", as stated in the second verse of the Bible "And the spirit of Elohim hovered over the surface of the waters."

---

72   Zohar, tome III. Le livre de la splendeur. Par Jean de Pauly. Maisonneuve & Larose, 1985, p. 478.

73   Le Zohar, Cantique des Cantiques. Collection « les dix paroles ». Verdier, 1999, p. 210.

74   Le Zohar, tome 1, collection Les dix paroles. Traduit par Charles Mopsik, Verdier, 1981, p. 151.

75   Ibidem, p. 110-111.

According to Kabbalah, the three Patriarchs formed the sun "**The sun is Jacob**"[76], but also the Body of God. Abraham is the right arm, Isaac the left arm and Israel the Body. The Hebrew letter Chin' ש (pronounced Ch or S) is the allegory of the three lights of Abraham, Isaak and Jacob. It marks the three phases of the sun related to the three prayers, morning, mid-day and evening. We find this symbolism with the three Magi guided by the star announcing the birth of Christ the King of Israel, or the three moons where the child Moses (light of Israel) was hidden. But more than that, the Yod contains the secret of **"the light of Jehovah [Adonay]"**[77]

"Yod represents the Central Point, the Cause of all things, which remains hidden from all worlds, which is unknown and will remain eternally unknown; it is the supreme mystery of all things"[78]

Kabbalah also states that the three Yod of Chin' ש form "the three Yod of the sacred name," the crown of Yahweh that symbolizes the three branches of the Patriarchs, the Fathers of the world. "The letter Chin' ש stood before the Holy Spirit bearing the three sacred crowns of the Patriarchs"[79];

"The Chin' of Shabbath symbolizes the three branches of the Patriarchs".[80]

Abraham, Isaac and Jacob form the oneness of God, the One in three, and are also the "three suns" of the day (morning, noon and evening) that participate in his creation. A text from the Zohar relates the discussion of three rabbis and a traveler.

---

76   Le Zohar, Genèse, tome III, Vayéchev, Mikets, collection « les dix paroles ». Traduit par Charles Mopsik. Verdier, 1991, p. 207.

77   Le Zohar, tome IV, Le livre de la splendeur, op. cit., p. 40.

78   Ibidem.

79 Le Zohar, tome III. Le livre de la splend., op. cit, p. 241, 54a.

80 Le Zohar, tome V, Le livre de la splendeur, op. cit, p. 92. Les patriarches sont aussi comparés à trois branches de laurier.

"... [The traveler] answered them: "One day I was traveling, and I saw a light that divided itself into three, walked before me, and then hid itself. I thought I had a vision of the Shekhina [the light of God, Israel]. Now I see that the three lights that appeared to me were announcing your meeting."

The Chin', the Mess and the sign Benou or YAHOU (Light) and the sceptre of Osiris participate in the same symbolism, the light of God, the One divided into three.

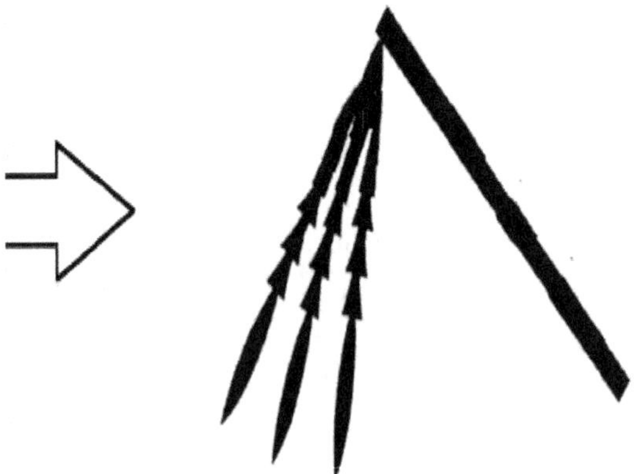

It is clear that the powerful symbolism of God, the One Principle turned into three, conveyed by the Kabbalah, agrees with the cosmogony of the SA-RÂ kings, issued from the High Priests of Heliopolis.

MONOTHEISTIC EGYPT HAS NEVER BEEN IDOLATROUS

The sacred texts and hymns reveal the origin of monotheism, from the Yods of the Nile Valley.

For about two millennia, first Judaism, then Christianity and Islam, the three great monotheistic religions have denounced the ancient Egyptian civilization as a pagan cult, idolatrous, devoid of any morality and law. A cult sunk in sin, devoted to the cult of statues, accusing it of a crime against humanity for having put the Hebrews, the Children of Israel in slavery and for having thrown their children into the Nile. This religion, although having many gods turns out to be monotheistic in its essence. Contrary to what Sigmund Freud thought, who did not have access to the Egyptian documents we have today, the ancient Egyptians were monotheistic from the beginning, long before the time of Akhenaten. After him, the kings continued to remain monotheistic until the end of their empire. In this case, what about their idols, their statues, the countless effigies of the multiple gods of Egypt? Did idolatry have another meaning? Monotheistic? Cosmotheism? Since Champollion, archaeology, the deciphering of sacred texts in hieroglyphics reveal a historical reality radically opposed to the alleged idolatry conveyed by religions. Many writings bring us the proofs that the Egyptian civilization was profoundly religious, moral, not bellicose, balanced, and of a very high quality, non-belligerent, balanced, founded on a monotheism in which "the gods" were only the imaginary representations of the unique god, of God revealed to all by his creation. According to Kabbalah, the idols of Egypt were images of God observing and judging the behavior of men, and particularly that of kings, who had the audacity to pretend to be God while they were alive or After their death.

"The Scripture says, "And the idols of Egypt shall be shaken before his [God's] face. The Scripture does not speak of the stones that formed the idols, but of the heavenly rulers who direct all the acts of the people here below."[81]

Yes, Jews as well as Egyptian worshippers of Osiris had the right to make images of God, the constraints brought by the god of the Bible did not exist.

During more than three millennia of civilization, ancient Egypt has left us monuments, temple remains, paintings, drawings, writings, books of commandments, wisdoms centered on the faith in a unique god, sprung from nothingness, hidden from the eyes of men, with a true name forever unknown.

This god, immensely silent, in whom everyone believed because he was revealed every day as the light of the world, the light of every day, this god whom the kings worshipped at the highest level, had created the sky and the earth. The idols, the stone statues were not worshipped for themselves, but they formed a huge reading grid, hieroglyphs intended to teach how the one god - the One Light of the universe - had come out of nothing and created the world. All the images, the colossi, the hieroglyphs were only the expression of his appearance, forming a syntactic bridge between the known world and the unknown. The religion of the kings of the Nile Valley was fundamentally monotheistic, advocating the uniqueness of light.

"As far as "monotheism" is concerned, each sanctuary worshipped only one great god, and in Thebes, even Amun was called "the One""[82].

There was an important caste of initiated priests from the ancient capital On'/Heliopolis, priests initiated into the worship of a single god, named RÂ (or RAÂ) or YAHOU. According to Jan Assmann, the goddess Isis was called ONE. Akhenaten only took up the old monotheistic ideas from the One Principle

---

81   Le Zohar, tome III, Le livre de la splendeur, op. cit., p. 29.
82 Christiane Desroches Noblecourt avec Daniel Élouard. Symboles de l'Égypte. Éditions Désclée de Bouwer, 2004, p. 76.

of the priesthood of the ancient city of On'. In the course of the dynasties, by syncretism, Ra was associated with other deities, in particular Amun, which became Amun-Ra, but this was only a verbal way of representing the ONE GOD, immanent by the multiplicity of his works and transcendent by the fact that the cosmos was unique, "Hidden from the eyes of men" (= Amun), no one knew his true name. Ancient Egypt was by no means idolatrous, let alone perverse, as the sacred writings have always led us to believe.

I know that it is not easy to be convinced of this, after more than two millennia of conditioning by religions. That is why the texts which will follow, translated from hieroglyphs, clearly establish that the ancient Egyptians were true monotheists.

They made abundant use of the images of the gods, which far from being idols formed a pictorial, initiatory language. In each city, each temple, each god or "Neter" was adored in the Holy of Holies as the image of the Unique God, says the Egyptologist Claire Lalouette:

"EVERY GOD IS THE GREATEST, THE ONLY, THE PRIMORDIAL"[83].

Each god of the Nile Valley is a form, a syncretic part of the Body of Osiris or Atum, the Reed Yod, which forms the universe, the Pyramid Texts of more than four millennia ago tell us. The sarcophagus n° 761 confirms that all the 'idols', all the Elohim/Yods/Neteru יִיִי, as we said, formed the members of the Body of Osiris, which is the Light of the world:

"There is no member in you that is not deprived of God"[84]

Another text in hieroglyphs specifies:

"It is Ra who created the names of his members, that is to say: the gods who are after him came into existence." [85]

---

83 Claire Lalouette. Thèbes ou la naissance d'un empire. Flammarion 1995, p. 243.

84   Spell n° 761. Textes des Sarcophages du Moyen Empire Égyptien. Claude Carrier, tome III. Éditions du Rocher, 2004.

85 Adolphe Erman, Hermann Ranke, La civilisation égyptienne, op. cit., p. 443.

Each god was GOD, a manifestation, the very expression of the unique god, whose omnipresence is clearly expressed in the Holy of Holies of the temples. The most sacred location of the so-called Egyptian temple, whatever the name of the god of the city, proclaimed not only the uniqueness of God, but also the fact that God was unknown, with an unknown true name, "Hidden" in the darkness of the sanctuary, invisible to the eyes of men. The Egyptologist Claude Traunecker notes that in the Ramesside era, supposedly polytheistic, religious thought was indeed monotheistic: **"The scholars of the Ramesside era admitted the idea of a transcendental and unique deity, close to the transcendental and unique divinity, close to the great monotheistic systems"**[86]. Guy Rachet attests that the Book of the Exit towards the Light initiates to monotheism (papyrus of Ani 1300 BC): **"It seems clearly that we have here an initiatory itinerary which led to a monotheistic and universalist vision of the world"**[87]

During nearly three millennia, the pharaoh son of Ra, SA-RÂ, incarnated the single god of the empire. In order to establish his royal authority, the king amalgamated his own body with the totality of the gods. He was the expression of the multiplicity melted in the divine unicity par excellence. Indeed, since the Pyramid texts, each part of Pharaoh's body symbolized the numerous Neteru 𓂝𓂝𓂝, the so-called gods or idols embodied on the contrary the manifestations of God and his perfect uniqueness, thus ensuring the perfect cohesion of monotheism in the Pharaonic empire. The body of the pharaoh symbolized the integrity of the "Commandment": as in Judaism where the 248 positive commandments form the parts of the body of the universal man, the Body of God. The expression "I am God" in ancient Egypt has exactly the same meaning in the Bible for Yahweh יהוה.

---

86   *Op.cit.,* Claude Traunecker. *Les Dieux de l'Égypte,* p. 98.
87   Guy Rachet *Dictionnaire de la Civilisation égyptienne.* Larousse-Bordas, 1998, p. 161.

"I AM RA" IN ANCIENT EGYPT "ANOKHI YAHWEH" IN THE BIBLE

Chapter 163 of the Book of the Dead, considered as the most sacred "Book" of the ancient "Egyptians", confirms that God defines himself as I AM, Yahweh-Adonay, the god of the Bible:

"I AM HE WHO IS..."[88]

In Chapter 153 of the Book of the Dead, the unique god of Egypt expresses himself as "I am the Lord", and in this expression, "I am" is said "Anokh'", in the same way that the god of the Bible says "Anokhi" (I am + Yod in Hebrew):

"I AM THE ETERNAL, I AM RA..."

In the Sarcophagus Texts (sarcophagus n° 80), God reveals his name Anokh' = Anokhi of the Bible:

"ANOKH' ☥ IS MY NAME"

In the same texts, on the sarcophagus n° 112 God confirms his perfect unicity89:

"I AM THE ONE WHO IS ALONE"

Another writing from the Sarcophagi (n° 304) confirms that the unique God of Egypt is expressed through his numerous manifestations, "the gods of Egypt", which form a syncretism, a Whole in One, melted in the unicity of God:

---

88   Le Livre des Morts des Anciens Égyptiens, chapitre 163, p. 234.

89,   Spell n°112. Textes des Sarcophages du Moyen Empire Égyptien. Claude Carrier, tome I. Éditions du Rocher, 2004, p. 285

"I AM THE ONE, THE QUINTESSENCE OF THE GODS"

Another Text of the Sarcophagi (n°) attests that the god of Egypt, Amun, is "hidden", invisible:

"HE WHOSE FORM IS INVISIBLE."

Other sacred writings confirm the general idea of the unique and hidden god of the pharaonic civilization:

"He whose name is not known."[90]

"He whose name will always be ignored."[91]
"He whose name and face are hidden"[92]
**"I am that One who crosses the No
and whose name men do not know
whose name men do not know".**[93]
"I AM ATEM OUT OF THE NU"[94]

Let us recall that Atum is the YOD, the image of God coming out of the primordial waters. Thus, several religious texts recited or sung in the so-called Egyptian temples confirm, with irrefutable historical evidence, the existence of a pure monotheism, well before the Bible or the Koran, a unique god, immanent by his manifestations and transcendent by his hidden power, his omnipotence and his omnipresence.

---

90   Textes des Sarcophages. Ibidem, spell n° 353, p. 877.
91   Textes des Sarcophages. Ibidem, spell n° 146, p. 347.
92   Textes des Sarcophages, spell n° 147, p. 349.
93   Textes des Sarcophages, spell 487, p. 1205.
94   *Le Livre des Morts des Anciens Égyptiens.* Littératures anciennes du Proche-Orient. Les Éditions du Cerf, 1967, chapitre 7.

HYMN TO AMON OF LEIDEN [95]

**Unique is the Hidden One (Amun)
Who remains veiled for the gods,
without his true form being known.
None of them knows his true nature
Which is not revealed in any writing.
No one has been able to describe it,
It is too vast to be apprehended,
Too mysterious to be known.
Whoever speaks its name will be struck down.**

The hymn to the unique god, engraved on the Stele of Lyon, was sung in the temples of Amun, Ptah, Isis, etc. :

**You are the One,
You are the being whose manifestation
existed before the manifestation.
You are the creator of heaven and earth
Who unceasingly offers fullness to all beings.**

The powers of nature although called "the gods", Elohim/Yods/Neteru in Egyptian, do not know the true nature and the true name of the unique God-Light, but recognize his existence. The goddess Athena, avatar of the goddess Isis will later teach the eternal mystery of the uniqueness of God-Light on the pediment of the temple of Sais:

"I am all that has been, all that is and all that will be, and my veil no mortal has lifted. The fruit that I bore became the sun"[96]

---

95   Christian Jacq. La sagesse vivante de l'Égypte ancienne. Robert Laffont 1998. P. 39.

96   Plutarque. *Isis et Osiris*. Par Guy Trédaniel. La Maisnie. 1992, p. 43-44.

Centuries before, chapter 174 of the "Book of the Dead" shows that the dog Anubis (the idol of Egypt par excellence) teaches and proclaims the worship of a unique god:

"Words of Anubis: 'O God absolutely unique, unique God who has no equal'..."[97]

What is the difference between the plural monotheism of Amun and the exclusive monotheism of Akhenaten? What is the difference with rabbinic monotheism, Christianity and Islam? Around 1350 B.C., the pharaoh Amenotep IV (Amenophis in Greek) who became Akhenaten had destroyed the syncretism of the temples of Amun, by channelling the believers into the cult of his own person. For that, he changes his name in Akhenaten (the living Spirit of Aten), destroys the concept of Amun (the unique god, the "God of gods", the "Hidden" god), by a visible monotheism, centered on his person identified with the sun, the king being adored as the unique image of Aten... He decreed the new cult with a terrible repression in the whole country, transformed the temples, drove out the priests and destroyed the names of Amun and replaced them by another unique god, visible, symbolized only by the sphere of the sun Aten (or the solar disc according to the sources), thus removing the priests of Amun and with it all the other hidden or visible manifestations of the divinity - he drove out the priests, but the Stela of Restoration interprets this event as the banishment of the gods - who had lived in symbiosis for almost two millennia.

"YOU ARE THE ONLY ATON, THERE IS NO OTHER".

However, it can be said that in order to make himself worshipped, Akhenaten had distorted the hymn of Amun - syncretic and universal - which advocated the uniqueness of God, unknown and mysterious in his essence, but visible only through the

---

97   *Le Livre des Morts des Anciens Égyptiens.* Littératures anciennes du Proche-Orient. Les Éditions du Cerf, 1967, chapitre 174, p. 260.

beauty of his creation, through the cosmos, perceptible in the multitude of forms of its manifestations. Images of the gods symbolizing the manifested divine power were allowed and not forbidden as in the Bible and the Koran, under penalty of death. Hymn to Amun:

"... God unique and without equal,
You create the universe, according to your
heart's conscience,
when you were alone...
...You eternally extract thousands of forms
from yourself,
You dwell in your unity...
...None of the beings generated by you exist
not to contemplate thyself alone..."

Amenhotep III, father of Akhenaten, knew perfectly well that he had inherited from his fathers a hidden god, Amun, omnipresent and omniscient, unique, creator of the sky and the earth and of man in his own image, conforming in every way to the unique god of the Bible. These hymns of Amun or Aten are well situated at the very foundation of the Bible and the Koran: the adoration of a unique God, creator of the universe and of man in his image. Particularly the great hymn to Aten which is found textually in Psalm 104 of the Bible, the latter is dedicated to Adonai/Yahweh. The Bible and the Koran proclaim the same unicity of God, revealed to Abraham, Moses and to the Prophet Mohammed for the Koran. Bible (Deuteronomy 6-4):

"Hear, O Israel, Adonai is our God, Adonai is one".

For Islam, the testimony, in Arabic the Chahada states:

"There is no God but God (Allah) and Mohammed is his Prophet."

Would the monotheism of ancient Egypt be the only heritage reported by the Bible? No, of course not: we will continue to explore the texts of ancient Egypt and discover that the Bible inherited the fundamental rituals and all the wisdom of these so-called Egyptians who proclaimed themselves the Yod reeds of God. It is precisely this spiritual heritage that is described under the metaphor of the "treasures of Egypt" brought back by the Hebrews/Jews/Yudaïos when they left Egypt in the book of Exodus. The land of the Pharaohs has been invaded several times in its history. From the seventh century B.C. (the so-called Low Period), the Nile Valley was successively occupied by the Assyrians, the Babylonians, the Persians,

the Greeks, the Romans, until the great Arab invasions in the seventh and eighth centuries of our era. Before this period of invasions, for almost three millennia, the sacred names of kings - so-called pharaohs - were read in the language of hieroglyphics. The kings had many names, like Osiris, and the basically monotheistic priests testified that Osiris was the One, ancestral God of many names.

The millennial power of Osiris disturbed the new conquering emperors, because Osiris represented, in addition to the single god and the light of the world, the avenging power of God on the secular, even millennial enemies of Egypt. Also, the conquering kings endeavored to break, even to annihilate this power by attacking the various clergy, mainly the priests of Ra and Osiris originating from Heliopolis. Why did they bother so much? They were the holders of the ancestral religious power, initiatory, monotheistic, but syncretic, on which was based all the religion known as Egyptian: the gods of MISRÂ known as "Egypt", formed the Body of Osiris, the universal god known as IS-RÂ. They formed the caste of Yahout or Yahouds, which Egyptologists translate as heirs or officials. But this name is much more powerful, because the kings of the Nile Valley bore the supreme title of Yahud at the time of their enthronement...

The conquering kings will thus attack religion, dogmas, rituals, sacrifices, and finally initiatory knowledge. They will crown themselves " Pharaohs kings of Egypt ". But to do this, it was necessary to completely reprogram the myth of Osiris and make it disappear forever. It was necessary to melt the aforementioned "Pharaohs kings of Egypt" in Greek mythology with universal vocation. After more than two millennia of demonization and blind anti-Semitism, it is time to demonstrate that the ancestors of the Jews were the true pyramid builders, the builders of the ancient holy city of Heliopolis, named On' in hieroglyphics, On' in the Bible as attested by the Septuagint. Their "history", which became the Bible - including the Torah, the Prophets and the Writings or Hagiographers - was rewritten and transformed on the orders of Pharaoh Ptolemy II Philadelphus, in the island of Pharos in the third century BC.

Chapter VI

TUTANKHAMUN IS A KING OF ISRAEL

Like all the kings of the Nile Valley, Tutankhamun was never an "Egyptian" nor a "pharaoh". Like all the kings of the Nile Valley, he bears the royal title SA-RÂ, which reads IS-RÂ (Son of God), which is the name of Osiris, the origin of Israel. The enthronement papyrus found in his tomb proclaims him YAHOUD: Jew. According to the Kabbalah, the heavens and the earth are the two twins of God, a myth inherited from the ancient Heliopolis.

The IS-RÂ kings images of OSIRIS, falsely named Pharaohs were embalmed, buried in sarcophagi. Why? In order to present themselves and justify themselves before the heavenly court of God. Not as "Osiris" in Greek, but as IS-RÂ in hieroglyphics. The Kabbalah says exactly the same thing about the kings of Israel, which we will see in a later chapter. In this case, with so many coincidences and similarities, we understand why no one has ever found the slightest trace of any of the kings of Israel, neither in Israel nor in Palestine - with the exception of the royal seal of Hezekiah - because they were all kings of the Nile valley called Yahu-Da, "the Land of God". A commentary by Rashi from the Babylonian Talmud (words of Rabbi Meir) tells us that the kings of Israel are all buried in Egypt. In Zoan, a city whose name has been translated as Tanis, which is said to be the place of ancient Pi-Ramses. But Zoan also symbolizes On'/Heliopolis or Thebes, the equivalent of «Zion'» (Jerusalem) Thebes being the city of a hundred gates of the ancient Egyptians.

"Egypt on the other hand, occupied the first rank among all other countries, as it is said "as a garden of God, like the land of Egypt" (Gen. 13-10), and Tsoan [Tanis or Heliopolis (On')?] was the privileged one of the land of Egypt, IT WAS THE RESIDENCE OF THE KINGS, as it is said "His princes are in Tsoan" (IS., 30-4)"[1]

If we take into consideration the data of the previous chapters, it is clear that in 1923, Howard Carter discovered the tomb of a king of Israel. But because of the deep modification of History imposed since the third century B.C. by the Ptolemies, he ignored that Tutankhamun was neither a pharaoh nor a king of Egypt. Tutankhamun was circumcised at birth for the same reasons as Abraham. Namely that in the Book of the Dead, his ancestor RÂ/Osiris/IS-RÂ had circumcised himself that his name of TUT (the image) ANKH (the vital light) HOU (the divine breath) AMON' (the Yod coming out of the waters), had been given to him by his mother as for the main characters of the Bible. His royal name was divided into five names, just like the kings of Israel. Carter did not know that Tutankhamun had undergone the ritual of having his hair cut, weighed on a scale and replaced by gold. That the little king made his "Bar-Mitsvah" at the age of ten, that he prayed three times a day and took ritual baths, that he washed his hands ritually, that he knew the equivalent of the Kaddish of the dead. He wore a "cabalistic" skullcap with the ten names of God, with the seven serpents divided into 4+3, a diadem with the Serpent of Amun, like all the kings of Israel, like the Shekhina, the god of the Jews. The king had the supreme title of YAHOUD meaning dignity, the royal office. The king had the supreme title of YAHOUD meaning dignity, the royal office. Never Pharaoh. Never Egyptian.

We have seen to what extent the reed Yod $\int$ determines the Being, the Self, the individuality, as attested by Allan Gardiner and Gaston Maspero. To understand the true reading of Tutankhamen's name, meaning the **living image of Amun in peace,** it is necessary to explore the sacred hieroglyph Amun.

---

1   Pentateuque selon Rachi. La Genèse. Samuel et Odette Lévy. 1993.

Amun means the "Hidden God", the mysterious, the sacred Yod ⌇ Reed that came out of the celestial waters 〰〰 . The Reed is at the origin of writing, thus of the images of God. Amun is the creator, the architect of the universe through the multiplication of the Reed or the primordial point. Another oracle of Amun addressed to King Amen-Hotep III (meaning **Amun is at peace** but renamed Amenophis by the ancient Greeks), confirms that Amenhotep III, grandfather of Tutankhamun, is indeed the image of the ME of ⌇ 𓀭 Amun-Ra. Thus, Amun, like RÂ, like Osiris or Atoum, are one and only God in Peace, that is to say, silent, representing the universe revealed at each moment. Whereas the god of the Bible is a speaking god, the god of the Word, of the Logos, even **"a man-of-war"** who leads the Children of Israel to war with the Nations.

Exodus 15:3: **Yahweh is a man-of-war; Yahweh is his name!** Septuagint Exodos 15:3: **It is Kyrios κύριος who crushes the armies; Kyrios κύριος is his name.**

Consequently King Amenhotep, like all the kings of the Nile Valley, is the image of AMUN the Reed YOD ⌇ , the image of God in Peace and of men - images of Atum coming out of the heavenly waters - living in peace, although there were periods of war. Let us take up the translation of the oracle of Amun to Amenophis III:

"Come, my son, Neb-Ma'at-Ra [Amen-Hotep III, Ra Lord of Truth-Justice], **heir** [Yahut/Yahud] **of Ra, son of Ra Amenophis, prince of Thebes! I hear your words; I have seen your monument. I am Amon** [⌇ 𓀭 or 〰 ⌇ Amon = ⌇ or Atum = ⌇] **your father** [Father is also written YT ◠⌇ or Yod], **who created beauty. I gave birth to you together with Shu and Tefnut, after you came out of my body before them. I raised you when I** ⌇ 𓀭 **came from the initial waters** 〰〰 [as Atum the Yod came out of the Nun],

...I created this earth in its length and width [the primordial brick ▭], **to do what my Ka wishes. I have given it to you to rule over it as I once did when I was a king of Upper

and Lower Egypt. I have created it with my loving heart. You are my beloved son, who came out of my limbs, THE IMAGE OF ME [= ⌐ 𓀀 = 𓈖 = NY = ANY אֲנִי the image of the Yod] **THAT I GAVE TO THE EARTH. I HAVE MADE THEE TO REIGN IN PEACE OVER THE EARTH, for thy club hath crushed the heads of all foreign lands. I accept the monument that you have made for me...**"[2]

In another text, the princes address a prayer to Rameses II, calling him the living image of Atum, the living Reed, before addressing the king:

"You are the living image on earth of your father [Father = Atum = Yod 𓇌] **Atum** [Yod 𓇌] **of On'** [of Heliopolis Atum = Yah =Yahu]. [...] **Your words are fulfilled every day, and the thoughts of your heart are realized like those of Ptah, when he creates works of art. Thou shalt live forever, and thy thoughts shall be performed, and all thy words shall be obeyed, O king, our master!**"[3]

It is obvious that Amun is the God/World itself begotten by Atum, the Yod. Amun generates the world by his word, as in the Bible Elohim creates the sky and the earth by the Word. It is indisputable that King Amenophis III who is translated Amun-Hotep (Amun is at peace) is the image of the ME 𓀀 of Amun/Atum, thus the image of the primordial Yod 𓇌 . Consequently all the kings that we name by mistake "Egyptians", all the men of the Nile valley, are all images of the I-Yod 𓀀 of Amun, the image of God. Same thing for the hieroglyphs of Atum, Aton or Anubis. Let us repeat, as we explore the symbolic reading of the hieroglyphs, Atum is the universal demiurge god, the first Reed god of creation, assimilated to Aten and Amun. All these names prove the duplication from the original divine reed, the Yod 𓇌 emerged from the celestial waters 〜〜〜 , or primordial waters, the Noun, the celestial "Nile".

---

2   Philipp Vandenberg. Nefertiti. Editions Pierre Belfond. 1987. P. 87.

3   Claire Lalouette. L'empire des Ramsès. Librairie Arthème Fayard, 1985.

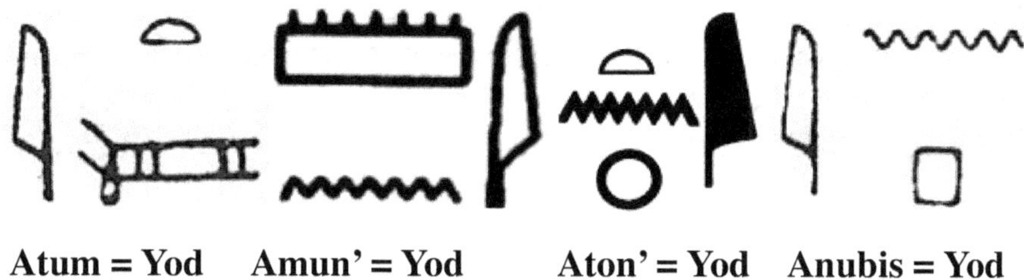

Atum = Yod   Amun' = Yod   Aton' = Yod   Anubis = Yod

All the following demonstrations prove that the kings and men of the Nile Valley cannot be "Egyptians" for the reason that they are all reeds of God. Atum then multiplied into billions of Yods, forming the universe and all the deities according to the different Enneads. Finally, the One God generating "the gods" is not a pantheistic polytheism like the ancient Greeks, with jealous gods waging war against each other, but an exponential multiplication of the First Principle. One God being the Infinite, the Unique, the God/World manifested at each moment, **the first Alpha and Omega,** immanent and transcendent at the same time. Which is why it is said in the *Pyramid Texts* that the "visible" gods who have come to earth each form a part of the Body of God.The numerous gods form thus - like Elohim אלהים in the Bible refers to the gods forming the Body of Yahweh יהוה - the celestial Body of Osiris or Amun, the Hidden, Unknown God. Thus, the figurative of God and the gods are written with one ן or three flags ןןן. The flag being in reality a Yod reed signifying the Father or the three primordial Fathers. Or the three primordial Fathers meaning the kings or priests and Great Priests, for they all form part of the Body of the primordial Yod. Like the scarab and like the Yod of Atum, the reed was multiplied in three to create "the gods" ןןן, the number three being the symbol of the plurality, of the multiplicity of the reed, the origin of the triptych and of the Trinity, as if to signify to us that they came from the division in three of the First Principle, Unique Atum/Yod.

To be convinced of this, it is enough to consider that the symbol forming the plural of the words in hieroglyphs is written with three superimposed Noun 〰. The reed scepter of Osiris ⋀ is divided into three rays. These three waves, these three rays, are the three energies forming the diversity of creation, the diversity of the gods, which are the luminous emanations coming from the creative scepter, the celestial reed of the demiurge. The Mystery of the Yod of the god Atum is indeed at the origin of the gods or Neteru ٦٦٦. He is thus at the origin of all creation, by the diffusion of the demultiplicating energy of the Yod. This explains why Atum says **"I am the One who became three"**. Atum is called the "One with millions of forms". The gods are consequently his emanations from the reed of creation, as Erik Hornung attests:

"The gods are fused with each other"[4]

"...When he [Atum, the Yod] became Three" This is nothing but the simplest formula to say that, from a unity, a multiplicity develops"[5]

The three-branched scepter of Osiris ⟋⟍ , which can be seen on the three sarcophagi of Tutankhamun, is a royal Reed that symbolizes the Yod of Atum, the Spirit of the primordial celestial reed divided into three. The three symbols from which creation was triggered, thus the very matrix of Osiris. The latter is the primordial Man who died and resurrected in RÂ and the Father of humanity. It is easy to see that the three-pronged scepter of Osiris ⟋⟍ has the same configuration as the hieroglyph Mess of Childbirth ⫴. The scribes are confirming here the creative power of Man, of the King, of the Son of Ra, but also the begetting of all creation from the genesis of the primordial reed for the gods of the Great Ennead of Heliopolis. The hieroglyph ESS ∫ or ISS of RameSS ∫∫ is also a reed or a curved rush and symbolizes Man as the Son of God.

Indeed, RameSS means that God, RÂ ⊙, gave birth to Man, the Son (∫ ∫ = twin Shu and Tephnut), giving birth to Hor (Horus) the solar child. Ramses is born from the matrix MESS located in the Noun, the celestial womb of the goddess Nut.

---

4 Erik Hornung. Les dieux de l'Égypte. Le un et le multiple. Éditions du Rocher. 1986. P. 7

5 Erik Hornung. L'Esprit du temps des pharaons. Philippe Lebaud Editeur / du Félin, 1996, p. 39.

The MESS-ESS symbol of childbirth and the resurrection of the Son/Sun, which is found in the Reed Scepter of IS-RÂ/ Osiris. The MESS symbol of the three energies of childbirth thus has the same symbolism as the three-pronged royal scepter, the matrix of the triple creative energy described in the Kabbalah.

Name of Ramses, the Yod of AMON-RÂ gives birth to MESS - S- S.

The hieroglyph of the Mess childbirth expresses what Eric Hornung calls the radiance[6], i.e. the luminous divine matrix emitting a triple radiation from a unique point, from which is born the son of God. Born to the light, often translated by <u>son of the sun SA-RA or IS-RA</u> whereas it is about the

6   The principle of radiance, in Egyptology as in Kabbalah, is the common foundation of both religions. For more details, read Erik Hornung, L'Égypte ésotérique, Le Rocher, 2001. Also Erik Hornung, Les dieux de L'Égypte. Le un et le multiple, Le Rocher, 1986, p. 119-120.

emanation of the original light, the divine light. We find these three creative branches on the crown of Serapis, the new god Osiris Hellenized by the Ptolemies. Consequently, all the kings that we falsely name "Pharaohs" are above all reeds coming from the divine, primitive light, the images of the Yod of God. And for good reason, in the hieroglyphs, it is the Yod reed that determines the image of Atum, Amun-Ra, Aten, Isis, Anubis, Thoth, etc. Finally, the YOD symbolizes the EGO, the universal consciousness, the Idea, the Spirit, the Being, the Principle, the image of the creative god. If you look at the name Rameses itself, it means Ra the original light (not just the sun) - MESS gave birth - SS the Son, born from the twin powers Shu and Tephnut. It is a perpetual birth and rebirth, a "daily" resurrection of the sun and the men who emanate from all the light of the creation. Here is my point. The heavens and the earth are symbolically the two twins with which Man and Woman are identified, themselves coming from this double Matrix. We will see that this process of birth of the so-called Egyptian world, which may seem a bit complex, is re-explained by the Jewish Kabbalah, the Zohar.

This is essential because the real name of the kings of the Nile valley, the «Sons of RÂ», SA-RÂ is read as SA-RÂ as well as IS-RÂ 🐦, and designates the land ——*—— of the reeds, the land of the Yods. According to the legend, Isis and Osiris formed the first royal couple of mankind, symbolizing heaven and earth, that is to say Egypt below and Egypt above ▤ the two worlds. By syncretism, Ramses is written in Hebrew רמעססם, and in hieroglyphs ⊙𓀠𓂧𓂧, meaning the Matrix Ra or Isis/ISET gave birth to the two twins, 𐤎𐤎, S-S 𓂧𓂧 Shu and Tephnut as we have said (or two celestial placentas). But also with the "two worlds" (engendering the two gods, the heavens - the world above - and the earth, the world below).

IN THE BEGINNING, RA CREATED THE HEAVENS

AND THE EARTH!

AND NOT UPPER AND LOWER EGYPT!

In fine, all the creation is concentrated in the Son of light Horus, and in all the cases, the reed or the rush ISS or ESS symbolizes God, the Man, the creation starting from the light left the primordial waters... This scaffolding was of course used by the scribes of the Septuagint/Torah to create the myth of Moses saved from the waters of the Nile, meaning born of the womb, the Noun. Wallys Budge's dictionary uses ESS 𓇋 to refer to the Son. To say "the children" one writes either MESS-ESS-ESS-ESS ⟹ 𓇋𓇋𓇋 (the three marks the plural).

Rec. 32, 82, ⟸ 𓇋𓇋𓇋, children.

messu 𓄟𓇋𓇋𓀔 𓏭 , IV, 614, children.

This comparison confirms that the sound ISS or ESS designates the Son of God, which confirms that SARA is read ISRÅ.

The name Rameses is read either with two rushes SS 𓇋𓇋 meaning ***the two twins*** or the two lions 𓃭 𓃭(heaven and earth). But also with two horizontal bars ☰, which are read "SS". The scribes replaced the two rushes with the two bars, proof that they mean "the heavens and the earth" ☰ and not the Two Earths, in accordance with the cosmogony of On'.

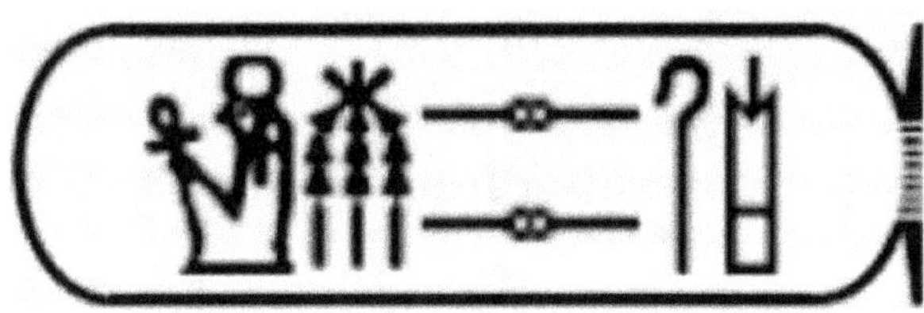

Name of Ramses: Ra begat ☰ the heavens and the earth.

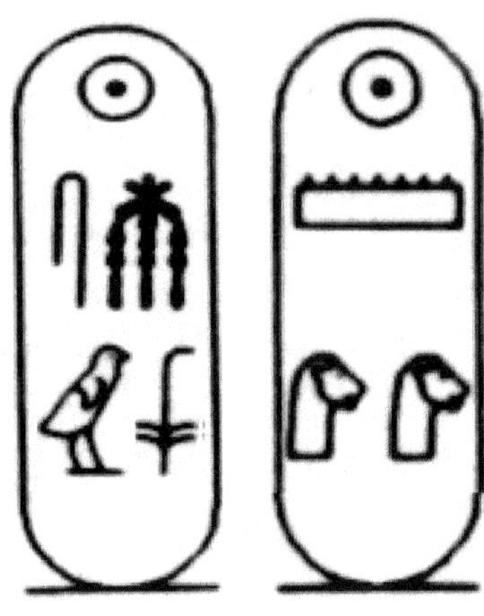

Cartouches of Rameses I. The sign Nu ∿∿∿∿ in the second cartouche has been replaced by the lion. Two twin lions symbolize Shu and Tephnut, the sky and the earth coming out of the Matrix Mess. Long before the Bible, Ramses means: Ra gave birth to the heavens and the earth.

In another form of the name of Ramses I given by Nicolas Grimal, the latter represents the Spirit Hou (the chick), the light coming out of the waters, as it is for Moses. Indeed, from the sign Nu ∿∿∿∿, the waters, come two lions head . The sun coming out of the roaring waters like the lion embodies the immense allegory of the birth of heaven and earth for the ancient "Egyptians". The Kabbalah has preserved the memory of Israel, the birth of the two twins Heaven-Earth, but also the emblem of the sun, the cosmic egg where the twelve chicks Sons of the Sun are the Sons of Israel: un, Son of Israel:

"The chicks": these are the twelve tribes from above. "Or the eggs": it is Israel from below which are like the clothing of the body" [7]

According to Plutarch, the egg is the birthplace of the King, the Principle Atum, the Yod at the origin of the universe:

---

7   Le Zohar, Livre de Ruth, collection «les dix paroles ». Traduit par Charles
    Mopsik. Verdier, 1987, p. 69.

"the egg was consecrated as a representation of the sovereign Being, who produces and understands all things"[8]

We thus have the written proofs, in the Bible, the Kabbalah and the hieroglyphs that the reading of the name Osiris corresponds to Israel. The title Son of RÂ, SA-RÂ is read and written with the cosmic egg IS ◯ and in this case it is read IS-RÂ, as the Wallis Budge dictionary attests. Thus, whenever we see the symbol SA-RÂ, it can be read IS-RÂ, the origin of Israel. We see that the hieroglyph of the sacred duck (or goose) is read SA by Egyptologists by pure convention. The historical reality of symbols attests that the pictogram SA is read IS because it designates the cosmic egg ◯. At the same time, it designates the earth of the reeds and the IS Son of Ra:

It is scientific evidence, neither Tutankhamun, nor Ramses II, nor Amen-Hotep III - nor any king of the Nile Valley - have ever been "Pharaohs", and even less "Egyptians", except for the Greek kings.

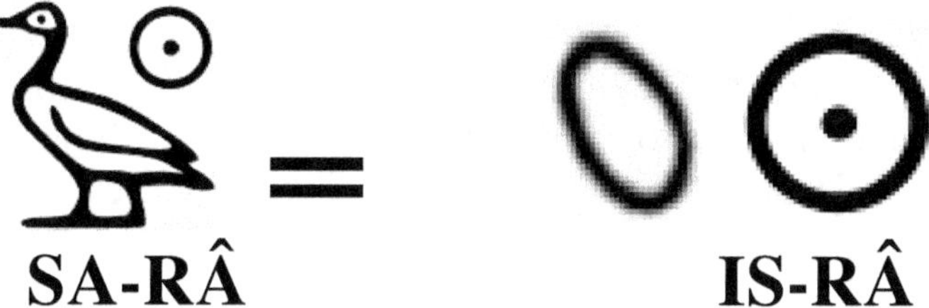

---

8   The solar egg gives birth to the gods, to the manifestations of the unique divine. Plutarque. Isis et Osiris. Par Guy Trédaniel. La Maisnie. 1992, p. 150, voire la note 1.

Royal Reed of Amun

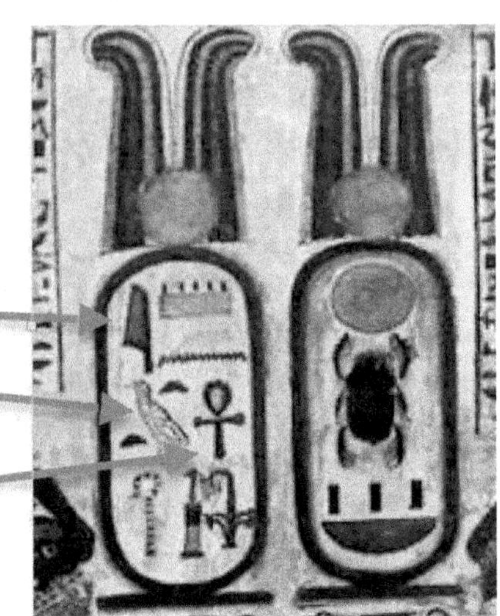

Poussin symbol of the creative Word and image of God

Ankh symbol of life and divine light

Septers of Osiris and rush, image of the sacred Reed the Yod of Atum

du roseau sacré.

Double cartouche of Tutankhamun

Let us observe carefully the cartouche of Tutankhamun: the three lines **I I I** below the scarab express the first Trinity, that is to say the multiplicity from unity. They symbolize three initial Yods (the hieroglyph Yod can be drawn by a vertical line, "**I**"[9]). One can read: **"The Lord NEB, the World KEPEROU and the Sun Ra are issued from the triple transformation of Atum"**. This means that the king is the living image of Tem (the One Reed became three to generate the World). Amun is thus the living image of the Yod that rises above the heavenly waters. The inscriptions specify that the king is the living image (TOT = T-HOU-T) HOU is the (Ankh) of Amun. The king is at the same time the chick Hou, meaning the creative Word/breath, and the reed that came out of the Nun, materialized by the scepters of Osiris. On the top of the cartouche, one notices indeed that dominates the YOD of Amun, the god Yod coming out of the Nun, the celestial waters, the image of Atum, as in the second verse of the Bible where God hovers above the primordial waters.

---

9   Egyptian hieroglyphic dictionary. Wallis Budge, op. cit., 15 a.

Now YOD, ANOKHI, HOU, AMEN are the names of the god of the Jews.

The cartouche of Akhenaten means that the king is the spirit AKH emanating from the light of Aten placed above the symbol of light RÂ, always imagined by the same reed YOD coming out of the waters of Noun and which is read Aten or Aton-Ra.

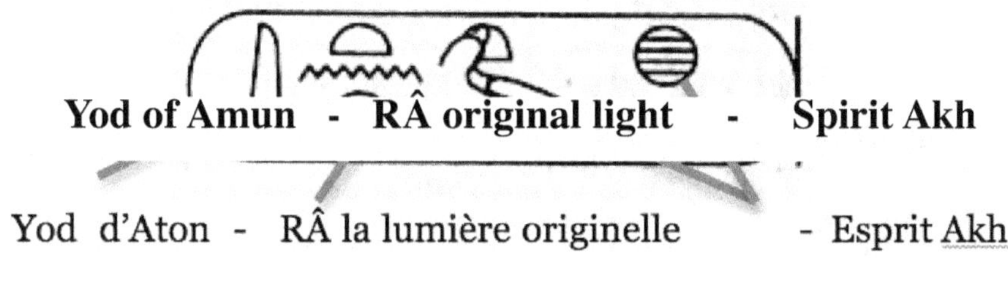

Royal cartouche of Akhenaten

The cartouche of King AY inscribed in the tomb of Tutankhamun means "His Father - God - I am the reed of God - Yod Yod", as attested by the figurative of the man pointing his finger towards him, followed by the reed Yod (= Me, I). The three scarabs signifying the transformation of the world by the demultiplication of the primordial YOD, Atum, which is divided into three Yods, express the original transformation of the world, from One into three energies. This is the reason why Atum affirms, "I am the one who became three".

This form of the unique god become three is at the origin of all the symbolic forms of the Trinity, the symbolism of the Hebrew Chin formed of three YOD, and designating the Spirit of God. Like the three Yods of the name of Osiris.

Indeed, the pictogram is included in the symbolic forms of the name SAR, or SARA of Osiris. This is the origin of the first Trinity, the symbolism of the Hebrew Chin' formed of three YOD, and designating the Spirit of God divided into three, as the divine Shekhina, and this goes up to the origin of the Christian Trinity. No wonder, the first Christians were Jews.

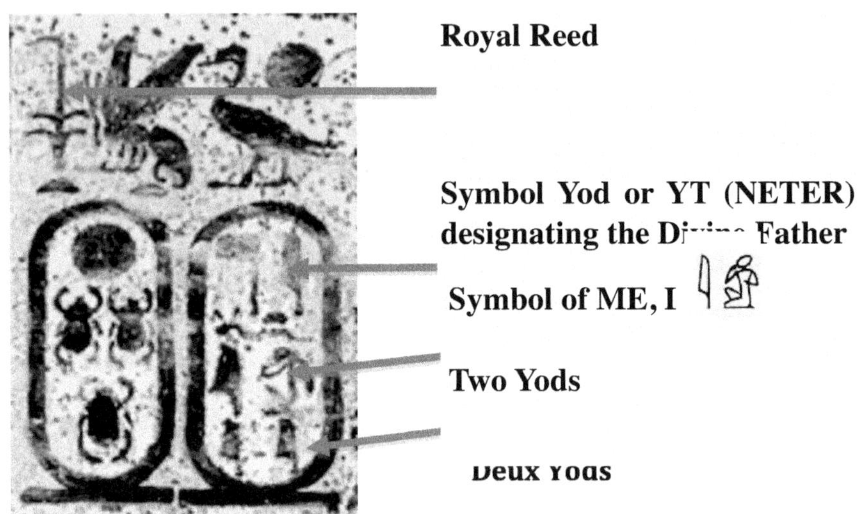

Double royal cartouche of King Ay.

Let us explore more closely the double cartouche of the pharaoh Ay. This cartouche brings the proof that the hieroglyph called "Néter" ⌐ - in the plural the gods ⌐⌐⌐ the Neteru - by the convention of the Egyptologists, **the famous flag ⌐ is none other than the figurative of the reed YOD ▮**. It designates God, but also the gods ⌐⌐⌐ the kings, the priests, the Fathers builders of the Nile Valley. Because the Yod forms here the hieroglyph Father of God, symbolically the king is the image of the Father. Consequently, the cartouche of Aÿ says: "I am - Yod Yod ▮▮- the image of God and the Gods, of the celestial Father resulting from the triple transformation of Ra/Atum", as if Aÿ were affirming at the same time to be the Father of Tutankhamun and the image of God himself, the Yod of Amun ▮. The expression "Father of God" refers directly to the Yod, which is confirmed by the Zohar for whom the Yod ▮ is the most sacred image of God, even the symbolic crown of God.

Now the flag ⌐ is the figurative of the expression "Father of the God" ⌐ ▮, supreme title of the High Priest that we find in the cartouche of the pharaoh Aÿ. This formula of the High

Priest ⌐〉 dedicated to Amun, Ra, Atum or Osiris is capital, because it brings the proof that the flag of Osiris ⌐ is indeed a Yod 〉 reed designating the priests and the High Priests, as for the Children of Israel are the priests who form the Body of Elohim.

Dieu T ou d Yod (Y)

Expression "Father of God" designating the High Priest.
The flag ⌐ is the figurative of the Yod 〉.

The cartouche of King Sethy I means that he is either the image of Set beloved of Amun, or the image of Osiris emanating from Ma'at the Truth Justice wearing the crown of the Yod, these two images being both followed by the two primordial Yods, which formed with Seth or Osiris a triad.

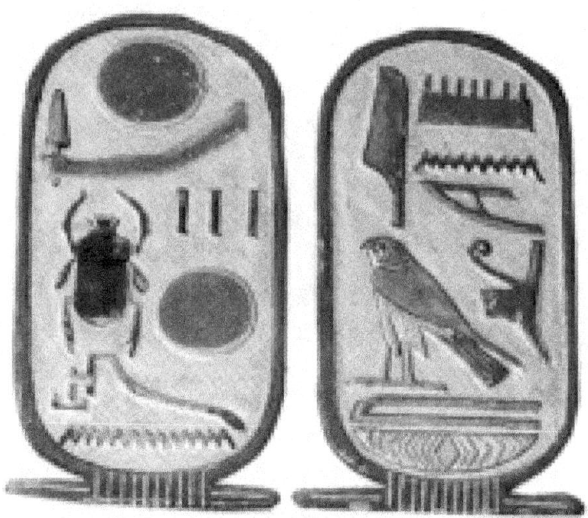

Yod reed of Amun with the image of Horus. Cartouche of King Horemheb..

Reeds of Sethy I with the image of Set and two Yods.

Sethy I with the image of Osiris/ISRA.

On several stelae of the Ptolemaic period, one sees the High Priest represented by Ptolemy V Epiphanes (who like Ptolemy Philadelphus used the false title of "Pharaoh"), making the offering to the bull Apis of the symbol of the three Yods resting on the sign of the earth. This hieroglyph with the three reeds designates the domain of Amun, or the kingdom of Osiris, the domain of **"the land built on water"**, thus the land of IS-RÂ.

Recall that for Kabbalah, the name of God is two, or three Yods. God wrapped a serpent around the divine Shekhina. The two Yods of the name of God are the two twins Heaven-Earth. Israel is none other than the valley of the Nile, the river that forms the crown of God. And consequently the crown of all the kings of Israel that we falsely name «Pharaohs»:

"The land of life built on water; for everything flows from the supreme river which comes out of Eden, which forms a crown for the sacred King and nourishes the worlds"[10]

Israel *IS the land of the Nile Valley*, the heavenly Garden of Eden of the Duat, the post-mortem world or Egypt above... Image of the land known as Egypt, it is also called "field of reeds" or "field of offerings", as attested by the Wallis Budge dictionary. The scenography of the stele confirms the capital importance of the hieroglyph of the *Field of the Reeds* translated by the *kingdom of Osiris*.

It is yet another clear proof that the ancient Nile Valley is none other than the original land of the Yods whose name will be usurped and will become the land of Egypt. This offering was also engraved on other stelae, in particular one representing Ptolemy II Philadelphus offering the same symbol of the kingdom of Osiris (or the domain of Amun), the land of the reeds Yods to the bull Apis, which symbolizes the beginning again, Amun/Osiris, god of abundance, fertility and fecundity and whose name the king will later transform into the land of ÆGYPTOS.

---

10   Zohar, tome V. Le livre de la splendeur, 1985, § 45 b, p. 126.

Ptolemaic stele where Ptolemy II Philadelphus makes an offering to Happi/Amun/Osiris of the symbol of the land of reeds .

Above the above stelae, one can see the emblem of the winged sun YAHOU with curved wings which is the symbol meaning "Osiris of light", "IS-RÂ-GOD" of light. This same emblem is found on many stelae and as we will see in detail on the royal seal of King Hezekiah which is called HAZAK-YAHOU, meaning the luminous power of Yahu/Osiris over the two worlds .

Ptolemaic stelae where Ptolemy II Philadelphus makes an offering to Amun and Osiris of the symbol of the land of reeds.

THE DECODING OF THE TWO CARTOUCHES OF ATON REVEALS THAT THE GOD OF EGYPT IS A PRIMORDIAL YOD

Around 1350 B.C., at the time of King Amenophis IV or AmenHotep IV, who renamed himself Akhenaten, the High Priests of Heliopolis (of Osiris) and of Amun bring us a definition of the name of the God. This is a discovery of first importance, because it gives us for the first time the possibility to explain the meaning of the name of the god in the ancient Nile Valley. And this is whether it is ATUM, RÂ, AMUN, OSIRIS or ATON. God is deciphered in a phraseology engraved on two divine or royal cartouches. Between the year 1 and the year 9 of Akhenaten called the Theban period. Because the king was initially named Amen-Hotep, after his father Amen-Hotep - Amun brings Peace - renamed Amenophis by the ancient Greeks.

The scribes wrote that Horus or Horakhty Ra, embodies the original light of God, the visible life force Ankh ☥ appeared on the eastern horizon in the name of Shu who is in Aten. The Egyptologists rely on a phonetic reading. They do not say more about this didactic name and leave us wanting more. Two enigmatic cartouches, to say the least, because it is indeed a synthesis of the name of God, Amun, Ra or Aten. There is another level of reading of the cartouches.

As we shall see, the Spirit of Life Ankh ☥ and the three suns of the day, ☉ correspond to the Tetragrammaton YHVH, the Alpha and Omega of Christ. I propose to push further the deciphering of this formula of Ra or Aten, by the symbolic, allegorical reading of the hieroglyphs. We will see that it leads us directly to the generic meaning of the YOD, the sacred reed, the image of God, whether it is Ra, Yahu, Osiris, Amun or Aten.

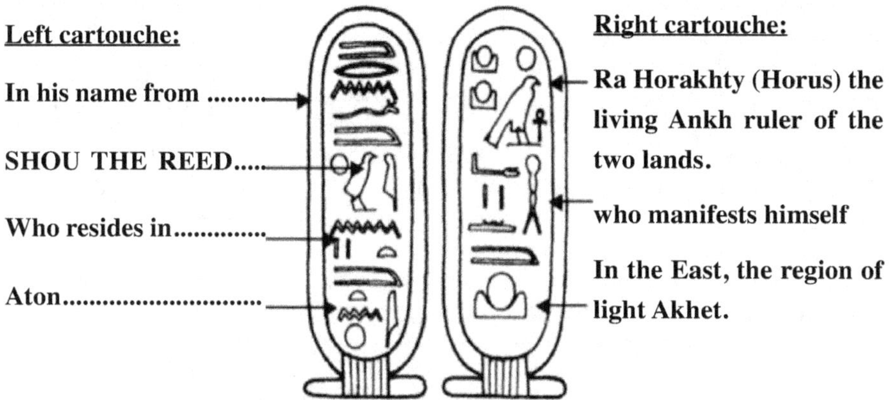

First didactic form of the title of Aten-Ra

Indeed, in the right-hand cartouche, the scribes tell us the meaning of the word REN, which means the «name» of Amen or Aten. REN is in front of the three suns or three lights. On the right, the symbol of the mouth ⬭ of RA ⊙ «R» and the symbol «N» of the Nou 〜〜, the nothingness, the Noun, the primordial ocean. The mouth ⬭ introduces the word coming from the Nun 〜〜, the creative Word coming out of the celestial Nun. The Word manifests itself in the second cartouche, the word of Ra ⊙ manifests itself to men through the feather of Shu 𓆄 (CH) followed by the chick 𓅱(HOU the Breath, the Spirit of God). The feather 𓆄 is another expression of the reed of God, the calamus of Truth-Justice carried by the goddess Maat. As proof of this, five years later, in the same title of Aten, the scribes will replace the feather of Shu 𓆄 by a reed Yod 𓇋.

The double cartouche of Aten confirms that the Nu is the matrix 〜〜 of God. The primordial ocean where God, ATUM, RÂ, manifested himself in the form of a Reed, a sacred calamus to enter into relationship with humanity. Atum, the demiurge, claims to be the reed that came out of the Nun. To draw and produce the images of all creation, the images of God (the hieroglyphs), Ra, Amun and Aten, the scribes teach us that Ra manifested himself in the form of a calamus, a Yod, Unique 𓇋 origin of the multiplicity of the creation.

Let's resume our investigation, which is very important because the Kabbalah has preserved this idea that the Yod is the origin of all creation. Below the mouth and the Nun are the hieroglyphs of the CH ⌡ reed of the HOU chick considered as "Him the Breath" and the creative Word coming out of Ra's mouth ⬭. Thus, the Spirit of God is identified with the chick and the reed Shu coming out of the Nu 〜〜〜.

Now it happens that these two elements CH and HOU correspond to HOU and SIA, the attributes of breath and knowledge at the time of Ra's circumcision.

"This is the blood that flowed from the phallus of Ra when he undertook to circumcise himself. Thus came into existence the gods who accompany Ra, Hou and Sia (who) accompany Atum every day in his race"[11]

Ra circumcised himself like Abraham. Circumcision causes the outpouring of the Spirit of God in the newborn. This is exactly the same explanation that we find among the Jews, we will come back to it.

Moreover, the scribes tell us that the hieroglyph of the reed CH ⌡ is located or ''resides in ATON''. But if we observe carefully the hieroglyph of Aten (or Amun), the only Reed that represents at the same time God, the creative Word and the divine Breath is the Yod of Atum ⌡ which comes out of the Nun:

Aton, the Yod that came out of the Nun to engender the world.

---

11 The Book of the Dead of the Ancient Egyptians. Ancient literatures of the Near East. Les Éditions du Cerf, 1967, p. 59. The translation of Guy Rachet in the Papyrus of Ani speaks about «drops of blood of the phallus of Ra, after the latter had mutilated himself». The Book of the Dead of the Ancient Egyptians. Unpublished translation and comments by Guy Rachet. Éditions du Rocher, 1996, p. 82.

The study of the first double cartouche of Aten allows us to understand that the sacred word, the breath and the creative Word of God, initially symbolized by the mouth ⬯, the chick 🐦 and the reed of Shu 𝄞, are manifested in fine by the YOD ⎮, the sacred calamus coming out of the celestial waters. The first title of the Theban period of Aten reveals to us that God himself, Amun, RÂ, Aten, Horus, Osiris, are the images of the Yod of Aten and are expressed by the Yod ⎮. Therefore the cartouches of the kings, allegedly called pharaohs, are based on the Yod of God. This finally confirms that the God of the ancient "Egyptians", whatever his name, is a Reed, a Yod, kings and men being in his image. By chance, in the ninth year of his reign, during the Amarna period, Akhenaten's scribes made syncretic modifications on the two cartouches of Aten. A second titulature that will confirm our demonstration.

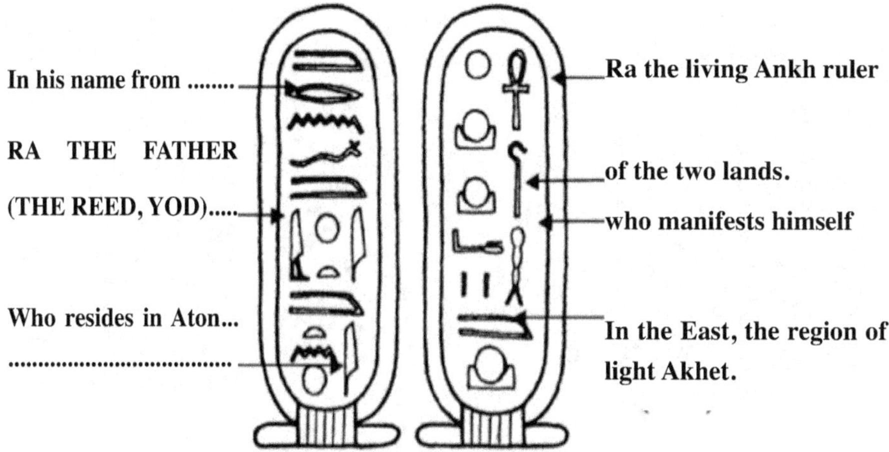

Second didactic form of the name of Aten. Shu, the chick and the reed have been replaced by the Yod of Aten.

As we can see, the three suns or three lights dividing the day into three parts are present, and this for the two periods, Theban and Amarna. The hieroglyphs demonstrate whether it is about Amun or Aten, that the very idea of God was centered on the Yod, the First Principle coming from the celestial calamus, which became three. Therefore, when Atum says "I am Atum (or RÂ) Out of the Nun" or "I am the One that became three", Atum refers to himself as the primordial Reed, in a way the calamus of God's artistic expression.

It is obvious that the scribes replaced the Shu reed and the chick by a YOD reed, designating Ra, the Father, thus Atum. By syncretism, Shu became "Ra the Father" or Ra became the YOD. Thus, the God of those whom we falsely name "Ancient Egyptians" is a sacred Reed, Yod. Thus the hieroglyph formed by two parallel lines linked together means, on the one hand, that the two worlds are linked by God. On the other hand, the preposition "in" (M), "inside", symbolically the womb of the woman. It recalls the Hebrew Beth ב which also means "in, inside".

Analogy between the Hebrew Beth and the hieroglyph of the sky and the earth, according to the Kabbalah and the cosmogony of Heliopolis, where the god Shu separates the sky from the earth.

The Zohar states that the Beth ‎ב refers to the house of God, the heavenly Temple, ‎ב formed by heaven and earth separated by the power "He" of God. This parable corresponds to the god Shu separating the sky Nut from the earth Geb. This comparison is essential because the symbolism of the Beth given by the Kabbalah reveals that the waters of the world above (heaven) are said to be feminine, while the waters of the world below (earth) are said to be masculine. Once again, the Kabbalah has preserved the memory of the two twins of Atum (Shu and Tephnut), the cosmotheism of On'/Heliopolis, the historical syncretism of the ancient "Jewish" religion.

"Rabbi Yehuda said: «The Beth (‎ב) is composed of two horizontal bars and a third vertical one that unites the other two. It is the image of God who unites heaven and earth. Rabbi Eleazar says: It is the image of the three supreme and sacred lights which form only One and which are the synthesis of the Law"

Two bars indicate two worlds. This scenography is described by the Kabbalah:

"Union of the masculine and feminine engraved in the imprints of the letters……Consider the intimate meaning (‎ב): the letter b (two) of the word bereshit (In the beginning) indicates that first of all there are two worlds which in turn create worlds; one creates the world above, the other the world below... ... The world above is filled and impregnated like a woman becoming pregnant after being impregnated by a man, then it gives birth to two twin children, one male, the other female, which are heaven and earth"

According to this explanation, the Beth ‎ב responds precisely symbolically and visually to its counterpart the hieroglyph ▬▬‎ב. But also to the cosmogony of On'/Heliopolis, where the god Shu symbolizes the divine breath separating the sky Nut from the earth Geb. These are derived from Shu and Tephnut, the twin powers represented by the two lions, the two wings of the sun, the two S's or the two horizontal lines, inscribed in the name of Ramses. The allegory of the two twins, Heaven and Earth, is taken up in the first verse of the Bible.

In conclusion, the two cartouches of Aten from the Theban and Amarna periods bring us the archaeological proof that the God of the Nile valley, whether he is unique or multiple, was undoubtedly manifested by the reed YOD. Whether it represents uniqueness like Aten, or whether it is unique and multiple by its manifestations like Amun, thus by pictorial syncretism, the YOD symbolizes God or the gods, (like El and Elohim in the Bible). The Yod is the god of Tutankhamun, which is why we find it dominant in Atum, Tutankh-ATON, Amun, Osiris, Thoth, Anubis, etc. Reasons why those whom we name "ancient Ægyptos" and their kings "pharao'" have absolutely nothing to do with the Greek nominations, imposed by the great Hellenization of Ptolemy.

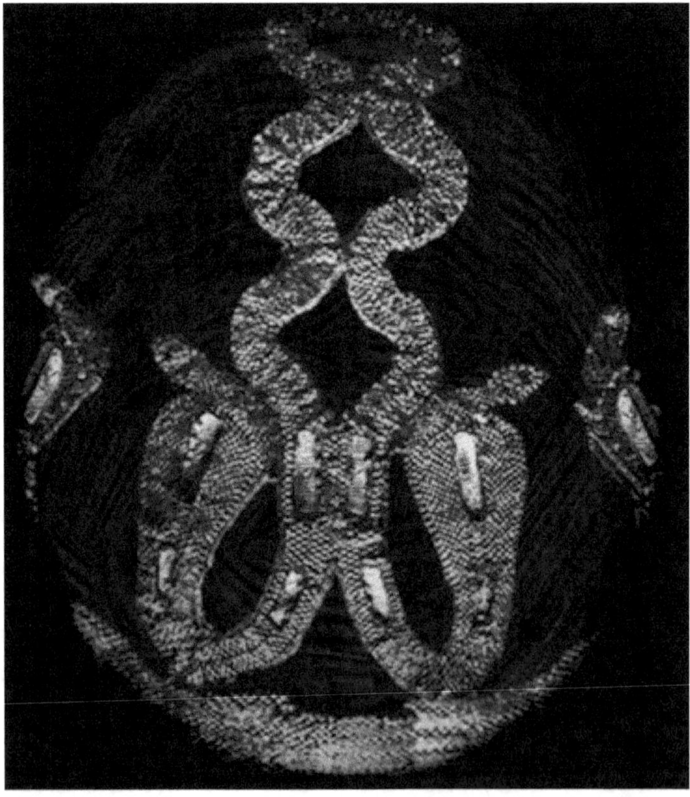

Monotheistic cap of Tutankhamun with the snake divided into four snakes, and bearing 10 times the name of Aten.

THE METAPHYSICAL CAP
OF TOUTANKHAMON

I now propose to penetrate the secrets of the Kabbalah's metaphysics, for they allow us to uncover the perfect similarity between the crowns of the kings of Israel and the SA-RA kings called Pharaohs. Here again, it is no longer a matter of mere coincidence between two civilizations. There is only one civilization, that of the Yod reeds that came out of the celestial waters of the Nun. The symbols of life, death and resurrection of the crowns and the cap of the kings of the Nile Valley, as well as the "Egyptian" secret of circumcision confirm their identity as kings of ancient Israel.

But before that, it is worth reminding the reader of the memory of the serpent crown of the kings of Israel, as preserved in the Kabbalah. It is said in the book of Kings that David took the crown of Nahash the Ammonite - translated as the Serpent of Amon - and girded it on his head. According to a passage in the Zohar, this crown of the serpent is the perpetual testimony of the recognition of the kings of Israel.

"With Amon, King David crowned himself, this crown being a testimony for the stock of David, as the verse indicates: "he imposed on him the crown and the testimony" (II Kings 11: 12) which came from Milkom degree of the Amonites, according to the words: "he (David) took the crown of Milkom" (II Samuel 12: 30) Milkom is indeed the degree of the children of Amon, it is written [on this crown]: "it was placed on the head of David". IT WAS A PERPETUAL WITNESS TO HIS DESCENDANTS, for by it is recognized who is the son of David to whom the kingship is due..."[12]

---

12   Le Zohar, tome II, collection 'les dix paroles ». Traduit par Charles Mopsik. Vayera, Hayé Sarah, Toldot, Vayetsé, Vayichlah. Verdier, 1984, p. 116.

Another passage of the Kabbalah evokes the great secret of the double crown of Yahweh/Elohim/Yod-Yod, of the two degrees of the red and white crown of Israel, again, an image of the crown of God, the two gates of the other world, united in one:

"Rabbi Simeon says: A tradition teaches us that there are two crowns that unite together and that constitute, as it were, the gate of all other crowns. The tradition also tells us that one of these crowns is rigor, and the other is clemency, one male and the other female. Clemency reigns on the side of the male, rigor on the side of the female. The one is white, and the other is red; and it is to mitigate each other that they unite together."[13]

As we have seen, the crown of the kings of Israel is linked to the notion of a "door" to the beyond. The white crown of the kings of the Nile Valley takes the form of the sun emerging from the red crown, which is none other than the Matrix, the famous Red Sea - or Sea of Reeds - from which the king SA-RA emerges. The *Texts of the Pyramids* give us the explanation. The red crown - the letter N in hieroglyphics - symbolizes both the famous river of fire where the sun regenerates (of which Akhenaten speaks in his *Great Hymn to Aten*), but also the serpent of the Nou or the Noun, the divine Matrix of the Sun Ra:

---

13   Le Zohar, tome V, Le livre de la splendeur, op. cit., p. 41.

"The king's mother is a great serpent, and it is a serpent of fire, THE RED CROWN, which gives birth to him; he is himself a reptile with many folds, provider of vital powers"[14]

This double crown thus gives metaphysical, eschatological power to the king, who becomes in a way the supreme guide of humanity towards the hereafter. The double crown of the ancient Egyptians symbolizes not only the daily rebirth of the sun, but also their «exit from Egypt» to the world beyond through the Red Sea... It is this exit from Egypt that is explained in the secrets of the Kabbalah.

The royal skullcap that adorned the head of King Tutankhamun allows us to understand, in a precise manner, how the emblematic images of the crown of the afterlife, belonging to the initiated priests "Egyptians" have reached the Kabbalah. For it is indeed a cap - a Kipa representing the celestial vault - both monotheistic and polytheistic. Found under the headdress of the young king's mummy, it is formed by the four snakes of the lower world, which symbolize the four rivers. The skullcap bears ten times the name or royal cartouche of the unique god Aten, thus ten times the symbol of the reed Yod coming out of the Noun, confirming by ten times the monotheism of the king of Egypt, resting on the Principle Atum.

According to many Egyptologists, Tutankhamun would have abandoned the religion of Akhenaten to return to the religion of Amun. In that case, why doesn't his cap bear the name of Amun ten times? In reality, the cap stamped ten times with the name of Aten shows that the young king had returned to the ancestral syncretism of Amun, where God was both unique and multiple. Amun means "the Hidden One", unique in his essence and multiple in his manifestations. Aten symbolizes the visible image of Amun, or Atum, the heavenly Father, whom the SA-RA kings will join after their death. Terrorized by the darkness - and consequently by Amun and Osiris, all that represented the gods and the images of the beyond - Akhenaten deified the light Aten, the sun, as the only form of the divine, repudiating all the beliefs relative to the celestial world, said underground of Amun or Osiris.

---

14 Christian Jacq, La tradition primordiale de l'Égypte, op. cit., p. 265.

Several passages in the Zohar attest to the vital importance of the transfer of the legacy of the ancient Egyptian civilization to the rabbis of Kabbalah. In particular, the secret knowledge of the initiation of the kings of Egypt. It is said that Pharaoh, the king of Egypt, dedicated all his actions to the Wisdom «from above» (which means according to the sacred Law of Ma'at), the king «Pharaoh» is the great **"Master of the knowledge of the ten lower crowns"**[15] of God... of Yahweh...

"Come and see: the wisdom of the Egyptians consisted in everything they did, they did it by referring to the Wisdom from Above. Pharaoh was the most knowledgeable, for no king was enthroned in Egypt unless he was the most knowledgeable"[16]

"Come and see: all the Egyptians were scholars, and from the side of the Power proceed many armies, many camps and many degrees, reaching to the lower degrees; the Egyptians were therefore sorcerers and experts in those lower degrees through which they knew the mysteries of the world"[17]

All the "Egyptians" - allegedly idolaters by our three monotheistic religions - and all the kings of the Nile Valley were therefore Yods - Jews - ruled by the Wisdom and power of God... an idolatrous god!!! That is, the god of the Jews originally was idolatrous! This primitive idolatry was broken by Hellenization. For according to this explanation stating that everything the Egyptians did, the god Yahweh of the Jews was none other than the god Yahu of the so-called Egyptians, which the hieroglyphs demonstrate. Only the Yahud High Priests of On' alias Heliopolis, called "Egyptians", could transmit the secrets of the crowns and of the wisdom coming from Above... If this explanation seems to us a priori obscure, it is because it has never been confronted with Egyptology. It is part of the esoteric language of the hieroglyphic thought and in particular of the Book of the Dead, transmitted from ancient Egypt to the scholars of the Kabbalah.

---

15 Le Zohar, tome III, Le livre de la splendeur, op. cit., p. 236-237.

16 Le Zohar, Cantique des Cantiques. Collection «les dix paroles ». Verdier, 1999, p. 173.

17 Le Zohar, tome IV, collection «les dix paroles ». Vayigash Vayehi. Traduit par Charles Mopsik. Verdier, 1996, p. 199

According to the Talmud, **"Four rivers surround Israel"**[18].This statement suggests that Israel was originally a huge territory, stretching from the Nile to the Euphrates. Does this recollection of the ancient topography of the Garden of Eden come from the symbolic memory of the four serpents surrounding the head of Tutankhamen, who became an IS-RA, or Osiris, at his death? Four rivers surrounding Israel would mean four symbolic snakes surrounding the skull of Osiris.

The Old Testament relates that in the beginning, the River of Eden was divided into four. The shape and metaphysical symbolism of Tutankhamen's royal cap are consistent with a passage in the Kabbalah, which describes the four rivers of the Garden of Eden as the four serpents/rivers of an empire that corresponds to Egypt, stretching from the Nile to the Euphrates. The four serpents of the river of the Garden of Eden include the Nile and the Euphrates (Genesis chapter I). In secret, they would correspond to the four great invasions of Egypt, that of the Assyrians, Babylonians, Persians and Greeks. Yes, the four rivers of the Garden of Eden already announce, in the secret of the dispersion, the death of the Egyptian civilization. Moreover, only the kings that we falsely call "pharaohs" wore a crown symbolizing the sacred river, the Nile. These kings had built their civilization on land annually invaded by the floods of the sacred river.

Only the Nile corresponds to the River identified with the royal crown of the Sons of Ra, the cosmotheistic crown where God was one with the universe. The Nile is the first river of the Garden of Eden of the Old Testament. The Nile was the crown of the "kings of Egypt", formed by the Uraeus serpent, a metaphor for the river of Osiris, the long nourishing serpent of the Nile Valley. A Kabbalah commentary states that the crown of God, Sephira KETER' (the divine breath of the Royal Crown) is the place where all the springs of life flow. In ancient Egypt, the Nile and its tributaries are symbolized by the serpent of Osiris divided into several heads, a parable of the creative multiplication of the Yod of Tem/Atum.

---

18   Aggadoth du Talmud de Babylone. Op. Cit., B.B. 74b.

Another Kabbalah commentary confirms that the Garden of Eden is Egypt, where Pharaoh is described as the primordial celestial serpent:

''the Master of the Ten Lower Crowns: Pharaoh» was the greatest of all the magicians; he was well versed in the knowledge of the [ten] "lower crowns" " [19]

Archaeology confirms what the Kabbalah says. Egyptologists have discovered that ten crowns participate in the ceremony of the sacrament of the king by the god Amun. The example is given to us by Queen Hatshepsut. Ten crowns are worn by ten goddesses who parade before the "queen pharaoh":

"Their retinue seems regulated by a canonical order."[20]

In esoteric language, this means that Pharaoh is the master of the ten "sephirot", the ten fundamental attributes of the god of the Bible... Now the ten sephirot constitute at the same time the Tree of Life and the Body of the Primordial Man, Adam Kadmon', Adam being at the same time the image of Yahweh and image of Israel. The Kabbalah goes even further in this Osirian configuration: like the crown of Tutankhamen it makes the link between the name of God, the unique god and the royal crown:

"The crowns of the king constitute the sacred name"[21]

The explanation of the four serpents is found in the *Sarcophagus Texts*. The serpent Ureus called the guide of the soul towards heaven, on the luminous path of the skull of Ra, breathes into the king's skull the breath of Hou - the Spirit - and and Sia - the knowledge - in direct connection with the self-circumcision of Ra (who we have seen, brought by this means the breath and the knowledge into his mind) :

---

19   Le Zohar, tome III, Le livre de la splendeur, op. cit., p. 236-237.

20   Marie-Ange Bonhème, Annie Forgeau, Pharaon. Les secrets du pouvoir, op. cit., p. 274-275.

21   Ibidem, p. 21.

"I know the dark paths by which Hou and Sia (the breath of the Spirit and knowledge) enter in four dark snakes, luminous for those who follow them (and) those who precede them. I want to enter between them through a secret path that is on the top of the skull of Ra"[22]

Let us not forget that the Kabbalah looks at the crown of God as the image of the supreme river of the Garden of Eden, that is the Nile, or rather ancient Israel named the land of life:

"The "land of life" is built on water; for all things flow from the Supreme River that flows out of Eden, which forms a crown for the sacred King and nourishes the worlds"[23]

Kabbalah confirms us that Israel aws the ancient name of Egypt, that **"Four rivers surround Israel"[24]**. All these elements, which cannot be coincidental, allow us to understand why Jan Assmann has drawn the following conclusion. Even if there is no historical trace of Moses and the kings of Israel, one fact remains undeniable: the Jewish people has its historical roots in ancient Egypt, but the Bible, the Torah of Moses, has definitely broken the link of historical filiation between the Jews and the ancient Nile Valley.

As we said, in the Hebrew Bible, the name Yahweh יהוה is made up of four letters, the secret of which symbolizes "Pardes", a Greek word meaning paradise, the Garden of Eden, composed of four rivers, the first of which is the Nile. But the name Yahweh is also written with two י י, or three Yods י י י, which shows that originally Yahweh/Yahu יהוה corresponded to the multiplication of the Yod י of the so-called "Egyptians". Let us now look at Tutankhamen's tiara placed above the cap with the four serpents. The tiara bears three snakes, of which the upper one has the shape of the meanders of the Nile.

---

22   Spell n° 759. Textes des Sarcophages du Moyen Empire Égyptien. Claude Carrier, tome II. Éditions du Rocher, 2004, p. 1701.

23   Zohar, tome V. Le livre de la splendeur. Par Jean de Pauly. Maisonneuve & Larose, 1985, §45b, p. 126.

24   Aggadoth du Talmud de Babylone. Op. Cit., B.B. 74b.

**Crown of the Nile snake of
Tutankhamun**

**Crown of God, the Sacred
King, the River according to
the Kabbalah**

Tutankhamun's three-serpent tiara

The metaphysical arrangement of the cap and tiara into
seven snakes divided into three for the tiara and four for the
cap is found on the upper case of the tiara of the tefilin or
philacteria of the Jews, which form the royal crown of God.
The crown of Yahweh/YHVH/YAHOU is thus formed by the
Sacred River, the Nile, the first river of the Garden of Eden, as
was the crown of the ''kings of Egypt'', formed by the Uraeus
serpent, a metaphor of Osiris, the long serpent of the Nile.
In addition to the symbolism of the sacred river, Tutankhamun
bears the symbol of the seven original serpents, forming the
seven names of Ra or seven Bâou of Ra:

**"Ra has seven souls and fourteen Ka; he is also given twelve
names"[25]**

---

25 Le Livre des Morts des Anciens Égyptiens. Littératures anciennes du Proche-
Orient. Les Éditions du Cerf, 1967, chapitre 15, note n° 5, p. 46.

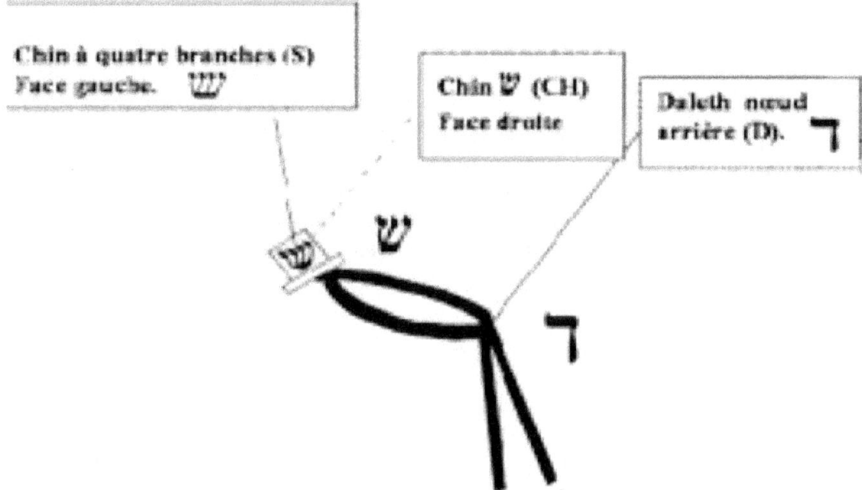

The crown of the tefilin of the Jews, symbol of the crown of God.

These seven lights (Yods) are comparable to the light of the seven days of the resurrection of the dead in the Kabbalah; they are reproduced by the seven rings of resurrection arranged in a "Christian" cross, on the mummy of the Pharaoh Tutankhamun. The metaphysical comparison between the king's tiara and the mummy is clear. On the upper case of the tefilin, a three-branched Hebrew Chin' is engraved on the right side and a four-branched Hebrew Chin' on the left side, which gives a total of seven branches, seven luminous powers, seven lights of the soul according to the Kabbalah. Seven branches or seven Yods are associated with the ten commandments contained in the text of the Deuteronomy in the case.

These seven lights correspond to the seven golden rings that were found in the strips of the mummy of Tutankhamen. The cabalistic symbolism of Abraham, Isaac and Jacob takes up this idea of the Principle of Oneness of the Body of God, the One in three. It is said in the Gemara that th e Jews who wear the phylacteries or Tephilines are assured, if their conduct is perfect, to live again after death in the Garden of Eden. This is equivalent to passing through the seven heavenly worlds to reach Paradise.

"The letter Chin' appeared before the Holy Spirit bearing the three sacred crowns of the Patriarchs"[26] ; "The Chin' of

26   Le Zohar, tome III. Le livre de la splend., op. cit, p. 241, 54a

Shabbath symbolizes the three branches of the Patriarchs"[27]

One may then ask whether the Torah really does discard the images of God from the gods. Is not Adam, the first man, himself the image of Elohim? Abraham is called Elohim, Moses is an "Elohim for Pharaoh". Several texts of the Kabbalah describe each character of the Torah as an image, an anthropomorphic allegory, a Sephira, an emanation of God. Abraham, Isaac and Jacob form the attributes and symbolic Body of God. Abraham is the right arm, Jacob embodies the sun and the Body, Isaac the left arm. The twelve sons of Jacob also designate the twelve parts of the Body of God (as well as the twelve constellations), Joseph designating the phallus of God. It is a true solar Osirian configuration, "heliopolitan" that the metaphors of the Kabbalah project.

The three Patriarchs are also the "three suns" of the day (morning, noon and evening) who participate each day in the creation, a single sun divided into three, a metaphor that is found on the cartouches of Aten. Thus, on the case fixed between the eyes of the faithful Jews, one finds the Osirian configuration, the metaphysical configuration of the crown of Tutankhamen. Thus, the metaphysical crowns or diadems of the Jews correspond to the crown and diadem of Tutankhamen. One can compare the prayer shawl, the tsitsit, the skullcap and the tefilin of the Jews to the royal, priestly dress of Tutankhamun, a dress that only the initiated High Priests of the Nile Valley could keep in mind. TUTANKHAMUN IS AN ISRAELI.

---

27 Le Zohar, tome V, Le livre de la splendeur, op. cit, p. 92. Les patriarches sont aussi comparés à trois branches de laurier.

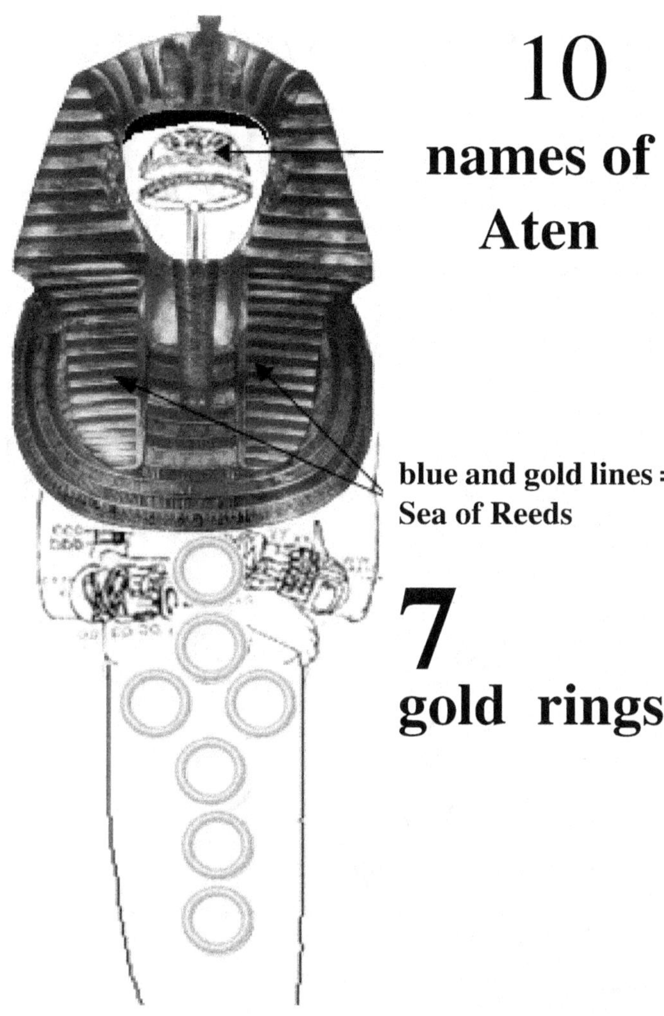

The soul of King Tutankhamun passes into the afterlife through the magical power of the seven golden rings, which symbolize the seven stars of the Great Bear, and the ten names of Aten on the king's cap.

TOUTANKHAMUN IS AN ISRAEL

To understand the deep, symbolic nature of Tutankhamun, it is necessary to insist on the fact that this King is never a pharaoh **but an Osiris, an IS-RÂ**. His first function is, as High Priest, to fight in the underworld, in order to guarantee the solar cycle, to fight symbolically against the Serpent "King" of darkness named Apophys or Mehen. Each daybreak is a victory, a new IS-RÂ , a new beginning of the world, of the God-World. We will see the parallel with the fight between Jacob and the Angel, which is none other than an Osirian cosmic fight against his twin brother Esau.

But As We Know, In the first reading of the Bible, Israel designates the Patriarch Jacob. But the Kabbalah informs us that Jacob is the sun, it is God himself... the solar god fighting Esau the god of darkness. So That ALL THE BIBLE IS THE STORY OF THE SUN-ISRAEL, THE GOD, THE LIGHT EXPELLED FROM EGYPT.

"The sun is Jacob"[28]

To give another view, the fight between Jacob and the Angel ends with the victory at daybreak of Jacob, who becomes Israel = IS - RÂ - ELOHIM. This myth conceals a cosmogonic scenography, cosmic, between Jacob the sun and Esau who would be the celestial serpent of darkness named Amalek (the King of Darkness) or, says the Kabbalah, Samael. «Jacob is the sun and Esau is the serpent. Thus, the characters of the Bible are not human, but they conceal a real cosmogony where the cosmic powers are sometimes at war, sometimes at peace, to explain the cyclic passage from day to night and vice versa. The Kabbalah confirms that Jacob ISRAEL is a solar man:

"Jacob prevailed, his reign being exercised during the day"[29]

---

28   Le Zohar, Genèse, tome III, Vayéchev, Mikets, collection «les dix paroles ». Traduit par Charles Mopsik. Verdier, 1991, p. 207.

29   Le Zohar, tome II, collection «les dix paroles ». Traduit par Charles Mopsik.

Let us now observe carefully the image of the pyramid of Khenzer where Yahu symbolizes the winged sun that we have identified with the power of Yahu. Below, we can see on the left Horus (Hor in hieroglyphic means the bearer of light), the son of Osiris, who transfers the solar falcon to Atum on the right. The falcon serves here as a relay, the cyclical passage of the sun from the world of night to the world of day. The Resurrection of the sun is done by the transfer of the divine falcon.

Transfer of the solar falcon bird RÂ from Horus (day) to Atum (night). Pyramid of Khenzer.

We understand that after this nocturnal combat that we find in the tombs of the Valley of the Kings, Jacob is named Israel, meaning at the same time in the Bible Son of God and the one who fights against Elohim, and Sun in the Kabbalah, attributes that are those of Osiris IS-RÂ-GOD.

"You shall say to Pharaoh, thus says Yahweh: Israel is my Son, my Elder" (Exodus V, 22, 23)

"Israel will be called «SONS OF KINGS"[30] = SA-RÂ

Verdier, 1987, p. 292.

30   Le Zohar, tome I, collection "les dix paroles ». Traduit par Charles Mopsik. Verdier, 1981,   p. 157.

RAÂ IS THE SECRET NAME OF YAHVE-ELOHIM

This is exactly the same cosmogonic symbolism in the Bible between the twin brothers Jacob and Esau. Rashi states that Jacob and Esau were already fighting in their mother's womb for the domination of the world and especially the domination of the sun. The Zohar reports that Jacob/Israel named TAM, the Perfect Man (the name of Atum), embodied the sun of the day (like Horus), while Esau, the red man (Esau is named Edom = red), embodied the darkness of the seven days of the creation of the world, Esau being the celestial serpent is assimilated to the biblical tohu-bohu and darkness: **"The darkness (Isaac) overcomes the face of the abyss (Esau)"** [31]

"And Elohim called the light "day" (Gen. 1:5) refers to Jacob [the sun, the Light God]. **"And the darkness he called "night" refers to Esau** [Greece, Rome]. **"And it was evening" refers to Esau, "And it was morning" refers to Jacob"**[32]

It is very important to remember in this chapter that rabbinic tradition compares Esau to the rule of Rome. But in the context of the Septuagint, Rome was not yet dominant. Esau necessarily and secretly symbolized Greek domination, the darkness and hustle and bustle of Genesis **refer to Greece, to Hellenization**, to the hold and terror of the Ptolemies over the Jews. The Bible confirms that Esau is a God-King who wants to take over the sun, and not a man, qualified by Jacob as Elohim (Genesis XXXIII, 10): Although the rabbinic tradition compares Esau to the domination of Rome, this proves that in the Septuagint period Esau necessarily and secretly symbolized the darkness and turmoil of Hellenization due to Greek domination[33], the

---

31 Le Zohar, tome I, op. cit., Traduit par Charles Mopsik. Verdier, 1981, p. 98.

32 Midrach Rabba, tome I, Genèse Rabba. Collection «les dix paroles ». Verdier, 1987. P. 52 § 3.

33 According to rabbinic tradition, Esau is compared to the serpent of the darkness of creation, but especially to the darkness linked to the domination and exile of Rome. But we have seen that in the secret tradition, before the domination of Rome, it was ancient Greece that dominated, Greece moreover compared to the darkness of creation.

hold and terror of the Ptolemies over the Jews. The Bible confirms, moreover, that Esau is a God-King wanting to seize the sun, and not a man, qualified by Jacob as Elohim, Genesis XXXIII, 10:

Jacob answered [Esau] **"Oh no! If I have found favor in your eyes, you will accept this homage from my hand; for I have seen your face as one sees the face of Elohim"**

What kind of tribute is this? Precisely the light of Ra, the god of the Nile Valley. One commentary tells us that at nightfall, Esau having triumphed over Jacob, the latter offered him his falcon named Ra'a ראה in Hebrew[34], the favorite solar bird of Jacob/Israel, the emblem coveted by Esau: **"According to Bahya, Jacob sent him a falcon, Esau's favorite bird, the one he liked to 'hold in his hand' "**[35]

But more than that, Moses himself is a falcon, **"a bird wounded in a thorn bush"**[36], which is called Raah the hawk in Hebrew. Reason why Yahweh addresses Moses as "I have seen" writes ראה .

"I have seen [ראה], I have seen the misery of my people who are in Egypt" (Exodus III, 7)

The Bible relates that Jacob prostrates himself seven times before Esau before speaking to him. Now the ritual of the seven prostrations is Osirian: it is an act of submission in connection with the course of the sun, the seven souls (Bao) of Ra or Osiris, as attested by the numerous letters discovered at Amarna, written during the reign of Amenophis III and Akhenaten. Letter EA 141 is addressed to the latter:

"Rib-Hadda says to his Lord, great king, king of all countries: I fall at the feet of my Lord, the king, seven times and seven times"[37]

---

34 Élie Munk, La voix de la Torah. Le Deutéronome, op. cit., p. 139.

35 Élie Munk, La voix de la Torah. Le Deutéronome, op. cit., p. 338, voire la note du verset 14.

36 Midrachim de nos sages, Exode, transcrit par Maurice Stern, op. cit. Tome II, Chemoth Rabbah, p. 30.

37 According to the letters of Amarna, one prostrated seven times on the stomach, and seven times on the back...

Thus we have evidence that the scribes of the Bible knew the traditions and customs of the Nile Valley, but also the allegorical secrets of the pyramid of King Khenzer, which dates from the Middle Kingdom about 1700 B.C. The Kabbalah has preserved the memory of the cosmotheism of Osiris and his forty-two judges, forming the cosmos - all humanity - the ancient Israel. The twelve tribes and seventy sons of Jacob arriving from Canaan to settle in Egypt are decoded by the Kabbalah to the "cosmos" - all humanity - settling in Egypt. Jacob - renamed Israel - is the sun and the old man from above. The twelve tribes formed the twelve constellations of the cosmos following God, the sun ISRAEL. Israel thus corresponds to the cosmogony of Osiris, the primordial solar elder and his forty-two judges installed in the Nile Valley (Book of the Dead) :

"Rabbi Simeon says: "When the Shekhina [the Spirit of God, Yahweh/Elohim] **descended into Egypt, she took the form of a Haya** [the original Light, the living solar power of God = ANOKHI = the Ankh φ of the «Egyptians»] **who bears the name of Israel** [Yahweh/Elohim is a solar man]**, and whose image resembles that of the old man** [from above]**. Forty-two holy angels destined to serve the Shekhina came down with her. Each of these angels carries a sacred letter of the divine name composed of forty-two letters"**[38]

Jacob/Israel came down to Egypt with his forty-two angels. This means that the God of Egypt, Israel, comes down to fulfill the Law, the forty-two commandments, harmony, flooding, fertility, etc. Following the example of Osiris and his forty-two judges, symbols of justice and cohesion of the world, it is said in the Zohar that the forty-two letters from the serpent not only form the sacred crown of God, but also that they were melted together, in a universal syncretism, to create the earth which was tohu-bohu (the darkness of Greece):

"The earth was Tohu and Bohu" (Gen. 1: 2) it did not become consistent as long as it remained in the state of Tohu-Bohu, it remained so until the world was inscribed with forty-two letters, it could then subsist. These letters

---

38 Zohar, tome III. Le livre de la splendeur. Par Jean de Pauly. Éditions Maisonneuve & Larose, 1985. P. 74.

form the crown of the holy name. When these letters were fused together [the harmony of the forty-two parts of the Body of Israel/Osiris] **the world could finally exist... With the staff of the great serpent they struck the ground...»**[39]

The English version differs, stating that "the letters struggled against the great serpent" to build up the world. Finally, the forty-two letters form the integrity of the body of God, the body of Israel, a cohesion necessary to fight against the abyss where the great serpent Leviathan reigns, an obvious reminder of the serpent Apophys, the cosmic enemy of Osiris and Ma'at, the serpent of the night which must never be killed but subdued every day, because the night is indispensable for the balance of cosmic forces. In the tombs of the Valley of the Kings, the king in the form of Ra or Atum fights Apophys all night long, until early morning. The aim is not to kill him, but to master the powers of evil within him. Thus domesticated, Apophys becomes again the "good snake", the protective uraeus, placed between the eyes of Pharaoh. The Kabbalah attests to the double function of the serpent: **"But sometimes the snake also serves to save man just as it also serves sometimes to kill him"**[40]

Atum/Osiris fighting nightly against Apophys the serpent of darkness. Tomb of Ramses I.

---

39   Le Zohar, tome I, collection 'les dix paroles'. Traduit par Charles Mopsik. Verdier, 1981, p. 172.
40   Le Zohar, tome III, Le livre de la splendeur, op. cit., p. 304.

The Kabbalah has kept the memory of Apophys, the "divine" image of the serpent Leviathan, the great serpent that surrounds the world by eating itself, the Ouroboros of the ancient Greeks. The Zohar gives another meaning: **"This serpent with its various folds and bends [...], the Holy One, blessed be He, constantly tramples it underfoot to prevent it from straightening up"**[41]

The Kabbalah relates that God takes the form of a snake surrounded by the divine Shekhina: the world is itself surrounded by a placental cosmic snake whose eyes are the sun and the moon. This is nothing less than the cosmotheistic configuration of the Ouroboros/Uraeus serpent of the so-called ancient Egyptians, forming the Matrix MISRAIM:

"The Holy One, blessed be he, rolled a serpent around the Holy One"[42]

"The Scripture adds: "And Elohim said: Let luminous bodies be suspended in the firmament of heaven. These words refer to the serpent making a circle. What is the meaning of the serpent making a circle? It is this serpent that surrounds the world"[43]

It is clear that the Kabbalah has preserved the double memory of the Serpent, the image of Darkness, the other God, the enemy of the God of Light. But the double Serpent - half Light and half Darkness is also an « image of God » - formally forbidden by the third commandment - in the form of the Ouroboros/uraeus of ancient Judaism in the Nile Valley. So it is not surprising when rabbinic commentaries state that at the time of the exit from Egypt, the Children of Israel - thus the Sons of the Sun - are symbolically protected within a pillar of light by day and a pillar of fire by night. Israel, the new sun, the new Israel, was born from the Ouroboros, which is an extraordinary message from the scribes of the Septuagint/Torah.

41　Ibidem.

42　Le Zohar, tome IV, Le livre de la splendeur, op. cit., p. 77 et 234.

43　Zohar, tome III. Le livre de la splendeur. Par Jean de Pauly. Maisonneuve & Larose, 1985, p. 169.

Let us take stock. The kings of Israel wore the crown inlaid with the serpent of Amun, calling this symbol the «perpetual sign» of the kings of Israel. Thus, the forty-two letters fused together to create the world and formed the symbolic Body of Israel spoken of in the Kabbalah are the forty-two parts of the Body of Osiris or forty-two nomes forming the symbolic Body of Osiris! According to the Kabbalah, the god of the Bible, the god of the Jews is the god of "Egypt". His name is "Israel".

This god has another secret name composed of forty-two letters. Forty-two angels form his heavenly court. Forty-two corresponds to the number of the members of Osiris, the forty-two judges of his court. From then on, no doubt is allowed. Israel makes the waters of the Nile rise, Israel is the winged sun, fighting every night against the celestial serpent, Israel the Man forming the symbolic body of the celestial elder... embalmed in a sarcophagus and mourned by all the... "Egyptians"... Like Osiris...

Israel is therefore the name of the divine Shekhina, the other name of the winged sun, the name of the God of the Nile valley located at the entrance of the temples.

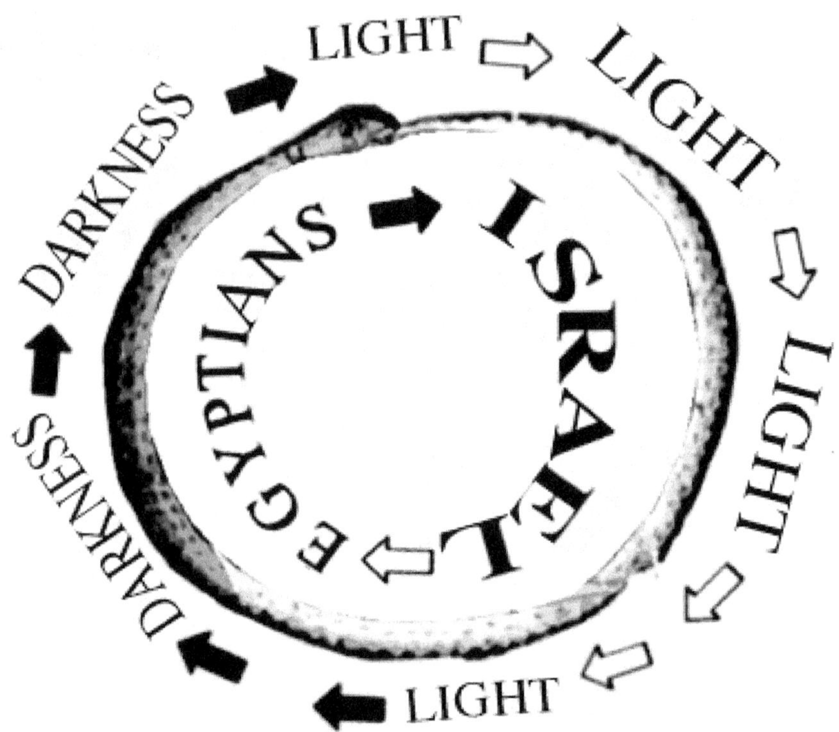

Allegorical scheme of the Egyptians pursuing Israel, the darkness pursuing the light, according to the Kabbalah.

Chapter VII

HEZEKIAH IS OSIRIS : THE KING
OF THE NILE VALLEY

*Archaeologists have noticed something "curious about the royal seal of Hezekiah, king of Judah, but they did not know or did not want to spot its symbolism. The hieroglyphs engraved on the royal seal of Hezekiah incontestably show that this king was exiled from the Nile Valley, but attached to the cult of Osiris, to the Two Lands, that is to say to the two worlds, terrestrial and celestial. Consequently Hezekiah pretended to be king of Judah was in reality a YAHOU-OSIRIS, i.e. a king of the Nile Valley. **This is the irrefutable proof that the hieroglyph YAHOU is the origin of ADONAY/HAHVE/ YHVH/JEHOVAH.** The historically untraceable kings of Israel were the kings of the Nile Valley. The kings falsely named "Pharaohs" by Ptolemy Philadelphus are all Yod reeds, Yahu-SA-RÂ-Osiris-Israel, which is confirmed by their royal cartouches.*

The recent discovery of the royal seal of Hezekiah, according to the Bible penultimate king of Judah, shows that Hezekiah (seventh century B.C.) was one of the last kings of the Nile Valley who lived historically. The seal of Hezekiah **is a mini Rosetta stone, because it contains two writings: archaic Hebrew (or protosinaitic) and three hieroglyphs.** One centimeter wide, it brings us the flagrant proof that the name of Hezekiah is none other than the hieroglyph of YAHOU engraved on his seal. Hezekiah, name hellenized by the Lagides. is said in Hebrew "Hazak Yahou" meaning the power of YAHOU/YAHVE, knowing that YAHOU is one of the names of Osiris. Indeed, the three hieroglyphs contained in the royal name of Hezekiah mean **"the power of Osiris"** over the Nile Valley.

In Egyptian mythology, Isis and Nephthys are venerated throughout the Mediterranean basin. They symbolize the protective goddesses of Osiris. Indeed, on many figures of the time, they are represented with two large wings under the arms, that is to say by the two protective snakes of the world. It is the solar symbol that we find on the pediments of the temples of the Nile Valley, but also on the royal seal of the king of Israel Hezekiah.

Royal seals of Hezekiah king of the Nile Valley armed with the winged sun or the winged scarab meaning Yahu, the light, the name of Hezekiah.

There is no doubt that if these three hieroglyphs had been engraved in the royal seal of Ramses II, Egyptologists would have interpreted them as follows. The first hieroglyph, the winged sun with three rays, translates precisely into the power of the wings of Ra-Osiris, the light of Osiris, the famous winged sun found on many pediments of the temples of the Nile Valley. On other seals discovered by the same king, the winged sun is replaced by a winged scarab, the sacred image of Ra-Osiris reborn in the light, **proof that Hezekiah practiced the cult of Osiris**. Jewish tradition speaks of the two protective wings of YAHVE or YAHOU, which the Kabbalah calls "the two wings of the divine Shekhina", which is a memory of the power of YAHOU, Ra or Osiris, Hazak Yahou in Hebrew. In the Bible, God defines his name as the winged sun or justice:

"But to you who fear my name shall the sun of righteousness arise, and healing shall be under its wings"[1] (Malachi 4:2)

And therefore, Hezekiah king of Judah was not a kinglet reigning in the land of Palestine or in the land of Canaan, but he was the sacred image of Osiris who dominated the valley of the Nile in the seventh century B.C. But what is the meaning of the two wings found on both the sun and the beetle? Primordial father of humanity, true biblical Adam, a kind of legendary Hercules, Atum, as a demiurge god, begets Shu and Tephnut, two breaths of the primordial power, or the god He or Shou, who supports the celestial vault on his shoulders. He separates the sky from the earth with his two arms, or his two wings. As we said, the Kabbalah never fails to mention the protection of the "Children of Israel" under the two wings of the Divine Shekhinah (the residence, the throne of God). According to Rabbi Eleazar, son of Rabbi Simeon Bar Yohai, the glory of God יְהֹוָה (Adonaÿ/ YHVH) **"is the image of the sun spreading its wings"**[2].

---

1   Le Zohar, tome 1, collection Les dix paroles. Traduit par Charles Mopsik, Verdier, 1981, p. 518.

2   Le Zohar, tome I, collection "les dix paroles ". Traduit par Charles Mopsik. Verdier, 1981, 596.

Thus, the Jewish priests kept the secret memory of the fundamental hieroglyph of God to designate the kings of Judah or Israel.

Winged sun, symbol of Yahu, origin of Yahweh.

A passage from the *Sarcophagus Texts* states that **"the light that splits the water**[3] [that separates the heavenly waters from the waters of the earth] **is the name of the two wings"**[4]

According to Rashi, the letter He ‫ה‬ represents the feminine element of the divinity. The breath separating the sky from the earth. In the same way as the "Egyptian" god He (= Hou, the breath or Ruach), the god who separated the waters of the primordial ocean. In the following scene, the god He stands opposite Atum (written with the hieroglyph Yod) also called The Great Green[5], the god of the sea. The text specifies: **"Who is this? It is the horizon of his father Atum..."**[6].

Atum thus embodies the Father, the Yod ‫ י‬of light coming from the sea, coming out of the matrix waters, the one who separates with his hands the two blue lakes of the primordial ocean on the right and on the left, which signifies the West and the East, death and rebirth. The two oceans are described as

3   This theme prefigures the opening of the Red Sea, since according to the Kabbalah, it is the celestial ocean that Moses symbolically opened.

4   Claude Carrier. Textes des Sarcophages du Moyen Empire Égyptien. Tome II. Éditions du Rocher, 2004, Spell 405, suite 2, p. 999

5   Or Oudjouri. The Great Green is the name given to the lake of Heliopolis which symbolizes the primordial ocean. The Book of the Dead of the Ancient Egyptians, note p. 81.

6   Le Livre des Morts des Anciens Égyptiens. Traduction inédite et commentaires de Guy Rachet. Éditions du Rocher, 1996, p. 80.

the "basin of natron and the basin of nitre", the ingredients of mummification and resurrection. This is indeed the genesis of the world, a cosmic metaphor for the resurrection of man. A formula from the *Book of the Dead* (chap. 101) reminds us that Atum is: **"He who split the water, who came out of the primordial waters"**[7]..

The god He of celestial spaces proceeds to the formation of the universe. Before him, Atum separates the waters - the feminine element - of the creation of the world. British Museum.

Let us recall that Abraham, named Etan' the sun and Jacob/Israel, the sun, have two wives symbolizing the He of God. Kabbalah states that the world was created symbolically by Abraham, the name Abraham being broken down into AB-RÂ-AMON, (which means Father Amon of the Nations): **the Father of Humanity is the light of creation**. Yahweh adds a He to the name Abram (called the He of circumcision), which becomes AbraHam, the breath of life and creation. It is as if Abram, having swallowed the He, had become the Patriarch Ab-RÂ-Amon, secretly concealing another Beginning. Another "Bereshit", a cosmogony of On, called Heliopolis, creating the world where God and Abraham would be merged in the creative breath. In the same way, the Sarcophagus Texts affirm that Horus had received the divine power by swallowing He, the god of the breath of life:

---

7   Le Livre des Morts des Anciens Égyptiens. Traduction inédite et commentaires de Guy Rachet. Éditions du Rocher, 1996, p. 138.

"I am the Great One who came out of the horizon! I am Horus who swallowed He!"8; "I am He, I am Ra, I am the Master of Life"9

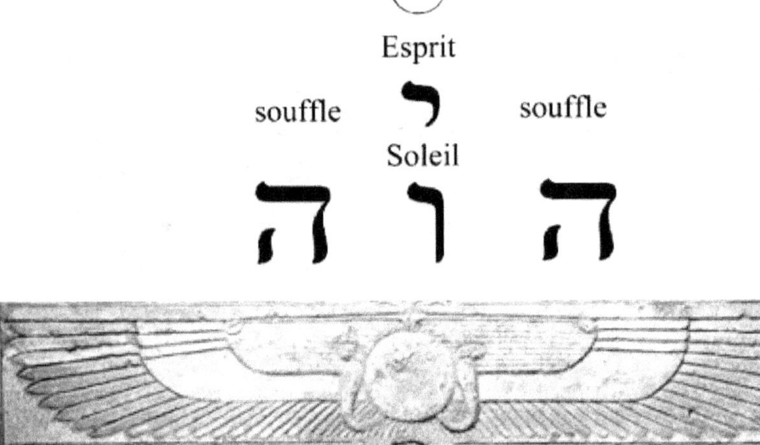

Winged sun with two protective snakes or winged scarab on the façade of the temple of Hathor.

It is undeniable that the symbol of the sun of justice and the two wings of Ra embodies since the first dynasties the highest degree of royalty, the throne of God. The protective symbols of the winged sun or the winged scarab adorn almost all the façades of the temples of the Nile Valley. The royal seal of Hezekiah allows us to affirm that the winged suns or winged scarabs clearly designate Yahu/Amon as the god of 'Egypt', the original light, thus making Hezekiah a king of the Nile Valley.

In <u>terms of Kabbalah</u> symbols, the Tetragrammaton Yahweh or

8   Spell n° 841. Textes des Sarcophages du Moyen Empire Égyptien. Claude Carrier, tome III. Éditions du Rocher, 2004, p. 1837.

9   Spell n° 441, ibidem, tome II, p. 1061.

YHVH יהוה is in fact the secret image of a Triptych formed by four letters in Three + One, with a divine and solar vocation.

The first hieroglyph of Hezekiah allows us to decipher the symbolic value of the Tetragrammaton יהוה of the Jews.

The Yod י of יהוה, the first letter, represents the hidden luminous power, the Spirit of Spirits, the primordial point. The two 'He' ה, images of the breath of God, are separated by the Vav ו, symbol of the sun, and allegory of the Tree of Life located in the center of the Garden of Eden, a tree that the Kabbalah identifies with Jacob, and therefore with ancient Israel. They also represent the separating and generating power of light over celestial and terrestrial forces. It is the solar and phallic power of the Vav, ו, symbol of the male, between the maternal thighs formed by the two breaths He' ה, symbols of the female. We can affirm that the Hebrew Tetragrammaton originated on the pediment or the central lintels of the temples of the Nile Valley, from the most sacred symbols of the ancient 'Egyptians', which are in fact Jewish symbols. The Kabbalah has never failed to express God through symbolic images, which of course goes against the third commandment of the Decalogue. According to the Kabbalah, the image of God is expressed precisely by the sun spreading its two protective wings, called the two wings of the Divine Shekhina.

Indeed, it is written in the Zohar that the two wings of the sun create two breaths to revive the Spirit. The breath and the sun of peace and justice are two notions that are found in the cartouches of the kings of the Nile Valley:

" We have learned that Rabbi Eleazar son of Rabbi Simeon stated, "When the sun spreads its wings to soar in its mighty revolutions, it strikes with its hooves the leaves of the trees of the Garden of Eden [a garden that the Kabbalah locates in Egypt] "[10]

Thus, for the Kabbalah and contrary to common belief, the name of God or Tetragrammaton formed by the four letters YOD-HE-VAV-HE יהוה is an "image of God" meaning the Spirit (Yod) the breath (He) the Sun (Vav) the breath (second He).

---

10   Le Zohar, tome I, collection "les dix paroles ". Traduit par Charles Mopsik. Verdier, 1981, 17 d, p. 596.

It is clear that the Tetragrammaton which is read "Yahu"

has its origin in the solar hieroglyph of Yahu engraved on the royal seal of Hezekiah, a winged sun which is found on the facades of the temples of the Nile Valley. Let us go further. The throne of Tutankhamun is that of the sun which protects the king with its wings. The winged sun is the symbolic top of the pyramidion located on all pyramids, as can be seen in the diagram of the pyramidion of the pyramid of Khenzer dating from the Middle Kingdom, 2000-1700 BC.

Symbols of the two wings of the sun, protectors of Yahu/Ra, the fertilizing luminous power of the sun Ra-Horus = Yahu, origin of Yahweh. Pyramidion of Khenzer.

Isis-Nout protected by the two symbolic wings of Ra gives birth to Horus, the central Reed-Yod, the sun, the Light of the world.

In the scenography of the pyramidion, the two folded wings of Ra protect Horus and Atum who carry the falcon, the solar bird. In another image we see the two folded wings of the sun and the two snakes that protect Isis giving birth to the sun Horus. The sacred name YAHOU symbolizes the top of the pyramid. Now YAHVE pronounced JEHOVAH is read YAHOU in Hebrew. The ostraca of Elephantine and the Greek documents bring the proof that the Jews adored Osiris and pronounced YAHÔ, YAHOU/YAHVE the name of Osiris.

It is easy to see that the Tetragrammaton YHVH יהוה is written in Hebrew at the top of the rose windows of cathedrals, churches and of course synagogues. This is the flagrant, archaeological proof that it is the same god, the god of the Jews, Christians and Muslims. As we can see, the two texts of the Kabbalah that clearly attest that the god of the Jews is the god of Egypt are confirmed by the hieroglyphs.

The symbolism of YAHVE or YAHOU is a perfect replica of the so-called "Egyptian" scenographies.

Hieroglyphic of Yahu, origin of Yahweh (YHVH) the light of Ra-Osiris with the figurative of the sun with three rays[11]

The symbolic arrangement with the Yod, the two birds symbolizing the two breath, and the central sun correspond to the Tetragrammaton יהוה YHVH.

---

11 Egyptian hiéroglyphic dictionary. Wallis Budge, Dover Publica

tions, inc, New York. published by General publishing Company, 1978, 23 a.

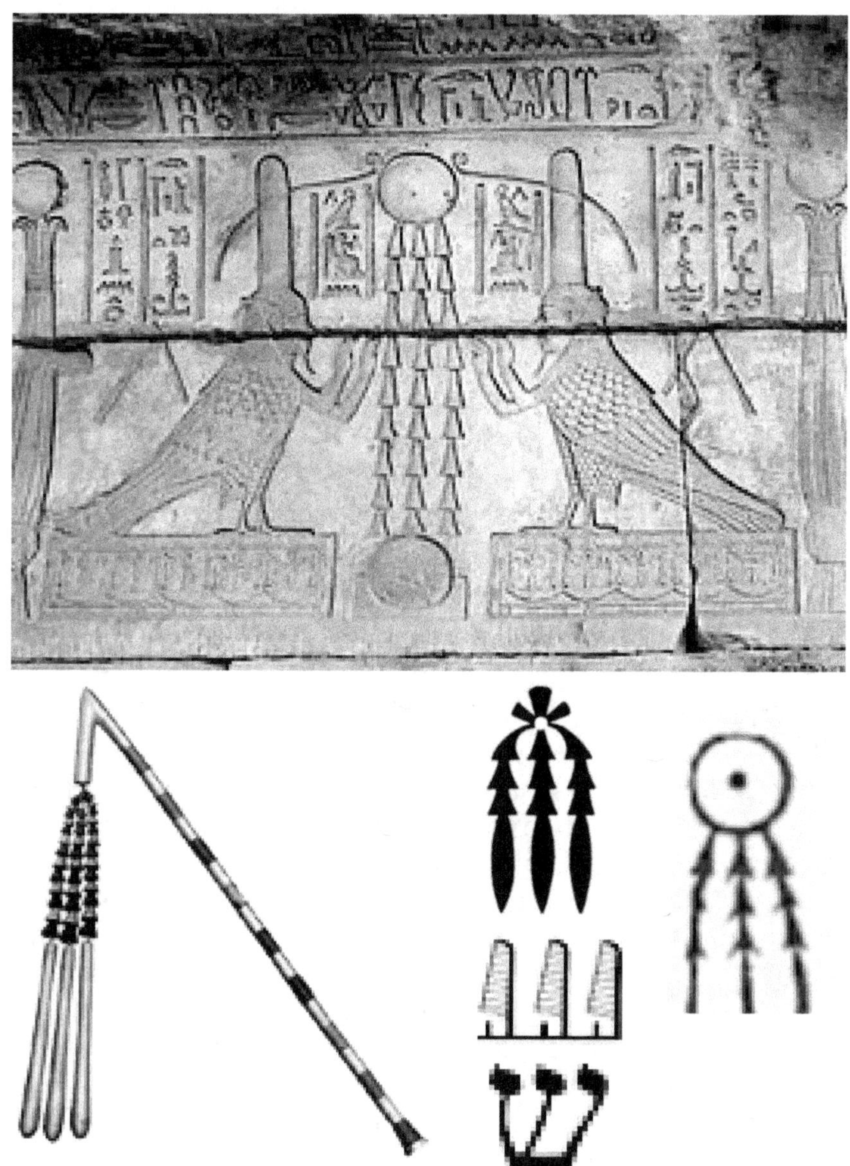

The three-rayed sun symbolizes Yahu or Amon-Ra, the image of the solar scepter of Osiris. In this illustration, we can see the birds with human heads evoked by the Zohar, the three-rayed sun of the seal of Hezekiah and the two curved wings symbolized by rounded lines.

These elements allow us to understand why King Hezekiah, three centuries before Ptolemy, not subject to the constraints of the Septuagint, proudly affirms on his royal seal that he is the king of the Nile Valley, the king of the world above and the world below, symbolized by the hieroglyph of the two lands ═.

The royal seal of Hezekiah proves that he practiced the cult of Osiris, and that consequently, all his people, the Children of Israel, whatever the names they would later be called, Jews or Egyptians, practiced the same religion: they were all Yods, the reeds of God. Osiris is the grandson of Atum whose hieroglyph is a Yod reed from the Nun. He is at the same time the serpent of the Nile and the earth of the Nile Valley. The earth is divided into forty-two nomes, which form the forty-two parts of the Body of Osiris with which Hezekiah identifies himself. The royal seal of Hezekiah proves indisputably that the Jewish king of "Israël"is a king of Egypt, even if this denomination is inappropriate. A historical reality - and no longer symbolic - that the Septuagint Codex has erased by naming the kings "Pharaoh".

Ptolemy destroyed this harmonious civilization by virtually driving it out of a country renamed Ægyptos. Indeed, according to the Septuagint, the Children of Israel are supposed to have come from the land of the Greek god Ægyptos. Whereas, according to the Hebrew Bible, they come out of the womb of Ra, the Nun, Mistraim. Those whom we call the ancient Egyptians knew perfectly the meaning of the words MESS, MESRÂ, IS-RÂ, MESS-IS-RÂ-YAM meaning that Ra gave birth to Man or the Reed from the celestial waters, the Nun. Moreover, the name Ramses breaks down into RA-MESS-ESS-OU which designates the MESS 👤 matrix of Ra ☉ which came out of the primordial waters and gave birth to Man IS or ES. Osiris is represented by a solar egg, cosmic IS ◖, or by a living reed Yod ▎, like all the kings of Egypt, because they are all the living image of Atum. As we saw, Atum is himself the primordial Yod reed ▎, the demiurge situated on a sledge. Osiris, as we have said, is read SAR, SARA, ISRA in hieroglyphics. MESS-RÂ which will be found later in the Hebrew Bible under the form MITSRAIM מצרים, MISRAE in Aramaic, MISRA or MISR' in Arabic, designate a name which refers directly to Osiris, the son born of Ra. On the other hand, Ægyptos, Egypt, formally designates a Greek god belonging to the family tree of Zeus. Ægyptos is the son of Poseidon who also symbolizes the god of the primordial ocean. Despite this similarity, Ægyptos son of the ocean Poseidon does never correspond to Osiris son of Nut. We thus understand the process of spoliation of the ancient Greeks. The royal seal of Hezekiah is the absolute proof that not only could no distinction be made in his time between Jews and Egyptians, **all being Yods**, but also that there were no "Egyptians", this word being a creation of Ptolemy. The Ægyptos were deliberately invented by the ancient Greeks, in order to usurp the great Ennead of Heliopolis, several thousand years old, and to create a cosmogonic correspondence, allegedly "historical", between a new god of the earth, Ægyptos son of the ocean incarnated by Poseidon, and Osiris son of Nut, whereas these Greek notions did not exist in the hieroglyphs. It was necessary to forbid to the true "Egyptians", to the Jews, the hieroglyphs or images of God so that they would never meet again with their historical past (we will return to it).

This is how the ancient Greeks, strangers to the History of the Nile valley, succeeded in making the names and titles of SAR, SA-RÂ, IS-RÂ and Osiris disappear from History, monopolizing the new land of God, Osiris/Misraïm coming out of the Noun having become Ægyptos son of Poseidon... As we have seen, the scribes of the Hebrew Torah and the Septuagint have left us messages, sometimes subliminal, hidden, and sometimes visible, incontestable. Let us return to the sun with the three rays of the seal of HAZAK-YAHOU said Hezekiah. A text of the Zohar relates the discussion of three rabbis and a traveler.

"... [The traveler] answered them: "One day I was on a journey and I saw a light which divided into three, walked before me, and then hid itself. I thought I had a vision of the Shekhina [the light of God, Israel]. Now I see that the three lights that appeared to me were announcing your meeting"

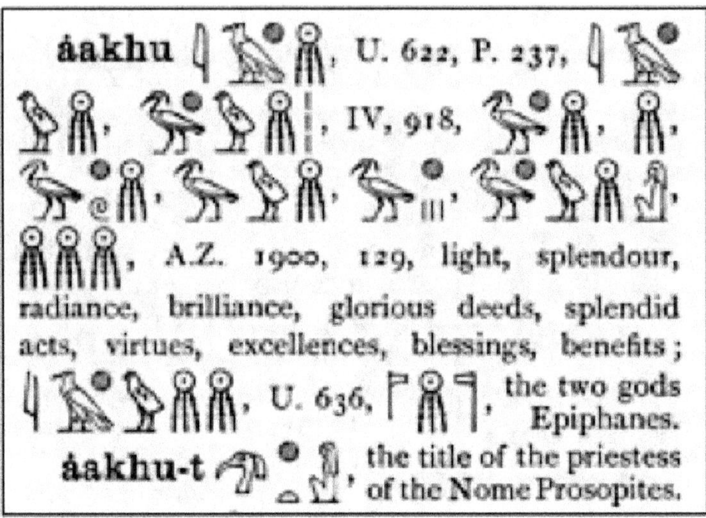

Hieroglyphs of YAHOU and YAHOUT (YAHOUD) of the divine light of Ra, Osiris, Horus, etc[12].

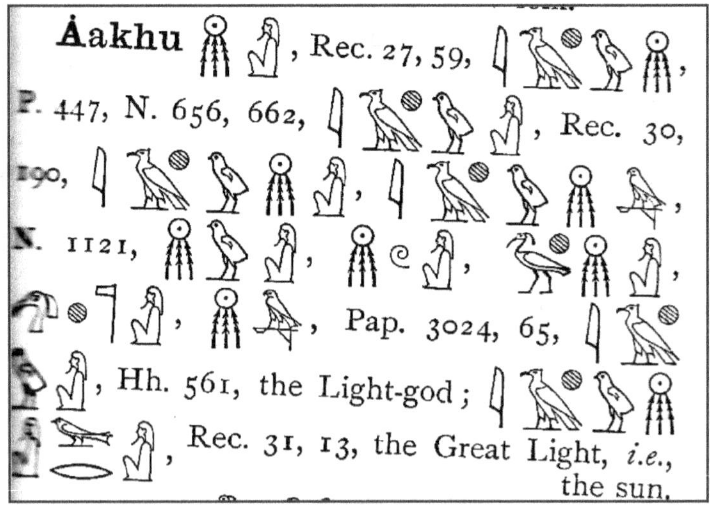

Other hieroglyphs of YAHOU.

---

12 Dover Publications, inc, New York. published by General publishing Company. Egyptian hiéroglyphic dictionary. Wallis Budge, 1978, tome 1, p 23 a.

We thus have archaeological evidence that Ra is Yahu/ Yahweh. For the Kabbalah, the Aleph א is the luminous Life Force of God[13], the archetype of the divine Shekhina divided into three lights:

"Principle of three that are One, three Lights are part of the letter Aleph"[14]

"The letter Aleph forms a body with two arms. It is the image of the divine essence; the supreme degree is in the middle and the other two degrees are at its side. It is of these two degrees that the Scripture says: "It is a path that no bird has ever seen" "[15]

This light of the Aleph א, God separated into three (three lights or three Yod which will multiply to create the world) corresponds obviously to the Ankh ☥ which defines the god of the Nile valley, the 'One become three' named Atum, YAHÔ, YAHOU, YAHOUT, YAHOUD, origin of the Tetragrammaton יהוה and origin of the Jewish word (YOD, YAHOUD) as we have shown. The royal seal of Hezekiah is not a new coincidence as some people who are disturbed by the truth claim. Like the other kings of the Nile Valley, Hezekiah had the basic hieroglyphs of kingship engraved on his seal. He is the three-rayed sun YAHOU ruling and living in the two lands ▬, as the Wallis Budge dictionary attests.

---

13   Le Zohar, tome I, op. cit., 21a p. 121.

14   Le Zohar, Cantique des Cantiques. Collection 'les dix paroles ". Verdier, p. 110-111.

15   Zohar, tome V. Le livre de la splendeur. Editions Maisonneuve & Larose, 1985. P. 502.

An enlargement shows the crouching man, wearing the beard of Osiris, who is the figurative of God, facing the sun with three rays. The three rays symbolize the three branches of the scepter of Osiris, the three energies of creation.

The second hieroglyph inscribed on the seal of Hezekiah is precisely an Ankh ⚥, meaning the vital power of Yahu, of Aton" or Adon", of Ra or Osiris, but also the living and existing kingship of Hezekiah over the Nile Valley. This kingship over the Nile Valley is confirmed precisely with the third hieroglyph: the two parallel lines ▬▬ located below the Ankh designate the two lands. Hezekiah, HAZAK YAHOU in Hebrew means the power of Osiris/Yahu or the power of Yahweh over the two lands or the two worlds, the earthly world and the heavenly world of Osiris. **Only a king of the Nile Valley could be invested with such power given by the hieroglyphs,** and bear such a title. According to Herodotus, the secrets of the hieroglyphs were never to be revealed to foreign peoples, symbol of Set, war and darkness.

(SON OF) ACHAZ YAHOU (Ra-Osiris) HAZAK (power)

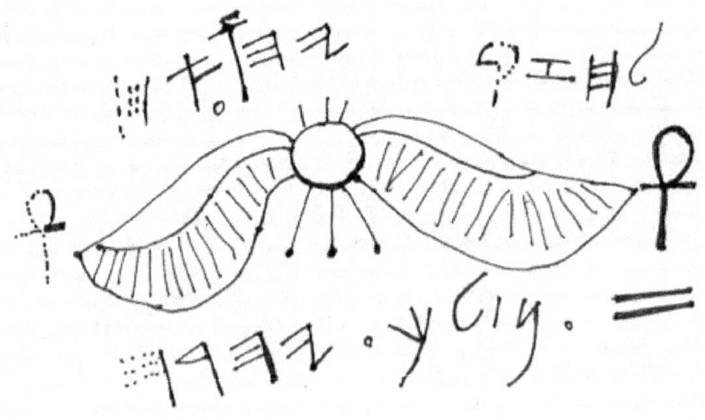

YAHOUDAH (Judah) MELEK (King)

Royal seal of Hezekiah: YAHOU or Ra-Osiris, living and ruling in the two lands of Yahu-dah, the Nile Valley.

We thus have written confirmation that Ra, Osiris, Yahu, the sun with the three rays engraved on the seal of Hezekiah, is none other than the symbol of the god of the Nile valley, the name of Yahu or Osiris living and reigning on the two lands ▬▬belonging to Yahu/Osiris. In proto-Hebrew writing, one can read just above the winged sun the mention in so-called proto-Sinaitic or proto-Hebrew writing " **Hazak-YAHOU (Hezekiah), son of Asab king of Yehudah"**

Unquestionably, the name Yahu-dah, land of YAHOU corresponds exactly to the sign of the two lands ▬▬ that Egyptologists read by convention in reverse: Ta-yes with a question mark (?) showing that they do not yet have the proof of the pronunciation of the hieroglyph of the two lands. **The royal seal of Hezekiah is a small Rosetta stone.** It translates YAHOU, the god of heaven and earth. Moreover, let us recall that in the texts of Hermes Trismegistus, Isis instructing her son Asclepius teaches him:

"Do you not know, O Asclepius, that Ægyptos is the copy of heaven, or, to put it better, the place where all the operations governed and implemented by the celestial forces are transferred to below?"[16] Marie-Ange Bonhème and Annie Forgeau attest to this: **"there is no representation of the kingdom in its totality"**[17], therefore no cartography of the high and low Egypt. The only cartographies describe a celestial Egypt and not terrestrial. It is written for queen Hatshepsut:

"Your border will extend to the width of the sky and to the limits of the confused darkness"[18]

These notions confirm that the hieroglyph with two parallel lines designates the earthly Egypt TA (or DA) and the heavenly Egypt YAHOU. We are talking here about a land

---

16 Hermès Trismégiste. Corpus Herméticum. Traités XIII-XVIII Asclépius. Les Belles Lettres, 1946. Chapitre IX p. 326.

17 Marie-Ange Bonhème, Annie Forgeau, Pharaon. Les secrets du pouvoir, op. cit., p. 231-232.

18 Ibidem, p. 227.

above and a land below, as the Kabbalah attests. As we have said, for the Zohar, Heaven and Earth are the two twins of God, an obvious reminder of the cosmogony of On'. Based on current geographical conventions, **Egyptologists have falsely interpreted the upper and lower worlds as Lower Egypt to the north and Upper Egypt to the south.** One more misinterpretation, a phenomenon all the more dramatic because it was universally accepted as a postulate, rejecting the biblical studies demanded by Champollion. But as we have seen, this is not the only imposture in this story. It is a fact, the seal of Hezekiah confirms that the two lands ▬▬ reading Yahu-Da, the Land DA of Yahu the Sky, Hezekiah of whom one will later make the king of Judah, **is in fact the king of the Nile Valley**.

Let us not forget that the letters of Amarna attest that the kingdom of the Nile Valley also extended over Judea and Israel. But the History wanted by the Ptolemies when writing the two *Book of Kings* will restrict the kingdom of Hezekiah and all the kings of Judah and Israel to the land of Canaan only, as we will demonstrate in a future work, studying the psalm "Israel is a vine taken from Egypt" which proves that the root of Israel is the land of the Nile Valley. Thus, we have the evidence that the name Israel meaning the sun and the divine Shekhina in the Kabbalah, or the Son of God in the Bible, as well as the Man Jacob who fights against his brother, corresponds to Osiris. Israel is the real name of Osiris written in hieroglyphics. Hezekiah is an ISRA/Osiris king, which is demonstrated by his royal seal.

The <u>name of Osiris S</u>A-RÂ is read IS-RÂ-GOD origin of Israel[19]

19   Dover Publications, inc, New York. Op. cit., Wallis Budge, 1978, tome 1, p
     83 a.

ACCORDING TO THE BIBLE, THE KINGS AND CHILDREN OF ISRAEL DID NOT KNOW THE LAW OF MOSES... AND FOR GOOD REASON : THEY WERE THE HIGH PRIEST, THE KINGS WORSHIPPERS OF OSIRIS/ISRAEL.

Some passages of the Bible, one of which is about Hezekiah, reveal truths that have been kept silent, because they agree on a "pagan" religion, therefore "idolatrous" of the Children of Israel, that is to say of RÂ or Sons of the Sun, in which Moses and his Law were simply unknown. Thus, according to Edward Will and Claude Orrieux, the reform of Ezra imposing the Law of Moses on the Jews took place under the Ptolemies. Four texts in the Bible confirm that the Judeans, the Children of Israel and the kings of Israel did not know and therefore did not follow the Law of Moses. In the second Book of Kings, while we have just demonstrated by the inscriptions on his seal, that King Hezekiah ruled over the Nile Valley, it is written that this same king destroyed the idols as well as the primordial serpent worshipped by the Children of Israel from the beginning.

"He (Hezekiah) made the high places disappear, broke the statues, cut down the idols, and cut in pieces the brazen serpent which Moses had made, for the Children of Israel had burned incense before it until then: it was called Nehushtan" (II Kings XVIII, 4).

King Hezekiah could not know Moses and his Law any more than the Jews of Elephantine. He could not destroy the bronze serpent of the Septuagint/Bible, especially since this serpent symbolizes Ra and Osiris, the winged sun, the Ankh, the kingship over the Nile Valley, etc. Nehoushtan' breaks down into Nahash, the primordial serpent, and Aten, the god of the Nile Valley symbolized by the sun and the serpent, representation of the crown of Amun-Ra of the kings of the Nile Valley. The scribes of Ptolemy have obviously tried to bring the Law of Moses into existence at the time of king Hezekiah and the iconoclastic scene where he breaks the high places, the statues, the idols and the serpent, which correspond to the demonization of ancient Egypt, allegedly at the time of Hezekiah.

Another text in the Book of Kings confirms this attempt, making the Law of Moses appear again fifty years later, with king Josiah. Before that, it is worth noting that in the *Book of the Exit to the Light*, it is written that the Book of Thoth was **"found for the first time"** in the holy of holies of the temple: **"This formula was found in Hermopolis, under the feet of the majesty of this august god"**[20]. In chapter 137 A, the sacred book is found in a box and written by the hand of the god himself... In chapter 148, devoted to the seven celestial cows representing the seven gates of paradise, it is specified that the sacred book was discovered in the past, at the feet of the Majesty of the god by the prince Djédefhor, gone to inspect the temples. It is specified that the prince **"reported it as a marvel to the king when he saw that it was something very secret, neither seen nor seen"**[21]. Let us see how similar this configuration is with the discovery of the Torah, under king Josiah.

Indeed, the second Book of Kings relates that Josiah, king of Judah, in Hebrew ICH-YAHOU = "Man image of Yahou", is the son of Amon. **Josiah is considered by the Bible as the only one of the kings of Judah to have discovered and respected the Law of Moses** later on. Josiah claims to have discovered for the first time the Book of the Torah of Moses (the Deuteronomy according to Israel Finkelstein). In contradiction to the text quoted above, Josiah states that the kings of Israel and Judah (and therefore his great-grandfather King Hezekiah with the royal seal of Osiris), **did not follow the Torah of Moses.**

"Great is the wrath of Yahweh/Kyrios, which is kindled against us, BECAUSE OUR FATHERS [thus Hezekiah] **HAVE NOT OBEYED THE WORDS OF THIS BOOK AND HAVE NOT PUT INTO PRACTICE ALL THAT IS PRESCRIBED TO US"**

(II Kings XXII, 13)

---

20 Le Livre des Morts des Anciens Égyptiens. Littératures anciennes du proche Orient. Les Éditions du Cerf, 1967, chapitre 31, p. 76.

21 Ibidem, p. 181.

We must note the inconsistency of the Bible with history. Historically, the royal seal of Hezekiah confirms his authority over the whole Nile Valley, without any separation between the so-called tribes of Judah and Israel. We have just seen that the hieroglyphic inscriptions designate him as the king of Judah/Yahudah and the king of ISRÂ-EL - OSIRIS, the living and ruling power over the two worlds, earthly and heavenly. The two dynasties of the kings of Israel left no trace, no royal palace, no temple, no inscription because they are fictitious, created from scratch by the scribes of Ptolemy. **Hezekiah, not knowing the Law of Moses, had no reason to break the temples, the idols and the brazen serpent, symbols of his god Israel/Osiris! His royal seal proves that he himself is the incarnation of ISRAEL-OSIRIS!** In all the territory of Egypt/Israel. The scribes mean that the ten tribes forming the northern kingdom of Israel were not only "idolaters" but also practiced the cult of Osiris. The sarcophagi of dignitaries (the Jews) embalmed in Israel have been found to contain amulets in the form of scarabs, which confirms on the one hand the symbolic value of life and resurrection of the scarab-sun god-Ra for these people, and on the other hand that it was still the religion of Osiris that predominated in the region. Such an observation invalidates the idea that the two tribes of Judah and Benjamin forming the little kingdom of Judah would have been in their great majority governed by idolatrous kings with the exception of Hezekiah and Josiah who would have supposedly discovered and followed the Law of Moses !...

Of the forty or so kings of Israel and Judah of whom the biblical texts speak, nothing has been found, apart from the royal seal of Hezekiah. If there had been two opposing religions, that of Osiris and that of Moses, a civil war would have broken out between Israel and Judah on the one hand, and Egypt on the other, which would have left many archaeological traces, as was the case after the Septuagint, which pitted the Hellenized Jews against the Jews who were newly adept at the Septuagint.

Moreover, Josiah's statement in chapter 22 contradicts the biblical text of chapter 18 of the Book of Kings, stating

that Hezekiah, Josiah's great-grandfather, had destroyed the high places and idols of Egypt before him, in order to apply the Law of Moses. This is historically impossible.

The hieroglyphs engraved on Hezekiah's royal seal demonstrate beyond doubt that this king was attached to the cult of Osiris and to the Nile Valley, the Two Lands 〓 of which he was king. If we pay attention to the length of the reign of the main chiefs, judges and kings of Israel, the allegorical figure of forty years comes up nine times out of ten, which is statistically impossible: at the beginning, the Hebrews who came out of Egypt were condemned to remain in the desert for forty years with Moses as their leader. After the death of Joshua, Otniel is judge of Israel for forty years (Judges, III, 8). Barak strikes Sisera and Israel enjoys peace for forty years (Judges, V, 31). Gideon subdues the Midianites for forty years (Judges, VIII, 28). Israel, which has fallen into sin again, is enslaved by the Philistines for forty years (Judges, XIII, 1). The prophet Elijah judges Israel for forty years (I Samuel, IV, 18). The prophet Ishbaal was forty years old when he reigned over Israel (II Samuel, II, 10). David's reign over Israel lasted 40 years (I Kings, II, 11). Solomon's reign in Jerusalem over all Israel lasted 40 years. (I Kings, XI, 42). Rehoboam son of Solomon was forty-one years old during his reign over Judah (I Kings, XIV, 21). King Asa's reign lasts forty-one years (I Kings, XV, 10). After the death of the prophet Elijah, his son Elisha cursed forty two children who were torn apart by two bears (II Kings, II, 24). The seventy sons of king Ahab are slaughtered (II Kings, X, 7). The prophet Jehu then had forty two brothers of Ahaziah, king of Judah, killed (II Kings, X, 14). In the seventh year of Jehu, Joash became king and reigned forty years (II Kings, XII, 2). Jeroboam son of Joash became king of Israel in Samaria; he reigned 41 years (II Kings, XIV, 3), etc... It is statistically impossible that each king of Judah or Israel reigned about forty years - without leaving any archaeological trace! - which casts serious doubt on their historical existence.

On the other hand, the historicity of the kings of the Nile Valley shows that they were at the same time the kings of Judah and Israel, the Yods image of Atum (the demiurge Yod), kings of ISRA-EL/Osiris and kings YAHOUDS. Although the Septuagint strives to make us believe in the existence of two dynasties, that of Judah and that of Israel, with the corollary that Judea and Israel were small monarchies separated from the kingdom of the Nile Valley, archaeology confirms nothing, being a pseudo-historical montage. A passage in the Book of Jeremiah calls into question the worship of the Law of Moses by the kings of Judah. It relates that some Judeans would have taken refuge in Egypt, rebelling against the prophet Jeremiah, but it tells us that all the kings of Israel and Judah were idolaters in that they practiced the cult of Osiris. Indeed, they claim to worship the Queen of Heaven, Isis/Nut, and I quote:

"'But we want to do as our mouth has declared, to offer incense to the Queen of Heaven and to offer libations to her, as we, our kings and our princes did in the cities of Judah and in the streets of Jerusalem. Then we had plenty of bread, we were happy and saw no evil' (Jeremiah. XLIV, 16-17)

This means that, like Hezekiah, all the kings of Israel and Judah, including David and Solomon, did not follow the Torah of Moses, but worshipped the Wisdom coming from the Queen of Heaven, the goddess Isis or Nut (Iset' in hieroglyphics), wisdom incarnated by the celestial placental serpent that had given birth to the sun, as the Pyramid Texts attest:

" The mother of the king is a great serpent, and it is a serpent of fire, the red crown, which gives birth to him"'[22]

The fourth text, from chapter 9 verses 32-38 of the *Book of Nehemiah* confirms, once again, that the Children of Israel enslaved by an unnamed king, reaffirm that the kings and priests of Israel did not observe the Law of Yahweh and Moses.

---

22   Christian Jacq, La tradition primordiale de l'Égypte ancienne selon les textes des Pyramides, op. cit., p. 265.

This text is essential, capital, because it allows us to situate the slavery of the Jews under the first Ptolemaic kings. Such slavery is described in the letter of Aristaeus. Here is the text of the Book of Nehemiah with my comments according to the context of the time, attested by the ostraca of Elephantine, where the Jews find themselves in a situation of slavery in Egypt, and then evoke a "covenant" which can only be the Septuagint because obviously the country is vast and fertile:

"Our kings, our chiefs, our priests and our fathers have not kept your Law [this is the Law of Osiris and the kings of the Nile Valley, not the 613 commandments of Moses], **nor have they paid attention to your commandments or to your warnings to them. While they were the masters** [the Pharaohs kings until the invasions by the Assyrian, Babylonian, Persian and Macedonian kings], **in the midst of the many benefits that you gave them, in the vast and fertile land that you gave them** [the Nile Valley, Canaan being neither vast nor fertile], **they did not serve you and they did not turn away from their evil deeds. And today** [in the time of Ptolemy], **we are slaves! We are slaves in the land which you gave to our fathers** [the Nile Valley], **to enjoy its fruits and its goods!** (Jeremiah 9:32-38)

Again according to Edward Will and Claude Orrieux, this text refers to the slavery of the Jews at the time of the Septuagint, described in the Letter of Aristaeus. Ptolemy had charged 20 drachmas per head, including women and children, for the liberation of the Jews from this first slavery organized by his father Ptolemy Soter, who in his perversity had given himself the name of "Savior". In his letter to the High Priest Eleazar, Ptolemy passes for the pharaoh liberator of the Jews. But in order to divide and conquer, he had prepared his incredible stratagem: to order in his letter the organization of the so-called "translation" of the Law of the Jews, which was only the Law of Osiris, while his real idea was to make the future "Revelation" of the Septuagint accepted. Thus, by freeing them from the slavery decreed by Ptolemy Soter son of Ptolemy Lagos, he was going to make the Jews fall into a second slavery, definitive this one, caused by their acceptance and their forced submission to the 613 commandments of the Septuagint.

Nephthys, feminine Principle, protects with her curved wings the king IS-RÂ, symbol of the light YAHOU (Horus in Greek).

Isis (previous page) and Nephthys protector of the light of
IS-RÂ = YAHOU (the symbolic child of the golden Horus),
with her two curved wings. Sarcophagus of Ramses III.

Chapter VIII

ISRAEL IS THE NAME OF OSIRIS, THE NAME OF THE NILE

The phonetic, philological and symbolic analogies between Israel and Osiris designating the latter IS-RÂ-GOD SA-RÂ, SAR, the numerous biblical passages where Israel is confused with Osiris leave no doubt. The scribes, the rabbinic tradition and the Kabbalah confirm what the hieroglyphs say: Israel is the ancient name of the Nile, and the memory of the god named Osiris/Osirios by the ancient Greeks.

In conclusion of this second work of our trilogy, we will take up again certain diagrams and quotations to fix the coherence of the discovery Osiris = Israel. If I affirm that the name of Israel does not come from the stele of Merenptah. We have demonstrated that it is the River of the Garden of Eden, the Nile, according to the biblical expression translated **I will be ACHER' I will be**, meaning **Breath - River, Sun - Breath**, corresponding to the image of Osiris. "And'yet, it turns'" said Galileo... The ancient name of Osiris had several verbal forms and is inscribed in the tombs of the pharaohs.

In a flagrant way, the initiated priests of Heliopolis knew, in the Mysteries, the sacred name of Osiris IS-RÂ, followed by the figurative of God. Not only does the name of Osiris have the same phonetic consonance as Israel IS-RÂ-GOD, but it has kept the same meaning, the secret symbolism of the archetypal Solar Man of God, the Righteous One, the son of God, guardian of the commandments, in the theological sense, and, of course, the allegorical and mystical meaning of Israel/Osiris concealed in the Bible, which we are going to discover.

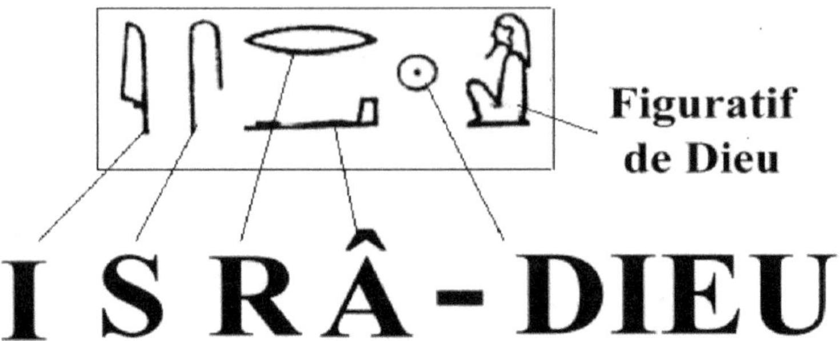

I S R Â - DIEU

Secret Name of Osiris, origin of Israel[1]

The hieroglyphs bring us the proof that every king falsely named "Pharaoh" is a SA-RÂ, an IS-RÂ, origin of IS-RÂ EL. Osiris is called SAR (prince in Hebrew שׂר), ASAR that we can bring closer to אשׁר ACHER' one of the names of Yahweh - the River - when he affirms "I will be ACHER' אשׁר I will be". Yahweh or YHVH still bears several names that we find without question in the hieroglyphs always designating Osiris/River, like YAH, YAHOU, HE, HOU. According to the secret tradition, Israel is not only a country, a land, but the Son of God. Jacob, whose name was changed by Israel in the Bible after his fight against the angel, is deciphered in the Kabbalah as the fight between two brothers, he Jacob against the Angel of Esau. It is a cyclical, solar cosmogony where each brother wants to get the sun, so that during the day Jacob wins, and at night Esau wins. The Kabbalah states that Israel is the name of God, the creator of heaven and earth, who came down with his forty-two angels. The Bible itself states that Israel is the eldest son of God. But the Zohar, the book of the Kabbalah, goes further, stating that God is Heaven, God is Earth. God is the creation. This means that Israel is at the same time Heaven and Earth, but also the Son of Heaven and Earth, **just as Osiris in the cosmogony of Heliopolis** is the son of the earth Geb and the sky Nut. But he is also the head of the heavenly court with its forty-two judges.

---

1 *Egyptian hieroglyphic dictionary.* Wallis Budge, Dover Publications, inc., New York. Published by General publishing Company, 1978, tome 1, p 83 a.

The Wallis Budge dictionary, brings us the confirmation by phonetics that the name of Osiris, read in general SA-RÂ (Son of King), or SAR (prince in Hebrew), is read IS-RÂ-GOD, root of Israel. Osiris name begins with a straight reed Yod (Being) followed by the hieroglyphic ∏ or ∏ . The Wallis Budge dictionary, brings us the confirmation by phonetics that the name of Osiris, read in general SA-RÂ (Son of King), or SAR (prince in Hebrew), is read IS-RÂ-GOD, root of Israel. The name begins with a straight reed Yod (Being) followed by the hieroglyphic ∏ ∏ , expressing the splitting of the rush/reed into two twin powers to engender heaven and earth and finally the primordial Man. Thus, the so-called "Egyptians" are above all the images of Man ∏ whose Spirit is embodied by the primordial reed Yod ⌇ , the creative Being, the image of the Father Atum (who is the Yod, the Demiurge) as attested by the symbolic name of Osiris (Man of God), the IS Man of the God Ra. The symbol of the mouth ⊂⊃ the creative Being, the image of the Father Atum (who is the Yod, the Demiurge) as attested by the symbolic name of Osiris (Man of God), the IS Man of the God Ra. The symbol of the mouth [2].

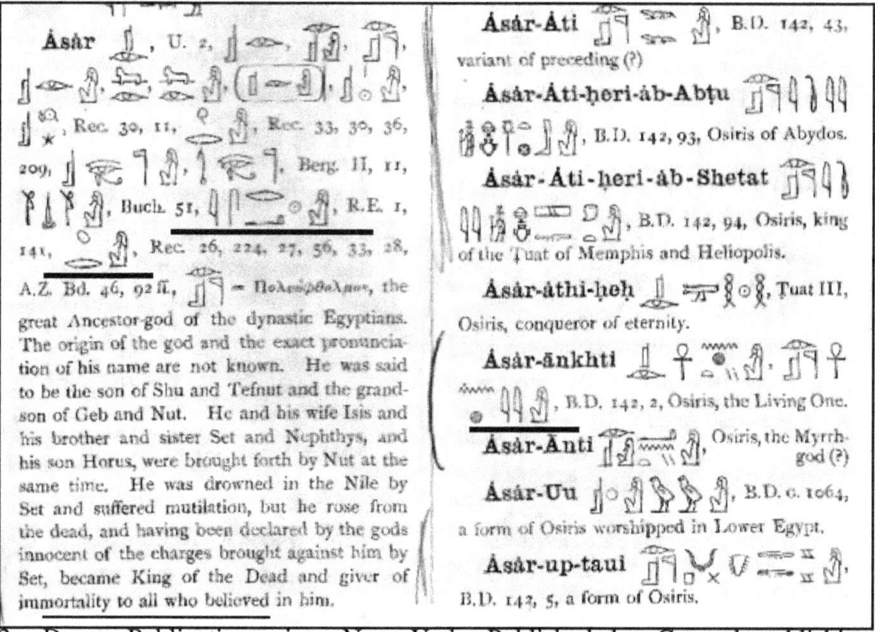

2   Dover Publications, inc, New York. Published by General publishing Company. Egyptian hieroglyphic dictionary. Wallis Budge, 1978, tome 1, p 83 a.

This is evidenced by the numerous hieroglyphs of Osiris meaning "God", "Man/God", "Man of God", "Son of God" (also translated by "Son of the sun") and even "Earth of God" (Geb Ra). More precisely IS-RÂ designates the begetting of Man from the sacred reed of Atum, the Yod ⎜, the original light of God. This formula is valid for all the kings of all the dynasties, since the First Empire until the Ptolemaic era. Every "Egyptian" identifies himself with the Yod reed, an "Osiris", an IS-RÂ, a formula written on all the royal cartouches and on all the tombs of the Nile Valley. A striking example is given to us by the Wallis Budje dictionary[3] : instead of the drawing of the bearded old man kneeling (Osiris), there is a snake of the River, a sign that reads, "L".

Another way of writing, "Son of Ra" where the River Serpent L serves as a figurative of the god.

Indeed, in Champollion's painting[4], the sound L is or R is given by the image of the mouth or the snake:

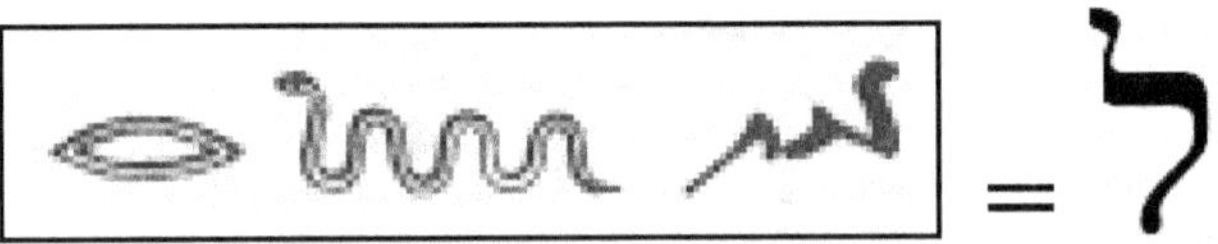

Table of letters of Champollion: the "L" symbolizing God, the mouth of Ra or Osiris is a snake erect that articulates "L" or "R".

---

3   Egyptian hieroglyphic dictionary. Wallis Budge, Dover Publications, inc, New York. Published by General publishing Company, 1978, p. 584 b.

4   Grammaire égyptienne de Champolion. Editions SOLIN 1997. P. 41. Les Secrets de l'Exode. Messod et Roger Sabbah. Jean-Cyrille Godefroy, 2000, p. 230.

The text of the Hebrew Massora reveals that the word "God" EL אֵל is also written with the Lamed ל erected in the form of a final Noun ן or River Snake on which a Yod rides. Thus, instead of reading Israel, יִשְׂרָאֵל, we read ישרי.

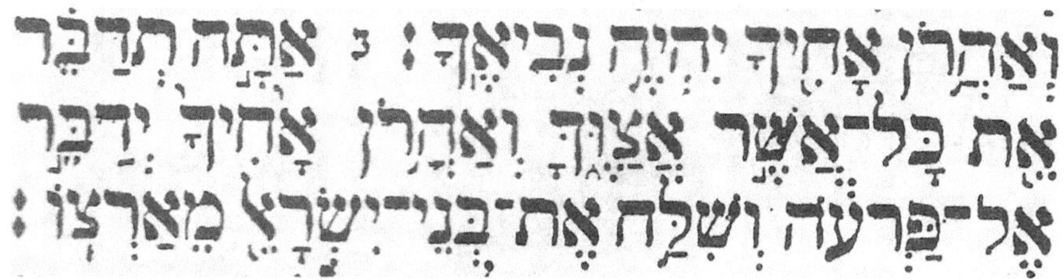

Example of the name Isra-ËL writing "God" in the form of the Yod riding the Lamed River/Serpent (Exodus 7:2)

This Yod represents the luminous Spirit of God riding the primordial serpent, compared to Osiris/himself a reed Yod seated on the primordial serpent symbol of the Noun figured in several tombs of the Valley of the Kings. Osiris, the god of light fighting against darkness, is thus represented as dominating the **serpent of the River that is the time**[5]. We notice that the ten stars correspond to the numerical value of the Yod: 10, symbol of the beginning again and origin of the ten "sephirot" or ten Breaths, lights, Spirits of the Tree of Life of the Kabbalah.

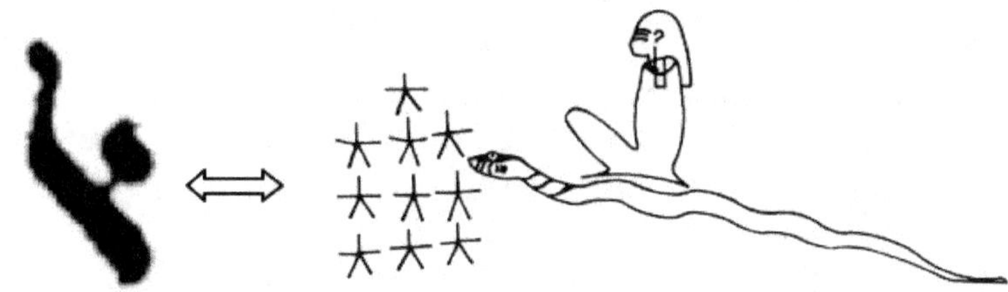

EL (God) in Hebrew and Osiris on the serpent of the River. Tomb of Amenhotep II (drawing by A. Brodbeck).

The hieroglyph of Amun, as well as the images of the tombs and papyri, in their syncretism, show the same symbolism with Amun-Ra in the place of Osiris, sitting on his throne on the serpent of River and the time.

---

5   Erik Hornung. L'Esprit du temps des pharaons. Philippe Lebaud Editeur / du Félin, 1996, p. 70.

As his name indicates, Amun is the Yod reed dominating the serpent of the River and the Time, symbol of the Nun .

Ancient Egypt is essentially based on the domination of the Serpent, a symbol of death and darkness. According to the Kabbalah, Samael, symbolizing the angel of death, broke into the Garden of Eden on the back of the primordial serpent. Samael would have inoculated Eve with the "defilement" through the serpent, in order to eat the fruit of the forbidden tree. The snake named in Hebrew Nahash symbolizes concupiscence, lust, carnal desire, sin, the world Below, the Angel of Death Samael... This is why the Kabbalah evokes the rejection of the defilement of the evil snake through circumcision. The foreskin would be "the secret of the other gods", "the other god", the "foreign god"[6], or "impurity", "mud", "the seed of the primordial serpent". Cain would not be the legitimate son of Adam, but the son of the serpent Samael, which is why he is motivated by the desire to kill his brother. Cain will give birth to a son named Seth... The flesh of the foreskin is the foreign part that man must banish from his body, while being perfectly aware of its existence and of its divine antagonistic value. Like a primordial snake, deeply rooted in the collective unconscious, it is a reminder of the fierce struggle between Horus and Typhon/Apophis/Seth. Perpetual fight of the good against the powers of the evil that the gods, as eternal enemy brothers, have mercilessly delivered to each other since the

---

6 Le Zohar, Genèse, tome III, op. cit., p. 354-355 et 164.

beginning of time, each wanting to possess the light...

We see with what precision the Yod astride the serpent Lamed ל designating God corresponds to the image of the god of the Nile valley, the King enthroned on the serpent of the Noun. We are faced with a major contradiction: the third commandment of the Decalogue formally forbids the Children of Israel, the Jews, to represent or draw the images of God, under penalty of a curse until the fourth generation, even under the penalty of death in Deuteronomy. We will see that this prohibition corresponds to the will of Ptolemy II Philadelphus, who purely and simply forbids the Jews to practice hieroglyphics, the writing of their fathers. Indeed, this commandment forbids the Hellenized Jews, living at the time of the alleged revelation of the Septuagint, to return to the sources of their knowledge, but the Hebrew Torah, the Talmud and **the Kabbalah will reject the Greek Septuagint, and will endeavor to explain each Hebrew letter as an image of God**, each one corresponding to a hieroglyph...

RAÂ/OSIRIS, THE GOD AND THE RIVER OF OLD

In the tombs of the Valley of the Kings, one sees Osiris or Ra on the celestial boat chasing the great celestial serpent Apophys, considered as the eternal enemy wanting to destroy Horus, the son of the god Osiris, symbol of the light of day. Deuteronomy (XXXIII, 25-28) notes the Osirian origin of Acher'/Yechurun (a name which also means Israel). Like Osiris on his boat or on the serpent, Acher "rides" the heavens and the heavenly clouds to rescue Israel, the light, the son of God. According to the Zohar, Acher' is the name of God when God reveals himself to Moses **"Ehieh Acher' Ehieh"** which is translated **"I will be Acher' I will be"**, while the Greek translation says **"I am the one who is"**. Acher' is the "ancient arm" of **the ancient god of Israel**, the light that drives out the hereditary enemy - the darkness - in the heavens:

He says about Acher' Blessed be Acher' among all sons! May he be privileged among his brothers and bathe his foot in oil! Let your locks be of iron and brass, and let your security last as long as your days. There is none like the God of Yeshurun, who rides on the heavens to help you, and the clouds in his majesty. The God of old [an obvious reference to the ancient god, Osiris] is your refuge. Here below, he is the ancient arm that drives out the enemy before you; he says: Destroy! Israel dwells in safety. The fountain of Jacob is set apart for a land of wheat and wine; the very sky distills the dew there.

The celestial boat of Ra/Osiris was replaced in Roman times by the winged horse, while the Torah refers to the exit from Egypt on the "wings of the eagle". Another text, just as telling, evokes the heavenly vessels of Yahweh bringing the Children of Israel back to Egypt:

"Yahweh will send you back to Egypt in ships or by a way that I said to you, 'You shall see it no more!' And there you shall go and sell yourselves to your enemies as servants and handmaids, and find no buyer."   (Deuteronomy 38:68.)

It is difficult to imagine that the god of the Bible, named Elohim אלהים from the first verse, was actually named Raâ, the name of the god of Egypt worshipped at Heliopolis. And yet, Elohim was really called Raâ! It is a verse of the Bible, from the book of Samuel which reveals it to us.

In the past in Israel, this is what people said when they went to consult Elohim אלהים: "Let us go to the seer" (ROE or Raâ) הראה, because instead of "prophet" as today, they used to say, "seer" (Samuel IX, 9).

To understand the significance of this verse, we must remember that the Israel of old was none other than the valley of the Nile. Ra was the "seeing" god represented by the solar eye. Akhenaten, worshipper of Ra-Aton, proclaimed himself, "Great of the Seers". By simply reading this verse in Hebrew, without taking into account the vowels, Elohim is not said Roe, but A-Raâ

הראה, he name of the god of IS-RÂ-EL, the name of Osiris, the god of Egypt. The Latin, French and other translations are insufficient, because they are based on a Greek reading and not a Hebrew reading:

In the past in Israel, this is what was said when going to consult Elohim: "Let us go to ARAÂ" הראה **, because instead of instead of "prophet" as today they used to say ARAÂ** הראה (Samuel IX, 9)

THE GENERIC NAME SON OF RÂ, SA-RÂ

IS READ IS-RÂ, ORIGIN OF ISRAEL

Finally, Yod-Yod, Yod-Yod-Yod, Elohim and YHVH symbolize the God/World, the "Supreme Matrix" coming from the Supreme Point -Yod, Atum - origin of all creation:

"The Name Elohim designates the sacred Point below which alone knows the paradise below and its mystery. For the very angels who dwell there do not know its essence. The Supreme Point casts a light..." [7]

Hieroglyphic of Ra: for the Kabbalah, it designates at the same time the sun and the primordial or supreme point at the origin of all creation. Ra (to see) designates all that is visible. All that is visible is God.

This passage requires the reader's utmost attention because we question the conventional reading of the hieroglyph, "Son of Ra" engraved in the protocol of the kings and adopted by Egyptology, which has deceived humanity, proving to be limited to one and only one pronunciation. According to

---

7   Zohar, tome IV. Le livre de la splendeur. Par Jean de Pauly. Maisonneuve & Larose, 1985, p. 219.

Gaston Maspero and Michel Vladimirovich Skariatine known as Enel, Osiris bore the epithet **"He who is in his egg"**[8], the seed at the origin of the gestation of the sun engendered by Nut, the archetype of the vivifying power of Nature on all the living beings. Is Tutankhamun, King SA-RÂ,   "Son of Ra", king of Israel/Osiris? Clement of Alexandria, Father of the Church, had declared in his Stromata that the symbols of the Hebrews, and therefore of the Jews - the ancient dignitaries of Egypt who were declassified by the Ptolemies - were the same as the symbols of the Egyptians. Above the double cartouche of the kings of the Nile valley, the two hieroglyphs of the sacred duck and the sun with a central point, are read SA-RÂ by pure convention. In fact they are also read IS-RÂ, the real name of Osiris, because we know today that Osiris Ὄσιρις is a Greek translation. Israel is the sun, says the Zohar (the body of Kabbalah works revealing secrets from the Old Testament).

The god of Israel is the god of Egypt, the Zohar also tells us. Israel is the divine Shekhina who came down to Egypt, whose name Misraim conceals the matrix "Isra-El". Israel has the same meaning as MIS-RA-YAM, a word meaning "the Son born by the sun and the waters". Israel and Osiris are at the same time God and Son of God. On this precise point of theological comparison, let us recall that the Bible affirms that Israel is the Son of Yahweh:

"Thou shalt say to Pharaoh, thus says Yahweh:

Israel is my Son, my firstborn" (Exodus V, 22, 23).

From this verse, it is possible to understand that Israel is a syncretic name meaning at the same time God, the God/sun and the Son of the sun, the one who fights against the darkness. This is the origin of the idea of Jesus, the solar man, the light, the Alpha and the Omega...

"THE SUN IS JACOB (ISRAEL)." [9]

"Truly, "Israel came to Egypt",

---

8   Énel. LeMystère de la Vie et de la Mort d'après l'enseignement des temples de l'Ancienne Égypte. Arka Éditions, p. 104.

9   Le Zohar, Genèse, tome III, Vayéchev, Mikets, Verdier, 1991, p. 207.

it is about the Holy One blessed be he"[10]

The Children of Israel are the Sons of the Sun and thus form the Solar Body of God: this is undoubtedly the memory of the syncretism intrinsic to the ancient "Egyptians" who constituted humanity without distinction of race, the memory of the myth of Osiris, knowing that the sun being born is the Son of God (Hor says Horus), and the sun descended in the West is Osiris, the Father of Men, going to death and resurrection in a new Horus. According to the Kabbalah, the primordial light is called Hor and Horus is read Hor in hieroglyphics. After defeating the angel of darkness, Jacob, who became Israel, is presented as God himself, the old man sitting on the throne of God (in the vision of Ezekiel). Jacob is the perfect Man, the Tree of Life, the image of Yahweh or Elohim, the Shekhinah, the **Old man** who came down to Egypt with his heavenly court, composed of **forty-two angels**, again an obvious reminder of Osiris and his court composed of **forty-two judges**:

Osiris, judge of the dead, sits in front of the forty-two judges. On his left (bottom right), the scales of judgment (British Museum).

Rabbi Simeon says: "When the Shekhina [God's luminous Spirit, Anokhi/Yahweh/Elohim] **descended into**

10   Le Zohar, Genèse, tome III, Verdier, 1991, p. 286, sq.

Egypt, she took the form of a Haya [God's luminous life power = the Ankh ☥ of the Egyptians] **who bears the name of ISRAEL, and whose image resembles that of the old man (from above). Forty-two holy angels destined to serve the Shekhina came down with her. Each of these angels carries a sacred letter of the divine name composed of forty-two letters"**[11]

Grandson begotten by Atum', Osiris was a solar man, an old man with a perfect body, accompanied by the forty-two judges of the celestial court. This passage in the Zohar states that the name of God, IS-RÂ-EL, is made up of forty-two letters of the divine name, thus forming the Body of Israel, an explanation that leaves no doubt as to the secret identity Osiris = Israel, because Osiris is made up of forty-two parts - the forty-two gods or images of God - that form the Body of the Nile, divided into forty-two names. Another meaning of Israel is given in the book of Genesis. Jacob receives the name Israel after his victory against the angel of Elohim during the night. Israel is divided into two words: ISRA, which means not only the "Son of God", but also the victorious battle against EL, short for Elohim. The pictograms lead us to another discovery. Osiris is written phonetically IS-RÂ. But before reading this name in hieroglyphics, if you observe carefully the obelisk of the Place de la Concorde, you will see that Ramses II never bears the name of Pharaoh, let alone Egyptian, but SA-RÂ or IS-RÂ the God.

---

11 Zohar, tome III. Le livre de la splendeur. Par Jean de Pauly. Éditions Maisonneuve & Larose, 1985. P. 74.

THE HIEROGLYPH OF THE THREE REEDS :

THE BODY OF OSIRIS, THE LAND OF THE FLOOD

Osiris is the Son of Ra, but also the grandson of Atum who is himself a Yod reed. Osiris is named Hapy, symbol of the flood. His name is written SA-RÂ or SAR, in Hebrew שׂר but also with the symbol of the field of the reeds, formed by the three Yods which symbolize "the very green", the land of the reeds, the land of the Yods, the Body/Kingdom of Osiris. Several hieroglyphs confirm that the name of Osiris is written with the pictogram with the three YODS meaning that the Body/Kingdom of Osiris IS the land of the flood (YAKOB in hieroglyphs **Ȧkeb**, name of Jacob), the land DA of YAHOU, origin of JUDA YAHOU-DA. These hieroglyphs confirm what we will see with the deciphering of the royal seal of Hezekiah, namely that the symbol of the two lands reads YAHOU-DA. We thus have the proof that the symbolic body of Osiris is as well designated by the three YODS designating the land of the reeds as by the sacred duck, also designating Geb God-Earth of the reeds, but also the cosmic egg which is read IS.

, U. 427, , T. 244, "field of offerings," the region of offerings of the Kingdom of Osiris in the Ṭuat ; plur. , N. 170, , U. 578.

The three reeds Yods form the Body/Kingdom of Osiris[12].

---

12 Egyptian hieroglyphic dictionary. Wallis Budge, 1978, tome II, p. 805 b.

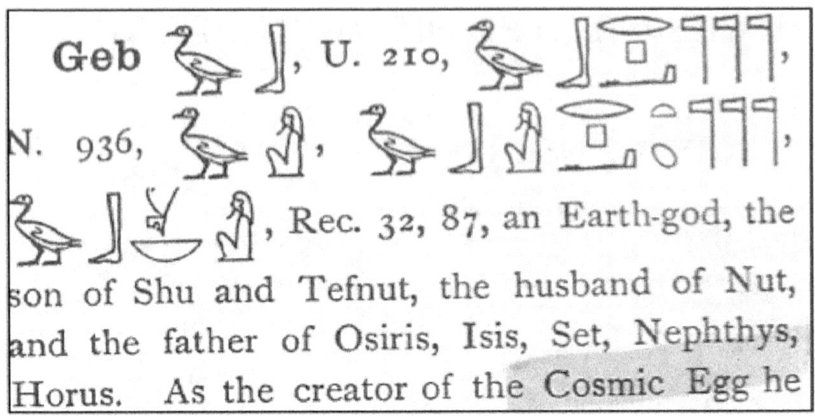

The Yod ⺁ brings us the proof that the God of the Nile Valley is a process of consubstantial generation from the Nun /Nu/ Nothing or promatter, a phallic Yod symbolically generating the Father, the Son or the Holy Spirit, the Idea, the Thought. God generated himself and the whole world from his matrix substance, the Yod ⺁ coming out of the Nun ᗯᗯᗯ. God is both One and Multiple. The Yod was multiplied to create the universe, which means that "All is God" according to the first Principle of "All in One" **Khen Kai Pan**. Isis was the One and the Whole of the world. All creation is God, the very substance of the Body of God. It was not worth the trouble for the Judeo-Christian and Muslim world to massacre each other for several centuries, to know if Christ was God or if he was an entity limited to the Son of God, or below God, or nothing but a mere apparition, or if he was begotten or created... The Pyramid Texts say that Osiris was symbolically cut into three parts forming a Solar Triad, the Son in the East (Horus), the adult in the Zenith (Re), the old man in the West (Atum) according to the movement of the rising and setting of the sun, taken up in the symbolism of the question of the Sphynx in Œdipus...

L   E (A)   R   S   I

ישראל

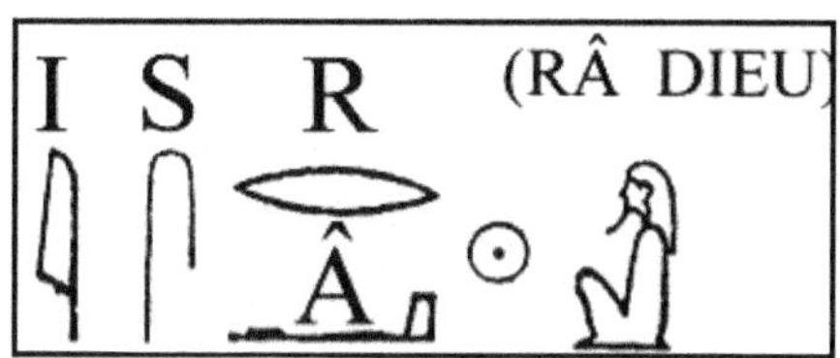

Phonetic name of Osiris IS-RÂ-GOD.

Israel responds to the SAR and ISRA hieroglyphs of Osiris.

The "three Yods ⁤ sacred name" are a reminder of the crown of the three reeds of Osiris SAR, SARA, ISRA. In the lower period, the crown with the three branches of Osiris becomes the crown with the three branches of Serapis, the Greek Osiris. Thus, the commonly accepted reading SA-RÂ of Osiris Son of Ra is also read IS-RÂ.

Crown of Isis made of the three reeds, like the three-flowered crown of Osiris in god Hapy, symbol of the flood. Temple of Denderah.

In fact, since the fifth dynasty, it is noted that the cosmic egg ◯ **read IS followed by the sign of RÂ ⊙ replaces the duck in the writing of the pictogram SA-RÂ** calling into question the conventional reading SA-RÂ. Consequently one reads SA-RÂ but also IS-RÂ.

Reading of the hieroglyph SA-RÂ which can be read in two ways[13] **:
SA-RÂ and IS-RÂ, written with the duck, or the cosmic egg IS
-RÂ.**

IS RÂ

In addition to designating the cosmic egg IS , the duck ,
SA or IS also designates the earth Geb, the father of
Osiris. The duck thus has several levels of reading as
Champollion had suspected. Osiris is also read SAR or
ISRA in hieroglyphs meaning "Prince", like the Hebrew,
SAR שׂר son of King. SAR is thus the root of the name
Israel ישראל. Now, as we have seen, **Israel means First
Born Son of God for Pharaoh** (Exodus V, 22, 23), the true
meaning of this verse brings us directly to the hieroglyph
"Son of the King for Pharaoh" read by convention SARA
but also read IS-RÂ   ISRÂ-ËL in the Septuagint and in
the Torah.

Let us summarize. Modern Egyptology has falsely named the
valley of the Nile, "Egypt" and "the Two Lands"   , whereas
in all the hieroglyphic texts, the latter is none other than the Body
or the Kingdom of Osiris divided into two worlds, namely the
terrestrial world and the celestial world. It was read by the name
of Osiris under the form SAR, SA-RA but also ISRA-GOD.
Now, the Yod of the Kabbalah is the "Supreme Point" of the
creation and resurrection of the dead. The Kabbalah affirms that

---

13 Egyptian hieroglyphic dictionary. Wallis Budge, Dover Publications, inc,
   New York. published by General publishing Company, 1978, 584 b, 588a,
   589a, 583a, M 217; N 589.

the three Yod of the Chin' שׁ of Israël ישראל which are found in the name of Osiris 𓇋𓅭𓏤𓀀 form "the three Yod of the sacred name", the crown of Yahweh which symbolizes the three branches of the Patriarchs, the fathers of the world. It corresponds to the crown of Israel formed with the hieroglyph of the three reeds, which participate in the sacred names of Osiris. Several pictograms[14] confirm that the name of Osiris is written with the glyph of the three YODS 𓇋𓇋𓇋 or the cosmic egg, ◯, IS-RÂ meaning that the Body/Kingdom of Osiris is the sky and the earth of IS-RÂ the GOD. Never "Egypt".

Two other forms of the name SAR or IS-RÂ says Osiris.

Osiris.

Re Names SAR/IS-RÂ/Osiris «Son of Ra» or the Serpent of the River (Wallis and Budge) [15]

Reasons why the body of Geb, the Earth, is covered with the reeds of the Nile, and symbolized by the hieroglyphic with the three YODS. 𓇋𓇋𓇋.

---

14 Egyptian hieroglyphic dictionary. Wallis Budge, 1978, tome II, p. 588 b.

15 Egyptian hieroglyphic dictionary, op. cit, p. 583a, M 217; N 589

Corps de Geb parsemé de roseaux Yods. Papyrus Tamoni.

Thus, the so-called "Egyptians" are all "ISRAEL" called "OSIRIS" after their death. The so-called "Egyptians" are totally unknown in hieroglyphics as Egyptians, for the simple reason that their sacred writings affirm that they are the images of God, the images of IS-RÂ/Atoum, the images of Yod, the primordial Principle, and that their God/Earth Geb is none other than the earth of the reeds, the earth DA issued from the light YAHOU. Osiris means Man IS of God RÂ and the priests of Osiris are the IS RÂ, the Men of God. To be convinced of this, it is necessary to specify that in hieroglyphics, man is pronounced IS (or ES as in Ramses: Ra gave birth to MES the Man ES). The cosmic egg ◯ is used to write the name of Isis, which is read ISET, IS-T ◯⌒ , and Nephthys which is written NEBET-IS, the Mistress NEBET of the IS egg. Thus, the pictogram IS ◯ of the cosmic egg followed by the earth and **the rising sun illuminating the vault of heaven** ⌒ because IS-ET and NEBET-IS are the daughters of Nut, the goddess of Heaven connected to the Earth. The celestial vault ⌒ Nut is positioned above Geb the earth, as can be seen in the temple of Denderah. T ⌒ expresses the feminine in general. More specifically, in the case of IS-T ◯⌒ , the T ⌒ expresses the feminine of IS ◯ (Solar Man being born every day from the womb of Isis/Nout). The goddess Iset, Isis in Greek, is simply the solar wife of the Man of IS-RÂ called Osiris (as ICH' אִישׁ in Hebrew).

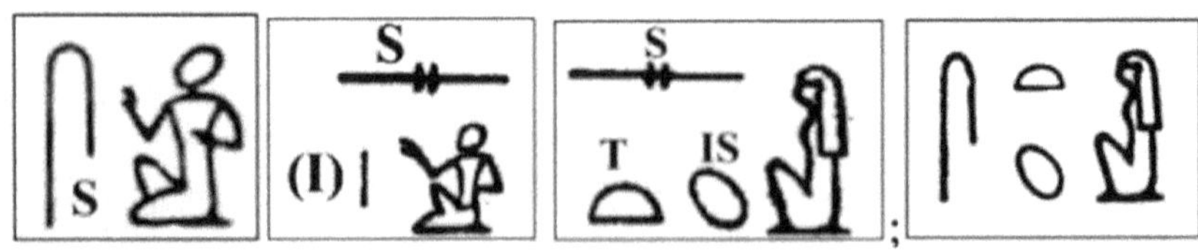

Hieroglyphs IS of solar Man and Woman IS-ET

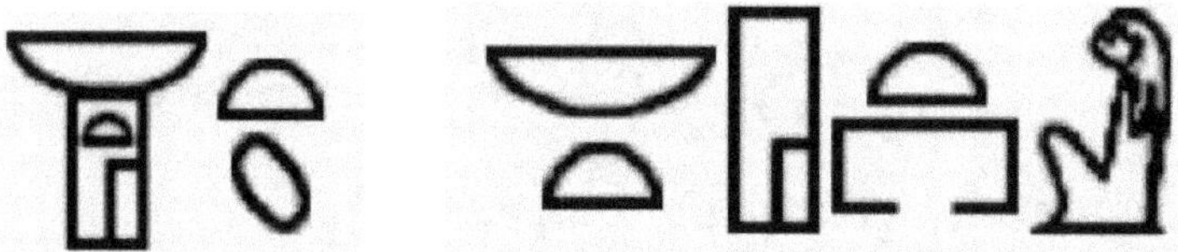

Hieroglyphs of Nephthys/NEBET-IS, the Mistress or guardian of the cosmic egg IS representing the Son and the duck. Nephthys is also the Mistress of the Solar Temple.

In Egyptian mysticism, the goddess ISET' - called Isis in Greek - is not only the wife and sister of Osiris. She is his feminine double, his complement, she designates both the sky and the earth of Egypt, the Matrix, the black earth according to Plutarch. The duck IS is here preceded by the Y (Yod) and is pronounced IS' represented by the horizontal line ESS or ISS ——*—— which can be found twice in the name of Ramses Ra-MES-SS: Isis/ISET and Nephtys/NEBET-IS designate both the daughters of Ra and the Heaven and Earth protecting the cosmic egg IS (the phonetic name of Isis is also read Ista, Istar). Finally, like the symbolic name ISRAEL יִשְׂרָאֵל of the Bible, the duck is said SA or IS because it designates Isis and Nephthys, the Sky Nut, the Earth Geb, thus the sun ⌂ coming from the Matrix Nun (Misraïm) as the Wallis Budge dictionary attests:

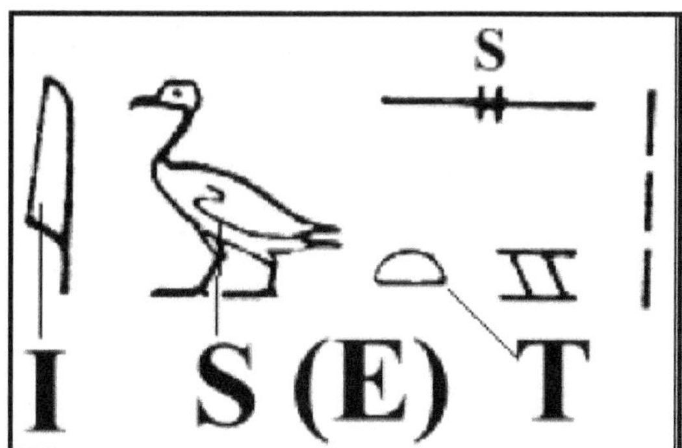

Hieroglyph of the earth. The duck IS ⟨ The duck IS named Iset (Isis) begets the sun ⌂ and the Earth[16]

---

16 Egyptian hieroglyphic dictionary. Wallis Budge, op. cit., 83a.

——⧓—— or the God Earth, origin of Misraïm.

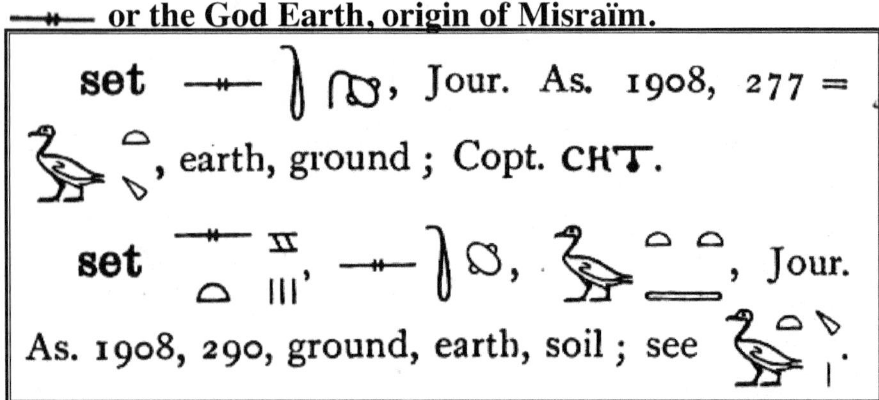

The earth is written with the symbol IS ——⧓—— or the duck SA or S (Geb).

Let us go as far as possible to see the many similarities between Israel and Osiris, understanding that this comparison is not only limited to the reading of hieroglyphs. The Bible tells us that Jacob fell in love with Rachel, the younger sister of Leah. One night, Jacob thought he was sleeping with Rachel, but in the morning, he woke up and found himself with Leah. An Egyptian legend tells the same story: according to Plutarch, Osiris having confused Nephthys with his sister Isis, had a love affair with the former and begat Anubis.

"Isis then learned that Osiris, in love, had mistakenly taken her for Isis herself, and that he had had relations with her sister Nephthys"[17]

The legend of Jacob/Israel concealing - again - the Osirian cosmotheism, is all the more explained that the sun sets with the star Venus/Nephthys and rises in the morning with Sirius/Isis. It is the heliacal rising of Isis/Septa/Sirius bringing the sun and the annual flood, considered as the resurrection of the whole land of the Nile Valley. It is important to give here another equally confusing example between Israel and Osiris. This analogy allows us to understand that the biblical narrative is a deeply symbolic and coded language. The parable of Pharaoh's dream deciphered by Joseph ends with the return

---

17 Plutarque, Isis et Osiris, Guy Trédaniel, La Maisnie, 1992, p. 61.

of Joseph's father, Jacob (renamed Israel). Jacob/Israel is said to bless Pharaoh. This blessing, the commentaries say, led to the first one, as well as to all the floods of the Nile. Everything happens in the Bible as if before the arrival of Jacob, renamed Israel, in Egypt, there had never been a flood... The ancient "Egyptians" had a vital need for the waters of the annual flooding of the Nile and worshipped Osiris, the sacred river, because Osiris had generated the first flood, and returned every year to trigger a new flood. For the river also bore the name of Osiris IS-RÂ **and never the name of the Nile, which comes from the Greek god Nylos from the Ptolemies**. After being murdered and dismembered by Set, the phallus of Osiris was thrown into the Nile and swallowed by a fish according to Plutarch. As a result, the water of the river was synonymous with flooding, life, divine energy, creative light, fecundity, fertility, even the blood or effluvium of Osiris murdered by Set. SA-RÂ/IS-RÂ (and not Pharaoh) embodies the river Osiris flowing and uniting with the earth Isis, a symbiosis disintegrated by Set, the desert or the salt sea, as attested by Plutarch, Greek historian and biographer of the first century AD:

"Osiris is the Nile which unites with Isis, or the earth, and that Typhon is the sea in which the Nile disappears and is dispersed"[18]

In the rigorous staging of the scribes of the Bible inspired by this legend, the pieces of a cosmic, Osirian drama are hidden at every moment, a war between light and darkness (Osiris is the light/sun against Set the darkness, Jacob is the sun against Esau the darkness) for the survival of the world and the equitable sharing of the waters of the desert, of the world and of the cosmos, which are necessary for all life. Jacob's coming to Egypt ends with Jacob's blessing, or rather Israel blessing to Pharaoh triggering the first flood of the Nile:

Joseph brought Jacob his father, and they stood before Pharaoh. And Jacob blessed Pharaoh. (Genesis XLVII, 7)

---

18   Plutarque, Isis et Osiris, op. cit., p. 111-112.

And Jacob blessed Pharaoh again, and departed from before Pharaoh (Genesis XLVII, 10). Here is Rashi's commentary:

"And Jacob blessed Pharaoh". And what blessing did he give him? That the waters of the Nile should rise to his feet, for Egypt receives no rainwater. It is the Nile that waters it with its floods. From the moment he was blessed in this way, whenever Pharaoh came to stand by the Nile, its waters came up to meet him and irrigate the land (Midrash tan'chumah Nasso 26)"

The message of the scribes becomes clear, without ambiguity: by blessing Pharaoh, Jacob/Israel blesses the whole so-called Egyptian civilization... its foundations. Jacob blesses the ancient Israel triggering all the floods... It is interesting to note that the hieroglyph of the Nile and the flood is read YAKEB or YAKOB. This hieroglyph contains the Yod and the heel. In Hebrew, heel is said EKEV because Jacob had clung to the heel of Esau (which is also called Edom meaning "Red, blood") when he came out of his mother's womb, so as not to drown in the amniotic waters mixed with the blood of the mother's placenta. Rachel, mother of the twins Jacob and Esau would symbolize the Misraïm Matrix of the sun Israel and the Serpent Esau/Samael, according to the reading of the Kabbalah. As if the birth of Jacob clinging to Esau formed a cosmogonic struggle for world domination, according to Rashi.

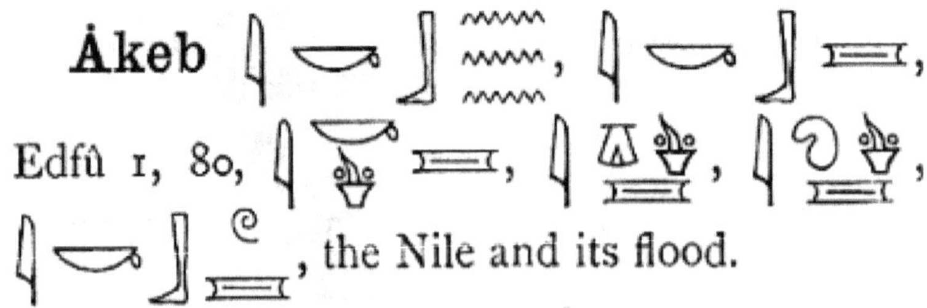

Hieroglyphs Yakob of the Nile and of the Flood[19]

The birth of Jacob/Israel would then be an allegory of the

---

19 Egyptian hieroglyphic dictionary. Wallis Budge, Dover Publications, inc, New York. Published by General publishing Company, 1978, p. 95 a. L'inondation se dit également AGEB ou AKAB, ibidem, p. 12a.

exit from Egypt from darkness to light, the sun against the Serpent... The Hebrew name of Jacob, YAAKOB, refers to the flood. Now we have seen, Jacob/Israel is the solar god bringing the flood. According to this commentary from the memory of the priests of the Nile Valley, the very first flood of the Nile only came about from the blessing of Jacob renamed Israel. This means that Israel has the attributes of Osiris. Thus, Jacob/Israel/Sun/Son of God is not only a Patriarch, but the god of Egypt, which is confirmed by another Kabbalah text, stating that Israel descended into Egypt is God himself, the divine Shekhina with two wings (thus the winged sun). Jacob alias Israel is a cosmogonic character hiding the Sun and God himself :

"Truly, "Israel came to Egypt", it is the Holy One blessed be He"[20]
"THE SUN IS JACOB (ISRAEL)"[21]

The myth of Israel conceals a cosmogony, the Sun God, the other name of Yahu - the hieroglyph of the divine light - or Yahweh, as Osiris is worshipped by the Jews under the names of Yahô, Ptah, Asar..., in the ostraca of Elephantine. We will go much further in the next work by confirming that the Bible gives the golden calf the very name of Israel, symbolizing the solar god Ra. Osiris grandson of Atum' was a solar man, an old man with a perfect body accompanied by the forty-two judges of the celestial court. Now Jacob/Israel is at the same time God and solar man, old man, the perfect man also called Tam, the name of Atum... The book of Genesis tells the story of Jacob, his nightly fight against the angel of God, his tense relationship with Laban, the father of his two future wives. To win his first wife, Leah, Jacob has to work seven years. He will have to work for another seven years to marry Rachel. The Kabbalah reports that the number seven is a symbol of fulfillment, purity, perfection, resurrection[22].

20 Le Zohar, Genèse, tome III, Vayéchev, Mikets, collection 'les dix paroles'. Traduit par Charles Mopsik. Verdier, 1991, p. 286, sq.

21 Le Zohar, Genèse, tome III, Vayechev, Mikets, collection "les dix paroles". Traduit par Charles Mopsik. Verdier, 1991, p. 207.

22 L'épouse royale de Salomon porte le nom de Bethsabée signifiant " la fille des sept ", ou fille issue des sept puissances de Dieu.

More than that; Jacob/Israel embodies the star of the East, swallowing the seven stars. Sirius is the brightest of the stars that precedes the sunrise. It is said that Sirius will "swallow" the seven stars of the Big Dipper, which will disappear with the coming of the sun to acquire the seven powers of divinity:

"The Star of the east points designates Jacob (cf. Numbers 24:17) who swallows seven stars in the north which are seven nations, seven (angelic) princes on the left side" [23]

Let's decipher the text of the Kabbalah that is more than two thousand years old, thanks to the Texts of the Pyramids that are more than forty centuries old. The hieroglyphs of the ancient On' which became Heliopolis, give us the key to the seven golden rings arranged in a Christian cross, in the mummy of Tutankhamun. The *Texts of the Pyramids* affirm that King SA-RÂ, the son of Ra alias "Pharaoh", comes from a cosmogony built from a **cosmic primordial Serpent of light which swallows seven snakes, the seven stars of the Great Bear.** It must be noted that the Pyramid texts attest to the same ritual stated by the Kabbalah concerning Jacob/Israel/Osiris:

"The king's mother is a great Serpent, and it is a serpent of fire, the red crown, who gives birth to him; he himself is a reptile with many folds, provider of vital powers, and a serpent named bull of the gods, WHO SWALLS HIS SEVEN URÆUS so that his seven cervical vertebrae come into existence. He gives orders to the seven Enneads and to the seven Arcs"[24]

---

23   Le Zohar, tome II, Op. cit., 1984, note 603, p. 155.

24   Christian Jacq, La tradition primordiale de l'Égypte ancienne selon les textes des Pyramides, op. cit., p. 265.

Tutankhamun symbolically "swallows" the seven stars of the Great Bear to come back to life.

"Ra possesses seven souls and fourteen Ka; he is also given twelve names..."[25]

As we have already demonstrated, the serpent would have swallowed the seven primordial serpents, seven stars, the seven vital powers, the seven senses ensuring him royalty over the whole Nile Valley... Let us return now to the Bible. It is said that the Egyptians embalmed Jacob/Israel for forty days and mourned him for seventy days. According to Diodorus, forty days, as we have seen, correspond to the time for the soul of Osiris (through the phenomenon of the Resurrection by the transmigration of souls) to be transformed into the Apis bull in order to renew the world. Forty days that the Children of Israel will choose to replace Moses (considered dead on Mount Sinai), by the golden calf, named "Israel", **the ancient historical Osiris - golden calf - replacing Moses...**

Let us recall here the message that came from the Pyramid

---

25   Le Livre des Morts des Anciens Égyptiens. Littératures anciennes du proche Orient. Les Éditions du Cerf, 1967, chapitre 15, note n° 5, p. 46.

Texts: **"It is in the form of a golden calf that the sun Ra appears in the sky"**[26]

Only the true "Egyptians" can have written the biblical passage of the golden calf - Ra, Israel in the Hebrew Massora - with precise memories, the most secret, whereas it was necessary to wait more than twenty-three centuries to decipher the Texts of the Pyramids and to discover the cosmogonic meaning of the golden calf named Israel. At first light, the star Sirius, called Septa in Greek, Sothis in Latin, shines in the East announcing the arrival of the new sun, so that the Pole Star and the seven stars of the Great Bear disappear, as if they were "swallowed" by the light of the sun reborn with Sirius. It is said in chapter 110 of the *Book of Leaving for the Light*:

"I am Yah (=Yahu = Yahweh = He = RÂ = God) and I have swallowed the darkness"[27]

The deceased king SA-RÂ or IS-RÂ Tutankhamun with the seven golden rings on the abdomen of his mummy - representing the seven serpents of the *Pyramid Texts*, the seven lights - symbolically swallows, in order to be fulfilled in life as well as in death, the seven stars of the Great Bear, the "immortals" of the Hermetic Texts, or the "adze of resurrection towards the light", towards a new world. According to the texts of Hermes Trismegistus, this is how he can recover his seven senses in connection with the seven souls of Ra and the seven orifices of his skull. This is why the Great Bear adze plays a decisive role in the ritual of the resurrection by opening the mouth and the eyes: the seven stars symbolically reanimate the seven senses of the king, a kind of integration of the soul BÂ of the Sons of Ra in the soul of Tutankhamen.

The serpent of fire is the image of the river of fire, the famous river of the underworld (taken up in Greek mythology, the Styx, the Acheron, etc.) where the sun is regenerated during the night,

---

26 Cf. Christian Jacq. La tradition primordiale de l'Égypte ancienne selon les textes des Pyramides. Grasset & Fasquelle. 1998. P. 264.

27 Le Livre des Morts des Anciens Égyptiens. Op. cit, 1967, p. 147.

the matrix of Isis or Nut, the sky or the nocturnal serpent which each day swallows the dead sun and pulverizes it into billions of stars. The serpent, the provider of the vital powers, embodies the sky, that is, the totality of the light and water contained in the universe. The seven Uraeus serpents embody, in addition to the seven souls of Ra, seven scattered lights, the dried-up, imperfect Nile snake, cut into seven sections, an allegory of drought, of exile in the desert for men, and of the dispersion of light in the infinite cosmos. The death of MISRÂ, Egypt, is inseparable from the death of Osiris, from the separation of light and its dispersion in darkness, a cosmic exile linked on earth to the drying up of the river and its separation into seven symbolic sections, as reported in a passage from the Book of Isaiah XI, 15:

Yahweh will dry up the bay of the Egyptian sea, he will wave his hand against the River in the violence of his breath. He will strike it to make it seven arms, and people will walk on it in sandals.

Everything seems to be based on the powerful symbolism of the number seven from the Pyramid texts. The Great Bear adze used by the High Priest Shem at the death of the king gives back to the soul of the deceased the use of the senses in the world of the afterlife, the Douat, and symbolizes the seven stars of the resurrection of the king IS-RÂ. Jacob unquestionably plays the role of Osiris/Israel in his ability to symbolically swallow the seven stars of the Great Bear, which gives him the royal, Osirian power of resurrection and flooding, which are part of the same process. The following table shows that according to the rabbinic texts and the Kabbalah, it can no longer be a question of simple coincidences between Osiris and Israel, but of a perfect similarity in the phonetic pronunciation, and in the celestial metaphysics of the ancient Nile Valley.

THE WISDOM OF EGYPT
IS THE WISDOM OF ISRAEL

In the millennium before the advent of Christianity, the enemies of Israel mentioned in the Bible and Jewish tradition are the Assyrians, Babylonians, Greeks and Romans. These four civilizations are, as if by chance, the same invaders of ancient Egypt, thus of Osiris, the invaders of the Nile Valley. While for more than two millennia Egypt has been structured as a state, as a united nation, it is curious that the reaction of the "Egyptians" to the invasions is only imprinted in the memory of the Jews... For the reason that they did not bear the name of Egyptians. Only the Jews seem to be concerned by the immense suffering resulting from the invasions and humiliations... The commentaries of the rabbis, who from Roman times onwards formed the Midrash and the Talmud, are eloquent on this subject. It is said that the Torah, especially the going out of Egypt is a huge metaphor, an allusion to the four great powers mentioned above, who had invaded "Judea, Israel, Jerusalem" following the example of King Nebuchadnezzar, while in history, these monarchs had invaded and plundered the entire Nile Valley, causing the said four exiles, four successive deportations of the Jews (no deportation of "Egyptians" on the horizon...) from the seventh century B.C. onwards. Have the Jews so lost the memory of their past? An entire passage in the TIKUNE AZOHAR explains, through the biblical text, the great secret of the first lost Torah, the one that contained the wisdom and commandments of the true Israel. It is clearly explained by the Zohar that the story of the Children of Israel, the myth of Adam and Eve expelled from paradise for having consumed the fruit of the Tree of Knowledge of Good and Evil, **is a coding, a scaffolding, a setting up of the expulsion of the Children of Israel from Egypt.** Banishment from paradise/ Egypt brilliantly encrypted in the stories of Noah, Abraham, Sodom and Gomorrah, Jacob, Moses. After being expelled from the land of Egypt, after worshipping the golden calf, the Children of Israel "ate and drank", then they found themselves "naked", their eyes became blinded, they sewed themselves clothes made of fig leaves, they lost all memory, they forgot the first Torah, the oral Torah, the Torah broken by Moses. ... like Adam in the Garden of Eden, because the story of Adam is the story of Israel, says the Kabbalah...

It is necessary to insist once again on this important point: according to archaeologists, there is not the slightest trace of the Hebrews of the Bible, not a word about a distant history of the slavery of the Children of Israel at the time of the ancient kings of the Nile Valley. One would have thought that the rabbinic commentaries had placed the slavery of the Children of Israel in the remote times of the ancient kings Khufu/Cheops, Ounas, Thutmose, Amenophis, Akhenaten, Ramses, etc., but this is not so... The story told in the Bible, in particular the slavery of the Hebrews submitted to the power of Pharaoh, refers, on the contrary, in a close relationship, welded, in the form of metaphors or parables, to the secular enemies, invaders of the land of SA-RÂ called "Egypt", enemies rightly qualified as responsible for the exile of Israel! For history shows that the same Assyrians, Babylonians, Perses, Greeks and Romans successively invaded, dominated, subjugated and humiliated the inhabitants of the Nile Valley. **The enemies of Egypt are indeed the same as the enemies of the Jews/Israel**, which is why the Kabbalah states that **"all of Egypt was in bondage; for it was the humblest of all other countries"**[28]... It is not at all about the slavery of Egypt but about the lost Garden of Eden of the Jews... And for good reason, the Egyptian wisdom was that of the ancient Jews, the wisdom of God: the Garden of Eden and its river, the Nile named Pishon', formed the allegory of Egypt, of the Nile whose drops symbolized the ancient Egyptian wisdom that has disappeared, forever lost for the Jews because it was symbolically scattered among the other rivers, the nations:

"What does this verse mean? (The River) uniting all the others is the Pishon', it flows into the land of Egypt and for this reason there was more wisdom in Egypt than in the rest

---

28   Zohar, tome III. Le livre de la splendeur. Par Jean de Pauly. Maisonneuve & Larose, 1985, p. 24.

of the world. When the sentence, stipulating the annihilation of the Egyptian wisdom was decreed, the Holy One, blessed be He, took the said drops [Egyptian wisdom] and threw them into the garden, into the river of the Garden of Eden [the Nile]... ...Now, this river gave birth to four other rivers, and the unifying one that was born of it was Pishon' [the Nile]. Since the drops of Eden have been taken away so that they no longer flow out of the garden, the wisdom of Egypt perishes."[29]

The four rivers of the Garden of Eden express the four exiles of Israel, Assyrian, Babylonian, Persian and Greek. They are one with the death of the Egyptian civilization, with the wisdom of ancient Egypt broken because of the four exiles. **The four enemy civilizations of Egypt and Israel are all compared to darkness**, all qualified as idolaters by the Kabbalah, the Talmud, which will be confirmed later by the Koran... They embody both the darkness and obscurantism that scattered the light of Israel and caused the exile of this light, which is none other than the ancient Egyptian wisdom.

The scattered divine light was a metaphor for the exile of the Jewish people. If the religion of the Jews is a transformation, an inversion by Moses of the "Egyptian" religion as Apion and Manetho claim, if the Hebrews or Children of Israel are the true heirs of Egyptian wisdom and of the land of Egypt - whereas there are no Egyptians in hieroglyphics and consequently no Egyptians in the entire history of the Nile Valley before the takeover of the ancient Greeks - then all of the history of the Nile Valley is that of the Yods, only Yods - so the whole civilization of the Nile Valley, those whom we call for more than two millennia, "ancient Egyptians" had another name.

Why in Jewish tradition are God and the Son of God referred to as Israel? The answer is found in ancient Egypt: every new day, the rising sun in the east is considered the Son of the dead

---

29 Le Zohar, tome II, collection "les dix paroles ". Traduit par Charles Mopsik. Vayera, Hayé Sarah, Toldot, Vayetsé, Vayichlah. Verdier, 1984, p. 207.

sun, the Son of the dead Father on the western horizon, and conversely, every setting sun dies and gives birth to a new sun, Hor in hieroglyphics, Horus in Greek. The Zohar translates Hor as "primitive light"[30].The Kabbalah evokes the crown of God formed by the three primordial branches[31] or "three Yod of the sacred name" of the divine Shekhina named Israel. For the Kabbalah, the configuration of the Body of God is, in the Sefirotic Tree, formed by Jacob renamed Israel, his right arm is Abraham, his left arm Isaac. Joseph constitutes the phallus of God (Sephira Yesod) because Joseph brings back abundance and gives life to Egypt. The configuration of the Sephirotic Tree designating the characters of the Bible as emanations of the symbolic body of Yahweh is unquestionably "Osirian". The Body of Osiris identified with the sacred Tree is adorned "with the gods", each forming a part or an organ of his body. The following examples attest to the primordial importance of the reed of God, as demonstrated by Michel Vladimirovich Skariatine, known as Enel, and the Egyptologists Maspero and Breasted, for whom the hieroglyph of Atum is written with the letter Yod, We will return to this in the chapter devoted to Yod [32] .

Ramses II as a child carries in his left hand the royal reed, emblem of royalty, of the calamus at the origin of all writing, of light and of creation, and his name RAMESSOU proves that he is indeed a king "HOU", one of the names of Yahweh which is read YAHOU, meaning the Word coming from Yod, the primordial light reed. The falcon Hor symbolizes the original light (Hor is confirmed by the Kabbalah as the light of creation) and the reed or rush symbolizes the calamus, the Spirit, the creative Word. Another symbolic reading of Rameses is RA-MESS-ESS-NESSOUT-HOU.

---

30   Zohar, tome VI. Le livre de la splendeur, 1985. p. 77.

31   Chaque lettre hébraïque est une couronne constituée de Yod. La lettre Chin est la couronne de Dieu, formée de trois Yod. Elle représente les trois patriarches.

32   La Langue Sacrée, Enel. Cf. Anthologie de l'Ancien Empire à nos jours. Maison Neuve Larose, 1997. p. 261.

This means that Ramses is the son of Amun or Atum, the primordial Reed, the Yod of the Kabbalah... RÂ ⊙ (Yah or Atoum, the divine light, the divine reed) gave birth to - MESS 𓀔 - HOU - 𓅭 the chick (for the Kabbalah, Yahou, Yah and Hou are the names of God), which is read "He the Spirit" or "He, the creative Word", followed by the royal rush or reed, image of the Being, image of the Yod 𓏤, image of the light God and image of the king Rameses is therefore the Spirit of the Word, the sacred reed given birth to by God, by the celestial light...

The solar child with his finger in his mouth to express his ME (Yod) coming out of the celestial waters Ramses II, protected by the Hor falcon holds in his left hand the reed of royalty. Cairo Museum.

ISRAEL: A SACRED NAME FOR THE TORAH, FOR THE GOSPELS AND FOR THE KORAN

In order to grasp the immensity of the hidden truth, which challenges the foundations of our civilization, it is necessary to return to our time. What is the relationship between the name of Israel and the current situation in the Middle East? As we know, after more than half a century of Arab-Israeli war, the so-called holy war, the Muslim world does not seem ready to concede any historical legitimacy to the Jewish people in the land of Israel, the ancient Judea and the ancient land of Canaan. According to the Bible, or rather the Torah (the first five books of the Old Testament, which together with the Gospels form the present-day Bible), the land of Canaan was granted by God, Yahweh, through Moses, as an inheritance to the Children of Israel... It is called "the land of the seven nations". But in the first book of the Torah (consisting only of the first five books of the Old Testament), Yahweh, the God of the Torah, had first promised Abraham a much larger land, a land that corresponded to the whole of humanity, made up of the seventy nations, an immense empire that contained Egypt, because it stretched from the torrent of the Nile to the Euphrates...

On that day the Lord made a covenant with Abram, saying: 'I have given this land to your descendants from the stream of Egypt to the great river, the river Euphrates (Genesis, XV, 18).

As we can see, from Abraham to Moses, the immense land of Israel has shrunk considerably to become the land of Canaan... Article 28 of the Hamas Charter (1988) summarizes in one sentence the anti-Jewish ideology of the Islamist movement:

"Israel, because it is Jewish and has a Jewish population, defies Islam and Muslims".

After the separation between Jews and Egyptians, Jews and Christians, a new separation is taking shape with Islam. The word, the very name of Israel, seems to be forever demonized, cursed in the vocabulary of the fundamentalists. Why, during the last two millennia, and even well before Islam, did Israel disturb people to the point of generating a real obsessive, neurotic hatred, marked by scenes of collective hysteria, leading to the great massacre of the Jews of Alexandria in the first century? Is Israel at the origin of a conflict of heritage, a conflict of civilization? The scientists, archaeologists, Jews, Christians, Muslims, fanatics and fundamentalists have never been able to solve this colossal enigma. And yet, Israel is the name that has subjugated and still subjugates the three monotheistic religions: humanity at war is always, consciously or unconsciously, searching for the truth: the Verus Israel. Reading the Hamas charter, one might think that the name Israel has been cursed forever by the Koran, by Allah, which is perfectly false. The verses of the Koran show that Israel and its children, the Bani Isrâ-îla, are as sacred to the Jews as they are to the Muslims. Israel is certainly the most sacred word in the Qur'an. Sura 2 -122, Allah glorifies the Sons of Israel.

O Sons of Israel, remember the raptures with which I have delighted you, favoring you more than the worlds.

The speeches of the Islamist leaders are full of comments or Hadîts, very often contradictory and hateful, filled with anti-Jewish hysteria. To the point of declaring that only a world purified of all Judeo-Christian presence, but also a world decontaminated of the presence of other infidels, polytheists, miscreants, idolaters, unbelievers, etc., will be harmonious, messianic. The world will find a true peace, a purification of humanity, fulfilling the Ummah, the community of believers, a peace necessary for universal messianism .... This indoctrination, which would require the sacrifice of a part of the human community, to satisfy the will of Allah, has existed

unfortunately for at least twenty-three centuries. A sacrificial ideology, purifying the Jewish people, had already been inspired in the third century B.C. by several false historians, real impostors in the pay of Ptolemy Soter and his son Ptolemy

Philadelphus, in particular Manetho who dared to claim to be a priest and an Egyptian, which would mean a man full of wisdom...

The speeches of the Islamist leaders are full of comments or Hadîts, very often contradictory and hateful, filled with anti-Jewish hysteria. To the point of declaring that only a world purified of all Judeo-Christian presence, but also a world decontaminated of the presence of other infidels, polytheists, miscreants, idolaters, unbelievers, etc., will be harmonious, messianic. The world will find a true peace, a purification of humanity, fulfilling the Ummah, the community of believers, a peace necessary for universal messianism .... This indoctrination, which would require the sacrifice of a part of the human community, to satisfy the will of Allâh, has existed

unfortunately for at least twenty-three centuries. A sacrificial ideology, purifying the Jewish people, had already been inspired in the third century B.C. by several false historians, real impostors in the pay of Ptolemy Soter and his son Ptolemy Philadelphus, in particular Manetho who dared to claim to be a priest and an Egyptian, which would mean a man full of wisdom...

Hebrew name : Israel

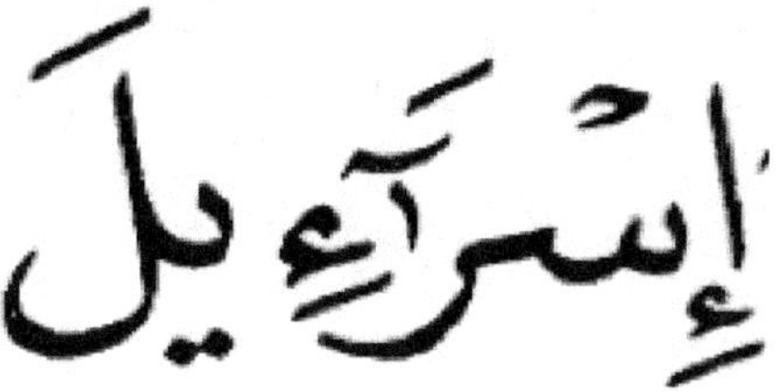

Koranic Arabic name : Îsrâïlâ

According to the Qur'an, Sura 28-4, an unnamed "Pharaoh"

"divided his people into clans and oppressed some of them, killing their sons and leaving only their daughters alive, for he was an evil being"

The Children of Israel are an integral part of the people of the Nile Valley. Pharaoh is blamed for creating a separation within his own people. More than a division, it is a real religious schism between Israel and Egypt that was created by this king. Is it necessary to ask who is this Pharaoh who divided Egypt, of which the Qur'an speaks? We answered this question in the first volume of this trilogy. Only the Greek pharaohs - who gave themselves the name of Pharao' which does not exist in the hieroglyphs - invaders of the Nile Valley correspond to the despoiling kings of the ancient religion of Osiris/Israel. They were therefore totally foreign to the immense civilization of the Nile Valley. Their inhuman, bloodthirsty, even demonic behavior could in no way fit into the framework of the ancient religion of SA-RÂ, ASAR, IS-RÂ, three times millennium old, called falsely Egyptian.

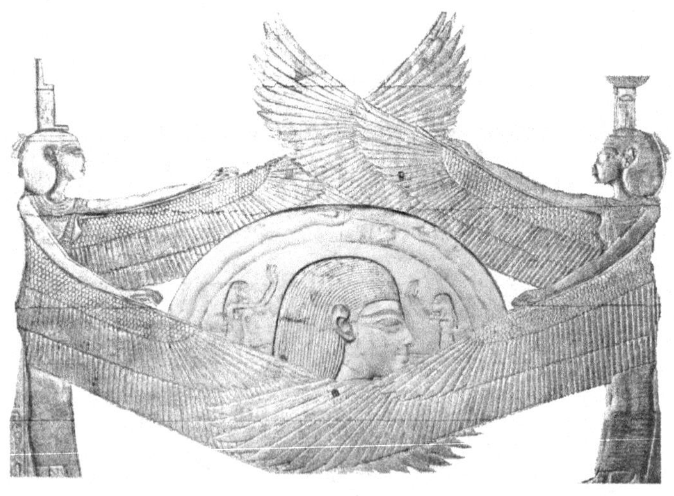

BIBLIOGRAPHY

Adolphe Erman ; Hermann Ranke. *La civilisation égyptienne.* Payot & Rivages. 1994.

Aggadoth du Talmud de Babylone. La source de Jacob/ 'Ein Yaakov. Collection « Les dix paroles », Verdier, 1982.

Agnès Cabrol. *Aménophis III, le magnifique.* Le Rocher. 2000.

Albert Soued. *Les symboles dans la Bible.* Jacques Grancher. 1995.

Alberto Silioti. Égypte *Terre des Pharaons* ; Gründ 1994.

Alberto Siliotti. *La vallée des rois.* Gründ 1996.

Allan Millard. *Trésors des temps bibliques.* Sator-Cerf 1986.

André Chouraqui. *Moïse.* Flamarion. 1997.

Annick de Souzenelle. *L'Égypte intérieure ou les dix plaies de l'âme.* Éditions Albin Michel, 1991.

Aventure des écritures. Naissances. Bibliothèque Nationale de France, 1997.

Bahir. Livre de la clarté. Collection « Les dix paroles ». Verdier, 1983.

Barry J. Kemp. *Ancient Egypt. Anatomy of a civilization.* 1989 ;1991. Routledge.

Betro Maria Carmela. *Hiéroglyphes. Les mystères de l'écriture.* Flamarion Paris 1995.

Bible. Traduction intégrale hébreu-français. Nouvelle édition 1994. Sinaï. Tel-Aviv. Israël.

Bill Manley. *Atlas historique de l'Égypte ancienne.* Autrement. Collection Atlas/Mémoires. 1998.

Champollion. *Le Panthéon Égyptien.* Bibliothèque de l'image. 1997.

Champollion. *Le papyrus de la pesée de l'âme;* le Rocher 1996.

Chemot Rabbah, Exode. Tome II. Copyright by Maurice Stern, 18, Garrick AV.

Chapitres de Rabbi Éliézer. *Pirké de Rabbi Éliézer.* Collection Les Dix Paroles. Éditions Verdier, 1983. LONDON N.W. 11. P.

Charles Novak. Jacob Frank, le faux Messie, L'Harmattan, 2020.

Christian Jacq. *Nefertiti et Akhénaton.* Ed. Perrin. 1996.

Christian Jacq. *Le petit Champollion illustré.* Robert Laffont 1994.

Christian Jacq. *Grammaire égyptienne de Champollion.* SOLIN 1997.

Christian Jacq. *La sagesse vivante de l'Égypte ancienne.* Robert Laffont 1998.

Christian Jacq. *La tradition primordiale de l'Égypte ancienne selon les Textes des Pyramides.* Grasset & Fasquelle. 1998.

Christian Jacq. *Voyage dans l'autre monde selon l'Égypte ancienne.* Épreuves de métamorphoses de mort d'après les Textes des Pyramides et les Textes des sarcophages. Le Rocher, Paris 1986.

Christiane Desroches Noblecourt. *Amours et fureurs de La Lointaine.* Stock-Pernoud. 1997. P. 168.

Christiane Desroches Noblecourt. *La Reine Mystérieuse. Hatchepsout.* Pygmalion. 2002.

Christiane Desroches Noblecourt. *L'ancienne Égypte. L'extraordinaire aventure amarnienne.* Les Deux-Mondes. 1960.

Christiane Desroches Noblecourt. *Ramsès II La véritable histoire.* Pygmalion 1996.

Christiane Desroches Noblecourt avec Daniel Élouard. Symboles de l'Égypte. Éditions Désclée de Bouwer, 2004.

Christiane Desroches Noblecourt. C.D. ROM Toutankhamon. Syrinx 1997.

Christiane Desroches Noblecourt. Hachette 1963. *Vie et mort d'un Pharaon.*

Christiane Desroches Noblecourt. *Sous le Regard des Dieux.* Éditions Albin Michel, 2003.

Christiane Desroches Noblecourt. *Le Fabuleux Héritage de l'Égypte.* Éditions SW-Télémaque, 2004.

Christiane Ziegler, Hervé Champollion. *L'Égypte de Jean*

François Champollion. Copyright Diane Harle, 1997.

Claire Lalouette. *L'empire des Ramsès*. Librairie Arthème Fayard, 1985.

Claire Lalouette. *Sagesse sémitique de l'Égypte ancienne à l'Islam*. Albin Michel. 1998.

Claire Lalouette. *Thèbes ou la naissance d'un empire*. Flamarion 1995.

Claude Traunecker. *Les Dieux de l'Égypte*. Collection Que sais-je ? Presses universitaires de France.

Claude Vendersleyen. *L'Égypte et la vallée di* Nil, tome 2, Nouvelle CLIO ;1995.

 Colette Sirat. *Écriture et civilisatio*n, du CNRS. 1976.

Colette Sirat. *Les papyrus en caractères hébraïques trouvés en Égypte*. CNRS. 1985.

Cyril Aldred. *Akhénaton roi d'Égypte*. Ed. SEUIL ; 1997.

Cyril Aldred. *Les Égyptiens. L'empire des pharaons*. Armand Collin, 1985.

Dictionnaire de civilisation juive. Jean Christophe Attias Esther Benbassa. Larousse Bordas 1997.

Dictionnaire des dieux et des mythes égyptiens. Roland Harari et Gilles Lambert. Le Grand Livre du Mois, 2002.

Dictionnaire de la civilisation égyptienne. Posener G. Sauneron S. Yoyotte J. Hazan, Paris, 1970.

Dictionnaire de mythologie et symbolique égyptiennes. Robert Jacques, Thibaud. Dervy. 1996.

Dictionnaire des pharaons. Vernus et Jean Yoyotte. Noésis, Parais. 1996.

Dictionnaire Encyclopédique du judaïsme. Le Cerf 1993.

Dictionnaire encyclopédique du judaïsme. Geoffrey Wigoder. Éditions du Cerf. 1993.

Dictionnaire Français-Hébreu Larousse. Achiasaf publishing house LTD. Tel Aviv 1997.

Dictionnaire. Petit lexique d'Égyptien hiéroglyphique à l'usage des débutants; Menu Bernadette. Geuthneur 1997.

Diodore de Sicile. *Bibliothèque Historique.*Éditions Les Belles Lettres, 2003. Première édition 1993.

Documents Araméens d'Égypte. Littératures Anciennes du Proche-Orient. Éditions du Cerf, 1972.

Dominique Marie. *L'Égypte éternelle*. EDITA S.A. 1995.

Dominique Valbelle et Geneviève Hudson. L'État et les institutions en Égypte, des premiers pharaons aux empereurs romains. Armand Colin Éditeur. 1992.

Dominique Valbelle. *Histoire de l'état Pharaonique*. PUF 1998. Collection THEMIS.

Edmond Fleg. *Moïse raconté par les sages*. Albin Michel, S.A., 1997.

Eggebrecht Arne. *L'Égypte ancienne*. Bordas. 1984.

Égypte ancienne (L'histoire de). Présentation Pierre Grandet. du Seuil. Collection Point. 1996.

Egyptian grammar Gardiner. Third. Oxford university presse, Ely house, London, W.i 1969.

Egyptian hieroglyphic dictionary. Wallis Budge, Dover Publications, inc, New York. Published by General publishing Company, 1978.

Élie Benamozegh. *Israël et l'Humanité*. Albin Michel, 1961.

Élie Munk. *La voix de la Thora*. La genèse. Fondation Samuel et Odette Lévy. 1980.

Élie Munk. *La voix de la Thora*. L 'Exode. Fondation Samuel et Odette Lévy. 1980.

Élie Munk. *La voix de la Thora*. Le Deutéronome. Fondation Samuel et Odette Lévy. 1998.

Élisabeth Laffont, *Les livres de Sagesses des pharaons*. Collection Folio Histoire. Gallimard 1979.

Énel. *LeMystère de la Vie et de la Mort d'après l'enseignement des temples de l'Ancienne Égypte*. Arka Éditions.

Énel. *Le message du sphynx*. Arka. 1998.

Énel. *Les origines de la Genèse et l'enseignement des temples de l'ancienne Égypte*. Maisonneuve & Larose, 1963.

Énel. *Trilogie de la Rota ou Roue Céleste*. Trois traités d'Astrologie et de Cabbale. Dervy Livres, 1973.

Erik Hornung. *L'Égypte Ésotérique*. Éditions du Rocher, 2001.

Erik Hornung. *L'Esprit du temps des pharaons*. Philippe Lebaud Éditeur / du Félin, 1996.

Erik Hornung. *Akhenaten and the religion of light*. Translated by David Lorton. Cornel university press, 1999.

Erik Hornung. *Les dieux de l'Égypte.* Le Un et le Multiple. Éditions du Rocher, 1986.

 Étienne Drioton. Jacques Vandier. *L'Égypte.* Presses universitaires de France. Collection « Clio » 7ème édition. 1989.

Fabre d'Olivet. *La langue hébraïque restituée.* l'Age d'Homme. Delphica. 1991.

Flavius Josèphe. *Contre Apion.* Éditions Les Belles Lettres, 2003. Première édition 1930.

France. Collection « Clio » 7ème édition. 1989.

Freud. *L'Homme Moïse et la religion Monothéiste.* Gallimard 1986.

Friedman Richard ; Qui a écrit la Bible. Exergue 1997.

Georges Roux. *La Mésopotamie. Essai d'histoire économique, politique et culturelle.* 1985. du Seuil.

Gérard Huber. *Akhénaton sur le Divan.* Éditions Jean Cyrille Godefroy, 2001.

Gérard Huber. *Moïse et le retour des Dieux.* Safed éditions, Gilbert Wendorfer, 2003.

Gérard Huber. *Abraham, Moïse et la stèle d'Israël.* Éditions l'Harmattan, 2011.

Goyon Jean-Claude. *Rituels funéraires de l'ancienne Égypte.* Traduction et commentaires, Éditions du Cerf 1997.

 Graves Robert et Patai Raphaël. *Les mythes hébreux.* Fayard 1984.

Gros de Beler Aude; *la Mythologie Égyptienne.* Molière. 1998. Collection Splendeur.

Guy Rachet *Dictionnaire de la Civilisation égyptienne.* Larousse-Bordas, 1998.

Hérodote. Histoires II. Les Belles Lettres. 1982.

Haïm Potock ; *une histoire des juifs.* Ramsay 1996.

Heike Owusu. *Les symboles des Égyptiens.* Guy Trédaniel, 1998.

Henri Stierlin. *Les Pharaons bâtisseurs.* Pierre Terrail. 1992.

Hermès Trismégiste. Corpus Herméticum. Fragments extraits de Stobée. I, XXII. Les Belles Lettres, 1954.

Hermès Trismégiste. Corpus Herméticum. Poimandrès. Traités II-XII. Les Belles Lettres, 1946.

Hermès Trismégiste. Corpus Herméticum. Traités XIII-XVIII Asclépius. Les Belles Lettres, 1946.

Hermès Trismégiste. Corpus Herméticum. Fragments extraits de Stobée. XXIII, XIXX. Les Belles Lettres, 1954.

Howard Carter, *La tombe de Toutankhamon.* Pygmalion 1978.

Israël Finkelstein, Neil Asher Silberman, *La Bible Dévoilée.* Bayard Éditions, 2002.

Jan Assmann. *Maât, l'Égypte pharaonique et l'idée de justice sociale*, Julliard Parais 1989.

Jan Assmann. Moïse l'Égyptien. Aubier. 2001.

Jan Assmann. Mort et Au-delà dans l'Égypte ancienne. Éditions du Rocher, 2003.

Jaques Champollion. Les Égyptiens. Minerva., S.A., Genève. 1971.

Jean Capart. Tout-Ankh-Amon. Vromant S.A. éditeurs. 1943.

Jean Vergote. *Joseph en Égypte à la lumière des études égyptologiques récentes*. Publication de l'université d e Louvain. Genèse Chapitre 37-50. 1959.

John Adams Wilson. *Vie et mort d'une civilisation*. Arthaud. 1961.

Joyce Tylsdeley, Nefertiti, du Rocher. 1998.

Kitchen K. Ramses II. *Le pharaon triomphant*. Le Rocher, Paris 1985.

L'aventure des écritures. Sous la direction d'Anna Zali et d'Anie Berthier. Bibliothèque Nationale 1997.

La Torah vivante. Traduction du Pentateuque Bésée sur les Sources Juives Traditionnelles. Commentée par Rav Aryé Kaplan. Éditions l'Arche du Livre, 1996.

L'Égypte ancienne. Les grandes époques de l'homme. Lionel Casson. 1969 by TIME inc.

L'Égypte. Sur les traces de la civilisation pharaonique. könemann. Imprimé en Allemagne ISBN 3-89508-914-1.

La Hagada de Pâque. David Berdah. Alpha Magium 1986.

La Kabbale dévoilée. Éditions Rosicruciennes. 1972.

La Vallée des Rois. Sous la direction de Kent.R Weeks ; photographies de Araldo de Luca. Gründ, 2001.

Le Déaut. *Targum du Pentateuque.* Tome 1 ;2 ;3 ;4 ;5. Collection source chrétienne. Éditions du Cerf.

Le commentaire sur la Torah. Jacob Ben Isaac Achkenazi de Janow. , collection « les dix paroles ». Traduit par Jean Baumgarten. Verdier, 1987.

Le Livre des Morts des Anciens Égyptiens. Traduction inédite et commentaires de Guy Rachet. Éditions du Rocher, 1996.

Le Livre des Morts des Anciens Égyptiens. Littératures anciennes du proche Orient. Les Éditions du Cerf, 1967.

Le Livre des Morts. Albert chapoor. Albin Michel. 1993.

Le Livre Hébreu d'Hénoch ou Livre des Palais. Collection « les dix paroles ». Traduit par Charles Mopsik. Verdier, 1981.

Les origines égyptiennes du droit civik romain. Eugene Revillout. Forgotten Books publisher.

Les Secrets de la Bible. Roger Sabbah. Éditions Carnot, 2003.

Les Secrets de l'Exode. Messod et Roger Sabbah. Jean-Cyrille Godefroy, 2000.

Le Zohar, tome I, collection « les dix paroles ». Traduit par Charles Mopsik. Verdier, 1981.

Le Zohar, tome II, collection « les dix paroles ». Traduit par Charles Mopsik. *Vayera, Hayé Sarah, Toldot, Vayetsé, Vayichlah.* Verdier, 1984.

Le Zohar, Genèse, tome III, Vayéchev, Mikets, collection « les dix paroles ». Traduit par Charles Mopsik. Verdier, 1991.

Le Zohar, tome IV, collection « les dix paroles ». *Vayigash Vayehi.* Traduit par Charles Mopsik. Verdier, 1996.

Le Zohar, Cantique des Cantiques. Collection « les dix paroles ». Verdier, 1999.

Le Zohar, *Lamentations.* Collection « les dix paroles ». Verdier, 2000.

Le Zohar, *Livre de Ruth,* collection « les dix paroles ». Traduit par Charles Mopsik. Verdier, 1987.

Les Lettres d'El Amarna. Le Cerf, 1987.

Henri Lhote, *Le chameau et le dromadaire en Afrique du Nord, Sahara.»*Groupe Média International. Paris.

Livre Hébreu d'Enoch, collection « les dix paroles ». Verdier, 1989.

Lubavicch, Rabbi Chélomo de. *Réflexions sur la vie juive.* 2ème édition 1987.

Madeleine Della Monica. *Thoutmosis III le plus grand des pharaons.* Le Léopard d'Or. 1991.

Marc Gabolde. *D'Akhénaton à Toutankhamon.* Diffusion de Boccard 1998. *Institut d'Archéologie et d'Histoire de l'Antiquité.* Maison de l'Orient, Université Lumière-Lyon 2-CNRS. 1998.

Marguerite Harl, *La Bible grecque des Septante : Du judaïsme hellénistique au Christianisme ancien.* Auteurs: Marguerite Harl, Gilles Dorival, Olivier Munnich, Initiation au christianisme ancien. Éditions du Cerf, 1988.

Marie-Ange Bonhème, Annie Forgeau. *Pharaon. Les secrets du pouvoir.* Armand Colin 1988.

Maurice Bucaille, *Moïse et Pharaon.* Seghers éditions. 1995.

Maximes des Pères. Introduction de Maïmonide. Les huit chapitres. Les éditions Colbo 1992.

Merkos l'Inoynei Chinuch. *Anokhi, le « mot des mots »,* source likouté-si-hot, vol. 3 892-895.

Michael Molnar. Sigmund Freud. *Chronique la plus brève.* Carnets intimes 1929-1939. Albin Michel. 1992.

Midrach Rabba, tome I, *Genèse Rabba.* Collection « les dix paroles ». Verdier, 1987.

Midrachim de nos sages, Exode. Par Maurice Stern. Tome II, Chemoth Rabbah. Copyright by M.Stern 18, Garrick Av. London N. W. 11. 1997.

Millar Burrows. *Les manuscrits de la Mer morte* ; Robert Laffont 1973 ;

Moïse. André Chouraki. Rocher, 1995 et Flamarion, 1997.

Mordrzejewski Mélèze. *Les Juifs d'Égypte de Ramses II à*

Hadrien. Ed. Quadrige PUF ; 1997.

Nicolas Grimal. *Histoire de l'Égypte ancienne*. Fayard, 1988.

Nicolas Reeves ; inter-livres 1995 ; Thames and Hudson 1990. *À la découverte de Toutankhamon*.

Nicole Maya Malet. Moïse Hébreu, *Moïse Égyptien*. 143 Éditions du Cerf 1997. Revue d'éthique et de théologie morale.

Philipp Vandenberg. *Nefertiti*. Pierre Belfond. 1987.

Philon d'Alexandrie. *De Vita Mosis* I-II. Éditions du Cerf, 1967.

Pierre Bordreuil, Françoise Briquel-Chatonnet. *Le Temps de la Bible*. Éditions Fayard, 2000.

Pierre Grandet. *Cours d'Égyptien hiéroglyphique*. Bernard Mathieu. Khéops 1997.

Pierre Grandet. *Hymnes à la religion d'Aton*. Le Seuil 1995.

Pierre-Henri Salfati. *Le Premier Mot « Au Commencement » Béréchit*. Histoire d'un contresens. Éditions Fayard, 2020.

Plutarque. *Isis et Osiris*. Par Guy Trédaniel. La Maisnie. 1992.

Plutarque. Œuvres Morales. Traités 24, 26. Dialogues Pythiques. Les Belles Lettres, 1974.

Frédéric Portal. *Les symboles égyptiens*. de la Maisnie 1985. Paris 1957, 1993.

Rachi, commentateur de la Bible au Moyen Âge. *Pentateuque selon Rachi*. La Genèse. Samuel et Odette Lévy. 1993.

Rachi, commentateur de la Bible au Moyen Âge. *Pentateuque selon Rachi*. L'Exode. Samuel et Odette Lévy. 1990.

Rachi, commentateur de la Bible au Moyen Âge. *Pentateuque selon Rachi*. Les Nombres. Samuel et Odette Lévy. 1977.

Redford, « *An Egyptological Perspective on the exodus Narrative* ».

Richard Lebeau. *Une histoire des Hébreux*. Tallandier 1998.

Robert Ambelain. *Le Secret d'Israël*. Énigmes de l'Univers. Éditions Robert Laffont, 1995.

Robert Vergnieux. Michel Gondran. *Aménophis IV et les pierres du soleil. Akhénaton retrouvé*. Arthaud 1997.

Rolf Krauss. *Moïse le Pharaon*. Éditions du Rocher. 2000.

Rosenthal Franz. *Grammaire d'Araméen biblique*. Traduit par Paul Hébert. Beauchesne éditeur 1988.

Ruth Shumann-Antelme. Stéphane Rossini. *Lecture illustrée des hiéroglyp*hes. Champollion ; du Rocher. 1998.

Saadia Gaon. Commentaire sur le Sepher Yetzira. Verdier, 2001.

Saintes Écritures. Traduction du monde nouveau. Watch tower Bible and tract society of New York, U.S.A. 1995.

Saitoti Tepilit Ole. *Les Massaï*. Carole Beckwith. Éditions du Chêne, Paris 1980.

Samivel. Trésor de l'Égypte. Arthaud. 1954.

Serge Sauneron . *Les prêtres de l'ancienne Égypte*. « Le Temps qui Court ». Éditions du Seuil, 1957.

Sepher Yetsirah. *Le livre de la création*. Rosicruciennes. 1989.

Sortie d'Égypte, par Gustave d'Eichthal, d'après les écrits du Pentateuque et de Manéthon. Paris, de Soye et Fils, 1850-1872.

Symboles du Judaïsme. Assouline 1995.

Textes des Sarcophages du Moyen Empire Égyptien. Claude Carrier, tome I. Éditions du Rocher, 2004.

Textes des Sarcophages du Moyen Empire Égyptien. Claude Carrier, tome II. Éditions du Rocher, 2004.

Textes des Sarcophages du Moyen Empire Égyptien. Claude Carrier, tome III. Éditions du Rocher, 2004.

Wildung Dietrich.Égypte de la préhistoire aux Romains. Taschen. 1997.

Zohar, tome III. *Le livre de la splendeur*. Par Jean de Pauly. Maisonneuve & Larose, 1985.

Zohar, tome IV. *Le livre de la splendeur*. Par Jean de Pauly. Maisonneuve & Larose, 1985.

Zohar, tome V. *Le livre de la splendeur*. Par Jean de Pauly. Maisonneuve & Larose, 1985.

Zohar, tome VI. *Le livre de la splendeur*. Par Jean de Pauly. Maisonneuve & Larose, 1985.

www.ingramcontent.com/pod-product-compliance
Lightning Source LLC
LaVergne TN
LVHW050953200726
843508LV00001B/38